THE BEAUTY OF GOD'S HOUSE

The Beauty of God's House

Essays in Honor of Stratford Caldecott

EDITED BY

Francesca Aran Murphy

CASCADE *Books* · Eugene, Oregon

THE BEAUTY OF GOD'S HOUSE
Essays in Honor of Stratford Caldecott

Cascade Books
An Imprint of Wipf and Stock Publishers
199 W. 8th Ave., Suite 3
Eugene, OR 97401

www.wipfandstock.com

ISBN 13: 978-1-62032-436-3

Cataloging-in-Publication data:

The beauty of God's house : essays in honor of Stratford Caldecott / edited by Francesca Aran Murphy.

p. ; cm. — Includes bibliographical references.

ISBN 13: 978-1-62032-436-3

1. Caldecott, Stratford. I. Murphy, Francesca Aran. II. Title.

BX4827.C30 B49 2014

Manufactured in the U.S.A.

Contents

List of Contributors | *vii*

Introduction—*Francesca Aran Murphy* | 1

1   It Is a Wonder, How Much the Clay Can Be Imprinted with the Beauty of Its Potter! Saint Ephrem the Syrian, *Hymns on Virginity*, XXV—*Francisco Javier Martínez* | 3

2   The Beauty of Being Christian—*Marc Ouellet* | 23

3   The Loss of Beauty and the De-naturing of Faith —*D. C. Schindler* | 36

4   An Observation about Saint Thomas Aquinas's Idea of the Intellect—*Jean Borella* | 63

5   Wisdom Has Built Her Beautiful House for Liturgy —*David W. Fagerberg* | 73

6   Eating Fire and Spirit: The Eucharist and the Blessed Trinity—*Nicholas J. Healy Jr.* | 89

7   "Wisdom Hath Builded Herself a House" (Prov 9:1): A Meditation on Mary as the Temple of God's Beauty —*Adrian Walker* | 99

8   Health and Hope—*Michael Cameron* | 121

9   Stratford Caldecott: Ecology on One's Knees—*Mary Taylor* | 129

10   Beyond the Binary Logic of Market-Plus-State:
      A Sane Social Order for the Global Liberal Age
      —*David L. Schindler* | 149

11   The Politics of the Soul—*John Milbank* | 189

12   The New Atheism and Christian Cosmology
      —*Aidan Nichols* | 205

13   Many Mansions in My Father's House: A Qur'anic
      Interpretation—*Reza Shah-Kazemi* | 220

14   What Is the Place of the Nude in Sacred Art?
      —*David Clayton* | 232

15   Newman for a New Generation—*Carol Zaleski* | 255

16   The Prayer of Saint Francis and the Grammar
      of Communion—*Derek Cross* | 270

17   Stratford Caldecott: A Brief Biography
      —*Philip Zaleski* | 273

      Afterword—*Léonie Caldecott* | 281

      Bibliography | 289

Contributors

JEAN BORELLA is a French philosopher whose works include *Esotérisme guénonien et mystère chrétien* (1997), *Histoire et théorie du symbole* (2004), and *La charité profanée*.

LÉONIE CALDECOTT is a writer living in Oxford, UK. With her husband, Stratford, she founded the Centre for Faith and Culture and the international review *Second Spring* (www.secondspring.co.uk). She is the author of *What Do Catholics Believe?* (2008) and several plays. She also edits *Magnificat* (UK and Ireland edition) and *Humanum*.

MICHAEL CAMERON is a physician in general practice near Glasgow, Scotland.

DAVID CLAYTON is an Englishman living in New Hampshire, USA. He is an artist, teacher, published writer, and broadcaster who holds a permanent post as Artist-in-Residence and Lecturer in Liberal Arts at the Thomas More College of Liberal Arts.

DEREK CROSS is a priest of the Toronto Oratory, where he serves. He also teaches philosophy at St. Philip Neri Seminary.

DAVID W. FAGERBERG is Associate Professor of Liturgy at the University of Notre Dame du Lac and Senior Advisor of the Notre Dame Center for Liturgy. His most recent volume is *Liturgical Asceticism* (2012).

NICHOLAS J. HEALY JR. is Assistant Professor of Philosophy and Culture at the John Paul II Institute in Washington, DC. He is the author of a monograph about Hans Urs von Balthasar and the editor of the American *Communio*.

FRANCISCO JAVIER MARTÍNEZ is the Archbishop of Granada, Spain.

JOHN MILBANK is the founder of the Radical Orthodoxy movement and Professor of Religion, Politics, and Ethics at the University of Nottingham. He is the author of the benchmark work *Theology and Social Theory* (1990),

The Religious Dimension in the Thought of Giambattista Vico (1991), and most recently, in collaboration with Slavoj Žižek, *The Monstrosity of Christ: Paradox or Dialectic?* (2009) and *Paul's New Moment: Continental Philosophy and the Future of Christian Theology* (2010).

FRANCESCA ARAN MURPHY is Professor of Systematic Theology at the University of Notre Dame du Lac and the author and editor of numerous books, including *God Is Not a Story* (2010) and *I Samuel* (2010) in the Brazos Theological Commentary series.

AIDAN NICHOLS is a Dominican friar and currently the prior of the Dominican house in Cambridge. He is the author of a number of highly readable books, including the finely illustrated volume *The Chalice of God* (2012).

MARC OUELLET is Prefect of the Congregation for Bishops and President of the Pontifical Commission for Latin America. Associated with the journal *Communio*, Cardinal Ouellet is the author of *Divine Likeness: Toward a Trinitarian Anthropology of the Family* (2006).

D. C. SCHINDLER was until recently Associate Professor of Philosophy at Villanova University. He has now become a professor at the John Paul II Institute in Washington, DC. He is the author of *Hans Urs von Balthasar and the Dramatic Structure of Truth* (2004) and *The Catholicity of Reason* (2013).

DAVID L. SCHINDLER is Edouard Gagnon Professor of Fundamental Theology at the John Paul II Institute in Washington, DC. He is the author of *Heart of the World, Center of the Church: Communio Ecclesiology, Liberalism, and Liberation* (1996) and *Ordering Love: Liberal Societies and the Memory of God* (2011).

REZA SHAH-KAZEMI is an authority on Islam, Sufism, and Shi'ism. He is the founding editor of the *Islamic World Report* and a Research Associate at the Institute of Ismaili Studies. He is the author of a dozen books, including *The Sacred Foundations of Justice in Islam* (2007).

MARY TAYLOR has published in *Communio* and *Second Spring*. She and her husband raise organic vegetables and beautiful children, one of whom is studying for the priesthood. She loves the Red Sox and celestial navigation.

ADRIAN WALKER is an associate editor of *Communio*. At one time he was Joseph Ratzinger's translator. He currently lives and works near Freiburg, Germany.

CAROL ZALESKI is Professor of World Religions at Smith College in Northampton, Massachusetts. She is the author of *Otherworld Journeys* (1988) and *The Life of the World to Come* (1996). She is coauthor with Philip Zaleski of *The Book of Heaven* (2000), *Prayer: A History* (2005), and an intellectual biography of the Inklings forthcoming from Farrar, Straus & Giroux.

PHILIP ZALESKI is a Research Associate in Religion at Smith College in Northampton, Massachusetts. He is the author of *The Recollected Heart* (1995) and *Gifts of the Spirit* (2009); coauthor with Carol Zaleski of *The Book of Heaven* (2000), *Prayer: A History* (2005), and a forthcoming intellectual biography of the Inklings; and the editor of the annual Best Spiritual Writing series.

Introduction

Francesca Aran Murphy

It is a privilege to write an introduction for a book of essays dedicated to Stratford Caldecott. It would not be accurate to say that Stratford Caldecott has "promoted" the connection of imagination and Christianity in England for the past twenty-five years. It would be better to say that, along with his wife, Léonie, he has *lived* the bond of imagination and Christianity for most of his adult life. This living witness to the beauty of Christian faith has been important for the survival of Christianity in "England's green and pleasant land." If William Blake had had the good fortune to know Stratford and his wife, Léonie Caldecott, there might have been less talk of "Nobodaddy," and more of "Christ the Imagination." In the ambiance of the Caldecotts, it was natural not merely to see our shared homeland through Blake's satirical lens, as littered and unpleasant, but also to envision it as that "fairest Isle" of which Dryden wrote in Purcell's opera, *King Arthur*. This was not because the Caldecotts harbored any fake ideas about accentuating the positive, but because love sees the best in all things. If, as Cardinal Marc Ouellet writes in this volume, grace is a form of love, then we may say that the Caldecotts taught their many friends, associates, and pupils to envisage the world in the light of grace. All of the authors who contributed to this book were eager to do so, in order to thank Stratford Caldecott for his witness to the beauty and thus the truth and goodness of Christian, Trinitarian, and incarnational faith. For all of them, perhaps, Stratford Caldecott helped them not only to see, but to envision the truth. He lived amongst those who readily believe that King Arthur will return in England's darkest hour ("and [some] say, the sooner the better," as C. S. Lewis once put it).

This volume assembles essays about Mariology, Thomas Aquinas's epistemology, aesthetics, liturgics, economics, cosmology, ecumenism, homiletics, Tolkien, and John Henry Newman. The single thread that runs through them is perhaps the principle that in order to know ourselves and to know all else beside, it must participate in what Augustine calls "the light which shines above my mind," the divine light. That Platonic and Augustinian theme is appropriate, for it typifies Stratford Caldecott's orientation to all reality, worldly and other worldly. "Other worldly" is a phrase that naturally comes to mind when one thinks of the Caldecotts, and a note of otherworldliness can be heard throughout these essays. By his life and thought, Stratford Caldecott has testified that other worlds exist, in imagination but also, *and therefore*, in reality.

I thought that I was editing a Festschrift, which almost by definition is a collection of disparate essays. I find, however, that by the magnetic force of his personality, Stratford Caldecott's name has evoked an exemplary primer in theological aesthetics. In its own way, each of these essays is about the beauty of God—how that beauty is known (Borella), expressed in poetry, literature, and liturgy (Martínez, Cameron, Fagerberg), exhibited in art and in nature (Clayton, D. C. Schindler, Nichols, Taylor), apparent beyond the scope of Christianity (Shah-Kazemi), bodied forth in human lives (Milbank, both Zaleskis, and Cross), most especially the life of the Mother of God (Walker), and how it is or can be incarnate in society (D. L. Schindler). All of the essays are about the manifestation of the beauty of God. It is a great tribute to the Caldecotts' force of personality that they have stimulated such a lively, deep, and unitary collection of papers.

It is impossible to imagine Stratford without his wife, Léonie. I conclude this brief introduction with Dryden's immortal words, which remind us of an England beloved of Venus:

> Fairest Isle, all isles excelling,
> Seat of pleasures and of loves,
> Venus here will choose her dwelling,
> And forsake her Cyprian groves.
> Cupid from his fav'rite nation
> Care and envy will remove;
> Jealousy that poisons passion,
> And despair that dies for love.
> Gentle murmurs, sweet complaining,
> Sighs that blow the fire of love,
> Soft repulses, kind disdaining,
> Shall be all the pains you prove.
> Ev'ry swain shall pay his duty,
> Grateful ev'ry nymph shall prove;
> And as these excel in beauty,
> Those shall be renown'd for love.[1]

1. From *King Arthur*, Act 5, Scene 2. Words by John Dryden. Music by Henry Purcell.

1

It Is a Wonder, How Much the Clay Can Be Imprinted with the Beauty of Its Potter!

Saint Ephrem the Syrian, *Hymns on Virginity*, XXV

Francisco Javier Martínez

The authentic hymns of Saint Ephrem of Nisibis, or Saint Ephrem the Syrian as he is more widely known, are considered today among the best pieces of Christian theological poetry ever written. Saint Ephrem, who lived in the fourth century (between roughly 306–373 AD) in northern Mesopotamia, in Nisibis and Edessa—the modern-day cities of Nusaybin and Urfa, in eastern Turkey—was considered in his own era "the harp of the Holy Spirit."[1] Even in our time, Robert Murray SJ, a leading scholar of early Syriac theology and literature, has written that Ephrem is "the greatest poet in the Patristic period, and perhaps the only poet theologian to be placed next to Dante."[2] Interestingly, Hans Urs von Balthasar does not include him in his list of great poet-theologians in the Christian tradition studied in volumes 2 and 3 of *Herrlichkeit*, a list that includes, besides Dante, Saint John of the Cross, Charles Péguy, and Gerard Manley Hopkins. I have the impression that Balthasar only came to know Ephrem when these volumes of *Herrlichkeit* were already well on their way or almost finished (the first quotation of Ephrem's works appears in volume 6, and the way it is introduced in a footnote looks very much as a discovery),[3] and I often think that

1. Theodoret, *Correspondance*, 3:190.

2. Murray, *Symbols of Church*, 32.

3. Balthasar, *Glory of the Lord*, 6:40. The note is a long quotation of the German version of Edmund Beck from the hymn *De Fide* XXVI, published (in the original Syriac and in its German version) in the Corpus Scriptorum Christianorum Orientalium at Louvain in 1955. Balthasar's original publication in German is from 1965. There are other quotes in the *Theo-Drama* (vol. 2, 186–87, 215, 221) speaking about freedom and

if he had known Ephrem's works before, he would have doubtless included him among his collection of great Christian writers for whom the glory of God—the infinite beauty of God manifested in the beauty of God's love—is a major theme, first in their Christian experience and then in their poetic language. For Saint Ephrem, indeed, this is not only a major theme: it is *the* theme of his writing. When I have tried to think about a phrase that would present a synthesis of his theology, it is this one that comes to my mind: "The Lord's glory, or the divine in the flesh." Saint Ephrem is really the poet of the sacramentality of all creation, as the necessary implication of the incarnation of the Son of God. This sacramentality is a perception most strange to the modern worldview (and also, for this reason, one of the most needed if modernity is to be saved from its own self-destructive forces). In Ephrem's view, it is this sacramental sense of creation that unites the whole work of God in creation and redemption, in nature and grace, leaving no space for any dualism, ancient or modern. This divine presence in the flesh, and indeed in the whole material world, happens in Ephrem's view in various ways and degrees: its summit (the *princeps analogatum*) is the physical body of Christ himself, inhabited by the Logos. This presence is mysteriously prolonged in the waters of baptism, or in his body and blood in the Eucharist. Then there is also Mary and the church (the church as a whole and every single member of the church), where he also dwells. His presence in the church is truly a mysterious one, just as that presence is mysterious in the Eucharist, although in a different way and in different degrees. Just to give one example of this, let me quote this stanza of his hymn *De Fide* XIV, 5. Saint Ephrem is singing about the eucharistic celebration:

> The soul is Your bride; the body too is Your bridal chamber,
> Your guests are the senses and the thoughts.
> And if a single body is a wedding feast for You,
> How great is Your banquet with the whole Church![4]

---

quoting in the first of these references from several passages of Saint Ephrem's hymns *De Paradiso*, and in the last one from the hymns *Contra Haereses* XI (but in both cases from French or German translations different from the one in Beck's edition). In vol. 3 of *Dramatis personae: Persons in Christ*, the references multiply: see 291, 302, 305, 320, 323, 326, 352. All of the passages treat the vocation and the mission of Mary, especially in relationship to the church: Balthasar quotes from the hymns *De Nativitate*, *De Paradiso*, and *De Ecclesia*. To my knowledge, there are no other references to Ephrem in Balthasar's great theological trilogy. One thinks how many possibilities hymns like *Carmina Nisibena* XXXV–XLII or LII–LXVIII would have given Balthasar as an account and representation of the original "Theodrama."

4. Hymn *De Fide* XIV, 5. For this text, see Brock and Kiraz, *Ephrem the Syrian*, 219. This anthology is also a nice introduction to Ephrem's poetry. Most of the authentic works of Ephrem have been published in the original Syriac text, accompanied by a

Finally, there is his presence in history and in nature. He is present first of all in history, that is, especially in the symbols, types, images, and titles of the Old Testament. But also contemporary history is judged in the light of Christ's presence: good examples of this are the "Carmina Nisibena I–XII," on the difficulties and sieges suffered by the city of Nisibis, harassed by the Persians between 337–361 AD, and the hymn "Against Julian" (the Apostate), written in 363 AD, on the occasion of Julian's corpse passing through Nisibis, and the city being handed over to the Persians in the peace treaty that followed the emperor's defeat. In both these instances, as true heir of the prophetic tradition of the Old Testament, which saw history from God's covenant with Israel, Ephrem sees all the events of history from their fulfillment in Christ. As regards nature, Christ is also present in the things and events of nature, whose silent language speaks permanently about him. They not only speak about Christ, they in some way contain him. Also, the realities of nature constitute symbols full of Christ to those who look with the "luminous eye" of faith. Saint Ephrem has been able to compare the Lord's Incarnation in the womb of the Virgin Mary with his incarnation in the realities of nature. He could write, without the slightest reticence, "Creation was pregnant with the symbols of Christ, like Mary had been pregnant with His members."[5]

Of course, this small paper is not the place to make any introduction to Saint Ephrem's hymns or to his other works, and even less to his theology, which is quite articulate and complex. On the other hand, there are several excellent introductions in English relating to his biography, to the cultural context in which he lived, to his ways of thinking, and even to his theological methods.[6] My goal in this paper is just to offer an English version of one

---

German translation, by Beck in the series Corpus Scriptorum Christianorum Orientalium (CSCO). When it is needed, we will give in this essay just the CSCO number and the page, first for the text and then (between parentheses) for the translation. For the *Hymns on Faith* XIV, 5 the reference is CSCO 154, 62 (155, 46–47).

5. See hymns *De Virginitate* VI, 7. Cf. CSCO 223, 23 (224, 23).

6. We have already mentioned Robert Murray's work, which is doubtless the best general introduction to early Syriac literature and theology (although one can explain differently some of the points he makes in it, especially in the Introduction, for instance, about the meaning of the undeniable connections between early Syriac tradition and Qumran literature). Besides this excellent work, the following should be mentioned: Brock, *The Luminous Eye*; Griffith, *Faith Adoring the Mystery*; McVey, *Ephrem the Syrian* and "Ephrem the Syrian"; Mathews, Jr., "General Introduction." This last introduction describes with some detail the scholarly enterprise made during the twentieth century of recuperating the true image of the life and work of Saint Ephrem in the light of his authentic works and of the oldest and more credible Syriac testimonies about him. This recuperation was badly needed because of the long and steady hagiographical tradition that had deformed his image, making of him a monk of the kind described

of his beautiful hymns, one in which some of his theological themes appear in quite a creative manner, and to add some comments to my English version of it.

In his efforts to maintain and foster the communion of the Syriac-speaking church with the main body of the Nicaean church in the cultural melting pot of Mesopotamia, Ephrem struggled with four main difficulties, two from outside the church and two from inside. On one side there were the pagan cults alive in Mesopotamia and Persia in the fourth century and the attraction of the Jewish tradition (as a more articulated and established tradition increased by the fact that a number of Christians came from Jewish communities in the area). On the other hand, from "inside" the church, there were the Gnostic groups (mainly the followers of Mani, Marcion, and Bardaisan) and the heresy of Arius. It is mainly against these last two threats to Christian faith and identity that Ephrem used all the resources of his wit and intelligence. Reading adequately the "books," both of scripture and of nature (on these two books, see *Hymns on Paradise* V, 1-2), or playing harmoniously with the three lyres of nature, the Old Testament, and the New Testament (see *Hymns on Virginity* XXVII–XXX), the truth that God

by Theodoret of Cyrrhus in *The History of the Monks of Syria*. That deformation started already with the *Lausiac History* of Palladius at the very beginning of the fifth century. Both the authentic works of Saint Ephrem and the most reliable texts within the Syriac tradition instead make of him a pastor, possibly a "deacon," who helped his successive bishops both in Nisibis and Edessa with the liturgy and catechetical work, composing mainly hymns (*madrâšē*), the part of his work which has always been considered the best. He composed also metrical homilies (*mēmrē*) and other prose texts, including commentaries on the *Diatessaron* and on certain books of the scriptures, always with a didactical concern. He is credited with the "founding" of the "school of Nisibis," and later on, in his last decade of life (363–373 AD), after Nisibis had been turned over to the Persians, with the founding of the "school of the Persians" in Edessa (named also simply "the school of Edessa"), which would become famous during the christological controversies in the fifth century. Whatever his role in the "founding" of these schools, the fact is that his teaching and writing activities, coupled with the nature of his works and with his innumerable allusions to commerce and city life (including theater, circus fights, trade, fishing, etc.), call into question his portrait as a "Syrian monk" or hermit living in caves in the mountains. For the critical edition of two Syriac representatives of both readings of Ephrem's life and work, see Amar, *A Metrical Homily*. This work, a metrical homily written by a former student of the "school of Edessa" about forty years after the death of Ephrem, portrays Saint Ephrem as a new Moses, as a teacher of the truth, and is mainly devoted to defending (probably from more rigid views coming from Byzantine monastic practices) the practice established by Saint Ephrem of women choirs singing in the liturgy. As for the *Vita Syriaca*, a work from the sixth century heavily influenced by the Byzantine hagiographical tradition, but still a major source for Ephrem's life, see Amar, *The Syriac* Vita *Tradition of St. Ephrem the Syrian* (CSCO, 629; Script. Syri 242). Amar is now preparing a work under the title *Ephrem the Syrian: A Cultural and Intellectual Biography*.

has revealed to us for our salvation comes into light. Saint Ephrem explicitly stated in another of his hymns the goal of his writing: "Blessed is that one, O Lord, whose tongue has become for You as a cithara, and with it he sings songs able to cure those who listen to them"; only revealed truth "cures those who listen" from the "poison" of "false teachings" (*De Fide* II, 15).

To sing in order to cure, that is, in the defense of the revealed truth about God, the poet draws from the treasure house of the church two "medicines." One is the insistence regarding the ineffable and absolute transcendence of God (compromised, in spite of superficial appearances, by both the Gnostics and the Arians, but especially by the dialectics used by the latter). The other is the recognition of God's presence (of Christ's presence) in nature and in scripture, in material things (olive oil, a pearl, the sea) and in human beings, in the events of history (like the already mentioned sieges of Nisibis by the Persians or the death of the emperor Julian), in Mary and in the church, and in the mysteries/sacraments of the church, which are "symbols" (really anticipations, "secrets," rÅzæ), opening for us the life of the kingdom in heaven. Broadly speaking, and perhaps somewhat unfairly, one could say that the affirmation of the transcendence of God points more to the anti-Arian polemic, while the emphasis on God's presence in creation and in the Old Testament has a more anti-Gnostic ring.

In the particular hymn whose annotated translation I offer in this paper,[7] both aspects are present, so that it can be considered a fairly good example of Saint Ephrem's writing and procedures: a strong statement of the absolute transcendence of the impenetrable Mystery that is God (so much that it is absolutely impossible to fathom the begetting of God's son), and a beautiful insistence on the presence of that Mystery, not only in the incarnate Son, in "the Baby in the manger," but also in those who are close to him (Mary and John at the cross, Simon's mother-in-law, the old prophetess Anna, the myriads of virgins who are his spouses). May this translation of a pearl of early Christian literature serve as an homage of gratitude for

7. I am fully aware, of course, that this hymn, as well as all the others from the collection *De Virginitate*, are already translated into English by my dear teacher Kathleen E. McVey in her previousy mentioned *Ephrem the Syrian: Hymns*, 259–468. Although it should be obvious that I have had McVey's translation always at hand, still, the present version is based on my direct work on Saint Ephrem's text, and at some points my reading or my interpretation of that text differs from hers. I am convinced too that the presentation of an isolated hymn (or of a small group of them) could perhaps help to highlight their beauty and their manner of thought (perhaps even could attract the reader to go to other hymns), more than the prospect of having to face the whole of some of Saint Ephrem's great hymn collections, given the considerable cultural differences with our world and other difficulties that the hymns have for us.

Stratford Caldecott, a brother and a friend in whom it has always been easy to recognize the image and the presence of our common Lord.

Although the hymn *De Virginitate* XXV is part of a collection of fifty-two hymns that in the old manuscript Vat. Syrus 111, from the year 522 AD, bears the title *De Virginitate*, it is known that this collection is composed of a number of smaller collections or *excerpta* of such collections: the hymns dealing with virginity constitute only the first of the smaller series of hymns included in it, and that series embraces only hymns I–III.[8] Allusions to virginity, and to the life of the consecrated virgins (both male and female) within the church, are scattered of course all through the work of Ephrem, and we will find them also in this hymn.

De Virginitate XXV is presented as an *encomium* of the Apostle John (title, strophe 1), but the truth is that strophes 1–12 develop in an exquisite way the wonderful relationship between Jesus, Mary, and John, using as a point of departure the Gospel episode in which Jesus, from the cross, entrusts Mary and John to one another (John 19:26–27). The central theme of the text is, then, the relationship between Jesus, Mary, and the church, represented here by the beloved disciple. But, and this is characteristic of Ephrem's work, the poet does not make any abstract consideration. Beginning with this Gospel episode, he instead illustrates, in a very beautiful and concrete way, what we have said above is *the theme* of Saint Ephrem's theology: the divine presence in the flesh. This presence is seen first of all in the humanity of Christ (strophe 12); in Mary and in the consecrated virgins (strophes 10 and 11); in John, who to some extent represents the other apostles (strophe 5); and in all the souls "betrothed" to Christ (strophes 17–18). Then, and in a way that gives the impression of having been put together in a random manner—which might indicate that the hymn is not complete—there are Simon's mother-in-law (whom Jesus's presence cured from her fever; see Mark 1:29–31) in the strophes 13–14, and the prophetess Anna, who met the Baby Jesus at His presentation at the temple (Luke 2:36–38), in strophes 15–16. All of these have been transfigured, blessed with Christ's presence in one way or another. The apostles, the virgins (both male and female), and the "betrothed souls" (the baptized) continue, in a certain way, the union between divinity and humanity that came to happen in Jesus, with the Incarnation, in Mary's womb. For this reason, in the church, in looking at one another we come to recognize in others the living presence of Christ (strophe 9). In this sense, Mary is, in the deepest way,

---

8. I have used for the translation the critical edition of E. Beck, *Des heiligen Ephraem des Syrers Hymnen De Virginitate*.

a "type" and a beginning of the entire mystery of the church, even if this particular hymn does not say this explicitly.

Strophe 1 in the hymn is introductory. Relying on the Lord's goodness, "Who has condescended to give Himself even to the hideous ones so that they might become attractive," the poet asks for the mercy of being like the beloved disciple, John (who is not named), and "trades" with the Lord this particular mercy: Ephrem will sing the praise of the disciple in order that the Lord might be merciful with him and give the poet the same beauty that he gave John.

In strophes 2 and 3 the poet speaks to Mary. Jesus, her "Lord and son," gives his mother into the custody of "the son of His bosom," John, configured in such a way to the image of Christ that—so the poet says—the image of Christ was "painted" in him. The two strophes emphasize with some detail the parallelism between Mary's motherhood in respect to Christ and Christ's fatherhood in respect to John. By entrusting Mary to John's custody, Jesus repays the debt he owed her, "the debt of His upbringing." Especially suggestive is the image of the last verse in strophe 2: "Everything you had lent Him, He repaid to you when He was crucified." What Mary "had lent" to Christ was his flesh, his humanity. And Christ returned that to Mary by giving to her his disciple, configured to his own image. What this implies is that Jesus is mysteriously present in the disciple. In his disciple, Christ's humanity mysteriously abides once he has concluded his earthly ministry and "gone to the Father" (John 16:28). This thought, of course, does not come from Ephrem, but from the scriptures, in texts such as, for instance, John 13:20: "Truly, I tell you, whoever receives one whom I send receives me; and whoever receives me receives him who sent me." In the following strophes, Ephrem develops this thought with a variety of nuances, first around the constellation Mary-Jesus-John, then in a few other figures including Peter's mother-in-law, the prophetess Anna, and finally the virgins and the betrothed souls in whom Jesus dwells.

Strophe 4 is like a parenthetical reflection in the midst of the poet's address to his mother. The theme of the insertion is the likeness between John and Jesus, a fruit of the disciple's love for his Master. That love brings the disciple to an imitation of the Master to such a point that the image of the Master is imprinted in the disciple.

In strophes 5 and 6, the poet speaks to Mary again. In strophe 5, Jesus's coming to Mary is related again to his coming to all men in the Incarnation through his disciples: "[He] sent Himself to those who were far away." The sentence refers indeed both to the Incarnation and to the mission of the apostles. It is worth noting the bold and clear statement of the divinity of

Christ: although Christ wants to come to every human person (as the Good one, a title for God already used in the first line of the hymn), he as God is already there, even where he is not known. He is also, says Saint Ephrem, "entirely present to every one who seeks Him." Unfortunately, in strophe 6 there is almost a verse and a half missing because (as happens in several other places, in this and other hymns of this collection) the manuscript is somewhat damaged (it fell into the river Nile when it was being transported from Egypt to Rome). However, the general idea is clear enough (and I make a suggestion to fill here the resulting gap): Christ "imprinted" himself in his disciple to comfort his mother so that Mary, when looking at the disciple, could see her Son, could see Jesus.

A first climax of the hymn appears in strophes 7–9. In these, the poet is not speaking to Mary anymore. In strophe 7, he underlines the difference between the images of the kings of this world and the images of Jesus. By merely making this comparison, he implies that Jesus is both king and Lord, the two expressions he uses for the worldly masters. The images (probably meaning "the statues") of kings are all of them mute, dead images. The images of Christ, on the contrary, are living persons, able to speak. Although Ephrem does not explicitly say so, the implication is that both Mary and John are living images of Christ. These images are not just living, but free: images that freely sing the glory of their Maker. This thought of Mary and John as living images of Christ, which is the core and the center of the hymn, begins to be uttered in strophe 8 when the poet speaks of the wonder of John at Mary, in whose womb the Most High had dwelt, and of the wonder of Mary at John, who had grown so much that he could "fall on God's breast." The deepest reason for that twofold wonder is just insinuated in strophe 8, but is told in full clarity and beauty in the following strophe (9): when looking at one another, they saw Christ. In this, they have given us the key to any relationship between Christians, which is recognizing the presence of Christ in his images.

In strophe 10, after this first poetic (and also theological) climax, begins an exhortation to honor Christ in the sanctuaries in which he dwells today, and more specifically, to respect his presence in the consecrated virgins.

In the same *parenetic* vein starts strophe 11, giving as examples Joseph and John, who venerated and respected Mary. And the text gives the reason for this respect: Mary was like the tent, the temporary tabernacle of God's glory (see Heb 9) that Israel had built in the desert. Already in that tabernacle Immanuel ("God with us") was accompanying God's people, and by that, Saint Ephrem means that it was Christ who accompanied Israel. From there, the poet goes on to consider the disproportion between the external, visible dwelling and the Immensity it bears, inviting us not to despise this last one because of the littleness of the first one.

This thought brings Saint Ephrem to a new polemic development having to do with Arianism. This development fills the last two verses of strophe 11 and all of strophe 12. No matter how strange this might seem, because it is not expected from what precedes, it is the real climax and the key to the whole hymn. The perspective from which the Arian question is approached is quite interesting: it looks as if Saint Ephrem were diagnosing the Arian position as a certain inability to perceive the transcendence of the divine presence in the created realities in which God dwells. More specifically, he sees it as an inability to perceive that transcendence in those sanctuaries who are the consecrated virgins and that sanctuary which was Mary's womb, where the Logos has "put on" our flesh. The poet makes his thought fully explicit only in strophe 12, by mentioning the "Baby in the manger," unfathomable to our limited thought in both his greatness and his ability to self-limit himself. What is behind all the developments in the text now becomes clear. It is the mystery of the Incarnation, from which all other presences of Christ in his images derive. Christ is present in the apostles, in the sanctuaries of the Christian virgins; all the baptized are in some sense an "extension" of the Incarnation in time and space.

The hymn has six more strophes yet. The themes of these strophes continue the idea of the blessing of Christ's presence in different contexts: the cure of the fever of Simon Peter's mother-in-law (strophes 13–14), and Anna the prophetess (strophes 15–16). The text ends by establishing a contrast between Solomon, whose many wives brought him to paganism, and the pure marriage of Christ with myriads of myriads of souls through baptism (strophes 17–18). Although one could signal the unity of thought that goes like a thread throughout all the strophes, the connection of these figures with one another and with the developments in strophes 1–12 is more than loose. So it is difficult to avoid the impression that the hymn here has been cut in one way or another and that the logic of those connections was clearer in the original, larger hymn.

On the Disciple Whose Blessing Was Great.[9]
(Thirteenth [hymn] with the same melody)[10]

1. Good One, you condescended to give yourself
    even to the hideous ones, so that they might become attractive
        with you!
    Make me also worthy to be adorned
    with that precious beauty of your disciple!
    I will seek refuge in him whom you loved, in order to find mercy;
    I will sing the praise of the one you cherished, to receive his beauty.
    I will sing, then, his love to you, that you might reward me
    with mercy, and not with a just wage.

Response: Glory to the Omnipotent One!

2. Blessed are you, O woman, because your Lord and son
    entrusted you to the one in whom His image was painted!
    The son of your womb has not been ungrateful to your love,
    and He has entrusted you to the son of His bosom.
    You caressed Him upon your lap when He was small,
    and upon His lap He also caressed him.[11]
    Everything you had lent Him, He repaid to you when He was crucified:
    the debt of His upbringing.

9. The "disciple whose blessing was great" is the Apostle John. The reason for that blessing is not made explicit in the title of the hymn or in the text of the hymn itself: it could refer to the fact that John reclined his head on the bosom of his Lord during the Last Supper (cf. John 13:23), or to the fact that Jesus entrusted him to the custody of his mother, as well as that he was entrusted with the custody of Mary (cf. John 19:26–27), or still, to the fact that he was the beloved disciple of Jesus (John 13:23; 19:26; 20:2; 21:7, 20).

10. Saint Ephrem's hymns, in the manuscript tradition, have always an indication about the melody with which they had to be sung. That melody is usually the *incipit* of a strophe, known to the community or to the choir, with the same syllabic structure as the hymn in whose front it is placed. When in the old manuscript tradition there is a series of hymns with the same melody, one can suspect in many cases that they belong together and that they formed a unity of some sort: perhaps they were composed (or used) together for the same occasion. Here, the group of hymns with the same melodic indication are hymns XIII–XXX in the collection *De Virginitate*. The melodic indication given at the beginning of hymn XIII is "Blessed are you, Ephrata!" This indication (and this type of strophe) appears also in other collections. Even the phrase is taken from (or at least it coincides with) the first verse of the hymn *De Nativitate* XXV. It could be interesting to note that many of the hymns associated with this melodic indication sing the blessing that Christ's presence means for certain persons, places, cities, etc. This is exactly the context of our hymn here. As for the actual practice of singing Ephrem's hymns, besides the homily of Jacob of Sarug already cited (cf. *supra*, note 6), see Kathleen E. McVey, "Were the Earliest *madrāšē* Songs or Recitations?"

11. The reference is to John 13:23. A note about vocabulary: "womb" and "bosom" translate the Syriac *ḥūbbā*, while "lap" translates *ḥedayyā*, literally, "breasts."

3. The Crucified, indeed, repaid all debts:[12]
   even this one which He had with you was repaid by Him.
   He had taken from your breasts the visible milk;
   so too John drank from His breast hidden mysteries.[13]
   Confidently Christ approached your breasts,
   and confidently John reclined upon the breast of Christ.
   As you were going to miss His voice, He gave you His lyre,[14]
   that he might be your comfort.

4. That boy so much loved Our Lord
   that he portrayed Him in himself, he put Him on, and resembled Him.
   In everything was he zealous to be like Him:
   in his speech, in his aspect, even in his ways.[15]
   The creature put on his Creator,
   even though he was not like That One Who really is.[16]

12. "The Crucified repaid *all* debts." *All* is a gloss of the translator. With this phrase, Ephrem alludes to Col 2:13–14, a text to which Ephrem appeals quite often. *Debts* is a usual image in Aramaic for *sins*, to the point of being almost synonymous. But if this sense of sins is clearly the meaning in verse 1, the debt of verse 2, instead, is only the debt of gratitude that Jesus has with his mother, like any son with his, and has no relationship whatsoever with the idea of sin: it is the debt of his upbringing, as the last verse of strophe 2 says.

13. The verb *drank* is a gloss of the translator to make more clear the text, which offers no doubts about its meaning. Equally, in the two following verses, the translator has added the proper names for the sake of clarity: in the Syriac text, the subjects are merely indicated by the conjugation of the verbs or by pronouns. Again, the poet is referring to John 13:23. The "hidden mysteries": McVey thinks, following Beck, that this expression might refer to the fact that Judas was to be the betrayer, and mentions John 13:21–30 and several parallel texts by Ephrem (*De Azymis* XIV, 11; *De Crucifixione* III, 15), although she says that "surely something more is meant"—perhaps the deep understanding of the mystery of the Incarnation that shows up in the Johannine writings, perhaps even the perception of paradise. Cf. Brock, "The Mysteries Hidden in the Side of Christ."

14. "His lyre": John is named here the *lyre* of Christ, doubtless because he sang, in the Gospel (cf. John 1:1–14) and in his letters (cf. 1 John 1:1–3), the divinity of Christ.

15. "In His ways": the text says, literally, "in His steps" (*halkâteh*). But obviously, the reference is not to the way of walking, but to the "way of life," to Jesus's conduct.

16. At the beginning of the verse, in the Syriac text, there is a Syriac word, *'etdammī*, which is omitted in the version, since it is probably a copyist mistake known as dittography. The resulting verse is just too long. In the case of maintaining the text as it is, the version should say, "and he resembled Him, although he was not like That One Who really is" (*'a[y]k haw lam d-hūyū*). In this last expression, *lam* is usually the indication of direct speech (which does not fit here) or of a quote. It goes always after the first word of the quote. I am not able to identify the quote here: the text is too short. The other possibility (the one I have chosen for the version) is that *lam* could be used to emphasize a word. That explains the nuance "like That One that *really* is."

It is a wonder, how much the clay can be imprinted
with the beauty of its Author![17]

5. He left you, and yet He did not leave you, for in His disciple
    He returned and came to live with you.
    He is the Good One, who sent Himself
    to those who were far away, although He was already there.[18]
    He inclined His good will to everyone,
    He sent His love everywhere.
    Even if He remains hidden to all, He is entirely present
    to everyone who seeks Him.[19]

6. When He saw that you could not wean your love
    from that son whom you had weaned,
    He imprinted and painted Himself, the Limpid One in
        the purified one[20]
    that you might see in His disciple[21]
    [your Lord, the son of your womb.]
    With precious [stuff] is the sculpture fashioned.[22]

17. In the two last verses of the strophe the image of the clay serves to express the divinization of humanity, exemplified in John. There is also a veiled allusion to Gen 1:26–27; 2:7 (although the term used by the poet is *tīnā*, "clay," instead of *'aprā*, "dust [of the earth]," as in Gen 2:7).

18. The phrase "to those who were far away" designates here probably the members of the human race, who, as creatures, are "far away" from God, or the pagans. In other texts of Ephrem, the opposition between "those near" and "those who were far away" represents the difference between the contemporaries of Christ, mainly Jews, and those who were not contemporaries of Christ, coming mainly from paganism, cf. the hymn *On the Nativity* XVI, 6–7. The distinction between "those near" and "those far away" has its source in scripture: cf. Isa 57:19 and especially Acts 2:39 and Eph 2:13, 17.

19. The phrase "to every one who seeks Him" alludes probably to Gentiles of good will, since the context of the strophe (cf. verses 3–6) speaks certainly of the mission of the apostles to the world (without ceasing to have in mind the Incarnation, the mission of the Son to the world, of which the mission of the apostles is only a continuation in history). Although this is less probable, the phrase could also refer to those who, like John, believed in him: the Syriac verb b'rā has the meaning both of "seeking" and "asking." In this case perhaps one should translate the phrase thus: "to those who call on Him."

20. "The Limpid One" (*šapyā*) is Christ, and "the purified one" or "the clean one" (*dakyā*) is John. In practice, both terms are synonyms. The poet wants to emphasize the similitude between John and Christ.

21. The words within brackets in the following two verses are a pure conjecture of the translator, since the manuscript is damaged here. I think, however, that the sense of the missing text could not be very different from the one offered here.

22. The conjecture "stuff" has no pretense whatsoever. The Syriac text could use any word (in the masculine gender, in the singular number) to denote the material with

> Here the eloquent came to stand for the Silent One,
> Who did not speak when He was judged.[23]

7. All the images of kings are mute,
   although their lords speak all the time.
   The images of Our Savior are a wonder,
   for their wills are their lyres.[24]
   The Word of that glorious Silence[25]
   (He whose manner of generation cannot be said)[26]
   is sung by a creature, and not by the Father or the Son,
   Who dwell in one another in silence.

8. The boy was seeing in the woman
   how much the Most High had lowered Himself:
   how He had come to dwell in a frail womb,
   and how He had come out to be suckled with weak milk.

---

which a sculpture could be made. The word translated here as sculpture is *ṣalmā*, literally "image," but meaning usually "statue," "idol." In the next strophe, however, we translate the plural, *ṣalmē*, for "images of kings."

23. These last two verses emphasize that John, "the eloquent," is the image of Christ the Word. John is named "the eloquent" (*mlīlā*) doubtless because of his writings, while Christ is named "the Silent One, Who did not speak when He was judged" because of His silence before the Sanhedrin (Mark 14:61) or, with less probability, before Herod (Luke 23:9). The motif of the eloquence of John and the silence of Jesus serves to prepare, in the next strophe, two other themes in the hymn: first, the contraposition between the "silent" images of the emperors and the "singing" witnesses of Jesus, and second, the wonder of a creature "singing" the generation of the Word that takes place in the eternal silence of divine life.

24. That is to say, "they sing freely." The difference with the images of the kings of this world could not be stated more sharply: first, not only the apostles and all the disciples of Our Savior do speak, while the images of the kings are mute, but, second, they sing, and they sing freely. The idea of freedom and free will is central to Ephrem's anti-Gnostic polemics against the determinism of the Gnostic teachings. E. Beck, *Ephraems Reden*, almost identifies free will with the *imago Dei*; T. Kronholm, *Motifs from Genesis 1–11*, pays attention to other aspects of the *imago Dei* as well. On freedom in the thought of Saint Ephrem, see Bou Mansour, "La Liberte chez S. Ephrem le Syrien"; "La defense"; and "Aspects."

25. "The glorious Silence" designates here the Father. For this motif, which seems to have connotations from the Gnostic vocabulary, see *De Fide* XXII, 10; *De Paradiso* IV, 11; and also Ignatius of Antioch, *To the Magnesians*, VIII, 2.

26. The word "generation" does not correspond to any word in the Syriac text. In this sense, it is a gloss of the translator. The poet says, literally: "The word [. . .], that one whose *how* cannot be said." The *how* refers both to the generation of the Son and to His way of being in and with the Father. The gloss is an attempt to help the understanding of the reader. A thought that Ephrem repeats often, especially in the *Sermones De Fide* and in the *Hymns on Faith*, is that we know *the fact* of the generation of the Son, but it is impossible for us to know and therefore to express adequately the *how*.

> But also the woman was amazed at him: how much he had grown,
> to ascend so much as to be able to fall on the breast of God.[27]
> Both were amazed at one another, seeing how they had been worthy
> to grow by grace.

9. You, Lord, were Whom they saw in one another
    when at one another they looked.[28]
    Your mother saw You in that disciple of Yours,
    and also he saw You in Your mother.
    That is to look well![29] They were seeing You, Lord, in one another,
    all the time, as in a mirror.[30]
    They showed us a type, so that we too, in one another,
    may see You, our Savior.

10. The boy honored the sanctuary in which You dwelt,
    in fear and in love, in order to teach us
    that today it is true, the King's Son dwells
    in the consecrated virgins.[31]
    Whoever has discernment and understands she is a sanctuary,

27. The poet alludes again to John reclining (falling) on Jesus's lap in the Last Supper; cf. John 13:23.

28. The manuscript is damaged here, also: in the first verse of the strophe three syllables are missing to complete the meter of the verse. The reconstruction we propose is *ba-hdâde*, "in one another," which, although it is repeated in the following verse, has another position in the sentence, so that it does not look like padding in Syriac. In any case, the sense of the missing text could not change sensibly the meaning, which is quite clear.

29. "That is to know how to look!" A somewhat free version of the Syriac phrase *'a(w)hazzâyê*, literally: "O the seers [spectatores]!," probably with the immediate sense of "What [amazing kind of] seers!"

30. The version "*as* in a mirror" weakens the strength of the Syriac expression, which simply says "in the mirror," that is to say, "in the mirror [that they were for one another]." On the image of the "mirror" in the works of Ephrem and its uses, see Beck, "Das Bild"; Beck, "Zur Terminologie." To the texts quoted there by Beck, one has to add the important text at the beginning of the *Letter to Publius*, a prose work of Ephrem discovered and published after the publication of Beck's first article; see Brock, "Ephrem's Letter to Publius."

31. "The consecrated virgins" translates *qaddīšatā*, literally, "holy." But in this context *qaddīšatā* cannot mean anything but "consecrated." Ephrem is referring obviously to the consecrated women known in early Syriac literature as the "daughters of the covenant," *bnât qyâmâ*. On them (and their correspondent "sons of the covenant," *bnay qyâmâ*), and the role of this old form of consecrated life in the early Syriac-speaking church, there is a wealth of literature. We should mention here only some important contributions. Besides the classic studies by E. Beck, "Ein Beitrag" and "Asketentum," see Griffith, "Asceticism in the Church of Syria."

is terrified of dishonoring your spouse.[32]
How harsh the curse for the one who dares
to dishonor the King in His own palace![33]

11. Joseph had honored also, like John did,
Your mother's womb, as carrying a mystery.[34]

32. "Your spouse": this expression shows how the *qaddīšatā* in verse 4 has to be understood.

33. The consecrated virgins are a "temple" or, more precisely, a "sanctuary," *nawsā* (Syriac transcription of the Greek ναός), in whom Christ dwells (verses 1 and 5). They are also a "palace," the mansion of the King. Even if the Syriac term *hayklā* (verse 8) means both *temple* and *palace*, the mention of the King in the verse makes preferable the version *palace*. The same alternation of temple and palace in the same context is found in the hymn *De Nativitate*, XVII, 5. It might be worth noting that, according to *Carmina Nisibena* XLVI, 1, Christ dwells also in the male virgins: "Our Savior, Who came down to dwell in Mary, today dwells also in the body of chaste men and chaste women."

34. The poet mentions Joseph's awe for the Holy Virgin also in the hymn *De Nativitate*, XVI, 16: "as carrying a Mystery" ('*a[y]k da-b-râzā*), literally, "as in a mystery." The Syriac term *râzā*, which appears here and in the following verse, is one of the theologically more loaded terms in the work of Ephrem and in the whole tradition of the Syriac-speaking church. It is also one of the most difficult to translate adequately. Sometimes it still keeps some of its original sense of "secret," and hence, its meaning "mystery" (in the sense of the Greek μυστήριον). For instance, in strophe 3 of this hymn Ephrem has said that in the Last Supper John "drank from the breast of Christ hidden *mysteries*" (*râzē*). In the vocabulary of typology, *râzā* means something similar to "symbol," but we need to keep in mind that in our present modern cultural context, the symbols tend to be understood (and to be) pure arbitrary human constructions (like the "icons" in the vocabulary of informatics or traffic signs). In the world of the Syriac-speaking church, "symbol" (*râzā*) is a visible, created reality, which is really always more than we can perceive. It always contains a greater reality, to which the symbol points. Only the luminous eye of the faith can hint at that greater reality, but it is always already there. This "real presence" of the greater reality in the smaller one is, on one side, what links the meaning "mystery" with the meaning "symbol," and the meaning "symbol/mystery" with the meaning "sacrament," especially the eucharistic species, which in Syriac also are named *râzē*. So, broadly speaking, the term refers in Syriac to three kinds of realities: the "symbols" of Christ in the nature "pregnant" of him (Ephrem's parlance); the "symbols" or "types" in the scripture, also mainly of Christ, but also of certain other persons, or events, or practices in the new "reality" created by Christ; and finally "the sacraments," which anticipate and contain and give "symbolically" or "mysteriously" the life of the kingdom. Besides *râzē*, the Syriac language also uses a certain number of cognate terms, that in some contexts can be entirely interchangeable: *tūpsā* (transcription of the Greek τυπος, which means properly "type," "sketch," "model"; *dmūtā*, "image," "likeness"; *pel'etā*, "comparison," "parabole"). It is very important to realize that *râzā* can refer equally to the earthly reality imbued by the divine presence as to the divine presence itself contained in the earthly "symbol." In a more technical language, in the context of typology, we could say that *râzā* can designate both the "type" and the "antitype." A similar point could be made with *tūpsā* or with the Greek term μυστήριον. On typology in Saint Ephrem in general, its vocabulary and its theological import, and

It is the mystery of the Tabernacle, like that temporal tabernacle
in which Immanuel was dwelling.[35]
Both Joseph and that tabernacle persistently admonish us,[36]
not to treat God lightly in his sanctuaries.
How dreadful is dialectics! That Highness that cannot be measured,[37]
we have tried to measure It with our inquiries.

12. Abyss not fathomable by the searchers!
Height too lofty for the mortals!
Length not to be measured as with cubits!
Breadth not to be calculated as with spans!
Even if you had the wings of the seraphim,
you would not be able to measure, by any means,
that Baby Who is in the manger, lowly in His aspect,
but great in His hidden reality.[38]

on the meaning of *râzā* in particular, see Beck, "Symbolum-Mysterium"; Brock, *Luminous Eye*, 53–84; Bou Mansour, *La pensée*. Having said all this, in the particular text we are working with here it does not seem fit to translate *'a(y)k da-b-râzā* by "as in a symbol": although the "honor paid by John to Christ's mother" is certainly a "symbol" or a "type," a "model" for the honor we should pay to one another as temples of Christ, it seems to me that the expression tries to explain the reason of that honor, and the little gloss I make in the translation tries to convey this. On the other hand, in the following verse (verse 3), we find again the term *râzā*: Mary, or more precisely, Mary's womb ("your mother's womb"), "is the *râzā* of the tabernacle, the temporal tabernacle." "The temporal tabernacle" is in Syriac the technical designation of the "tent" or the "tabernacle" in which the glory of the Lord dwelt and went with God's people from the time of the Sinai Covenant to the construction of the Temple of Solomon; see Exod 26; 33:7–11; 36:8–19; and especially Heb 8–9. If *râzā* were to be translated here as "symbol," the text would seem to mean that Mary (and the Christian virgins) are the "symbol" of the tent in the desert, when what the text is trying to say goes exactly in the opposite direction: although the poet says clearly that in the tent "Immanuel was dwelling" (like 1 Cor 10:4 says that "the stone [from which the Israelites drank in the desert] was Christ"), the "temporal tabernacle" is a provisory "symbol" or a "type" of Mary and the virgins, in whom the definitive gift of God dwells now: Jesus Christ, the Immanuel, "God with us."

35. "Immanuel." Saint Ephrem uses the same term as the Syriac Bible (*Pšittā*) for Isa 7:14, which merely transliterates the Hebrew expression.

36. "Joseph and the temporal tabernacle" is a gloss of the translator to clarify the referents of the Syriac text. This says only "Both of them persistently admonish us." The reference to the tabernacle "admonishing" might be to laws like the one in Num 1:51, prohibiting the approach to the tabernacle.

37. "Dialectics," in Syriac *drāšā*. Two other possible translations, even more "literal," could be "investigation" or "dispute." The term—common in Saint Ephrem's polemic with the Arians—serves in this context to designate the kind of formal reasoning of what has been called "the Second Sophistic," which was at the base of the Arianism known to Saint Ephrem. On the intellectual context of Saint Ephrem's polemic with the Arians, see Bruns, "Arius hellenizans?".

38. The whole strophe is a song to God's transcendence, told in simple but highly

13. Blessed are you, sick mother-in-law of Simon,
for the Physician from on high came down to visit you.[39]
Although He approached your hand, it was not to explore the fever,[40]
for He is the One Who has stretched out all the veins.
He hid the fever in them.
The source of perspiration united itself to the veins' fire.[41]
By a hint of their Lord, the two of them, both the fire and the source,
conquered and were conquered in one single body.[42]

14. In your body, O sick woman, dwelt a fever,
a hidden, invisible fire.
In the body of your Physician there was the fire from on high,
visible only to spiritual beings.[43]

---

expressive terms, and to the paradox of the Incarnation, his mysterious (and poetically abrupt) becoming "that Baby Who is in the manger." What is most significant about the strophe is that the paradoxical presence of God in the "lowly" humanity of Jesus constitutes really the paradigm and the *princeps analogatum* to the presence of Christ in his "other" sanctuaries: Mary, John and the other apostles (cf. strophe 5), the consecrated virgins, and those who are mentioned in the following strophes: Simon's mother-in-law and the old prophetess Anna, "the flock of the pure Lamb." Because of its content, this strophe is really the core, the *climax*, of the hymn.

39. Mark 1:29–31p. For the image of the Physician applied to Christ, traditional in the Syriac-speaking church, and very common in Saint Ephrem's works, see, for instance, *Commentarium in Diatessaron*, ch. VIII (according to Beck, of dubious authenticity, but that might only mean that the text has suffered certain manipulations) and *Carmina Nisibena* XXXIV. See also R. Murray, *Symbols*, 199–203. The designation "physician," in Syriac *'asyā*, is also used by Saint Ephrem for God—see, for instance, the hymn *De Ecclesia* LII, 4—and for the Holy Spirit—see the hymn *De Virginitate* IV, 4.

40. Both Mark 1:30 and Matt 8:15 mention the "taking of her hand," although Luke 4:39 does not. The "taking of the hand" (the pulse) was usually one of the means by which physicians estimated the strength of the fever. Saint Ephrem emphasizes that Jesus did not need to do that kind of examination, since he is the Creator of the veins.

41. As McVey observes, Beck has remarked in a note to his version of the hymn *De Epiphania* VII, 16, that perspiration was seen as a cure for fever. "The veins' fire": in Syriac simply "their fire."

42. The Syriac text has only "the two of them," without further qualification. The phrase "both the fire and the source (of transpiration)" is therefore a gloss of mine. It is not obvious at first glance "who" are "the two of them," and why they "conquered and were conquered." My suggestion is only tentative, but the idea seems to be that the "source of transpiration" (that fire that cures) acts as a "symbol" of the divinity of Christ, the true "source of health," of which the next strophe speaks openly. The paradox, in both strophes, is that two fires unite themselves to "cool" the fever. This was at once their victory (they won against the fever) and their defeat (because the fires "cooled" instead of "burning").

43. "Fire," in Syriac *nūrā*, is the image used more frequently in Saint Ephrem's world to refer to the divinity, and also to the "matter" from which are "made" the created spiritual beings, like the angels. For the angels, see Cramer, *Die Engelvorstellung*, 113–17. A

This is a wonder. Who would be able to speak of it?
For the fervor of mercy went in, cooled, and healed you.
The listeners were amazed at the fiery coal that allayed
the intensity of the fever.

15. Blessed are you, old woman, beautiful Anna,
because the silent Baby made you into a prophetess.[44]
His hidden silence thundered in your mind,
so that through you He might sing of His exploits.
Through you He advanced His deeds when He was just a child,
but He Himself would fulfill them when He became an adult.[45]
O Baby Who, although silent, are able to sing in every tongue,
for You are the Lord of all mouths![46]

---

clear text is the hymn *De Fide* XXX, 2: "The natures of the Watchers [the angels] are fire and wind [spirit]; the natures of the bodies are dust and water." See also *De Fide* X, 9. Even the soul, some have considered—Ephrem says in the hymn *De Fide* I, 7, referring to some of the Greek philosophers or to the Manichaeans—"is made of fire," which implies probably that it shares somehow in the divine nature. As for the image of the "fire" used for the divinity of Christ, see, for instance, the hymn *De Beata Virgine Maria* X, 14 (a hymn possibly authentic in this mostly unauthentic collection, edited by Thomas J. Lamy, *Sancti Ephraem Syri Hymny et Sermones*; see vol. 2, 561): "Of fire you are, also spiritual, Son of the divine Essence. You took a body from the daughter of David." Even more obvious is the text in the hymn *De Fide* IV, 2: "Fire came into the womb, put on the body, and came out." Many other examples could be easily gathered. On other occasions, the Syriac term used is *gmūrtā*, "fiery coal." So, for instance, *De Nativitate*, XI, 5: "If [Mary] could embrace You, it is because the fiery coal, merciful, protected her bosom." "Fire" is in Mary's womb, in the waters of the baptismal spring, in the eucharistic species; see the important hymn *De Fide* X. In *De Nativitate* XXII, 14, Saint Ephrem cries out, "Blessed the One Who has mixed His fire with us!" For the image of the divinity as fire, see Brock, *Luminous Eye*, 38–39, and for the image of the "fiery coal," 103–6, 8.

44. For the episode of Anna when Jesus was brought to the temple for the purification of Mary (Lev 12:2–4, 8) and the offering of the firstborns (Exod 13:2, 12), see Luke 2:22–24, 36–38. Saint Ephrem speaks of Anna also in his hymn *De Nativitate* XVI, 13–14.

45. The Gospel reads, "At that moment [when Jesus had entered the temple], she came, and began to praise God, and to speak about the child to all who were looking for the redemption of Jerusalem" (Luke 2:38). Ephrem obviously interprets this "speaking about" Jesus as a foretelling of his future exploits: his teaching, his signs, his passion and his triumph over Satan and death.

46. In my view, these two verses are an example of a typical phenomenon in Aramaic: the change of a sentence, in addressing someone directly, from the second to the third person. Examples of this phenomenon are quite common in the works of Ephrem: see, for instance, *Carmina Nisibena* LV, *Refrain*: "Glory to *You*, Son of the Lord of all, Who *has died* for all." In order to avoid these constructions, quite strange to our way of speaking, I keep the whole sentence in the style of direct address.

16. Blessed are you, old woman, treasure of foreknowing,
    for this old Baby has met you.[47]
    You, old woman, He espoused first of all,
    the Baby Who has come to espouse souls.[48]
    He made you the first fruits of all of them,
    and by your old age He put childishness in its proper place.[49]
    He polished a mirror. He set it up for the foolish girls
    so that they might learn modesty.

17. King Solomon had taken a full thousand
    wives: a very lascivious thing![50]
    Our glorious Lord has made disciples myriads of myriads
    of virgins: a thing both powerful and splendid![51]
    In that son of David a singular thing was seen,
    but in You, Son of David too, took place a miraculous thing!
    O Son of Jesse, from whose seed two sons[52]

47. "Foreknowing," in Syriac *ta'mā*, literally "taste." It could also be translated as "perception" (so McVey), or simply "knowledge." In light of what is said in verses 5–6 of the previous strophe, it seems that "foreknowledge" is preferable here. The adjective "old" applied to the Baby Jesus brings to the forefront the paradox of Jesus's divinity in the littleness of his humanity. It is an echo of a text like John 8:58: "Truly, I tell you, before Abraham was, I am."

48. The theme of the Incarnation as a marriage is common in patristic writings, and it is very prominent in the works of Ephrem. For the church as the bride of Christ and Christ as the bridegroom of the church in Saint Ephrem and in early Syriac literature, see Murray, *Symbols*, 131–42; Brock, *Luminous Eye*, 94–97, 115–30. In the hymn *Contra Haereses* XVII, 5, Ephrem sings: "The body gives You thanks, / for You created it as an abode for Yourself; / the soul worships You, because You betrothed it at Your coming." All this implies that Ephrem is not talking here anymore of the consecrated virgins, but of the baptized as such, the members of the church. The introduction of this theme here prepares the reader for the development of the two following strophes.

49. That is, Christ showed that the spousal love that he has come to give is not confined to childish passion or sentiment. In fact, that spousal love is again the *princeps analogatum* of all spousal love on earth, a love that, in the light of Christ's love, is fulfilled in the gift of the bridegroom's life for the life of the bride. The Syriac term *šabrūtā*, literally "childishness," has also the connotation of "foolishness," as the adjective *šabrātā* (which appears in the following line and which we have translated as "foolish girls") means also "childish girls." Both terms have also to do with "inexperience."

50. On Solomon's one thousand wives, seven hundred of them princesses and three hundred concubines, see 1 Kgs 11:3.

51. The poet says "powerful" because of the numbers, and "splendid" because of the purity of this unique marriage.

52. McVey translates "son of Isaiah," and refers Ephrem's text to the two sons of the prophet Isaiah, of whom it is spoken in Isa 7:3–4 and 8:1–4, explaining also their symbolic names. But the Syriac name *'īšay* is the name of David's father, Jesse in English (see Ruth 4:22), and this is the most natural reference in the context: "son of Jesse" is equal to "David." Clearly what the poet is doing in this strophe is comparing two "sons"

..................[53]

18. Solomon was turbid, as was his will;[54]
a fruit of the earth, as his root also was.
The will of the unsullied Child is pure,
and pure is His nature, as is His Begetter.[55]
Also the flock of the pure Lamb is chaste;
shameless instead is the herd of the lascivious.
The daughters of Tyre led him astray;[56]
but to You, Lord, worshipped a daughter of Tyre, as it is written.[57]

End of the one hymn on the disciple whose blessing was great.

In another of his hymns, *De Fide* XIV, 9, Saint Ephrem asks, "How could my lyre, Lord, rest from your praise? How could I teach my tongue ungratefulness?" In the text translated here, we have seen a few "crumbs" of the gratitude of Saint Ephrem for the Lord's mercy. Might the reading of this text, as deep as it is beautiful, increase in us the joy of that mercy and gratitude for the gift we have received and the fullness to which we have been called.

---

of David: Solomon and Jesus. For the denomination of Jesus as "son of David," see, for instance, Matt 1:1, 20; 9:27.

53. The last verse of the strophe is damaged in the manuscript.

54. The poet continues the comparison (and the contrast) between Jesus and Solomon: in this strophe, he compares the will of both of them, different as their "roots" were different (for Solomon, David; for Jesus, God the Father); and their "flocks," represented finally by how the "daughters of Tyre" behaved both with Solomon and with Jesus. On the importance of the will for the thought of Ephrem, see *supra*, note 24.

55. Ephrem, living in the fourth century, does not distinguish between the divine will and the human will in Christ. As McVey has noted, "this, in conjunction with his bold kenotic imagery, made his hymns especially open to the interpretation of later so-called Monophysite thinkers such as Philoxenus." McVey also refers here to the reflections of Beck, *Ephraems Reden*, 89–91.

56. See 1 Kgs 11:1–8. Sidon and not Tyre is mentioned in 11:1.

57. See Mark 7:24–30, the curing of the daughter of the Syrophoenician woman. The Gospel text speaks explicitly of "the region of Tyre."

2

The Beauty of Being Christian

Marc Ouellet

The word *beauty* evokes equally a landscape, a work of art, an athletic exploit, a gesture of love; that is, it evokes those symbols that attract human hearts and move us. Plato already knew that *the beautiful is that which pleases and attracts.* Beauty has the connotation of harmony, singularity, and even uniqueness, but at the same time it implies difference since one can only appreciate the uniqueness of a gesture or a work in relation to the background from which this gesture or work stands out and springs forth with the character of an exception, of splendor, in short, of miracle. Consider Michaelangelo's *Pieta* or Mozart's *Jupiter* symphony.

The beauty of the love-bond between a mother and child is greater than the many different social relations of exchange, sharing, and service, which do not achieve the intimacy, permanence, and intensity of the relation between mother and child. Despite all the increasing problems of our era, the wedding remains one of the most beautiful symbols of human life, and this is equally because of the love relationship it rests on as of the meaning of the life it celebrates. It is God's preferred means of describing the mystery of his covenant with the creature his hands have made.

On a theological level, the perception of beauty (glory) depends on divine revelation and on the conditions revelation lays down for being grasped by the human mind. Hans Urs von Balthasar figured that the manifestation of God in history appears in its absolute particularity precisely from the perspective of beauty. He writes that God's deed on man's behalf "is credible only as love—specifically, as God's own love, the manifestation of which is the glory of God." As von Balthasar views it, Christianity "can be interpreted . . . solely in terms of the self-glorification of divine love."[1]

---

1. Balthasar, *Love Alone Is Credible*, 8–9.

The conditions of the perception of this love require what Saint Thomas calls connaturality between the subject and the object. Perceiving the divine love in its precise glory necessarily takes more than the natural ability to admire the beauty of things, works of art or human relationships. It takes a gift of the Holy Spirit, which incites a person to faith, the faith of the church, a holy and Catholic faith. A faith that is not just the mind's assent to abstract truths or an emotional impulse to put absolute confidence in a mystery. A christological faith, which sees through Jesus's eyes, takes on his fundamental attitude of receptivity to the will of the Father and of an obedience that takes love to its furthest extremity. Such a faith is not acquired by imitation but by the free communication of the Holy Spirit. It is a gift that overflows from the beauty of Christ, out of his resurrection from the dead.

For Christ's resurrection is the effulgence of the glory of the Trinity. It bears witness to an excess of love at the heart of the Trinity, which erupts into history. Responding to the gift of the Father who engenders and delivers his Son through love, and to the consequent gift of the Son, the Holy Spirit makes the glory of God as absolute love to sparkle and glow in the flesh of Christ. The luster of this glory on the face of Christ announces the rebirth of the covenant between God and man, the birth of the church as spouse and body of Christ, and his evangelical mission, which embraces the entire cosmos.

Some would like me to write about the *beauty of being Christians*, because Christian identity is never purely individual but always implies others. We are created and re-created in Jesus Christ, to the image and resemblance of the Trinitarian God. This theme is fascinating but not often treated and, indeed, is intimidating, because traditionally people prefer to put Christianity forward under the angle of its truth and goodness rather than that of beauty. I shall jump in *in medias res*, by touching upon the glory of God manifested in the resurrection of Christ.

Is aesthetics really a fruitful path for us today? Kierkegaard armed himself against the superficiality of the aesthetic stage of existence, that of the dilettante who never gets personally involved in a deep or lasting way. Doesn't it actually happen that some aspects of Christianity, cut off from their lifeblood, are in danger of being frozen in the form of the cultural detritus of a bygone age? Does beauty have enough weight to start over again as an evangelizing force, in a world that is thirsty for values but which has turned away from a God whom it imagines it knows but whose face and Word is unknown to it? I pose this question as a challenge we must meet because it raises the stakes, letting us see that we are not just talking about social action for a good cause, but a dramatic response of the whole person and of the church to the absolute love manifested in Jesus Christ.

I would bet against the challenger on the way of beauty. I would do that because the ecclesial movements and new communities are rooting themselves in beauty. At the start of the third millennium are we perhaps called to return to the beauty of Christ? Do we owe our enthusiasm and our magnetism to a new perception of the beauty of Christ? Do we owe our energy to the example of Saint Francis, who was sent to repair the beauty of the church after he encountered the cross of Saint Damien?

Is the Beauty of the Church a Program?

At the outset I will say that the theme of beauty exhibits a summarizing and programmatic quality, especially since it was the theme of our beloved Pope Benedict XVI's first homily. His theological lesson on the charisms in the tradition has served theologically to situate the movements and the new communities in a better way and to make their identity and original importance universally understood. The footlights he laid out remain central for guiding the conciliar reform and renewal of the church along the path of a "hermeneutic of continuity."[2]

In his first encyclical, Benedict XVI put his money on beauty by tackling the harmony between divine and human love. The very positive response that he received indicates the pertinence of his choice, which aims to "call forth in the world renewed energy and commitment in the human response to God's love."[3] We are thus directed by him to live under the ensign of beauty and to communicate the joy of believing that dwells within us. But we do not call this a program because it is a matter of grace, the grace of holiness. The Holy Spirit gives it to those whom he wills and he does not refuse it to those who pray for it in humility.

To Perceive and to Be Ravished by the Figure of Christ

Hans Urs von Balthasar spent many years meditating on the Christian revelation through the lens of beauty. Meanwhile in Rome, as he wrote his seven-volume theological aesthetic, the fathers of the Second Vatican Council were experiencing the great Pentecost, which he called The Council of the Holy Spirit. Von Balthasar chose to envisage Christian revelation from this perspective because of his strong conviction that the perspective of glory

---

2. Benedict XVI, *Address to the Roman Curia Offering Them His Christmas Greetings*, December 2005.

3. Benedict XVI, *Deus Caritas Est*, 1.

(the theological word for beauty) is the widest and enables us to make evident the originality and the attractive power of Christian experience: "Who ever sneers at her . . . can no longer pray and soon will no longer be able to love."[4]

His basic intuition is summarized in the little book called *Love Alone Is Credible* where he shows how the way of beauty meets the deepest aspirations of the human heart by aiming, over the heads of rational considerations and affective needs, at the most profound dimension of being, where the person responds to the call of gratuitous love manifested in Jesus Christ. We will set out for this way by noting two preliminary points, one methodological, the other historical, in order to place our inquiry in the actual context of secularized cultures. Von Balthasar introduced his aesthetic method like this: "If all beauty is objectively located at the intersection of two moments which Thomas calls *species* and *lumen* ('form' and 'splendor'), then the encounter of these is characterized by the two moments of beholding and of being enraptured."[5]

To perceive the form of the glory of God in the face of Christ is to be so ravished by his splendor that one is taken out of oneself, dispossessed and redirected into the service of Trinitarian love in the church. Here, to put it in a nutshell, the Christian experience of beauty consists in a perception and the overflowing rapture of an authentic personal encounter. "Being Christian is not the result of an ethical choice or a lofty idea," writes Benedict XVI in his first encyclical, "but the encounter with an event, a person, which gives life a new horizon and a decisive direction."[6] This fundamental affirmation in the first paragraph gives his encyclical a solidly aesthetic orientation in the strongest theological sense, which first of all invites adoration, but which also includes the total gift of self to the following of Christ, the *diakonia*, which can go all the way to martyrdom.

It is an urgent matter today to explore this way of beauty because the perspectives of truth and goodness are less helpful in touching actual human beings who are marked by scepticism and relativism. To the skeptic, it seems, rightly or wrongly, that the affirmation of truth has led historically to intolerance and he thinks that the imposition of a universal moral Good is incompatible with his freedom. The harmony between truth, goodness, and freedom has been broken and the task of Christians consists in restoring this harmony out of the living experience of Christ, who awakens the heart

---

4. Von Balthasar, *Glory of the Lord*, 1:18.

5. Ibid., 12.

6. Benedict XVI, *Deus Caritas Est*, 1.

of the person and gives meaning to his life by opening it up to the totality of reality.[7]

The worst problem affecting secularized cultures is their inward-looking narcissism. It undermines genuine human relationships and pollutes the general atmosphere of society.[8] It's enough to take a look at the way customs, social mores, and laws regarding the family are going to test the social and cultural consequences of rupturing the living relation with the God of Jesus Christ.

This leads us to a historical observation about the theme of the beauty of Christian existence as a way to engage the world where it actually is. This condition is dramatic, implying an unceasing struggle with the spirit of the world. The *Letter to Diogenes* describes this in a way that is timelessly relevant. Externally, the Christian condition is the same as that of their contemporaries, but internally they are situated amongst tensions and conflict with the world around them: "They love the whole world, and all the world persecutes them. People condemn them without knowing them; people kill them and that is how they discover life. They are poor and yet are filled with good things. They lack everything and they have an abundance of everything. People despise them and in being despised they are glorified." Christians "are in the flesh, but they do not live according to the flesh. . . . The soul loves the flesh which detests it, because it belongs to it, and the Christians love those who detest them." The author concludes with the epigraph which says it all: "The post to which God has bound them is so beautiful that they are not permitted to desert it."[9]

After having cleared the ground, we can now go to the heart of the matter, to the heart of the beauty of being Christians in the plural, while remaining aware that plurality is not opposed to unity, for the divine love that shines in the face of Christ and of the Christians who are his disciples, renders each person unique and original. It awakens the "I" of each and every one, creating an ever-more-free personality.

One could say even more. By comparison to every other religion the unity of Christians consists in the paradoxical fact that it somehow absolutizes the "I" of each person *by wholly relativizing it*, that is, by rendering it wholly relational. This can be explained. The Trinitarian image of God in man, which is already recognizable in natural family relationships, calls the persons in communion to an ever-greater mutual self-giving. This mutual love tends to coincide to a personal maximum—Trinitarian noblesse

---

7. This problem is analyzed in John Paul II's *Veritatis Splendor*.

8. See Anatella, *Le règne de Narcisse*.

9. *Letter to Diogenes*.

oblige—love, gift of self and of self-realization. The "I" finds itself by losing itself in the we, in which it rediscovers itself as better integrated to itself.[10] Ask lovers how they feel when they are compelled to be separated, and to renounce an impossible love. They prefer death. Tristan and Iseult, Romeo and Juliet are the best-known expressions of this.

We come back once again to the heart of the matter. It bears a proper name, a singular name, but which is simultaneously universal, a name to which every Christian and all Christians together are accountable, a name venerated even by other religions that aspire to a plenitude we Christians are happy and conscious of calling Grace: full of grace!

Full of Grace

"From generation to generation," writes Benedict XVI, "we continue to marvel at the ineffable mystery [of the Incarnation]. Imagining that he was speaking to the angel of the annunciation, Saint Augustine asked, "Tell me angel of God, whence came this favor to Mary?" The messenger's reply is contained in two words of his salutation: "I salute you, full of grace."[11] Evidently the angel in going in to her did not call her by her earthly name, Mary, but by her divine name, as God had seen and credited her since forever: "Full of grace—*gratia plena*," which in the original Greek is *kecharitomene*, full of grace, the grace that is nothing other than the love of God, so that ultimately we can translate this word as "beloved" of God (cf. Luke 1:28). Origen observes that never before had such a title been given to a human being, that nothing like it is to be found in the whole of sacred scripture.[12] It is a title expressed under a passive form, according to the Holy Father, but this "passivity" of Mary, who since forever and for always has been beloved of the Lord, implies her free consent, her personal and original response: in being loved, and receiving the gift of God, Mary is fully *active*, because she personally opens her arms to receive the waves of divine love, which wash through her. In this way she is a perfect disciple of her Son, who through obedience to the Father fully achieves complete freedom, and in fact exercises liberty by doing this, by obedience.

Turning next to the Letter to the Hebrews, the pope refers to the beauty of the spousal form of the New Covenant: "Also, in entering the world, Christ said, 'I have come to do your will' (Heb 10:5–7). In the presence of these two 'here am Is,' the 'here am I' of the Son and the 'here am I' of the

10. Ouellet, *Divine Likeness*.

11. Augustine, cf. *Sermo*, 291.6

12. Origen, *In Lucam*, 6.7

Father mirror one another and give shape to a singular *Amen* to the loving will of God, we remain astonished, and, full of understanding, we adore."[13]

Kecharitomene in Greek, *gratia plena* in Latin: "full of grace." Why have we put this name at the center of our discourse? Because one can locate in it the beauty of the "whole in the part," to recall a title phrase of the great Swiss master. The whole means God, the church, humanity, and a woman who preserves the entire original task, perfectly transparent to the divine love, crowned with stars in the midst of sorrows, giving birth to eternal life in us. A woman, Mary of Nazareth, Mother of God and Mother of the church, who lives in us, her children, and who floods us with her incomparable beauty.

The beauty of being Christian draws on the beauty of Mary, for what she possessed as a unique privilege, she spreads through us integrally through her perfect harmony with the Trinitarian Spirit, which dwells in her. The Holy Spirit is in God the glory of love. It gives itself and effaces itself between the Father and the Son in order to glorify their mutual love. Thus Mary, the daughter of Zion, lives in the unity of the church, in perichoresis with the people of God, since she was raised to the station of the spouse of the Lamb by her standing at the foot of the cross. Mary has a deep communion in the night of faith with the abandonment of the Son of God, becoming bound to his abandonment and thereby fertilizing all the graces that flow from the cross and wash over human beings.

The beauty of being Christians in the plural thus passes from her to us by osmosis, less by imitation than by being given birth, for our reproducing her Christian beauty occurs by her efficiacious mediation, itself the work of the Holy Spirit. This unique experience Mary has is archetypal.[14] It is the living response of her immaculate heart to the grace of the love of God: 'the response of the 'spouse' who is moved by grace to cry 'Come!' (Rev 22:17) and who 'comes to me according to the Word' (Luke 1:38); of the spouse who 'carries in herself the divine seed" and consequently "does not sin" (1 John 3:9), but rather "preserves in herself these memories and meditates on them in her heart" (Luke 2:19, 51); of the wholly pure spouse who the love of God has made "totally glorious and immaculate' (Eph 5:26–27; 2 Cor 11:2) by his blood, and who, set before him "as a humble servant" (Luke

---

13. Benedict XVI, Homily to the Consistory, March 25, 2006.

14. There is a discussion of archetypal experience in Balthasar, *Glory of the Lord*, 1:301–65. It implies both the notion of a model and that of mediation: "The archetype, by its very nature, has a maternal form and under its 'protective mantle' it embraces the progeny that will imitate it" (340).

1:38, 48) "looks to him in reverent modesty, submissive before him" (Eph 5:24, 33; Col 3:18).[15]

The immaculate and unlimited *fiat* of Mary accompanies the event of the complete Incarnation of the Son of God, that is, of all his mysteries from his conception on, his birth, his passion, and his death, down to his resurrection, his gift of the Holy Spirit, and finally his Eucharist, which engenders his ecclesiastical body. The Virgin, "full of grace," pure and fertile, is rendered passively pliable and actively offers herself through the prevenient action of the Holy Spirit, which brings the divine fecundity of Christ about in her and, through her, in us. In all these mysteries that she espouses and meditates upon in her heart, Mary has "an experience for others—for all. It is an expropriated experience for the benefit of all . . . for the sake of the Church": 'Here is your daughter.'"[16]

The Beauty of the Church— Communion, the Plenitude of Humanity

Over the centuries, the Christian experience of beauty is expressed in countless works of art, architecture, painting, and music but it is incarnated above all in prayer and in actions, through the gestures, the forms of life, of personal and communal vocations, in a word in the church-as-communio whose task is to bear witness to the hope that dwells within it. The martyrs and the saints bear such a witness by their fidelity to the archetypal and original form of the witness of the church.[17] This original form is Trinitarian, christological, and Marian: "It is the glory of my Father that you will bear much fruit and become my disciples. As the Father has loved me, so I have loved you. Remain in my love" (John 15:8–9).

Three linked moments of the life of Mary show this form in action, and show the nuptial paradigm that marks the relationships between God and his people: first, the fact of being loved and of welcoming the divine will; second, the experience of fecundity in the Holy Spirit; third, the active accompaniment of the incarnate Word for the whole length of his earthly journey and his heavenly life. The saints each in his own way reproduce this

15. Balthasar, *Love Alone Is Credible*, 78.

16. Balthasar, *Glory of the Lord*, 1:340–41.

17. Balthasar (*Love Alone Is Credible*) notes that "the conditions for man's perception of divine love" are "1) the Church as Spotless Bride in her core, 2) Mary, the Mother-Bride, as the locus, at the heart of the Church, where the fiat of the response and reception is real, 3) the Bible, which as spirit (-witness) can be nothing other than the Word of God bound together in an indissoluble unity with the response of faith" (79).

figure which illuminates the life of the people of God and which shows the impact of faith on the sense and the beauty of human existence.

Communion with the mysteries of the incarnate Word sheds a decisive light on the beauty and the joy of human existence. At the heart of human life is God, the light of the love who confirms and fulfills the humanity of man and woman as modeled by the Holy Family of Nazareth. This is wonderful news for our dehumanized world! For it is beautiful to respond to the call of Love in every state of life and so to become fully human. How beautiful it is to love Christianly without self-regard, to study, to work, to wed, to give oneself to God in the priestly and consecrated life, to devote oneself to the poor, the sick, the afflicted. Saint Gianna Beretta Molla told her husband while reading a woman's fashion magazine a short while before her ultimate sacrifice that she longed for a beautiful dress if, after all, she survived her experience. The saints are close to the little things of life. The mystery of the Incarnation protects them from an esoteric spirituality. For all the realities of human life are illuminated, nourished, and transformed by the presence of Jesus amongst us and by the splendor of his eucharistic mystery: God with his church, the spouse who comes to consecrate the whole of human reality and to gather all of it into the unity of a single body and a single Spirit.

The Restoration of Beauty: Christian Unity

"I, therefore, the prisoner of the Lord," wrote Paul the Apostle to the Ephesians, "beseech you to walk worthy of the calling with which you were called, with all lowliness and gentleness, with longsuffering, bearing with one another in love, endeavoring to keep the unity of the Spirit in the bond of peace. *There is* one body and one Spirit . . . one Lord, one faith, one baptism; one God and Father of all, who *is* above all, and through all, and in you all" (Eph 4:1–6, emphasis added).

It is for the sake of this growth in unity that the ecclesial movements and new communities exist and flourish, as blessed John Paul II recalled at Pentecost 1998. Their purpose is to work in unity to witness to the love of God, which is made Word and sacrament in the church. They are to work for unity through the mark of mutual love by which Jesus's disciples are known. This love unifies and reconciles, it is a calling and an ecumenical vocation, maintaining respect for legitimate diversities and repenting for the wounds caused by the divisions in the church.

I recall a visit of a delegation of the Greek Orthodox Church to Rome in March 2002, the first official visit in a thousand years, which I had the good fortune to spend a week welcoming and accompanying to the Vatican. We cannot pray together, because from the strict Orthodox perspective, one cannot pray with heretics. But after the audience with the Holy Father John Paul II, we went to visit the magnificent chapel, Redemptoris Mater, the chapel of unity. When six members of the delegation saw and recognized the Eastern saints, their own saints, set amongst the saints of the West, who encircle the Mother of God at the center, they were captivated and they set themselves to singing a Marian hymn with us, which I have never forgotten. This was the summit of the visit! Isn't it an invitation to explore unity through the beauty of the ecumenical movement, flowing from the school of the saints and first of all from the school of Mary, Mother of unity?[18]

A Pedagogy of Beauty: The Example of the Brebis de Jésus

Before concluding, permit me to summarize all this by giving an example of the pedagogy of beauty from a movement founded in Quebec twenty years ago that has now spread to twenty countries: the movement of the Brebis de Jésus (Sheep of Jesus), founded by a Franciscan, whose testimony I reproduce here:

> "Come! You count for me, you are worth something in my eyes and I love you."
>
> "Come!" It all starts with a call, a call of Love. At each meeting, a Brebis de Jésus understands himself to be called in this way by his Shepherd. Everything begins in the heart of God. It is he who takes the initiative. Come! There is an invitation. The response to this invitation makes an entrance into the *beauty of love*, which inspires us to go.
>
> *You are worth something to me.* Each child is called personally and tenderly by his name. He is known by God. The mentor is invited to pronounce the name of the child to the image of Christ. Each time, he asks Christ for the following grace: that pronouncing his name will bring out the best in him. That he can give birth to what is unique in him, to his profound identity as a creature and son of God. Each child is an "original." The *beauty of love is passed on in unity.*

18. It is striking that amongst the ecumenical texts of recent years, the most significant are two bearing on the Virgin Mary, one from the Groupe des Dombes in 1997 and the other from the official Anglican-Catholic dialogue of 2005, which concluded by acknowledging that one cannot consider veneration of the figure of Mary as an obstacle to unity.

You are worth something in my eyes, a very great value, the price of redemption that adorns it in the splendor of glory, in a wonderful beauty. The Brebis de Jésus is invited to see himself within the same gaze with which the good Shepherd laid down his life for him. It is a long journey. It is not surprising that one of the fruits of the encounter is a conversion of his way of looking at himself. The child says, "I love myself more, I have confidence in myself."

I love you. To open oneself to a lover who loves one is the first objective of the Brebis de Jésus's pedagogy. This declaration of love runs through the whole Bible and wants to run through every person's life.

"*Whoever looks toward him will shine. On his face there will be no more shame.*"

All the meetings of the Brebis de Jésus are directed to the Word of God, a word that is understood, welcomed, shared, and tested out. Guided by the Holy Spirit, the mentor becomes the servant of the Word. He effaces himself so that its face can be shown to the child and produce the fruits of the kingdom in him. It teaches us to school our gaze, to decenter oneself to enable a higher light to illumine the depth of existence. Iconography has always wanted to transmit the light of the resurrection. Baptized by this, a Brebis de Jésus is called to become an icon of Christ. That is the grandeur and the beauty of his divine vocation.

The Brebis de Jésus is beautiful because he is wholly illuminated by the light of love. It is also his own responsibility to shine with this light. One stage in the journey is called "being received as a Brebis of the light." At the same time, it is a sore trial. One exercises the personal fidelity to live in such a way as to keep one's illuminated lamp from going out. Many obstacles place themselves in one's road in order to extinguish one's light. "You exercise my hands for the battle. You build me up for combat." There is a beauty in this struggle. It is that of fidelity or infidelity forgiven, of confident abandonment, of constantly handing oneself over to God.

There is also this engagement to shine with light, to share it despite the test of the road. The Christian is in the world, but no longer belongs to this world. There are Brebis of Jésus who with tranquility laugh at their own fidelity to the meetings. They say, "If they laugh at me, it is because they do not know Jesus. If they knew the love of Jesus, they would come to the meetings and they would probably be more fervent than I am." There is a *beauty in this regard for the other*, making for forgiveness, understanding, and the bearer of hope. Many Brebis de Jésus already experience the mystery of persecution. Christ whipped and crowned with thorns is already divinely beautiful. Love alone can contemplate this beauty.

The older Brebis de Jésus who pull through are guided by a conducting thread. *They intend to meet the heart of the Lamb who invites them to follow him.* This intimate relation puts them in communion with our Mother, the church. They know at heart that they are fostered, nourished, forgiven, and enlivened. They are amongst the little ones to whom the mysteries of the kingdom are revealed. They do not shout it from the rooftops but their everyday offering, united to that of Christ, raises the world and hastens Jesus's return. They live the beauty of the eucharistic life made possible by the sacrifice of the Lamb.

That is the witness of the Brebis de Jésus, taken as one example amongst many, which doubtless modestly encapsulates the pedagogical experience of many ecclesial movements and new communities. Every fertile evangelization comes about through the personal and ecclesial appropriation of the Word made flesh, which transforms the believer's vision of God, of others, and of himself. This real transformation always begins with a genuine encounter with Jesus and through prayer—personal prayer, liturgical, lay, and monastic prayer—whose beauty is tried, tested, ever rejuvenated, and bears fruit in peace, conversion, and hope. This transformation is fostered above all by the Eucharist, the source and summit of evangelization and of the life of the church.

Prayer opens us up to the poor and to those wounded by life, who become not only the beneficiaries of our charity but, as Jean Vanier has testified, our benefactors and our masters. The poor are the founts of the wealth of the church (Saint Laurent). Does not the face of the Crucified silently present this fact to this, appealing to compassion and the way of the first Beatitude?

"As the Father has loved me, so I have loved you. Remain in my love" (John 15:8–9). To be loved by God in Jesus, to remain in his love and to bear much fruit out of sheer delight in God: this is the beauty of being Christians. The love of Jesus is given abundantly and in many diverse ways in the ecclesial movements and new communities, in the joy of the Holy Spirit, for the sake of witnessing to the beauty of Christ and his church.

Conclusion

The beauty of being Christians is a grace that flows from Christ and Mary-church through the gift of the Holy Spirit. Saint Francis summed up the grace of his life in two words: Jesus and Mary! This grace is also a responsibility, a mission, *the* mission to evangelize. This evangelizing mission becomes in the real world the greatest priority: to evangelize and to shed the light of love through prayer, action, and passion and through reason and art, like the great witness Luigi Giussani of happy memory; to evangelize by the testimony of faith and by the example of a fully human life; and to evangelize also during persecution and trials, for our Christian and apostolic maturity is measured by our willingness to suffer for the name of Jesus. Love is not a feeling; it is a person, a vision, and an engagement in a mysterious covenant. It is for this reason that the beauty of being Christians is constantly sourced from and leading to the eucharistic mystery of the church.

"We are incessantly occupied in transforming and reforming this church to match the needs of the times, to answer her critics and to fit our own models," writes von Balthasar, "but has the single perfect model and archetype been lost from sight? Must we not, in our reforms, constantly ensure that our gaze is fixed on Mary, not in order to multiply in our church the feasts, Marian devotions, and *a fortiori* definitions, but in order to know for ourselves what the church really is, and what the ecclesial spirit and ecclesial behavior actually are?"[19]

The post to which God has assigned Christians is so beautiful that they cannot desert it, even if it costs them to participate in the passion of the Lord in order to enter into his glory. We remain at this post, working together in charity and unity, and to grow in eucharistic splendor we open ourselves ever wider to the Holy Spirit so that his grace, given in abundance, shall be offered through the church, sacrament of salvation, to the whole of humanity. As Saint Basil said so beautifully in his treatise on the Holy Spirit, with which I conclude, "The Holy Spirit brings the foreseeing of the future, the understanding of mysteries, the comprehension of hidden things, the distribution of spiritual gifts, the celestial city, the dance with angels, joy without end, the dwelling in God, the likeness to God, and the fulfillment of our desire to become God."[20]

19. Balthasar, *Marie, première Église*, 74.
20. Basil, *On the Holy Spirit*, 9.

3

The Loss of Beauty and the De-naturing of Faith

D. C. Schindler

In his monumental study, *The Nature of Order*, the architect Christopher Alexander explains that the ugliness of so much modernist architecture is more than just an errant aesthetic fashion; it is, more profoundly considered, the result of an inadequate conception of the *nature* of things.[1] He therefore proposes that a truly fruitful critique of this architectural style requires a recovery of a better sense of what order is, what matter is, and, in short, what *reality* is. According to Alexander, behind the modernist aesthetic is an ultimately mechanistic metaphysics, the roots of which can be traced back more or less to René Descartes.[2] This mechanistic sense of reality not only impoverishes our notion of order by fragmenting things, dissolving their deepest connections and rendering all relations extrinsic. It also undermines our capacity to detect this impoverishment by effectively separating subject and object. On the one hand, in a mechanistic view of nature, the subject is displaced from the world and turned into a detached observer, so that his participation in reality, and the intimacy with things this implies, no longer bears on the meaning of what he observes. On the other hand, and as a result of this, he is able to grant objective (real) significance only to the "quantifiable" aspects of the world—those that are (apparently) detachable from any particular subjective experience. The non-quantifiable aspects, by contrast, are relegated to the category of "mere" subjectivity. We thus get in architecture subjective elements that are wholly arbitrary because they lack any real measure, which are then "tacked on," to one degree or another, to the purely functional elements of a building, which alone can be measured and discussed rationally. The aesthetics of a building, thus, *intrude* on those elements according to the measure of the particular architect's audacity.

1. Alexander, *The Nature of Order*.
2. Ibid., 1:16–18.

Alexander refers to this problem as a "mass psychosis": having surrendered any connection with our evident experience of the reality, we come to admire buildings precisely because they shock or disturb us, or because they are the buildings the experts judge to be good. As a result we no longer really see what we see. In response to this problem, Alexander seeks to train us in a new way of judging that weighs the "deep feeling" a person has when viewing a design as revelatory of the truly objective quality of things. This way of judging arises from an enriched, more organic notion of order. In more classical language, one might summarize what Alexander is talking about as a crisis of *beauty*, since the notion in its classical sense includes both an organic notion of order in which the rational and vital principles converge and also a recognition of the fundamental unity between subject and object, the soul and the world. The proper response to this crisis is therefore an education in beauty, which means both a deepening of our understanding and a formation of our capacity to perceive and appreciate.

Stratford Caldecott proposes just such an education in *Beauty for Truth's Sake*.[3] In this book, he points to the same phenomenon of a kind of cult of the ugly in modernist architecture and, like Alexander, insists that what is at issue here is not simply a fashion in aesthetic taste, but more radically a conception of the meaning of reality as a whole. It is particularly striking that, in their reflections on this problem, both men focus their attention in a direct way on themes in physics and even mathematics. It seems to me that Caldecott goes beyond Alexander, however, in three respects. First, while Caldecott agrees with Alexander that the problems in modernist architecture are fundamental, he sees these problems as part of a larger whole: a deep ugliness can be found not only in modernist architecture, or even simply in material culture in general, which Alexander also affirms, but also in the realm of the spirit per se, in poetry, philosophy, and religion. This is one of the reasons his book centers specifically on education. Second, his reflection on this problem is not only a profound penetration into various cultural phenomena, as is Alexander's, but moreover it extends its roots into the tradition. In other words, he connects the contemporary issues with insights he recovers from ancient wisdom, both from the representatives of what can be called the perennial philosophy and from the specifically Christian tradition. This helps to save the diagnosis from being dismissed as somehow idiosyncratic. And, third, bringing these two dimensions together in a way, Caldecott carries his reflection on this theme to the specifically theological dimension, which he sees as the foundation for all the rest, even for the cosmological aspect that both he and Alexander make central.

3. Caldecott, *Beauty for Truth's Sake*.

The result is a glorious vision that sets the multiplicity of the problems of modernity into new relief by gathering them up in relation to a center: that center is beauty, which represents on the one hand the order that founds the intelligibility of all things in their truth and on the other hand the miracle of loving self-gift that draws all things forth as the good. This beauty has been contemplated in wonder and awe from the beginning of human reflection on the cosmos. It is ultimately revealed to be the convergence of logos and love—it is the logos *of* love in both the subjective and objective sense of the genitive. Indeed, beauty is the Logos who showed himself *to be* love in his hanging on the cross in which he brought to light the very love that is the logos of God in the inner life of the Trinity. With this vision as the ultimate frame, Caldecott calls for a rethinking of the formation of the soul in education, in all of its sophisticated differentiation, through a recentering on beauty, which means above all an attention to the significance of form in each of the areas of study and so a revivification of human culture more generally.

Inspired by this vision, what I wish to do in the following essay is reflect on the significance of beauty specifically for the theological virtue of faith. Caldecott talks about the fundamental importance of church architecture, and moreover closes the book by gathering all of its insights into a liturgical hymn. In both cases, he insists that what he is talking about exceeds in its significance the boundaries of the church; in other words, he is concerned with more than what happens simply inside a particular religious building. Instead, the architecture of sacred buildings expresses in a certain respect the paradigm of the meaning of architecture more generally, which is itself a human expression of the meaning of space simply. Similarly, liturgy is in a certain respect the paradigm of human action generally (liturgy = *leitourgia*, an "act of the people"), which is itself a culmination of the meaning of movement in time. The church and the liturgy celebrated in it is thus the consecration of space and time; it is the place and moment in which all spaces and moments receive their orienting center. It is therefore not irrelevant whether a church or a liturgy is beautiful. What is at stake here is in a certain sense the meaning of everything else. As has often been observed, a cathedral is an incarnate theology; in the spirit of Caldecott's book, we might add that it is also an incarnate metaphysics and therefore also an incarnate anthropology and cosmology.

But what is at issue in church architecture and liturgy is also, as Ratzinger says in a passage quoted by Caldecott, "making faith visible."[4] In addition to the metaphysical, anthropological, and cosmological implications,

---

4. Ratzinger, *New Song to the Lord*, 88, quoted in *Beauty for Truth's Sake*, 102.

the beauty of architecture and liturgy has implications for the nature, the quality, and the experience of the act of faith. To be sure, faith is an internal act, occurring within the soul of each individual. But that soul is, as human, always an embodied soul. The body is, as it were, the extension of the soul into space and time, and thus represents the involvement of the soul *in* the world and with other human beings.[5] In this respect, faith is not an essentially private affair, but is always enacted publicly (even if in a secluded place). It is thus a spiritual reality, if you will, that is always mediated concretely in and through the place wherein it is enacted. As we will attempt to show here, the quality of the place therefore bears on the quality of the act of faith.

What I intend to do specifically in this essay is argue for beauty as, so to speak, the natural correlate of faith, which I mean in a strong sense: for embodied human beings, without beauty there can be no faith in the proper sense; a faith that is turned into an exclusively internal act that is independent from and indifferent to the externals of the surroundings—paradigmatically architecture and liturgy—is distorted to the extent of being de-natured so that it ceases to be faith properly speaking. To show this, I will draw in a rather free way from insights of three philosophers of beauty from the ancient, medieval, and modern periods; I will be reflecting on a particular insight from Plato, Aquinas, and Heidegger, respectively. Each of these thinkers makes some fundamental point about beauty that serves to illuminate the nature of faith.

Plato

In the famous Second Speech of Socrates in *The Phaedrus*, Plato describes the ascent of the soul from its submersion in the body to the transcendent realm "beyond heaven," which is in fact its proper home.[6] This ascent is made possible by the wings of eros, which are generated through a vision of beauty. Now, it is often thought that Plato is expressing, in this image of the soul's flight from the body, a contempt for the physical world that results from a radical dualism in his thinking. Plato is accused of separating the spiritual and the physical, or the transcendent and the immanent, by an insuperable chasm. It is not possible in the present context to defend Plato against this charge, but we may at least note the light that beauty, as he presents it here, sheds on this problem. For Plato, beauty is—like justice, wisdom, or equality—one of the "forms," that is, an essentially transcendent

5. On the significance of the body in this regard, see Granados, "Taste and See."

6. Plato, *Phaedrus*, 247c.

reality that lies beyond space and time. But what distinguishes beauty from every other supra-material good is that, though it is of its essence an object for the soul or mind like all the others, it is at the same time able to be perceived by the senses (above all by sight).[7] Plato says that it alone (*monon*) possesses this quality: it is exceedingly radiant, so excessively bright, one might say, that even our eyes can see it. Beauty lies beyond human perception as a transcendent reality, but its transcendence exceeds itself into the physical world that we can perceive.

There is therefore a twofold aspect to beauty—and, as we will see, in fact everything about beauty is paradoxically twofold. This paradox has implications for our experience of beauty. The soul's response to this particular transcendent form is *eros*.[8] For Plato, beauty and eros are so closely connected as to be inseparable: there can be no eros without beauty, and beauty is not perceived as such except in the experience of eros. Now, Plato describes eros in the *Phaedrus* in vivid, dramatic terms as a painful, but pleasant, disturbance whereby the soul grows wings, that is, is elevated beyond itself.[9] The dramatic tones are appropriate because of what in fact occurs in eros. It is, for Plato, not just an emotion or feeling, at least not in the contemporary sense of the terms. Rather, the pathos of eros represents a profound transformation, a metaphysical movement, if you will, in which the soul's ontological status is changed. The soul that is influenced by eros is no longer in a mundane state, but now a heavenly, or even a supra-heavenly, one; it is out beyond itself. We speak of ourselves in this state as being "beside ourselves." Plato uses the phrase "divine madness" (*theia mania*) in order to speak of the soul in its ecstatic state; the soul is "out of its mind" (*mania*), but this particular mania is divine, which means it is outside in the sense of being above, rather than below, its normal condition. *Theia mania* is in other words a supra-rational, rather than an irrational, state, and so it is one that does not exclude (but in fact necessarily includes) the soul's reason even as it exceeds that reason.

There are two conditions that make this fundamental mania of the soul possible: on the one hand, the beauty that provokes eros, and so generates wings, has to be genuinely transcendent. The soul experiences an endless series of desirable objects in a straightforward, immanent way, and these do indeed move the soul in a certain sense by attracting it, prompting it to seek satisfaction: I am thirsty, and I drink a cup of water; I feel an itch,

---

7. Ibid., 250d. Plotinus adds hearing to sight as the senses affected by beauty: *Ennead*, I.6.1.

8. *Phaedrus*, 249d.

9. Ibid., 251d–e.

and I scratch it. Though I am moved by these desires, I would not speak of these experiences as radical disturbances; I am not shaken in my very core and brought outside myself. In a word, I am not transformed by them. But I can be moved in a genuinely *vertical* fashion, in contrast to these horizontal attractions, only if that which moves me lies above me. Therefore, beauty, which indeed does disturb the soul in its most potent instances, must be a transcendent reality.

In the second place, however, it has to be a transcendent reality that, without departing from its transcendence, nevertheless speaks directly to the bodily senses and appeals directly to the bodily desires. The movement of transcendence, as a movement, requires not only a proper "to" but also a "from." We said above that the physical goods that appeal to the sensible appetites move the soul only in a horizontal direction. It is also the case that merely intellectual objects—numbers, for example—fulfill this soul, indeed, but do not, in themselves, inflame the soul. The delight of solving a mathematical problem is different from a glimpse of beauty, because, while both appeal to the mind, the beautiful at the same time appeals to the senses and desires. It is the simultaneity of the simplicity of beauty with its twofold presence as transcendent and immanent that accounts for the unique excitement, the dramatic tension, the "fluttering of the soul," as Plato says.[10] Without something that is simultaneously both transcendent and immanent, the two levels of reality, so to speak, might remain at best parallel planes, which would not intersect even if extended to infinity. Beauty has the power to unify the soul by satisfying its highest desire but at the same time being able to speak meaningfully to the lowest. Perhaps we might express this best by saying that beauty speaks of the highest fulfillment but does so in a language intelligible also to our most basic, physical desires. There is no human being, however vicious, who is incapable of being moved by beauty. Beauty is, in this sense, paradigmatically catholic.[11]

Now, according to Plato, it is beauty *alone* that reaches the soul in its embodied state from above, from the intelligible realm, which is to say that it is beauty alone that is capable of elevating the soul. Without beauty, there is no transcendence. In the *Symposium*, Plato presents eros as an intermediate reality, a "go-between" or mediator, which joins together heaven and earth.[12] As we mentioned above, there is an essential connection between

10. Ibid., 249d.

11. To be sure, it is the case that the transcendence of every form is what allows it to be immanent to sense experience; on this, see Perl, "The Presence of the Paradigm." But one could say that to perceive the forms as such, that is, to perceive a physical particular to be expressive of a transcendent meaning, is precisely to have an experience of beauty.

12. See Plato, *Symposium*, 202d–3a.

eros and beauty. The mediating power of eros is a reflection of what we have called the "simple twofold" character of beauty. It is crucial, however, that we see the connection between eros and beauty in the proper order. The movement of transcendence is elicited specifically from above: eros is not in the first place an immanent power in the soul, or a drive or striving force that originates from below (though of course it is also this in some respect). Instead, it is a response of the soul, which is awakened by, and in a certain sense empowered by, not only an object external to it, but indeed one that is of its essence transcendent. The transcendence of beauty is what causes the soul's wings to grow.

It is this "from above causality" that makes the experience of beauty the proper natural analogy of the reception of faith. According to the Catholic tradition, faith is a gift of the Holy Spirit; it is a virtue of the soul—that is, a perfective actualization of the soul—but a specifically theological virtue, which means that it is infused from above. The gift of faith is what Saint Paul called an "upward call" (*hē anō klēsis*; Phil 3:14). There is a widespread tendency in the popular imagination to overlook the gift-character of faith, and it seems to me that a significant cause of this tendency is our having lost a sense of the connection between faith and beauty. Thus, we most commonly think of faith either as something akin to *pistis* in ancient philosophy, that is, a belief or opinion we happen to hold—in this case concerning divine matters—that is distinguished from knowledge (*epistēmē*) by its lack of certainty or direct evidence. Or we think of it as something controlled ultimately by our will: our faith is what we choose to believe, again because there is no objective evidence that would necessitate our acknowledgment.

The reason this impoverishment of the meaning of faith is connected with a loss of a sense of beauty, I suggest, is the following: though faith is a supernatural virtue, because it is a virtue of the human soul, the realization of faith necessarily includes a natural dimension. The natural dimension, thus, mediates the realization of faith. If the natural aspect is not apt for this mediation, the reality of faith will be compromised. Thus, for example, without an apt mediation, faith will be affirmed as a supernatural gift specifically in the sense that it lies outside of human experience. But in this case it will be simply posited; it will be something that is therefore not received into the soul (which, according to the scholastic dictum, always occurs in some sense "in the mode of the recipient"), but to which the soul relates itself wholly through an act of will, which is ultimately arbitrary because it is altogether spontaneous (i.e., non-receptive and so completely "from below"). If some human experience is correlated to faith, then, insofar as the experience is not taken to bear the relation of analogy to faith, it will be extrinsic to the nature of faith. Typically, faith will be associated with some feeling, insofar as feeling seems to lie outside of what is rational or objective; in this case, feeling is itself interpreted in subjectivistic terms. Though faith is thus affirmed to be something beyond the natural, it nevertheless cannot dispense with a natural mediation, for even the rejection of natural mediation turns out to be a particular natural mediation. Faith therefore inevitably ends up with a mediation that distorts it: paradoxically, the lack of an apt natural mediation results in the compromise of faith's supernatural character. We will come back to this point in our discussion of an insight from Heidegger.

When we say that the experience of beauty is analogous to the gift of faith, we mean analogy in an ontological and not merely metaphorical sense. In other words, we mean, on the one hand, that there is a certain simultaneity between the two: like the supernatural virtue of faith, beauty moves the soul essentially "from above," but in a manner that calls on and so includes all of the soul's own internal energies. Moreover, both imply an elevation of the soul and so a kind of ontological shift rather than simply the affecting of one passion or another, one power or another. By contemplating the analogy, one comes to see that, as an elevation, faith is not simply the insertion of a new content, or even a new activity, into the soul, which otherwise remains as it is, but a lifting up of the soul as it were into a new existential condition. Beauty is apt because it is of its essence a movement of the soul beyond itself, and so makes possible the reception of a supernatural gift from above without imposing conditions of possibility that would compromise its transcendence.

But, while analogy implies all of this, it means something more: interpreted ontologically, analogy indicates not only similarity, but real unity. What we mean by this is that the experience of beauty is, as it were, the shape that faith takes to the extent that it enters into nature. This does not necessarily mean that every experience of beauty is an experience of faith, though it does not exclude this possibility outright.[13] What it does mean, though, is that there can be no genuine experience of faith apart from an experience of beauty.[14] Without beauty, and the elevation of the soul it implies, faith will inevitably get reduced to some sort of immanent act, whether it be a mere

13. One might argue that every experience of beauty is a kind of implicit invitation to faith.

14. Of course, a person may possess faith without actively experiencing it, and this is in fact the usual state. But we ought not, for all that, to separate the state from the experience; instead, we ought to recognize that the experience lies implicitly within the state, so that the active experience is not the addition of something new but the "re-activation," so to speak, of something that is already present. We could compare this to eros: the experience that Plato describes is not constant, but it initiates a state and remains within it.

feeling, a mere act of will, or a mere notion or idea to which one decides to give one's assent. It is this that helps us understand the importance or indeed the indispensable necessity of architecture, liturgy, and even, as Ratzinger explains in the passage we cited, iconography, in the celebration of faith. One might also reflect in this context on the significance of the witness of the saints—that is, the radiant *Gestalt* presented by those who express the gospel in the form of their lives—in the effecting of conversion.

Aquinas

For our medieval testimony, we will consider the classic description of beauty given by Thomas Aquinas: *id quod visum placet*, "that which pleases when seen." In unfolding the significance of this formulation, Aquinas explains that, while beauty and goodness are the same in one respect, they differ insofar as goodness concerns appetite directly, whereas beauty also concerns the cognitive power.[15] On the other hand, beauty differs from truth, which directly concerns the cognitive power, insofar as it brings about delight rather than understanding. We may therefore say that, while goodness forms the proper object of the will, and truth forms the proper object of the intellect, beauty represents a kind of unity between goodness and truth and so forms the object of both the intellect and will at once. Beauty is perceived (*visum*) not only by the eyes but at the same time and more fundamentally by the intellect, as Plato showed, and this intellectual perception implies a kind of distance, which is lacking in the direct contact, the immediate presence, of the good as object of appetite. But beauty also "placet," like the good; it gratifies the appetitive power of the soul. It is something we enjoy. Once again, we see that beauty represents a simple unity that is at the same time irreducibly twofold.

Now, it just so happens that Aquinas defines the act of faith in terms that are analogous to his description of beauty: faith, he says (following Augustine), is "thinking with assent."[16] He goes on to explain that faith is principally an act of the intellect, but at the same time he acknowledges that it involves assent, which is an act of the will.[17] Because the difference between what Aquinas means by "will" and the conventional understanding might cause some confusion, it is important to add here that Aquinas defines the

15. Aquinas, *Summa Theologiae* (*ST*) I, q. 5, a. 4, ad 1.
16. *ST* II–II, q. 2, a. 1.
17. *ST* II–II, q. 2, a. 1, ad 3; cf. I–II, q. 15, a. 1, ad 3.

will itself specifically as an intellectual appetite,[18] though one that includes within itself the power to choose between alternatives (*liberum arbitrium*).[19] This means that, for him, the act of will is not in the first place a spontaneous impulse "from below," but instead includes a spontaneous moment of self-motion within a more basic receptive "being moved," that is, an attraction that characterizes the movement of appetite: assent, *ad-sentire*, indicates a movement toward, and so a kind of conformity to an object that lies beyond itself. As Aquinas puts it, this movement toward implies a "distance."[20]

It makes sense that the act of faith would be, on the one hand, an act principally of the intellect, and on the other hand an act that necessarily also involves the will. Both of these affirmations follow from the specifically theological character of faith, and the elevation of the soul that this character implies. In the first place, an object—we are speaking here of the truth of God as revealed or indeed of *revelabilia* more generally, that is, the meaning of things that come to light in God's self-revelation[21]—that transcends the soul would naturally be grasped by the highest faculty of the soul, which according to Aquinas is the intellect. On the other hand, however, the truth of God cannot be simply an object of the intellect, because the intellect, as an essentially receptive faculty,[22] takes its objects into itself, which means that it cannot attain an object that by its nature exceeds the soul as the truth of God so clearly does. By contrast with the intellect, the will is an act that terminates, as it were, outside of the soul: if the intellect internalizes, the will represents a movement of the soul outward, and so beyond itself.[23] Because the truth of God is above the soul, this truth—which, as truth, is indeed an object proper to the intellect—is nevertheless an object that the intellect must be brought outside of itself to attain. It is for this reason that the act of faith does not have the natural evidentiality of the created truths to which the intellect assents (more or less) on its own: as Aquinas puts it, faith shares something in common with the partially understood notions to which we assent with doubt, uncertain opinion, and suspicion.[24] But it is not because the object of faith is *less* than certain, that is, because the matter of faith falls below the evidentiality of the intellect's proper objects (as is the case

18. *ST* I, q. 59, a. 1.

19. *ST* I, q. 83, a. 4.

20. *ST* I–II, q. 15, a. 1, ad 3.

21. *ST* II–II, q. 1, a. 1: "If . . . we consider materially the things to which faith assents, they include not only God, but also many other things, which, nevertheless, do not come under the assent of faith, except as bearing some relation to God."

22. *ST* I, q. 79, a. 2.

23. See Aquinas, *De veritate*, q. 1, a. 2; cf. von Balthasar, *Grain of Wheat*, 41.

24. *ST* II–II, q. 2, a. 1.

with ancient *pistis*[25]), but instead because it *exceeds* that evidentiality. Faith represents, as it were, a kind of supra-certainty.

Because the act of faith is an elevation, a drawing of the soul above itself, it necessarily involves the whole soul all at once, even if it is an act principally of the intellect. Let us explore this aspect a bit further. In an endlessly provocative little book, *The Eyes of Faith*, Pierre Rousselot raises a dilemma with respect to the act of faith, which, as we have seen, involves in some sense both the intellect and the will.[26] The dilemma concerns the order of these respective acts: Does the intellect come first, followed by the will, or vice versa? In other words, do we first see the truth of God's self-revelation, and then, because we see its truth, give to that truth our assent? The problem with this interpretation is that it implies a denial that the truth of God is "above" the soul. If the intellect can receive into itself the truth of revelation without the "soul-transcending" act of will, it means that the soul stands somehow above the truth of revelation. This would be, of course, a deeply problematic, rationalistic reduction of faith.

Are we then to say, instead, that in faith the soul first gives its assent through an act of the will operating without the guidance of the intellect, and subsequently, as a result of this assent and the self-transcending motion it seems to imply, the intellect comes to understand the truth of God? This alternative, if anything, is worse than the other: in the first place, it implies that the act of faith is fundamentally arbitrary, that it is at its deepest level unmotivated in the sense of being without a reason. We would thus avoid rationalism only by falling into voluntarism, or indeed an irrational fideism. In the second place, this alternative, too, would end up denying the very transcendence of the act of faith that it sought to preserve. If the will were to operate without the intellect, its act would be wholly spontaneous and therefore "from below." It would become a kind of self-assertion, a sheer unelicited positing of the will, and therefore no elevation at all. According to Aquinas, in fact, the act of will always willy-nilly follows cognition; this is, indeed, what is implied in the definition of will as an intellectual appetite. The spontaneity of its choice always occurs within a more fundamental receptivity, which is the intellect's grasp of the object. To posit the will as operating first without the intellect is in truth to say that the will is simply operating in subjection to a poor intellectual conception of some reality.

And so we seem to be thrust back into the dilemma. Does the intellect follow the will or does the will follow the intellect in the act of faith? The only adequate answer to this question, as Rousselot shows, is yes. But

---

25. See, for example, Plato, *Republic*, book 6, 509d–11e.

26. Rousselot, *The Eyes of Faith*.

Rousselot does not, himself, elaborate what exactly it would mean for the intellect and will to act simultaneously in a reciprocal interdependence. We have an indication, on the other hand, of the direction to go in order to think about this reciprocity in the characterization of beauty we considered above. As we saw there, beauty presented itself as a sort of unity of truth and goodness, which involves both the intellect and will at once. What this means is that the perception of the intelligiblity and the assent, the movement toward, come about in the same moment—though this moment does not exclude the subsequent deliberate handing of oneself over and the explicit conceptualization that characterize the good and the true respectively in their proper order. It is just that beauty represents, as it were, both of these aspects together in embryo, in such a manner that they are then able to be unfolded in their proper integrity, which always includes within itself an intrinsic relation to the other transcendentals.[27] In any event, this simultaneity makes sense only if we think of the soul as being elevated as a whole, which means an active involvement, a moving itself in its being moved by another, and thus as actualizing the particular powers of the soul within the context of the properly ontological transformation that we have described as the essence of the experience of beauty.[28] If, by contrast, we were to think of the soul as standing in itself, so to speak, and operating either one or the other of its faculties, intellect or will, we would never be able to avoid the dilemma presented above; we would be left, instead, with the equally problematic alternatives of rationalism or fideism. Once again, we see that the act of faith requires the mediation of the experience of beauty.

As we saw in our reflection on Plato, beauty is analogous to faith both in the sense that the natural phenomenon of beauty shares certain features with the act of faith and in the more directly ontological sense that beauty is what faith looks like, so to speak, in the natural order. In the present context, we can see both of these aspects. The natural experience of beauty in religious art, for example, can dispose the soul to receive faith insofar as it is a natural elevation, an opening up to what lies above. At the same time, it is clear that the act of faith itself will transpire in and through an experience of beauty. One does not simply decide to believe in a deliberate and spontaneous way; neither does one simply reason one's way to faith in God—though one's decision or one's reasoning can be part of the act in

27. For a fuller explanation of this point and a discussion of its significance, see the chapter titled "The Primacy of Beauty, the Centrality of Goodness, and the Ultimacy of Truth," in my book *The Catholicity of Reason*.

28. Aquinas presents grace as affecting not just one or another of the powers of the soul, but its very essence (*ST*, I–II, q. 110, a. 4), and also understands faith to be something received in grace (*ST* I–II, q. 110, a. 3, ad 3).

some respect. Instead, one finds oneself moved by an image, person, act, or some teaching or passage from scripture because of its effective radiance. Finding oneself being moved—which is a way the experience of beauty can be described—is crucial in the act of faith since it indicates that the act is a gift, it is an act elicited from above. It is inside this being moved that one assentingly sees the truth of faith. This truth includes, to be sure, aspects that are rationally demonstrable in the strict sense, but the decisive evidence will always take the form of fittingness (*convenientia*), which is an (analogously) aesthetic category.[29]

Heidegger

Thus far we have focused our discussion on the *experience* of beauty; turning to Heidegger for our final aspect directs our attention to what we might call the ontological reality of beauty.[30] In his famous lecture "On the Origin of the Work of Art,"[31] Heidegger criticizes the reduction of the significance of art in what he takes to be the traditional collapse into aesthetics, that is, an absorption of its meaning in subjective experience, or a preoccupation with the deliberate maker of art. He focuses, instead, on the work of art, and indeed on *art, technē* itself, as the origin of the work as well as of the producer or artist. It is not possible to present the background of Heidegger's thinking, which would be necessary for a deep understanding of that lecture, or even to present the lecture as a whole, which would help illuminate the meaning and implications of the particular aspect we will focus on here. Instead, we will be abstracting this aspect and attending to it simply in relation to our present theme; but we hope to be faithful nevertheless to the spirit of Heidegger's insight. This last section will be a bit longer because Heidegger's language is so different from the common one.

Heidegger mentions beauty in a substantial way only once in this lecture,[32] in what is one of its climactic moments:

29. See Balthasar, *Glaubhaft ist nur Liebe*, 33–39.

30. In this last section, we will be using a lot of terminology that Heidegger would not himself use. As is well known, he developed his own language and vocabulary to present his particular "thinking of being." There is no space here to explain his language and discuss the reasons for the names he gives things. Instead, we will be to a certain extent translating him into more traditional language in order to connect him with our theme, namely, the relation between faith and beauty. Our aim is not in the first place to explore Heidegger's thought for its own sake.

31. Heidegger, "On the Origin of the Work of Art."

32. He also mentions the term in passing (ibid., 666) in his characterization of a conventional understanding that he is criticizing.

Thus in the work it is truth, not only something true, that is at work. The picture that shows the peasant shoes, the poem that says the Roman fountain, do not just make manifest what this isolated being as such is—if indeed they manifest anything at all; rather, they make unconcealedness as such happen in regard to what is as a whole. The more simply and authentically the shoes are engrossed in their nature, the more plainly and purely the fountain is engrossed in its nature—the more directly and engagingly do all beings attain to a greater degree of being along with them. That is how self-concealing being is illuminated. Light of this kind joins its shining to and into the work. This shining, joined in the work, is the beautiful. *Beauty is one way in which truth occurs as unconcealedness.*[33]

This passage reveals, first of all, the inseparable connection between beauty and truth, which we will interpret in the present context as the revelation of things in their deepest meaning. Heidegger, moreover, states that things disclose themselves precisely by being "engrossed in their own nature" (though we note that he is pointing precisely to artistic representations of things). And, third, he says that, by being engrossed in their nature and thus revealing themselves in truth, they are in fact making manifest not only themselves as "isolated" beings, but "what is as a whole": "all beings attain to a greater degree of being with them."

To understand what these affirmations mean and how they fit together, we need to consider a pair of key terms that Heidegger presents in this lecture: "earth" and "world." The "shining" of beauty is a result, we might say, of the unity-in-opposition, or the opposition-in-unity of earth and world. Here, again, we see that beauty represents a simple twofold. Now, we can best come to see the sense of these notions by understanding that Heidegger introduces them in the place of the traditional notions of matter and form, which he claims have never been adequate to account for what a thing is. The traditional terms, at least as conventionally understood,[34] take the act of manufacturing to be paradigmatic: one takes material of one sort or another and imposes on that matter a form in view of some intended use. In this case, the matter becomes a kind of inert "stuff," which has no real significance in itself, but only as a sort of means by which the form can be realized. Ideally, then, the matter would, as it were, put up no resistance to the form, but would instead disappear into it so as to enable the form to perform its intended function: the steel of the head of a hammer, for example, provides

33. Ibid., 682.

34. Heidegger presents a kind of caricature of traditional "hylomorphism" as a foil for the position he is developing; see ibid., 658–61.

the weight and hardness that allows the hammer to do its work, and any characteristics the steel might have besides these serviceable features are either accidental or intrusive. Heidegger claims, again, that the form-matter concept takes manufacture to be a paradigm for all things: if it was only implicit initially, and one made a distinction between beings that are "by nature" and artifacts, the convergence of this philosophical tradition with the biblical notion of creation makes it explicit. It thus does away with this distinction between the natural and artificial, insofar as the distinction can have only a relative, and not an ultimate, scope in this case: creation means that all things are made by a deliberate agent.[35]

Heidegger's notion of "world" is like "form" insofar as his term indicates intelligibility; but it does so in a decisively different way. Rather than signifiying the discrete intelligibility of an object for the mind—a particular meaning—"world" more basically means what we might call "meaning*fullness*." It is not a deliberate intention or a particular idea, but rather the open horizon within which we have intentions and ideas; it is the open sphere of meaning wherein we live, move, and orient ourselves. To illustrate, Heidegger takes one of van Gogh's famous paintings of peasant shoes: we see in these shoes not just a particular shape that indicates a particular function. Instead, we say that, in looking at van Gogh's depiction of these shoes, a "whole world" of meaning opens up to us: we see the life of the peasant woman who wears these every day, we see her work, the struggle with and celebration of the seasons, her sorrows and sacrifices, and so forth. All of these meanings are present in this image of shoes; a "world opens up" here. This opening up, this coming to presence of a world, this infinite configuration of deep human meanings that we perceive and experience in this particular image, is an example of what Heidegger means by the notoriously cryptic phrase "the worlding of the world."

The corresponding term is "earth," which represents we might say the world of nature, that in and on which a (human) world has its place. In this respect, there is a certain analogy between "earth" and the traditional term "matter," as that out of which a thing is made. But "earth" differs radically from "matter," at least in the conventional interpretation we sketched above, in the first place because of the emphasis it gives to the natural integrity of things, the meaning that they have in themselves, in some sense prior to and independently of the meaning that is given to them by human activity or the form that is imposed on them. In contrast to the openness of

---

35. Heidegger's interpretation of the metaphysics of creation is clearly a distortion of the traditional understanding, though we cannot discuss this matter in the present context. For a radically different interpretation that is truer to the tradition, see Kenneth Schmitz, *The Gift*.

world, Heidegger uses the word "closed" to describe earth: to quote one of Heidegger's favorite texts from Heraclitus, "nature loves to hide" (*DK* B123). Natural things are, he says, "self-secluding"; they have boundaries that belong properly to them, and they resist being "exposed" or "found out," not because they do not want to be known, as it were, but because the natural limits that shelter them are precisely what allow them to be present as themselves. In a word, *mystery* belongs to the very essence of the world of nature, so that knowing natural things cannot mean an elimination of their mystery. Instead, real knowledge would have to include an acknowledgment of their mystery and in some sense a protection of it. This is true not only of natural things, such as plants and animals, but even the most basic physical characteristics of natural things. As Heidegger puts it with an example: "Color shines, and wants only to shine. When we analyze it in rational terms by measuring its wavelengths, it is gone. It shows itself only when it remains undisclosed and unexplained."[36]

Now, Heidegger describes world as "open" and earth as "closed": these evidently represent principles of a sort that are in a certain respect diametrically opposed. But he has explained beauty as the unity of the two. We could think of the energy, the radiance (which is in a way both light and heat), as a result of the tension generated in the conflict between these principles. It is crucial to see that they are not properly understood as being brought together in an extrinsic fashion, in the sense of the imposition of form on matter in manufacture. We saw above that this imposition implied the domination of matter by form in a reduction of all things to mere tools of one sort or another, so that matter is "used up" by form.[37] What Heidegger has in mind here is, instead, a rather extraordinary event: a genuine work of art is an encounter between world and earth in which each on the one hand resists the other and on the other hand depends on the other in order properly to be itself.

There is a unity here coincident with an irreducible difference:

> World and earth are essentially different from one another and yet are never separated. The world grounds itself on the earth, and earth juts through world. But the relation between world and earth does not wither away into the empty unity of opposites unconcerned with one another. The world, in resting

36. Heidegger, "Origin of the Work of Art," 674.

37. Heidegger uses the term "tool," or as it is often translated, "equipment," in a positive sense in some contexts. The peasant shoes that van Gogh depicted, for example, are an example of "equipment." The point is not whether something is an instrument, but whether its "thingly character" is interpreted according to the conventional notion of form and matter, or instead in relation to Heidegger's notion of a "work."

upon the earth, strives to surmount it. As self-opening it cannot endure anything closed. The earth, however, as sheltering and concealing, tends always to draw the world into itself and keep it there.[38]

What this means can perhaps best be illuminated through an example. We might consider the grand "work" of a medieval cathedral. Here, stones are cut, stacked, and bonded together in order to soar way above the earth. In the shape of a cathedral, and its architectural design, is disclosed an entire theology, as Caldecott describes in his book. The building has a "meaning"; it is eloquent. It speaks, even if what it says is not just a determinate meaning or circumscribed intelligible content. An expert could list the symbolic significance of every single detail of the architectural design, and, however illuminating the list of features might be, that list could never substitute for the meaning present in the cathedral, which has to be experienced to be genuinely understood. The presence of the meaning is, as it were, an indispensable part of that meaning, not as one piece juxtaposed to all the others, but as a quality that belongs to all of its meaning in its meaningfulness. There is, in other words, a radiant whole here that is greater than the sum of its parts, an eloquence beyond any particular expression or formulation, no matter how exhaustive the explanation of the symbolism might pretend to be. To say that the actual presence of the cathedral is part of its meaning, so that the meaning cannot be adequately translated into speech, is to say that, in the cathedral, the "world worlds." It is just the "extra-conceptual" character of the earth that allows the world to be a revelation of meaningfulness within which the particular meanings disclosed in this world have their sense. If it were not rooted in the earth in this way, the work would be more or less an accidental vehicle through which a discrete set of meanings or a particular function is conveyed. Thus, it is the earth, in its resistance to world, so to speak, that in fact enables world to be itself.

Along the same lines, *"The work lets the earth be an earth"*;[39] the encounter with the world in the work reveals the "earthiness" of the earth in a decisive way. Caldecott makes an observation that illuminates what Heidegger is getting at here:

> The materials of which we make our buildings are just as eloquent [as the form we give them]. Traditional materials such as wood, stone, or clay speak an immediate connection with the earth. On the other hand, concrete and cement by their very nature represent the brutality of modernism—the reduction of

38. Ibid., 676.
39. Ibid., 674.

the world to particles in order to force it into shapes of our own devising. The shaping of concrete is done from the outside, by the imposition of mechanical force, rather than from inside by growth or natural accretion.[40]

The contrast with concrete is especially helpful: in this material, the resistance of nature is quite literally broken down; the natural elements are forced into submission by a power that overwhelms them. And so, when we look at a building made out of concrete, we do not really "see" the concrete. It is, instead, a mere "stuff" that makes the form or structure possible, and it is more or less the form exclusively that draws our eye. One does not typically admire, in such a building, the particular qualities of the concrete, its concreteness. In a stone building, by contrast, the weight, color, texture, and shape of the stones are all still very much felt even in being resisted and overcome or harnessed by and in the structure. The upward thrust of the building is achieved through a kind of "battle," to use Heidegger's word, in which the strength of the opponent is respected, admired, and even celebrated. The imposing weight of the stone makes the soaring arch that much more miraculous, and the arch in turn makes the earthy weight of the stone more evident. Similarly, the non-uniform color of the stone contributes to the beauty of the cathedral, as well as its slightly irregular shape and texture. The building would be less beautiful, in most cases, if it were covered in paint or cut systematically by machine in a way that simply ignored the natural contours.[41] The point is that the very resistance of the earth to the world is essential to the beauty of the order that comes about as a result; it is what allows the "worlding of the world," which in turn "shelters" the earth and puts it forward in its natural mystery. There is rest in this work, which is not a static inertness, but rather the vibrancy of an intimate tension, and this radiant vibrancy is what Heidegger means by beauty.

Now, there is a further point made in the initial passage we cited from Heidegger, which we need to reflect on before turning to the implications of all this for faith. As we saw there, Heidegger explains that beauty, understood in this way as a kind of unconcealment, that is, truth as the interplay

---

40. Caldecott, *Beauty for Truth's Sake*, 99.

41. This is not to say that the use of paint always diminishes beauty, or, more generally, that artifice always compromises the beauty of nature. To the contrary, the argument is that artifice (world) augments and enhances the beauty of nature (earth) to the extent that it respects the proper tension. The point is not to leave the natural element of earth untouched, but rather to avoid simply overwhelming it, or, in other words, dismissively overriding its natural character through the imposition of an extrinsic form. For a reflection on the relation between nature and artifice along these lines, see the profound meditation in Romano Guardini's *Letters from Lake Como*.

between openness and concealment, is not simply a quality that a thing possesses, alongside its other qualities, any more than truth is just a property of things. Instead, to put the matter in more traditional language, beauty, like truth and in intimate connection with it, is ontological. In its beauty, a work of art does not simply present the characteristics that belong to it alone as a particular item in the world; instead, in doing this—or, as Heidegger puts it, by being engrossed in its nature and entering into its own mysterious depths—a beautiful thing manifests being as such. But being is both what is most intimate to a thing and at the same time most universal. It is what is shared by all that is to the extent that it is. By radiating beauty, a work brings out, we might say, the beingness of things beyond their discrete significance for one purpose or another. This is in part what Heidegger means by a work of art "opening up a world"; it casts a light, so to speak, on the things around it, it discloses a context of meaningfulness within which things can have their own proper meaning. The more generously beautiful a thing is, the more it *is* simply, that is, the more it makes manifest the being that all things share.

As the Neoplatonic aesthetic tradition has held, the more beautiful a thing is, the more it is simply.[42] Beauty can therefore give a thing a priority in relation to its surroundings even if it comes later than they in a chronological sense. To illustrate this point, Heidegger takes the example of a Greek temple:

> The temple-work, standing there, opens up a world and at the same time sets this world back again on earth, which itself only thus emerges as native ground. But men and animals, plants and things, are never present and familiar as unchangeable objects, only to represent incidentally also a fitting environment for the temple, which one fine day is added to what is already there. We shall get closer to what *is*, rather, if we think of all this in reverse order. The temple, in its standing there, first gives to things their look and to men their outlook on themselves.[43]

The temple is not merely one thing among others, which happens to be placed among things and happens to possess the quality of beauty. Instead,

---

42. See Plotinus, *Ennead* VIII.9:267–69. "But the power in the intelligible world has nothing but its being and its being beautiful. For where would its beauty be if it was deprived of its being? And where would its reality be if it was stripped of its being beautiful? For in deficiency of beauty it would be defective also in reality [in being: *tē ousia*]. For this reason being is longed for because it is the same as beauty, and beauty is lovable because it is being. But why should we enquire which is the cause of the other when both are one nature?"

43. Heidegger, "The Origin of the Work of Art," 671.

as the encounter of earth and world, it opens up a sphere in which things have their place; it gives a meaningful order to the space that these things inhabit. So, even if it arrives later on the scene than the surrounding things, it opens up a world *for* them. There is a sense in which the majesty of the cliff becomes especially manifest with the crowning of the temple, the brightness of the sun comes forth, the violence of the stormy clouds, the vastness of the sky against the pillars, the shape of the surrounding bush and the animals that have their homes in it, and so forth. But most directly, it orders the human world, allowing a group of individuals to become a people, having a place to which they come to celebrate the feasts that define the significant periods of their existence and to pray, a center around which the particular activities and movements of their lives turn and weave together. It is crucial to see that, in this case, the human meaning is rooted in the earth rather than imposed on it and erected in spite of it. In the beauty of this work, the world makes itself felt as present simultaneously with the earth.

Before we turn, now, to consider what light Heidegger's notion of beauty sheds when we interpret it as an analogy of faith, a word of caution is necessary: whereas Plato represents a "preparatio evangelium," and Aquinas did his thinking *inside* of the Christian tradition, Heidegger placed himself more or less explicitly and deliberately *outside* of that tradition and sought in part to recover a pre-Platonic paganism as an alternative to the metaphysics of creation that arose from philosophical reflection on scripture. To fructify his deep insights from a Christian perspective would thus require a basic rethinking from a different standpoint. Most directly in relation to his notion of beauty, such as we have set it forth, we would have to rethink the encounter between earth and world as founded on something that lies deeper than the Heraclitean *polemos*, the strife between opposed principles in reciprocal dependence. This deeper reality would ultimately be the unity-in-difference and difference-in-unity of the inner life of the Trinity, which is most basically the play of love instead of an intimate battle. In this case, we would see the mystery of nature, for example, not primarily as a function of self-seclusion and concealment, but as a sign of the inexhaustible transcendence, the otherness, of generosity and letting be. In any event, as many have observed, it is also the case that, in his departure from the Christian tradition, Heidegger carried with him some profound elements of that tradition. As we will see, his rooting of beauty in nature represents a complementary contribution to the primary note of transcendence in Plato, and serves to bring to light a dimension of faith that is indispensable but often neglected, particularly in a modern liberal culture such as our own.

There are three aspects of Heidegger's notion of beauty that we can highlight in particular as properly analogous to faith. The first aspect that

becomes illuminated in faith insofar as it is mediated by beauty in the specifically ontological sense that Heidegger presents is its incarnational character. As we saw, Heidegger focused his discussion on the work of art in part
as a response to the modern drift toward subjectivism in its preoccupation
with aesthetic experience, on the one hand, and artistic creativity, on the
other. A similar critique could be made of the modern understanding of
faith: what the word means for us is the subjective act of assent, considered
apart from any particular content at all. What Heidegger shows in response
to the subjectivism of aesthetics is that beauty is an event of truth; it is not
just a manifestation of a being but is the manifestation of being, or more accurately, a particular way in which truth comes to pass. Now, this event lies
in the work, and, though it radiates as it were out from the work, it cannot be
separated from the work insofar as the work is understood as an encounter
between world and earth. As we saw, the earth is, so to speak, the material
element that cannot be translated without loss into concepts or otherwise
replaced. Instead, concepts are an attempt to articulate the meaning that
shows itself, makes itself present, irreplaceably in the work. Hans-Georg
Gadamer, a student of Heidegger's, describes this aspect of the beauty of art
as its properly symbolic dimension, which he says is one of the indispensable features of all art.[44] He interprets "symbol" in its original sense—symbol, a "joining together"—as what we might call the "physical presence" of
meaning in contrast to allegory, which is a pointing to an absent meaning
(*allos-agoreuein*, "speaking of something other"). From our perspective, it is
not an accident that Gadamer takes the sacrament of the Eucharist, according to the traditional, as opposed to the Protestant, interpretation, to be the
paradigm of the incarnation of meaning that symbol represents in art.[45] In
the Eucharist, the body of Christ is not simply indicated as an absent meaning, but is instead made really present *in* the wafer, which thus must be not
only understood by the mind but actually eaten.

The paradigm for art turns out to be the same for faith. It is not the
case that we believe, that is, give our credence to God, and then, as Catholics, happen to take the Eucharist to be one of the many objects of our belief
(which would differ from the objects of someone belonging to a different
religion, though we can be said both to have faith). Instead, faith is not
only the act of a subject (*fides qua*), it is also the object of that act (*fides
quae*). Moreover, the act of assent in faith is an entrusting of ourselves to

44. Gadamer, *Relevance of the Beautiful*, 31–39.
45. He makes the claim as a Lutheran, and explains that Luther defended the "old
Roman Catholic tradition" on this point in the controversy with Zwingli (ibid., 35).
Whether Luther in fact affirmed the Catholic tradition in this matter is an open question, but does not bear immediately on the point we are making.

that object: we do not only believe God (have faith in the things revealed) and believe in a God (have faith that God exists), but we also believe *in* God.[46] In other words, it is a handing of oneself over to God, and indeed, to a God who cannot be separated from his incarnation in Christ. And the incarnate God remains present in the flesh in history, in the sacrament. The Eucharist is, as it were, the incarnation of our faith, its reality. We speak of faith as an inward assent, but we also speak of *the* faith as *what* the church believes, and in the most proper sense we could point to the Eucharist and say, "This is our faith."[47] Just as in beauty, so too in faith, the matter *matters*. As Heidegger showed, it is the positive, "extra-conceptual" aspect that makes beauty an event of meaning that is not just the communication of discrete intellectual content that can be taken away, but instead must most fundamentally be received, contemplated, and beheld. Similarly, the contemplation of the Eucharist, the enjoyment, as it were, of its presence, is not simply one of the acts a believer might perform, but is in fact the very enactment of faith. As barbarous as the phrase sounds, it is appropriate to borrow Heidegger's language here: the celebration and contemplation of the Eucharist is the "faithing of the faith."

But is the Eucharist itself beautiful? It would be more fitting, I think, to say that it is the condition for beauty. We are speaking of an analogy between faith and beauty, and the difference is what makes the unity possible. Thus, though the matter of the Eucharist is indispensable, it nevertheless involves a kind of suspension of sense experience, a sort of hiatus: *visus, tactus, gustus in te fallitur*, as the hymn says. But this suspension is just what sanctifies or sacralizes the matter and the entire physical world it symbolizes. The setting apart of matter from its physical qualities is not an act of removal but of generosity; it is the transcendence that allows meaning to be given physically, and so it is what makes beauty possible. It is therefore not an accident that the churches in which the Eucharist resides and the liturgy in which the bread and wine are transformed have traditionally been given exceptional aesthetic quality. To the contrary, they *must* be beautiful, because their beauty is an extension of the presence of God in the Eucharist into worldly space and time. They are, so to speak, the body of the body of Christ. Now, to be sure, there is a radical difference between these two bodies; the relation of the matter of churches and liturgies to the event that occurs within them is in some respects much freer than that between the bread and body and wine and blood—for example, a great variety of

46. See *ST* II–II, q. 2, a. 2.

47. A full treatment would require a reflection on the whole range of meanings of the body of Christ, including the community of the church; see de Lubac, *Corpus Mysticum*.

building styles and materials are conceivable in churches—but to deny that *beauty* is significant is in a sense to deny the reality of faith; it is, irrespective of the intention behind it, to deny the incarnation of Christ. The church is not just a building in which believers happen to gather, but has much more central and fundamental significance: to use Ratzinger's phrase, it is faith made visible. If it is ugly, this is then a statement about the quality and significance of faith.

The second aspect can be explained more simply. The analogy of beauty sets into relief what we might call the integrity of nature in faith. Heidegger speaks of beauty as an "intimate battle" between world and earth, in which each strives against the other in the context of a reciprocal dependence. The very "striving against" makes each what it is. We proposed reinterpreting this in terms of generosity rather than strife, as a play of love rather than a "raging battle." The point that Heidegger is making is nevertheless an indispensable one: it is not just that the "earthiness" of the earth is respected and preserved in its interaction with the "higher meaning" of the world, but it is in fact liberated. The earth becomes "earthier" in relation to world. To put the matter thus immediately recalls the Catholic understanding of the grace-nature relationship. Grace does not eclipse or destroy nature; instead, it presupposes nature, heals it, and elevates it. In transforming nature, grace does not change it into something *else*, but in fact enables it first to be what it most properly is and was always meant to be. The transformation of nature (earth) in a beautiful work of art is a particularly vivid expression of the same paradox. The stones in a cathedral are "used," both to create the structure and to give glory to God. But they are not thereby "used up"; instead, as we have seen, they take on a far greater significance in this context (in this "world") precisely *as* stones than they would have lying on or in the ground. Their nature comes to dramatic expression. If "the very stones cry out" to bear witness to God, it is their very being that does so; their reality or inner being as stones becomes radiant. In this, they make explicit the perhaps otherwise unheard chorus of nature generally, all the creatures of which in their nature "bless the Lord," as the psalm says.

In seeing beauty as not only a transcendence of the physical world, but at the very same time as a liberation of it in its irreducible physical reality, the Heideggerian perspective on beauty adds a complement to the Platonic aspect we discussed at the outset—though it should be noted that this aspect is arguably already implicit in the "twofold" quality of beauty that Plato describes.[48] In any event, if Plato highlights the "from above" character, the transcendence of beauty, Heidegger shows that this does not exclude, but in fact requires, a kind of rootedness in the earth. In other words, beauty properly speaking does not elicit merely an ascent, which would threaten to leave the materiality of matter behind, but at the very same time therefore elicits a descent into the very depths of nature.[49] Charles Péguy famously observed that he expects the great cathedrals to be in heaven, because such beauty would never be left behind.[50] In the experience of the beauty of the liturgy, or church architecture, we feel *at home* in our body, and indeed especially at home there. The resurrection of the body, we might say, is, like the Eucharist, not simply one of faith's various objects, but a revelation of the very nature of faith. We can appreciate, in this context, one of the standards that Alexander offers for the judgment of good architecture: in looking in a focused way on this structure or this building, do I feel my humanity expand? Do I feel more profoundly *human*?[51] Though some qualification would be necessary,[52] we could also use this as a standard by which to measure the authenticity, the genuinely ontological reach, of faith: inside this faith, do I feel strengthened in my humanity?

The point is that faith is not simply a discrete act among others, distinguished from them by its specifically supernatural, that is, theological,

48. Robert Spaemann makes a crucial observation in this regard that nature can be in fact genuinely transcended only when it is fully and properly recollected—which implies that properly understood the liberation of nature and the transcendence of nature will always coincide; see his essay "Nature," in *A Robert Spaemann Reader*, forthcoming.

49. The order is important: the ascent entails a descent, rather than the reverse. To imply the priority of the descent would imply the kind of naturalism that generates a kind of shock rather than genuine transcendence, and it does so by means of repulsion rather than the attraction of the beautiful.

50. Péguy, *Basic Verities*, 229.

51. Alexander, *Nature of Order*, 1:354–56.

52. It would of course be disastrous to measure faith simply by its anthropological implications. We mean only to say that the anthropological implications are an essential *sign* of the authenticity of faith, without being its measure. Moreover, we also do not mean to identify this elevation of humanity simply with the positive pleasure of beauty. In a message to the Communion and Liberation meeting at Rimini, in 2002, titled "The Feeling of Things, the Contemplation of Beauty," Ratzinger presented the dramatic and paradoxical aesthetics that emerges from Christianity, above all from the contemplation of Christ on the cross. He explains that the tradition has always recognized this image as both supremely beautiful and supremely ugly, and sees this as an affirmation of the Greek notion of beauty along with its reversal. Christianity affirms the possibility that suffering, and the darkness it implies, can be genuinely beautiful insofar as it is assumed in love, but it does so without glorifying the ugly in a Nietzschean manner. It should be pointed out that Alexander himself does not intend to reduce beauty to the consoling.

nature (though this is of course also true). Instead, as transcendent of nature, faith is a world-opening act and at the same time one that liberates nature. Faith therefore "brings out the best in us" in a twofold sense: on the one hand, we bring our first fruits to lay down at the altar. One might think in this context of the jongleur de Notre Dame. A significant part of art history in the West is in fact a catalogue of Christian art: the human desire to give glory to God is spontaneously expressed in the creation of beauty. On the other hand, authentic faith is generative of culture beyond the literal walls of the church. Plato describes the state of the soul when it has reached the peak of its ascent, when it has achieved the fullest actualization of its humanity, not as a departure from the world, but as a desire *tiktein en tō kalō*, "to generate and to give birth in beauty."[53] In a different key, perhaps, the same phrase might be used to describe the act of faith. The very possession of faith is inseparable from an ongoing fruitfulness, not only in the order of grace but also in the order of nature.

The final aspect we wish to highlight is what we might call the "cosmological" dimension of faith, which comes to light through the analogy with beauty as Heidegger presents it. As we saw above, Heidegger conceives of the great work of art as opening a world by presenting, as it were, the irruption into the immanent sphere of space and time of an event of revelation, but a visible one, a structured event with its roots in the earth. This irruption presents the discontinuity of difference, which is what allows the otherwise homogenous monotony of geometrical space and linear time to acquire order and form; it presents a center around which things arrange themselves as they find their proper place and season. The role that Heidegger gives to the work of art turns out to be quite similar to that given to the sacred object or ritual by Mircea Eliade in his famous phenomenological and cultural anthropological study of religion, *The Sacred and the Profane*, which Caldecott discusses in his book on beauty. In setting apart a particular natural object as sacred, a religious culture transforms the natural order *tout court*, and so enters into an "enchanted" world: "For those to whom a stone reveals itself as sacred . . . [t]he cosmos as a whole can become a hierophany [a revelation of sacred order]."[54]

But Caldecott's interpretation of the matter brings to light something decisive, which is missing from both Heidegger and Eliade. In describing the Greek temple as opening a world, Heidegger says in fact that it is able to do so only "as long as the work is a work, as long as the god has not fled

53. Plato, *Symposium*, 205b.

54. Eliade, *Sacred and the Profane*, 12, quoted in Caldecott, *Beauty for Truth's Sake*, 127.

from it."[55] One might say, here, that Heidegger is implicitly acknowledging the analogy between beauty and religious faith, but at the same time he rejects the reality of faith. As a result, the difference between beauty and faith gets absorbed into beauty alone, and so beauty takes the place of faith; it is identified with the sacred. Thus, the Greek temple, from which the god has fled, is made relative for Heidegger to any great painting or poem, any great work of art. On the other hand, we might say that Eliade loses the analogy from the other direction: we have in every instance theophany *instead of* beauty, which amounts to a tendency similarly to "immanentize" religion. We do not have the "natural transcendence" of beauty in art and nature that is distinct from religious transcendence, but which, as we have been suggesting, makes it possible. In contrast to these, Caldecott presents the notion of beauty that is an image of Christ (who is the perfect image of the Father), which at once liberates the reality of beauty as radically different from the self-revelation of God, and at the very same time—indeed, for that very reason—allows beauty to be the eloquent presence of the ever-greater mystery of God. It is just this view of beauty that restores, as it were, the *nature* of faith.

With this, we come full circle; we reconnect with Caldecott's reflection on church architecture and liturgy as sanctifying space and time more generally. To return to Heidegger's profound reflection on the Greek temple that "opens up a world and at the same time sets this world back again on earth, which itself only thus emerges as native ground,"[56] we can see the beauty of the church from which the God *has not fled*, but in which he becomes real in the very matter of the Eucharist, as an ontological and cosmological event rather than a mere aesthetic decoration. It is not just the icon or stained glass window that is faith made visible, it is not even just the church and the liturgy that takes place within it. Instead, the visibility of faith in the full scope of its meaning is the beauty of the church that frames a town square in which people gather to walk, to eat, to celebrate, to do business, the church around which a town is built and ordered, a church whose steeple pierces the horizon and thus allows things not only to have space, but also to have their proper place. Our faith becomes visible in the recovery of the beauty of a natural order of life. Caldecott presents a program of education that aims to recover this order through a recentering of the various aspects of the world and human culture on beauty. Such a program both reconceives the various subjects of study as so many reflections of a single, harmonious cosmos and cultivates dispositions of wonder and praise and habits of

55. Heidegger, "Origin of the Work of Art," 671.
56. Ibid., 671.

gratitude and respect. We ought to interpret the entire vision he presents in this book, indeed, as faith made visible. Educating in beauty, Caldecott says, "will begin the process of building a society that is liturgical to the very core, in which the 'air' of grace can circulate."[57] Such a society would also manifest beauty in its structure, in the way that it gives shape to space. It is only in the circulating air of such a society that one can have and enact a faith that is more than a merely private set of beliefs, but is true to (its) nature. If beauty without faith is ultimately blind, faith without beauty is empty: "Western civilization has long since lost its sense that cosmic order has to be rooted in a 'Logos.' It is no coincidence that it lost its faith in God at the same time. If God is not connected with the universe by some kind of mediation, then he floats off into abstract space and faith starts to seem meaningless."[58]

57. Caldecott, *Beauty for Truth's Sake*, 130.
58. Ibid., 15.

4

An Observation about Saint Thomas Aquinas's Idea of the Intellect

Jean Borella

It's a good question whether what Saint Thomas Aquinas understands by "intellect" means intellectual intuition, an act identical to the Platonic *nous*, that is, to the vision of intelligible realities. Many experts think the opposite is true. Father Sertillanges says, "There is no intellectual intuition in Saint Thomas."[1] Maurice de Gandillac asserts, "Saint Thomas did not believe there is such a thing as an intellectual intuition."[2] This interpretation rests on the Thomist theory of knowledge, according to which the intellect's true activity is to abstract essences from sensible realities; it follows that these essences are not the intelligible realities themselves, but rather concepts. Nonetheless we think we can answer the initial question in the affirmative.

First, too many expositions of Thomism give the impression that it comes down to an intellectual system and that the Angelic Doctor expended all his energies in solving philosophical problems created by some interpretations of Aristotelianism, so much so that one can say, we find this philosophical notion in Thomas and we do not find that notion. Of course these categories apply to modern and contemporary philosophy, but they don't apply to the writings of Saint Thomas. One only has to read him to notice an omnipresent spiritual breath, coming from a mind that is perpetually directed toward God. Thomas's faith—his utter, loving submission to the Word of God—was not for him a launch pad from which to "construct" an autonomous philosophical system, which, once he had got started on it, absorbed his attention so much that he forgot his starting point and dedicated himself to building philosophical artifices.

1. Sertillanges, *Saint Thomas d'Aquin*, 2:145.
2. Gandillac, *Philosophie de Nicolas de cues*, 196 n. 1.

In reality, in Thomas's doctrine, everything looks to God, in the same way that, in his own personal existence, Saint Thomas lived constantly under the gaze of God: God was for him the only thing that matters at all. The entirety of his doctrinal discourse consists of asking himself, how can one speak accurately about God? That is, if God is such—and God is such—then what does he think of what I say of him? So theological discourse never does its job properly; it is always inadequate and on the verge of throwing in the towel. And for this reason, the reader cannot treat this discourse like an autonomous object, and, detaching little pieces from the assortment, interrogate them to see whether or not such a general philosophical concept is found therein. At the end of the day, Thomas would agree with us that the thought of Saint Thomas is utterly unimportant: what matters is the Truth.

Second, intellectual intuition really happens. This is a statement of fact, requiring no proof. So either there is an intellectual intuition in Thomas or there is not. And if there is not, and if its possibility is explicitly denied as in Kant and the moderns, then Thomism is missing something really important, because, outside of an intellectual intuition, there is no direct and infallible grasp of truth. The upshot would have to be that Thomism is false. This cannot be so, since under the inspiration of the Holy Spirit the church's magisterium has acknowledged it as the common doctrine of the Christian faith. It follows that Thomism of one sort or another must include the notion of the intellectual intuition.

Third, it is necessary to show what kind of Thomism presents an intellectual intuition. Without rambling too far, we simply mention the following points.

The Platonism of Saint Thomas

Father Romeyer has objected to the way Sertillanges' interpretation makes Thomas into a thoroughgoing Aristotelian.[3] It seems to be certain that if Thomas's external framework is Aristotelian, the interior dimension of his thought is implicitly Platonic. This is the case even if Thomas didn't directly know Plato's writings, because the Platonic teaching expresses the essence of all intellectual spirituality, and thus any given intellectual spirituality engages with Platonism. But, for Saint Thomas as for Aristotle, there is no intelligible world constituted of intelligible realities, which are the perfectly real targets of intellectual intuition. Hence, neither does that intellectual

---

3. Romeyer, "Philos, chrétienne III." See also Faucon de Boylesve, *Aspects néoplatoniciens de la doctrine de saint Thomas d'Aquin.*

intuition which represents the prototype of all noetic intuition exist for Saint Thomas.

However, if the intelligible realities do not exist for Saint Thomas, *in mundo*, as true realities, and if they are always inseparable from the sensible reality, even if distinct from it, unlike Aristotle he does affirm that they exist in the divine realm, in the divine Word, and they are known there by a genuine intellectual intuition, in the beatific vision. This vision, which can only rarely occur in this life, defines the perfection of the intellect and therefore its true nature. It follows that for Thomas the intellect is indeed a direct intuition of intelligible realities and even of the divine essence, but that, apart from exceptional cases, the character of the intellect is only realized after death.

Hence, the intuitive nature of the intellect remains relatively hidden to all degrees of knowledge, other than the highest. The intellect is forever intuitive, but an intuition which is unaware of itself and which gets to know itself gradually, in step with a person's realization of his spiritual destiny. In other words, there is no purely philosophical theory of knowledge in Saint Thomas. To look at it as if there were is to betray the essential perspective of a habit of thought, which narrowly considers everything in its relation to God and its capacity for attaining God. It is to define it by external similarities, and to forget the nearly infinite gap between a medieval man and a man of today.

The Three Degrees of the Intellect

"The intellect is naturally supernatural or supernaturally natural." Failing to grasp this truth, all the expert discussions of the intellect by this and that author who uses the term, cannot get anywhere. For Saint Thomas, whether it is at the level of natural knowledge, at that of supernatural knowledge or at that of beatific knowledge, it is always the intellect that knows.

So it is necessary to distinguish three degrees of intellect (one could distinguish even more and all our exposition can do is to point out a few things), which Thomas calls the natural intellect, the gift of the intellect, and finally the perfect intellect. The intuitive light of the perfect intellect is reflected in lowering itself to the two inferior levels, but it is always the same light. Of course, Thomas distinguishes natural knowledge quite clearly from supernatural knowledge, which is based on faith, and he distinguishes this knowledge from the fulfillment of its promise in the beatific vision; but for all that the sainted doctor uses one single term to designate this singular cognitive power, *intellectus*.

To consider the intellect purely on the level of natural knowledge is to consider what is just a shadow of intellection. It is to want to grasp the essence of the cognitive act on the level on which it cannot be met. At the end of the day, it is to consider that Saint Thomas could have been an atheist.

1) In Its General Definition the Intellect Is an Intuitive Knowledge

"The name *intellect* expresses a sort of intimate knowledge (of things); for *intelligere* means: *intus-legere*, to read in. And this is manifest if one considers the difference between sense and intellect. In practice, sensitive knowledge bears on the exterior and sensible qualities, whereas intellective knowledge bores right in to the essence of the thing."[4]

2) In Natural Knowledge or Intellective Reason or Imperfect Reason, the Intellect Is an Intuition which Is Unaware of Itself

Reason is nothing other than the intellectual nature obscured [*obumbrata*].[5]

That which is supreme in our knowledge is not the reason but the intellect which is the origin of our reason.[6]

The certitude of the reason comes from the intellect, but the necessity (of using it) comes from a defect of the intellect.[7]

However, because one cannot have knowledge without an intuition (because rational enquiry by itself never reaches an end), meaning, unless it grasps an intelligible *end point*, reason, which comes from the intellect also completes itself in intellect, because it is compelled to connect discursive thinking with intuition: "The intellect and the reason differ as to the mode of knowledge, because if the intellect knows by a *simple intuition* [*simplici intuitu*], reason knows things discursively, by coursing from one thing to another. Nonetheless, through discursive thinking, reason comes to know what the intellect knows non-discursively, that is, it knows the universal."[8]

4. Aquinas, *Summa Theologiae* (*ST*) II–II, q. 8, a. 1.
5. Aquinas, *In I Sent.*, d. 3, q. 4, a. 1.
6. Aquinas, *Summa contra Gentiles* (*SCG*) I, ch. 57, sec. 8.
7. *ST* II–II, q. 49, a. 5.
8. *ST* I, q. 59, a. 1.

So for human beings, while it is the reason that leads us into essences, the aspect of reason that grasps the objective essence of things is the intellect. This is why the intellect is intrinsically infallible, but human beings can err, because the intellect relies on the reason to get hold of its authentic target, in natural knowledge: "The human intellect does not acquire perfect knowledge by its first act of apprehension but . . . it first . . . compares one thing with another by composition or division; and from one composition and division it proceeds to another, which is the process of reasoning."[9] But "the proper object of the intellect is the essence of a material thing; and hence, properly speaking, the intellect is not at fault concerning this essence" but "the intellect . . . may be accidentally deceived in the essence of composite things, not by the defect of its organ, for the intellect is a faculty that is independent of an organ; but on the part of the composition affecting the definition."[10] We can say the intellect without the reason is impotent, and the reason without the intellect is blind. It is reason that pursues the essence of things in sensible realities, but it is intuition that perceives this essence.

Intellect exhibits itself in reason as a kind of instinct for intuition. The real object of this intellect is not the Idea in the Platonic sense, and so its intuition is not a Platonic intuition, but even so it is the object of an intuition, bearing not upon intelligible beings that are separated and stand alone, but on the abstracted objective essences *of* sensible things. And the task of the reason in abstracting the essence is only possible by dint of an intelligible light (actualized in the agent intellect) which illuminates the human intellect: "The intelligible species is rendered non-material by the active intellect which separates it from matter."[11] "A being is not perfected by a thing which is inferior to it. . . . It is evident, for instance, that the form of a stone or of any other material object is something inferior to a human being. So it is not in the form of the stone that the human intellect is perfected, insofar as it in some way becomes that form; it can only be by participating in something superior to the human intellect, that is to say, the intelligible light."[12]

So even knowledge of material things comes about by participation in the intelligible light. If it is only possible to speak legitimately of an intellectual intuition for an exclusively Platonic *noesis*, then of course, there is no intellectual intuition in Saint Thomas. But this is a singularly counterintuitive notion of intuition (even in relation to Plato's conception

9. *ST* I, q. 85, a. 5.
10. *ST* I, q. 85, a. 6.
11. *ST* I, q. 79. a. 3.
12. *ST* II–II, q. 3, a. 6.

of intuition). In addition, Thomas defines the intellect's way of knowing as intuitive knowledge (*simplici intuitu*), so it is fair to ask where in the texts of his writings Thomas rejects this notion. And if one answers from texts such as "in the conditions of this present life, the human intellect cannot know immaterial created substances,"[13] we have to observe that Plato never presumed that it was possible for the prisoner chained up in the Cave of the world to know intelligible realities.

3) The Intellect Sanctified by the Gift of Intelligence Grasps the Supernatural Truths that Are Necessary for Our Salvation

Saint Thomas's invariable teaching comes down to this: in its authentic nature, the intellect is a pure intuition of intelligible realities, but it cannot display itself in all its majesty here below because it is tied to a body. Man can thus not achieve the genuine nature of his intellect, at least of a *mutatio intellectus*, which is one and the same as his salvation and his immortality. This means that the whole of Saint Thomas's teaching about the intellect is driven by his understanding of the spiritual destiny of man and that the realization of the intellect is not a theoretical issue but rather lies in the realm of sanctification, so that one could somehow say this teaching touches upon sacralizing the intellect. And a human being does not see that his spiritual destiny is at stake in the knowledge of natural things. So it is necessary that the charismatic intellect descend through faith into the natural intellect in order to teach man that he has a knowledge which involves his very being; this knowledge is that of supernatural things which the charismatic intellect (or the gift of intelligence) allows him to grasp, by making the intellective power morph from nature to supernature.

> Hence we may speak of understanding with regard to all these things. Since, however, human knowledge begins with the senses, that, is, with the outside of things, it is evident that the stronger the light of the intellect, the further can it penetrate into the heart of things. Now the natural light of our understanding is of finite power; wherefore it can reach to a certain fixed point. Consequently man needs a supernatural light in order to penetrate further still so as to know what it cannot know by its natural light.[14]

> The intellectual light of grace is a gift of the intellect in the sense that the human mind becomes more pliable to the inspiration

13. *ST* I, q. 8, a. 3.
14. *ST* I, q. 8, a. 1.

of the Holy Spirit. And the effect of this inspiration is to make the human person understand the truth in relation to its proper end; so that the human mind has the gift of the intellect in so far as the divine inspiration makes him conceive an accurate idea of his end, some knowledge which gives him the light of the Holy Spirit. But to have an accurate idea of his end is not only not to err about the end, but also to attach himself to it as a supreme good, and no one can do this without sanctifying grace. No one has a gift of the intellect if he does not have sanctifying grace.[15]

But this does not change the fact that the charismatic intellect cannot produce its full effect during this life. So one must distinguish between the gift of the intellect in this life, which perfects the human intellect, and the gift of the intellect as it will be in heaven.[16]

Does that mean that Saint Thomas absolutely excludes the entire possibility of an intellectual intuition of the divine essence, and of Platonic intelligible realities, happening in this life? No, it does not.

Let's start by remembering that the *Summa contra Gentiles* assert that Plato's teaching concerning the prototypical Ideas is in a certain, qualified way true.[17] But it's especially important to consider this text, which relates to the contemplative life: "In the present state of life it is impossible for a human being to contemplate without corporeal images [phantasmata], because it is connatural to man to see the intelligible species in the phantasms, as the Philosopher states [*De Anima* iii, 7]. Yet intellectual knowledge does not consist in the phantasms themselves, but in our contemplating in them the purity of the intelligible truth: and this not only in natural knowledge, but also in that which we obtain by revelation."[18] And we can find them in the present life in two ways: in an effective or actual way, or in a "potential" way: "When the soul is united to the mortal body as its form, yet so as to make use neither of the bodily senses, nor even of the imagination, as happens in rapture; and in this way the contemplation of the present life can attain to the vision of the Divine essence. Consequently the highest degree of contemplation in the present life is that which Paul had in rapture, whereby he was in a middle state between the present life and the life to come."[19]

---

15. *ST* I, q. 8, a. 5.
16. *ST* I, q. 8, a. 7.
17. *SCG* I, ch. 54, *in fine*.
18. *ST* II-II, q. 180, a. 5, ad 2.
19. *ST* II-II, q. 180, a. 5, c.

4) In Heaven, the Perfected Intellect, United to the Divine Intellect, Enjoys the Intuitive Vision of the Divine Essence and of Intelligible Substances

A. The Obediential Potential

How can the human intellect be capable of an act of intellection that surpasses its own nature? Theology answers this question with the notion of an obediential potential. The term sounds weird and the question can sound vacuous. But it is tackling the eternal destiny of human beings. In theology one distinguishes between

—the objective potential: the simple possibility which does not imply a contradiction (any two lines can meet);

—the subjective potential: the real principle of an action or passion (the view).

Within this we can distinguish

—the active potential (for instance, the will capable of acting);

—the passive potential (for instance, the intellect, capable of receiving intelligibles).

Within the passive potential one can distinguish

—the natural potential: what is configured to the nature of the power;

—the obediential potential: the power to obey a perfection that intrinsically exceeds one's natural potential at the behest of the first Cause.

Insofar as God is the author of nature, the obediential potential which is in nature displays itself as a miracle.

Insofar as God is the author of supernature, the obediential potential only concerns intellectual beings and displays itself for instance as the intuitive vision of the divine essence.

"It is necessary to note that there is in the human spirit, as there is in all creatures, a dual passive potential: one which acts in relation to its natural agency (for the passive intellect it is the agent intellect); the other acts in relation with the First Agent and makes it pass to a more perfect act than that to which it led the natural potential; this potential is commonly called *obediential potential* in the creature."[20]

The power of obedience thus enables the human being to locate itself in the presence of God. This notion seems to correlate with that of the natural and supernatural character of the intellect. It provides a key to the mystical notion of deification.

B. The Beatitude of the Intellect

In itself beatitude is something created, but in its object it has the air of the uncreated. It is a created participation in uncreated Beatitude, for in God, beatitude is his very nature.[21]

In the state of perfect beatitude, the human soul is united to God by an operation that is one, continuous, and endless.[22]

This operation does not belong to the sensitive soul, not to the will, but solely to the intellect, for the will desires the supreme Good and it would love to possess it, but it cannot enter his Presence: "So the essence of beatitude consists in an act of intellect."[23]

This act is not the act of the practical intellect, but essentially that of the speculative intellect. "Now man's highest operation is that of his highest power in respect of its highest object: and his highest power is the intellect, whose highest object is the Divine Good, which is the object, not of the practical but of the speculative intellect. . . . In regard to the principal thing known, which is His Essence, God has not practical but merely speculative knowledge."[24]

The glorified intellect knows separated substances (Platonic Ideas), that is, the angels, and it takes part in their festivities. But that is not all there is to it. We do not say that Saint Thomas identifies the angels and Platonic Ideas, but that he establishes a correlation between them and calls them by the same name: "Plato only allowed for separated substantial forms,"[25] he writes. And, he adds, "the separated substances, meaning, the angels."[26] Thomas also heaps praise on Plato in the *Summa contra Gentiles*.[27]

20. *ST* III, q. 2, a. 1.
21. *ST* III, q. 3, a. 1.
22. *ST* III, q. 3, a. 2.
23. *ST* III, q. 3, a. 4.
24. *ST* III, q. 3, a. 5.
25. *ST* I, q. 115, a. 1.
26. *ST*, I–II, q. 3, a. 7.
27. *SCG* II, ch. 74, sec. 7.

"Because the soul can be separated from a given body, the intellect can have intellection of beings which are intelligible in themselves, that is to say of separated substances, by the light of the Agent intellect (the intelligible light in act) which, in our soul is like the intellectual light in the separated substances."[28] So "we will take part in the angels' festivals." But this is still an "imperfect beatitude."[29] We will still only be in the celestial paradise, "the second heaven where we will see the celestial spirits."[30] And in some way, this paradise is a "prison" for the intellect. "The highest part of the human being does indeed touch the base of the angelic nature, by a kind of likeness; but man does not rest there as in his last end, but reaches out to the universal fount itself of good, which is the common object of happiness of all the blessed, as being the infinite and perfect good."[31] For "the final perfection of the human intellect is by union with God"[32] and "contemplation of Him makes man perfectly happy."[33]

The intellect is only perfectly beatified in the vision of the divine essence. "For perfect beatitude requires that the intellect attains the very essence of the first Cause; and thus it obtains its perfection by its union with God, as with the only object in which human beatitude consists."[34]

So it seems that the obediential potential of the intellect is limitless, since it renders human nature capable of a deifying union, and thus it can only only be actualized by a grace which is infinite in its pure essence, even if it is finite in the subject in which it locates itself.[35] This is how the vision of the divine essence is brought about, in the light of glory, through which the intellect becomes "God-formed." "The created intellect is not intrinsically possessed of this faculty for seeing the divine essence, but sees it through the light of glory, which constitutes the intellect in 'God-formedness.'"[36] A God-formedness of the intellect, whose prototype is the hypostatic union of Christ Jesus to the eternal Word, for "when a created intellect sees God through his essence, it is the very essence of God which becomes the intelligible form of the intellect."[37]

28. *SCG* III, ch. 45, sec. 9.
29. *ST* I–II, q. 3, a. 7.
30. *ST* II–II, q. 175, a. 3.
31. *ST* I–II, q. 2, a. 8, ad 1.
32. *ST* I–II, q. 3, a. 7, ad 2.
33. *ST* I–II, q. 3, a. 7, c.
34. *ST* I–II, q. 3, a. 8.
35. *ST* III, q. 7, a. 11.
36. *ST* I, q. 12, a. 6.
37. *ST* I, q. 12, a. 5.

5

Wisdom Has Built Her
Beautiful House for Liturgy

David W. Fagerberg

S tratford Caldecott has always been interested in the points where heaven
and earth intersect.[1] Some of those points are regular and ritualized;
some of them are unsuspected and staggering; some of them are heaven
clothed in earthly matter, and others are earth clothed in celestial light.
"Splendor" means to shine, and whatever truth, beauty, and goodness exist
in this lovely world is the splendoring of heaven's truth, beauty, and goodness upon it. Without prejudice to God's freedom to surprise us unexpect-
edly, if he so wills it, the place where we regularly, routinely, and ritually
encounter this splendor sacramentally is the liturgy. We are therefore in a
constant search for sacraments, for symbols and theophanies, for the signs
of the eternal that populate this cosmic home in which we live, and we go
blind if we do not find them. Light is required for the capacity of sight; the
splendor of heaven is required to capacitate our humanity.

Our world, while graced, is not inadvertent. We do not inhabit an accident. We live in a cosmos, not a chaos, and the world is disposed, prepared,
ordered, and arranged, which is what *kosmein* means. To communicate this
fact, the book of Proverbs says that this world has been built by Wisdom.
The agent that orders and adorns creation is called Wisdom, or Sophia. She
is shy, and does not disclose herself very readily in either scripture or tradition, but one place her activity is described is in the book of Proverbs. "To
you, O men, I call; my appeal is to the children of men" (Prov 8:4). She
asks us to prefer her instruction to silver, and her knowledge to gold; she

1. It would be wise for us to be interested in these intersections, too, because if we
do not choose to stand there now voluntarily, we will one day stand there against our
will.

73

gives counsel and advice to anyone who will receive it, and by her sapiential gifts "kings reign, and lawgivers establish justice" (Prov 8:15–16). She is not stingy, but lavish, "granting wealth to those who love me, and filling their treasuries" (Prov 8:21). Wisdom instructs us about the rightly ordered life, the path of justice, the way to happiness. This Wisdom can do because she has full knowledge of natural things, and she has full knowledge of natural things because she knows how things are rooted in the mind of God, and she knows how things are rooted in the mind of God because she was present at earth's creation.

> The Lord begot me, the first-born of his ways,
>> the forerunner of his prodigies of long ago;
> From of old I was poured forth,
>> at the first, before the earth.
> When there were no depths I was brought forth,
>> when there were no fountains or springs of water;
> Before the mountains were settled into place,
>> before the hills, I was brought forth;
> While as yet the earth and the fields were not made,
>> nor the first clods of the world.
> When he established the heavens I was there,
>> when he marked out the vault over the face of the deep;
> When he made firm the skies above,
>> when he fixed fast the foundations of the earth;
> When he set for the sea its limit,
>> so that the waters should not transgress his command;
> Then was I beside him as his craftsman,
>> and I was his delight day by day,
> Playing before him all the while,
>> playing on the surface of his earth;
> and I found delight in the sons of men. (Prov 8:22–31)

In a lecture on the campus of the University of Notre Dame, Caldecott summarized her this way: "Wisdom, then, is God's original Idea of the world, and also the creation finally conformed to that Idea in the consummation of all things—for the divine essence contains all that is, and nothing is perfectly its own unique self until it coincides with God's thought of it."[2] Wisdom is the Logos and Holy Spirit enacting the Father's archetypical Ideas, refracting the glory of God through non-divine creatures. Wisdom

---

2. Caldecott, "Beauty for Truth's Sake and the Children of Wisdom," 8. The online copy has the same title as his book *Beauty for Truth's Sake*, but in his manuscript for the original lecture he subtitled it "And the Children of Wisdom." We will use that title in order to distinguish the lecture from the book.

then plays on the surface of the earth creatively, conducting and guiding the creative will of God.

Those who have eyes to see can perceive the value and purpose of things that Wisdom has arranged. "God does not create things simply to fill up space. He creates for a reason, and the ultimate reason for his creation is love. Each thing, and especially each living thing, is a word, symbol, a revelation. Each is a note, or theme, and some great music. At any rate, it is more than itself: that is, more than the thing most people see when they look at it."[3]

Wisdom sings the Creator's siren song in order to lure us back to God. Each created object is a note to break the spell that holds us back from glory. The falconer swings a lure above his head to call the falcon back to him, and God set the universe spinning in order to lure us to himself. Heaven is alluring. Everything Wisdom touches symbolizes some aspect of the divine. "The Catholic lives in a symbolic cosmos, in which everything—every stone, every flower, every neighbor—both exists in its own right and symbolizes some aspect of the divine. . . . In this sense the entire natural world is what we might call 'sacramental'—not a sacrament in the strict theological sense, but nevertheless a symbolic system apt for the communication of spiritual realities."[4]

Wisdom is God's creative activity turned outward. She was with Christ the Cosmic Geometer at the time when he, the Logos, laid out the measurements of heaven and earth. Thus the book of Proverbs next says:

> Wisdom has built her house, she has set up her seven columns;
> She has dressed her meat, mixed her wine, yes, she has spread her table.
> She has sent out her maidens; she calls from the heights out over the city:
> "Let whoever is simple turn in here; to him who lacks understanding,
>   I say,
> Come, eat of my food, and drink of the wine I have mixed!"
>   (Prov 9:1–5)

Little wonder so many Orthodox churches are named for her, including the Hagia Sophia (Holy Wisdom) in Constantinople: they house tables for even greater feasting. Little wonder that Wisdom has liturgical overtones: "There are icons of Sancta Sophia in the Greek as well as the Russian Orthodox Church: a great red and gold angel on a throne, sometimes bearing a musical instrument or book on her lap. . . . She is traditionally identified with the Shekinah or Glory of God present in the Temple."[5] She

---

3. Caldecott, *Power of the Ring*, 24.

4. Ibid., 60.

5. Caldecott, "Beauty for Truth's Sake and the Children of Wisdom," 6.

has built an edifice to house the mystery of God—we mean the cosmos, and we mean the micro-cosmos, the church. She plays liturgy in both places.

We can cite three of the great sophiologists to clarify the distinction between Wisdom and the Logos. They are not identical, and Sophia is not a person of the Trinity. Sergius Bulgakov says, "As divinity, Sophia is nonhypostatic (is not a 'fourth hypostasis') . . . [but] she *belongs* to the divine trihypostatic Person as this Person's life and self-revelation."[6] Wisdom is neither a hypostasis of the Trinity, nor a goddess on her own, nor an autonomous creature. "The Divine Sophia contains the entire fullness of divine being, but she does not exist in isolation from the divine trihypostatic Person."[7] Wisdom is the creative act of the Holy Trinity, the Trinity turned outward in divine creativity. God's own life is self-revealed by creating something that is not-God, by creating non-divine beings. The life of the Trinity becomes an eternal act, and "this act is the Divine Sophia, the self-positing and self-revelation of the Holy Trinity. . . . She is the creative act of the divine trihypostatic person."[8] Vladimir Solovyov agrees: "To speak about Sophia as an essential element of Divinity does not mean, from the Christian point of view, to introduce new gods."[9] Sophia is not a deity; she is a connection between God and the world, between the uncreated and the created, between the divine One and non-divine beings. As such, she solves two philosophical dilemmas. If the gap between God and the world is too large, we find ourselves left with dualism; if the gap between God and the world is too small, we find ourselves left with monism. Sophia allows us to say that creation is connected to God (it doesn't have its own source of being) and yet that creation is other than God (no polytheism). Thus Solovyov concludes that Sophia "occupies the mediating position between the multiplicity of living beings, which comprised the real content of her life, and the unconditional unity of Divinity, which is the ideal beginning and the norm of that life."[10] Pavel Florensky writes in a similar vein: "Sophia is the Great Root by which creation goes into the intra-Trinitarian life and through which it receives Life Eternal from the One Source of Life. Sophia is the original nature of creation . . . the Guardian Angel of creation, the Ideal person of the world."[11]

6. Bulgakov, *Bride of the Lamb*, 38–39.

7. Ibid., 39.

8. Ibid., 42.

9. Solovyof, *Lectures on Godmanhood*, 154–55.

10. Ibid., 173.

11. Florensky, *Pillar and Ground*, 237.

Wisdom was beside the Creator and was his craftsman, Proverbs says. She is the artisan of the work that was willed by the three-personed God. And what was that? What was willed by God as the purpose of creation? The Catechism of the Catholic Church summarizes it for us in the first three paragraphs of the second pillar, which deals with liturgy and sacrament. The mystery of the Holy Trinity and the plan of God's good pleasure for all creation is that the Father give "his beloved Son and his Holy Spirit for the salvation of the world and for the glory of his name."[12] This is principally accomplished in the paschal mystery, from which the church is born.[13] And "it is this mystery of Christ that the Church proclaims and celebrates in her liturgy."[14] Thus a liturgical alliance with God was in the plan of creation from the very beginning, and the liturgy of creation and the liturgy of the church are twinned. The liturgy is rooted in cosmology, so early Christians could say that the world was created for the sake of the church. The Christian vision of existence is therefore fundamentally liturgical, and Wisdom's house is a cosmic house for liturgy. That is why Caldecott can write with stereoscopic vision. He is as enamored of the order of number discovered by Pythagoras as he is of the order of the Mass celebrated by the ordained minister. He sees Wisdom organize a beauty in her house that is retraced in the beauty of the church as house of prayer; the ritual liturgy writ small is a revelation of the cosmic liturgy that Wisdom has writ large. It is a perception he shares with Benedict XVI. In the pope's book on liturgy we read the following:

> According to Pythagoras, the cosmos was constructed mathematically, a great edifice of numbers. . . . [T]his mathematical order of the universe ("cosmos" means "order"!) was identical with the essence of beauty itself. Beauty comes from meaningful inner order. . . . But a further step was taken with the help of the Trinitarian faith. . . . The mathematics of the universe does not exist by itself, nor, as people now came to see, can it be explained by stellar deities. It has a deeper foundation: the mind of the Creator. It comes from the Logos, in whom, so to speak, the archetypes of the world's order are contained. . . . In virtue of his work in creation, the Logos is, therefore, called the "art of God" (art = techne!). The Logos himself is the great artist, in whom all works of art—the beauty of the universe—have their origin. . . .

12. *Catechism of the Catholic Church*, ¶1066.

13. Ibid., ¶1067.

14. Ibid., ¶1068.

Yes, it is the cosmic context that gives art in the liturgy both its measure and its scope.[15]

Caldecott concurs that such a vision of human existence is fundamentally liturgical, which means the liturgy is not a purely human business, he says, but is rather related to the mathematical ordering of the cosmos because "our lives can be oriented toward God by prayer and action in such a way that the interior world of the human soul and the exterior world of the society and universe are brought into harmony."[16] A liturgy of praise is knit by Wisdom on a three-sided loom of space, time, and matter, and within that *eucharistia* we may attain intimate communion with God.

Cult produces culture. "If we are to renew our civilization by renewing our worship, we must understand also that liturgy is a way of being in tune with the motion of the stars, the dance of atomic particles, and the harmony of the heavens that resembles a great song."[17] Our cultic liturgy will yield a culture attuned to the archetype written into the harmony of existence. That harmony has been blotted from our memory by the fall of our protoparents, but by hearing the refrain again in the ritual liturgy we learn its notes once more when it is played for us on scripture and sacrament. And the purpose for learning it here is to put our whole life into tune with it there. Catholic liturgy takes us "to the source of the cosmos itself, into the sacred precincts of the Holy Trinity where all things begin and end (whether they know it or not), and to the source of all artistic and scientific inspiration, of all *culture*."[18] Three things are needed for such a culture, Caldecott says: a beginning, an end, and a liturgy that arcs between them. "The religious society orients itself toward God by having first a cosmogony or a creation story, second an eschatology, a doctrine of the 'last things,' of the endings of life and time, and thirdly a liturgy—that is, a set of rituals and a way of organizing time and space that situates us in relation to the beginning and end of things (*in via* or in process from one to the other)."[19]

The sacramental life unfolds Christ for us through the medium of matter. In Catholic theology, the order of grace is sacramental because all matter is pliable in the hands of God, and can be restored to its original symbolic function. All it takes is human petition and divine concession (this is called *epiclesis* in the liturgy). Olivier Clément says,

---

15. Benedict XVI, *Spirit of the Liturgy*, 152–54.

16. Caldecott, *Beauty for Truth's Sake*, 13.

17. Ibid., 125.

18. Ibid.

19. Ibid., 129.

In Christ the world is joined together again in symbol, in a profusion of symbols. The invisible part appears in the visible: the visible draws its meaning from the invisible. . . . Christian symbolism expresses nothing less than the union in Christ of the divine and the human—of which the cosmos becomes the dialogue—displaying the circulation in Christ of glory between "earth" and "heaven," between the visible and the invisible.[20]

Then, when we take our place within this Christ, installed by the Holy Spirit in his mystical body, we find the personal relationship that liturgy intends to communicate. In the sacramental life of the church Caldecott finds first human unity, then, in it, a cosmic unity. "The sacraments thus become the means for drawing all men—and through them the entire cosmos of space and time—into an intimate personal relationship with the Father, into the everlasting liturgy of praise that is the business of heaven."[21]

The coin of this realm is beauty, which is why liturgical theology is a better vehicle for it than rational theology taken by itself. This explains Caldecott's interest in Hans Urs von Balthasar, because what the latter called the "kingdom of beauty" is to be identified with "the radiance of Being with that strange, elusive, quasi-personal presence to which the Bible gives the name Wisdom, Sophia, Sapientia."[22] The beauty we find within liturgy is an icon of the beauty that Wisdom placed in creation, and when we experience this beauty it awakens within us a desire to find its prototype. It stirs joy, but a joy that is poignant as grief. "Joy in the sense of the German *sehnsucht* contains 'the stab, the pang, the inconsolable longing' that indicates precisely the gulf that exists between *esse subsistens* and *esse non subsistens*."[23] This is love in its erotic form. It stirs movement within the mind in a way nothing else does, bringing a noetic thirst for the ground of beauty.

As we search for this "lost wisdom of the world," we will keep coming back to a rather significant fact. As our own eyes reveal every day, the universe is *beautiful*. It has majesty, order, and loveliness; these three types of beauty are precisely what scientists themselves love to discover in the world. In fact, the greatest of them have usually been motivated less by curiosity than by love. Plato would not have hesitated to call the longing

---

20. Clément, *Roots of Christian Mysticism*, 219.

21. Caldecott, *Seven Sacraments*, 8.

22. Caldecott, "Beauty for Truth's Sake and the Children of Wisdom," 6.

23. Ibid., 5.

for truth that drives them onward to their discoveries a form of erotic desire.[24]

The human mind stretches itself out toward knowing, as Aristotle said at the beginning of his *Metaphysics*, and what we want to know is truth, reality. "But *why* do we desire truth? What makes truth attractive to us? Immediately these questions take us into the realm of *eros* and of beauty. We desire the truth because in some sense it is beautiful, it draws us towards it."[25] And this is how the church happened to find herself in the business of university education, with its varied disciplines. She did so in order to give glory to God. By the disciplines learned there, ears are trained to hear, and eyes to see, and minds to wonder.

> This is perhaps why tradition describes the seven Liberal Arts, and all the other arts, as the "children of Wisdom." That is how they are depicted in the allegorical carvings that adorn many Gothic churches and many Renaissance frescoes. It is in Wisdom that the Liberal Arts connect together, and it is because they connect together in this way that they are recognized as expressions of the same Spirit. Or else we might put it slightly differently, and say that it is from Wisdom that they all unfold and diversify, in their varied richness and spontaneity, without losing their interior unity.[26]

In every corner of creation one finds the craftsmanship of holy Wisdom, whose play philosophers, scientists, poets, and theologians have never tired of exploring. She provides a full and unending curriculum. "Music, architecture, astronomy, and physics—the physical arts and their applications—demonstrate the fundamental intuition behind the Liberal Arts tradition of education, which is that the world is an ordered whole, a 'cosmos,' whose beauty becomes more apparent the more carefully and deeply we study it."[27] In the liturgical cult, the play of Wisdom is known and it inspires a view of the world that is more than a utilitarian view: it is wisdom beheld.

There is a cost, however. There is a cost to grasping Wisdom's beauty. Many other topics can be approached while still keeping our real selves at a distance, under our control, in reserve, so to speak. But not this kind of beauty, not this kind of wisdom. It can only be known if the knower submits himself to an ascetical makeover. Mortification is the tuition fee. As

24. Caldecott, *Beauty for Truth's Sake*, 16.

25. Caldecott, "Beauty for Truth's Sake and the Children of Wisdom," 1.

26. Ibid., 9.

27. Caldecott, *Beauty for Truth's Sake*, 116–17.

Caldecott unflinchingly says, "Beauty in this sense, so closely identifiable with the Wisdom and Glory of God, may be witnessed and known only by those *who are in some way akin to her*."[28] He quotes Pavel Florensky when the Russian philosopher says, "Purity of heart, virginity, chaste immaculateness is the necessary condition for seeing Sophia-Wisdom, for acquiring sonhood in the Heavenly Jerusalem. It is clear why this is so. The heart is the organ for the perception of the heavenly world."[29] Caldecott therefore concludes, "Chastity, or purity, or spiritual virginity, turns out to be the very key to the knowledge of God."[30] Knowing Wisdom must be very different from any other ordinary kind of knowledge. Knowing that two plus two equals four requires of me a capacity to memorize, but it does not require of me a moral conversion. However, detecting the passage of Wisdom does. A conversion of mind—a *meta nous*—is required (*metanoia* = the Greek word for repentance). A person must have depth in order to know heights. Imagine! Episteme has an ascetical prerequisite. Virginity, chastity, and purity of heart are required for this *gnosis*.

In the desert tradition there were three ways by which an ascetic had to stage his life—that is to say, three stages of the ascetical life. *Praktike* disciplined the passions and brought a calm regard called *apatheia*; *physike* was knowledge of the created things; and *theologia* was knowledge of the Creator of those created things. Theology was knowledge of the Trinity. There are traces of the Logos in everything (*logoi*), and if the cataracts of sin could only be removed from the eye by asceticism then we could see them. Thus asceticism is required before contemplation, *praktike* before *physike*, and then the purified mind is able to contemplate the natural order (*physike* being the Greek for "natural") and understand its inner structure.

Wisdom has built her house, and it is a temple. It contains beauty and truth and goodness, all splendoring from the glory of God. She is the Shekinah in the tabernacle, in the temple. But our earthly temple is still embryonic. It still waits for perfection, and Wisdom waits impatiently, too. God is truly, really, and substantially present in our cultic liturgy, but we still ache for the kingdom to come. We await Sophia's fullness so that creation can be brought to God in pure and final sacrifice. There we will know God directly, because we will become light, and like will be able to know like. This is an astounding idea, Caldecott confesses, and his knowledge of non-Christian philosophies and religions sharpens the amazement he feels by the contrast they present.

28. Caldecott, *All Things Made New*, 99.

29. Ibid., quoting from Florensky, *Pillar and Ground*, 254–55.

30. Caldecott, *All Things Made New*, 99.

This is a staggering notion, and it should be contrasted with all of the religious notions of "enlightenment" and gnosis. It is true that, as with the Asian religions, the final state of perfection in Christianity is one of knowledge, since that is the paradigm of spiritual union. But for Christianity the vision of God, in which all happiness is comprised, is not our natural state, to be retained by some method of meditation or insight that will dissipate the clouds of ignorance we have wrapped around ourselves. It is something new, something of which we only become capable by being transformed. That transformation makes us "sons in the Son," *logoi* in the Logos. . . .

The Christian lives in the anticipation of the blissful Vision of God, but because he is a temporal creature the goal is not yet achieved. We do not yet experience the influx of the *lumen gloriae*; we are not yet incandescent. The infused virtue of faith must serve in the place of this light, for the time being. We know God but not by sight, rather by touch, like children in the dark holding their mother's hand.[31]

For the time being, faith must serve in the place of this light, as we grope after God. But the Christian virtue of hope properly orders our patience and our eagerness for the kingdom to come, for God's will to be done. "It is by love alone that the will of another can become my will."[32] It stirs us to make that will be done on earth, as it is in heaven.

Understanding the grounds of this enlightenment puts even apocalyptic literature within Caldecott's grasp, as he proved in his last book, *All Things Made New*, a study on the book of Revelation. It takes a certain skill set to interpret this literature: biblical literacy, in order to catch prophetic allusions; typological familiarity, in order to connect the two Testaments; acquaintance with the symbology of numbers from the ancient world and Hebrew Scripture; mystagogical sensitivity, in order to see the text's potency for formation in the mysteries of Christ and of the church; liturgical depth, because the liturgy is the organizational structure and contextual home of the book of Revelation; and, finally, a capacity for prayer, since John's Apocalypse opens out onto the life of mystery. The church has always spoken of two books of Revelation—nature and the Bible—and Caldecott traces Wisdom's steps whenever he is writing about creation.

The traces of Wisdom wait for perfection, because matter is intended to be building blocks for the temple, raw material for sacraments that will

31. Ibid., 78.
32. Ibid., 124.

yield their place when we reach the eternal sacrifice before the heavenly throne of God.

> Sophia is thus an image of the final perfection of creation, of holiness and beauty. For wisdom is the beauty of holiness. It is in human holiness that we glimpse the true and final order of the cosmos, and thus the beauty and the purpose of creation. What else of greater value can we seek than this? But important moral implications follow from such an interpretation of the meaning of Sophia. We are speaking of the fiery, transcendental Beauty that is the "unspotted mirror" of God's majesty and goodness, and into which no defiled thing can ever fall without being consumed. This Beauty is the radiance or self-gift of being.[33]

Sophia has moral implications, and the true glimpse of her is in the face of a saint. A man or woman who has been conformed to Christ by liturgical asceticism is an unspotted mirror, an icon, a display of the beauty that laid the foundations for being.

All things are directed toward their end: the eye toward sight, the mind toward truth, and creation toward its own apocalypse. One day the weight of grace will strip distraction and distortion from us, and truth will finally be told. *Kalyptein* means to cover or conceal, and *apo* has a spatial sense of "away" or "off," so the *apocalypse* will be like the removal of a mask in order that we might be seen by God. This is the fondest desire of every creature, which is why Paul Claudel says we yearn for Judgment. "Our conscience has found what it longed for above all else: a Judge. . . . There are so many things heaped up inside us all ready and only waiting to become an answer for the question to be put. A question, a challenge, a presence."[34] And, "On the day of the Last Judgment, it is not only the Judge who will descend from heaven, the whole world will rush forth to meet him."[35] It is a fearsome thing to desire Wisdom because Wisdom was present at our creation and knows the Idea God had of each one of us in his mind, and to what degree we have failed it. That is why this Judgment feels like an impingement on us: God has to press himself upon us, individually, each day. Dilating our eyes for the light of resurrection requires pressure from God.

> External circumstances, the practical life in which we are engaged, only allow us to live on the crust, to use the most superficial part, not necessarily the worst but the least authentic part of ourselves. Only profound emotion, the weight and painful

33. Ibid., 99.
34. Claudel, *Lord, Teach Us to Pray*, 19.
35. Claudel, *I Believe in God*, 151.

pressure of harsh and turbulent events, reach down to the gush-
ing salutary vein in the depths of us. Someone has fought his
way through to us. Someone is urging us to say outright the real
name, our own real name.[36]

We are waiting to be called by name—for Wisdom to disclose it to us, for
faith to discover it, and for a beatific hearing that will accompany the beatific vision in order to hear our name clearly for the first time.

George MacDonald picks up on this theme in his *Unspoken Sermons*
where he reflects on Revelation 2:17. The verse reads, "To him that overcomes will I give to eat of the hidden manna, and will give him a white
stone, and in the stone a new name written, which no man knows save he
that receives it." The giving of the white stone with the new name on it,
MacDonald says, "is the communication of what God thinks about the man
to the man. It is the divine judgment."[37] This name will be different from
our ordinary name, because an ordinary name has nothing essential in it;
MacDonald observes that it is only a label based on a scrap of our external
history, founded upon some external characteristic of the person. On the
other hand, our true name is what God means when he thinks of us, what
God intended by us, our truest self whom Wisdom knows. "The true name
is one which expresses the character, the nature, the being, the *meaning* of
the person who hears it. It is the man's own symbol—his soul's picture, in a
word—the sign which belongs to him and to no one else."[38] Who can give
such a name? Only God. And when will he give it? Revelation indicates it
will not be until the man has overcome. What does this mean? MacDonald
does not think it is because God does not yet know what any individual is
going to become. The Almighty knows "as surely as he sees the oak which
he put there lying in the heart of the acorn."[39] But we will not bear that name
until we have overcome; we will not bear that name until the image of God
in us has grown into the likeness of God; only the finished saint will know
it. Our vocation—the calling God makes to us—is the slow, steady creation
of this identity. MacDonald concludes, "God's name for a man must then be
the expression . . . of his own idea of the man, that being whom he had in his
thought when he began to make the child, and whom he kept in his thought

---

36. Claudel, *Lord, Teach Us to Pray*, 29.

37. *Unspoken Sermons*, 70. George MacDonald was a nineteenth-century Scottish
preacher whose mysticism and universalism did not sit well with his Presbyterian congregation, so was dismissed; he recorded his sermons in written form beginning in
1867.

38. Ibid., 71.

39. Ibid.

through the long process of creation that went to realize the idea. To tell the name is to seal the success—to say 'In thee I am well pleased.'"[40]

There is one of our race whose name is finished. Christ gave it to her. She is a finished human being, named Mary, the Virgin, Theotokos. Because of this, the Christian tradition has closely associated her with both Wisdom and with the church. Indicating these threads will bring us to our liturgical conclusion.

First, let us see Mary's connection to Wisdom. Caldecott can describe it from the top, so to speak, from a sophiological perspective. "Sophia is the original Idea of the world, but also the world resurrected. She is created Being glorified, the Bride of God, the rejoicing of God in his creation."[41] Then he can describe it from the bottom, from a Mariological perspective: "This is the mystery of *theosis*, of the creature's divinization. It is represented in the Coronation of the Virgin, the final mystery of the Rosary, in which Mary and Sophia become indistinguishable."[42] *Theosis* may be translated as "deification," as is more frequently done in Eastern Christianity, or "divinization," as is more frequently done in Western Christianity, but it amounts to the same. It is the full flowering of the theological virtues. "These three virtues in particular—faith, hope, and love—are called 'theological' virtues because they can make us holy, or God-like. (*Theo* means 'God' and *logos* means a pattern or design.)"[43] Creation may be said to have been constructed with this very end in view. The house that Wisdom has built is a habitat for divinity, a place into which God may come out of the Virgin, a staging for our deification.

Second, let us see Mary's connection to the church. Caldecott recalls Bulgakov saying that Sophia "was the revelation or glory of the Father as disclosed by the Holy Spirit together with the Son: 'The Son and the Holy Spirit, together, inseparable and unconfused, realize the self-realization of the Father in his nature.'"[44] This means that Wisdom refracts divine and spiritual light upon the created realm. Such divine and spiritual realities are the work of the kingdom, which is the very end that the church serves.

> God's Kingdom comes by the radiation or sending of the Holy Spirit, as in the crowning of the Disciples with tongues of fire at Pentecost. In that sense the Church is the Kingdom; but the

---

40. Ibid., 72.

41. Caldecott, "Beauty for Truth's Sake and the Children of Wisdom," 13.

42. Ibid. This is the footnote that accompanies the passage.

43. Caldecott, *Seven Sacraments*, 42.

44. Caldecott, "Beauty for Truth's Sake and the Children of Wisdom," 7.

> Church is only partially realized on earth until the times are
> fulfilled and all are safely gathered in. . . .
>
> The Kingdom is Sophia, God's Wisdom which is his majesty
> and beauty, into which the whole creation is taken up through
> the Incarnation of the Son, in the marriage of the divine and
> human natures.[45]

The kingdom is Sophia; the church partially realizes the kingdom on earth until the eschatological glory of the parousia; in the final mystery of the Rosary, Mary and Sophia become indistinguishable; Mary is mother of the church. (Jean Corbon calls Mary "the Church as it dawns in a single person."[46]) A deified human person stands in the center of these currents. The church fathers never ceased to marvel at the exchange: man is to become by grace what Christ is by nature. God became man so that man might be made divine. God was in-carnated and human beings will be en-godded. Vladimir Lossky expresses it this way.

> "To have by grace what God has by nature": that is the supreme
> vocation of created beings. . . . This destiny is already reached
> in the divine person of Christ, the Head of the Church, risen
> and ascended. If the Mother of God could truly realize, in her
> human and created person, the sanctity which corresponds to
> her unique role, then she cannot have failed to attain here below
> by grace all that her Son had by his divine nature. But, if it be so,
> then the destiny of the Church and the world has already been
> reached, not only in the uncreated person of the Son of God but
> also in the created person of his Mother. That is why St. Gregory
> Palamas calls the Mother of God "the boundary between the
> created and the uncreated." Beside the incarnate divine hyposta-
> sis there is a deified human hypostasis.[47]

Mary is the cosmos's destiny already reached; she is the end of the world. God called the cosmos into existence, and Wisdom was his craftsman. God calls each individual into existence, calls the adult from the child, and one day will call the living from the dead. God has been constructing our apocalyptic name our whole life long, training us to hear it, so that one day he can use it to call us from the grave on the day of Resurrection.

Mary has heard her name called, and answered.

45. Caldecott, *All Things Made New*, 123.
46. Corbon, *Wellspring of Worship*, 173.
47. Lossky, "Panagia," 34.

The woman whom Catholics call "Our Lady" is the center of the universe of beauty created by her Son. The natural beauties of landscape and forest, mountains and streams, and the moral beauty of heroism and integrity, friendship and honesty—all of which are celebrated in Tolkien's imaginative world—are gifts of God that come through her, and she is the measure of them, her beauty the concentrated essence of theirs.

For Catholics, the Virgin Mary has all the beauty that Eve lost, and just as Eve was the mother of all the living in the world that is passed, she is the mother of the world to come.[48]

That world to come is described in the book of Revelation as the New Jerusalem, which will shine with glory. But for now, during this time, that glory is mediated through the house that Wisdom has built. "Worldly beauty is the radiance of God's glory shining through created being."[49] Can we identify this divine glory with Wisdom? Caldecott believes so. Christ has received his own divine nature from the Father, and when he gives back in the Holy Spirit all that he has, it includes the world and the church joined to him, "and it is this spiritualized creation, creation purified and made perfect, that is the Wisdom of God who is mysteriously already present with him in the beginning as his plan and purpose."[50] Christ is the foundation for the heavenly Jerusalem, and the Holy Spirit guides all things to their teleological end. They co-operate on us. And although Western theology is often accused of being weak in its pneumatology, Caldecott thinks Mariology holds an ignored key. The Blessed Virgin is traditionally called the "Spouse of the Holy Spirit" because she is totally united with him. The graces she had received freed her to say "yes" to the will of the Trinity.

Her whole life was a journey ever deeper into God, for though she was "full of grace" from the start, grace always opens up new capacities for grace. This intimate intertwining of Mary's life and personality with the Holy Spirit is perhaps the reason why there has traditionally been less emphasis in Western theology on the Holy Spirit, on pneumatology, than in the East. In the West our theology of the Spirit has tended to take the form of Mariology.[51]

Wisdom has built herself a cosmos, and the church, as the fathers so often said, is a microcosm because in the church's liturgy you may find the alpha and the omega, spirit and matter, creation and redemption, Genesis

48. Caldecott, *Power of the Ring*, 52.
49. Caldecott, "Beauty for Truth's Sake and the Children of Wisdom," 8.
50. Ibid.
51. Caldecott and Caldecott, "Theosis."

and Revelation, the Big Bang and the apocalypse, the Uncreated and the created. We cannot read the cosmos without the liturgy, but through the liturgy we discover Wisdom's ways in the world, and no one has better read Wisdom's tracks in both nature and revelation than Stratford Caldecott. Well, maybe proto-monk Anthony. "A certain member of what was then considered the circle of the wise once approached the just Anthony and asked him: 'How do you ever manage to carry on, Father, deprived as you are of the consolation of books?' His reply: 'My book, sir philosopher, is the nature of created things, and it is always at hand when I wish to read the words of God.'"[52] They both had Wisdom for an instructor, and she taught them how to see God's creation in a liturgical light.

Wisdom has been playing before God on the surface of his earth, and she invites us to join her. "The human task is to build up the Liturgical City by turning our lives back into gift."[53]

52. Evagrius, *Praktikos*, para. 92, 39.
53. Caldecott, *Beauty for Truth's Sake*, 134.

6

Eating Fire and Spirit

The Eucharist and the Blessed Trinity

Nicholas J. Healy Jr.

Out of the darkness of my life, so much frustrated, I put before you the one
great thing to love on earth: the Blessed Sacrament. . . . There you will find
romance, glory, honor, fidelity, and the true way of all your loves on earth,
and more than that: Death: by the divine paradox, that which ends life, and
demands the surrender of all, and yet by the taste (or foretaste) of which
alone can what you seek in your earthly relationships (love, faithfulness,
joy) be maintained, or take on that complexion of reality, of eternal endur-
ance, that every man's heart desires.

—J. R. R. TOLKIEN

The doctrine of the Trinity . . . makes sense of human life as a whole.
It is the key that opens every lock, an insight that reveals
the center of the universe.

—STRATFORD CALDECOTT

In his "Religion and the Artist," Paul Claudel reflects on the catholicity at
the root of Dante's poetic genius:

> [He] received from God such vast things to express that only the
> entire universe will suffice for [his] work. . . . There is no mea-
> sure, according to the Psalmist, that can exhaust God's mercy or
> that is adequate to our debt of thanksgiving. . . . These billions
> of stars scattered with a sublime carelessness across the abyss,

this is not enough! It will never be enough to repay our debt of gratitude, says Beatrice.[1]

In our own time, Stratford Caldecott has kept alive the same spirit of wonder and gratitude for the entire order of creation and the new gift of grace. The beautiful order of nature and grace is held together without confusion or separation in the person of the incarnate Logos. Through the outpouring of the Holy Spirit and the sacraments of the church, we are invited to receive and co-accomplish the unity of nature and grace by way of sharing in the eternal gratitude of the Son of God who creates and redeems by receiving all things as a gift from the Father.

It is possible to discern in Caldecott's writings and in the many initiatives of the Centre for Faith and Culture a double movement. The first movement is directed toward the concrete figure of Jesus Christ in whom the "fullness of the Godhead dwells bodily" (Col 1:19). "It is through encountering [Jesus Christ] as a person," he writes, "that we are introduced to the true purpose and meaning of human life. In his every word and gesture while on earth, Eternity was expressing itself to man in the language of human existence."[2]

The second movement of Caldecott's thought is less a new direction than a discovery of the innermost secret of Christ's own life and mission. Christ is the eternal Son of the Father, sent into the world to bring the world back into communion with the triune God. At the heart of this double movement toward Christ and with Christ into the world and back to the Father is the idea of a "cosmic liturgy"—a holy exchange of gifts whereby the entire created order is received as a gift from God and, through the co-working of the Son and the Holy Spirit, offered back to the Father as a renewed gift.

One of the seminal insights that Caldecott received from Hans Urs von Balthasar and John Paul II (among others) is the idea that the liturgy of the church is an expression and communication of Trinitarian love. This theme, which runs like a thread throughout Caldecott's writings, is summed up in the following passage:

> [T]he celebration of the Mass . . . is an echo or symbol of a sacrifice that is eternally taking place in God. But the heavenly sacrament is not merely something that is being done by God: it *is* God. It is not done by the Holy Trinity: it *is* the Holy Trinity. The Father is always pouring himself out for the Son, the Son is eternally offering himself to the Father, and the Holy Spirit is the divine nature given and received—the "gift" that passes eternally

1. Claudel, "Religion and the Artist," 367.
2. Caldecott, *Seven Sacraments*, 6.

between them. The link or connection between this heavenly Trinity (this ecstatic and eternal act of love that is God) and our earthly Mass is, of course, the Incarnation. Here is a man who is also God, whose sacrificial act as a man is also the sacrificial act of God.

At the heart of the Mass is a self-sacrificial act that takes place both in heaven and on the Cross. The Mass is not an imitation of what happens in heaven between the Father and the Son, nor a repetition of Christ's sacrifice on Calvary, but a sacrament, which is to say that it makes both of these events "present" for us, wherever and whenever it is celebrated. Those who attend the Mass are standing with Mary and John at the foot of the Cross.[3]

My aim in what follows is to unfold this insight in light of Catholic doctrine on Christ's real presence in the Eucharist. The teaching that bread and wine are transubstantiated into the body and blood of Jesus Christ confirms and safeguards the truth that Christ has given us nothing less than himself. And, as Caldecott suggests, Christ communicates the substance of his life precisely by giving us something more, the Holy Spirit. In giving us the Spirit, Christ gives us a share in the eternal exchange of love between the Father and the Son. In the unsurpassable words of Saint Ephrem, "He called the bread his living body and he filled it with himself and his Spirit. . . . He who eats it with faith, eats along with it the fire of the Holy Spirit. . . . Take and eat this, all of you, and eat with it the Holy Spirit; for it is truly my body, and he who eats it will have eternal life."[4]

I. The Real Presence of Christ in the Eucharist

Toward the end of the Orthodox Coptic Liturgy according to Saint Basil there is a solemn confession of faith:

Amen, Amen, Amen, I believe, I believe, I believe. To the last breath of my life, I will confess that this is the life-giving body that your only-begotten Son, our Lord, God, and Savior Jesus Christ took from Our Lady, the lady of us all, the most pure mother of God. He has united it to his divinity without mingling, without confusion and without alteration. . . . He gave it up for us upon the holy wood of the cross, of his own will, for us all. I believe that his divinity has never, for a single instant, been

3. Ibid., 25.
4. Ephrem, *Sermo IV in Hebdomadam Sanctam.*

separated from his humanity. It is he who is given to us for the remission of sins, for eternal life and eternal salvation. I believe, I believe, I believe that all this is true!

At the Council of Trent, the church confirmed and handed on the truth of this mystery of faith by using the language of "transubstantiation" to describe the conversion of bread and wine into the body and blood of Jesus Christ. The *totum Christum*—body and blood, soul and divinity—is substantially present in this sacrament not only *in signo*, but *in veritate*.

In order to understand more deeply why the church teaches that Christ is substantially present under the appearance of bread and wine, it is necessary to contemplate the form and content of this gift. "The Church," writes John Paul II, "has received the Eucharist from Christ her Lord not as one gift—however precious—among so many others, but as the gift par excellence, *for it is the gift of himself*, of his person in his sacred humanity, as well as the gift of his saving work."[5] The language of transubstantiation signifies that in the sacrament of the Eucharist Christ communicates nothing less than himself. In offering us his body and his blood under the appearance of bread and wine, Christ loves us "to the end" (John 13:1) by giving us the substance of his life as our spiritual food and drink. The notion of substantial or real presence confirms the totality of Christ's gift: "This presence is called 'real'—by which is not intended to exclude the other types of presence as though they could not be 'real' too, but because it is presence in the fullest sense: that is to say, it is a substantial presence by which Christ, God and man, makes himself wholly and entirely present."[6]

There are two aspects to this gift of real presence that call for further elaboration. The first point is that the entire historical life of Jesus of Nazareth, especially his dying on the cross and his rising to eternal life, is included in this sacrament. The Eucharist does not come only at the end (or after) Christ's historical life, perhaps as a memorial of his former presence. Nor is it sufficient to consider the Eucharist simply as an application of the graces merited by Christ's passion. The "grace" or gift received in this sacrament is Christ himself, a gift that contains all of the "saving mysteries" of Christ's historical life.[7]

5. John Paul II, *Ecclesia de Eucharistia*, 11.

6. Paul VI, *Mysterium Fidei*, 39.

7. In *Ecclesia de Eucharistia*, 11, John Paul II indicates that the "saving work" of Christ ("all that he did") is included in the gift: "it is the gift of himself . . . as well as the gift of his saving work. Nor does it remain confined to the past, since 'all that Christ is—all that he did and suffered for all men—participates in the divine eternity, and so transcends all times.' When the Church celebrates the Eucharist, the memorial of her Lord's death and resurrection, this central event of salvation becomes really present

The historical events of Christ's life can be included in the Blessed Sacrament because the form of his earthly life was already eucharistic. The Greek word *eucharistia* means thanksgiving. From the first moment of the Incarnation in the womb of Mary, through his hidden life of work in Nazareth and his public ministry in Galilee and Jerusalem, to the culminating mystery of his passion, Christ received his existence as a gift from the Father to be offered back to the Father in gratitude. Both as God and as man, the incarnate Son gives thanks to the Father in all that he is and all that he does. As the one sent by the Father into the world, Christ receives not only his own existence, but the entire created order, as a gift from the Father.

Christ's coming from the Father and returning to the Father in communion with creation was accomplished under the sign of the Holy Spirit, who continues to unfold and communicate his historical life through the sacraments of the church. The resurrection and ascension of Christ are not a departure from history, but a taking up in the Spirit of the bodily and historical existence of the incarnate Son into the eternal life of God.

The mysteries of the life of Jesus, then, are not simply past events to be recalled or remembered from a distance. Every word and every gesture of Jesus as recorded in the New Testament is saturated with Spirit. The Holy Spirit bridges time and eternity in two directions at once. He continues to bring the Risen Christ (together with the saving mysteries of Jesus's life) into history at the heart of the liturgy (*epiclesis*); and he brings the faithful into communion with the historical events of Jesus's life—especially to the foot of the cross to contemplate with Mary and John the temporal and eternal outpouring of blood, water, and Spirit. As Caldecott reflects, "Those who attend the Mass are standing with Mary and John at the foot of the Cross."[8] Contemplating and receiving the outpouring of "Spirit, water, and blood" (1 John 5:7), the faithful are united with all the saints and angels in heaven and on earth, in time and in eternity.

John Paul II writes, "All that Christ is—all that he did and suffered for all men—participates in divine eternity."[9] If the Incarnation represents the indwelling of eternity in time, the co-working of the Son and the Spirit in

---

and 'the work of our redemption is carried out.'" Drawing on the work of Odo Casel, Hans Urs von Balthasar presents a similar account of the inclusion of the temporal dimension of the Incarnation within the gift of Eucharist: "Christ, in surrendering his sacrificed flesh and shed blood for his disciples, was communicating, not merely the material side of his bodily substance, but the saving events wrought by it. . . . The fundamental presupposition is that the person of Jesus is really present; but along with the person comes his entire temporal history and, in particular, its climax in cross and Resurrection" (*Theo-Drama*, 4:391–92).

8. Caldecott, *Seven Sacraments*, 25.

9. John Paul II, *Ecclesia de Eucharistia*, 11.

the sacrament of the Eucharist opens up the "time of the Incarnation" to the past and future time of the church. The Eucharist completes or fulfills the Incarnation in the sense that the hypostatic union is ordered to the accomplishment of God's plan set forth in Christ "to unite all things in him" (Eph 1:10).[10]

> The Eucharist in this way is inscribed into the sacramental logic of the Incarnation. It is instituted not only in memory of the Incarnation, for lack of something better, but in order to continue and "fulfill" ("*accomplir*") the Incarnation through the sacramental economy of the Holy Spirit in the Church. From this perspective, the sacrament of the Eucharist is in a certain way the pneumatological and ecclesiological modality of the Incarnation.[11]

The crucial point is that the Holy Spirit's work of opening up or interpreting the life of Christ in the church stems from and returns to the historical and bodily existence of the incarnate Son. "There can be nothing of the Spirit in the Church," argues von Balthasar, "that does not also coincide with Christ's reality, christologically, that does not let itself be translated in the language of Eucharist—the surrender of Christ's own flesh and blood, the streaming outward from Christ's self up to the very point of his heart being pierced and his side flowing with water and blood."[12]

The second aspect of the gift of real presence concerns the unveiling and communication of Trinitarian love at the heart of the sacrament. In the words of Saint Ephrem cited above, Christ "called the bread his living body and he filled it with himself and his Spirit."[13] In giving us the Holy Spirit, Christ gives us the totality of his life and something more—he reveals the love of the Father as the origin and end of his love. The doctrine of Christ's substantial presence in the sacrament of the Eucharist has its deepest roots in the mystery of the Trinity. "The first element of eucharistic faith," observes Benedict XVI, "is the mystery of God himself, trinitarian love. . . . In

10. In a key passage in his encyclical *Dominum et Vivificantem*, 50, John Paul II affirms the "cosmic significance" of the Incarnation. He writes, "The Incarnation of God the Son signifies the taking up into unity with God not only of human nature, but in this human nature, in a sense, of everything that is 'flesh': the whole of humanity, the entire visible and material world. The Incarnation, then, also has a cosmic significance, a cosmic dimension. The 'first-born of all creation,' becoming incarnate in the individual humanity of Christ, unites himself in some way with the entire reality of man, which is also 'flesh'—and in this reality with all 'flesh,' with the whole of creation."

11. Ouellet, "Trinity and Eucharist," 274.

12. Balthasar, "Spirit and Institution," 237–38.

13. Ephrem, *Sermo IV*.

the Eucharist, Jesus does not give us a 'thing', but himself; he offers his own body and pours out his own blood. He thus gives us the totality of his life and reveals the ultimate origin of this love. He is the eternal Son, given to us by the Father."[14]

Drawing on the eucharistic theology of Hans Urs von Balthasar and Joseph Ratzinger / Benedict XVI, Caldecott develops an understanding of church's "cosmic liturgy" that begins and ends with the mystery of the Father, who is "always pouring himself out for the Son."[15] Accordingly, the next step in our reflection is to consider how the real presence of Christ in the sacrament represents an unveiling and a handing over of the reciprocal love of Father, Son, and Spirit.

II. The Eucharist as a Sacrament of Trinitarian Love

In all three Synoptic Gospels the true Lord of the table in the eucharistic banquet is the heavenly Father, who sets out for us the best he has to offer. Similarly, the precious taste of the gifts welling up within all of the sacraments comes from the Holy Spirit, the Spirit of the Father who gives and the Son who allows himself to be given as food and drink. It is the Spirit who enables us, when we pray the Canon of the Mass with the Church, to address all thanks and gratitude, all honor and glory, through him and with the Son to the Father.[16]

Two principles need to be kept in mind in approaching the Eucharist as a sacrament of Trinitarian love. The first states "the whole divine economy is the common work of the three divine persons. For as the Trinity has only one and the same nature, so too does it have only one and the same operation."[17] The second principle states "each divine person performs the common work according to his unique personal property." The co-working of each person in the economy of salvation discloses or reveals their distinct relations of origin. The common and personal work of the three divine persons is a revelation that the very nature or being of God is love: "By sending his only Son and the Spirit of Love in the fullness of time, God has revealed his innermost secret: God himself is an eternal exchange of love, Father, Son and Holy Spirit."[18]

---

14. Benedict XVI, *Sacramentum Caritatis*, 7.

15. Caldecott, *Seven Sacraments*, 25.

16. Balthasar, *Epilogue*, 117.

17. *Catechism of the Catholic Church*, 258.

18. Ibid., 221.

The Father is "the source and origin of the whole divinity."[19] The unfathomable love of the Father is the origin of the Godhead and the source and end of the whole economy of salvation. As the Fourth Lateran Council teaches, "the Father gives his substance to the Son, generating Him from eternity. . . . One cannot say that he gave him a part of his substance and retained a part for himself . . . nor can one say that he gave it to the Son in such way as not to retain it for himself."[20] The Son, who eternally receives his being as a gift from the Father, is a perfect image or icon of the Father. The Holy Spirit proceeds from the Father and the Son as the form and fruit of their reciprocal love. In the words of John Paul II, the Holy Spirit is "Person-Gift": "It can be said that in the Holy Spirit the intimate life of the Triune God becomes totally gift, an exchange of mutual love between the divine Persons and that through the Holy Spirit God exists in the mode of gift. It is the Holy Spirit who is the personal expression of this self-giving, of this being-love."[21]

In going to the end of love by dying and communicating the substance of his life in the gift of the Eucharist, Christ reveals the mystery of the Father as the origin of the whole divinity. The deepest source of Christ's Eucharist is the Father who is eternally giving everything to the Son. While Christ's entire existence serves to make known the love of the Father, the gift of the Eucharist is a perfect image of a Father who holds nothing back in the generation of the Son and the procession of Spirit. "[W]hen the Son allows himself to be poured out," writes von Balthasar, "he directly reveals the love of the Father, who manifests himself in his Son's *eucharistia* . . . we begin to appreciate the ultimate meaning of Jesus's saying, 'He who has seen me has seen the Father' (Jn 14:9)."[22]

Christ's Eucharist is simultaneously a perfect of expression his own identity as the only-begotten Son of the Father. The Son eternally receives his being as a gift from the Father and offers himself back to the Father in love. The Eucharist expresses this receiving and giving insofar as it is the consummate expression of the Incarnate Son's readiness to give the whole of his life unto death and beyond death. In allowing his life to be taken and his side pierced so that blood and water flow forth (cf. John 19:34), Christ gives himself in a filial mode. He allows himself to be given or distributed by the Father and the Holy Spirit. He thereby opens up a space in his body for

---

19. Council of Toledo VI (638): DS 490.
20. Fourth Lateran Council (1215): DS 805.
21. John Paul II, *Dominum et Vivificantem*, 10.
22. Balthasar, *Theo-Drama*, 5:384.

creation to be gathered into a unity and brought into the heavenly sanctuary of God.

If the reciprocal giving of Father and Son is eternally fruitful of the Holy Spirit, the gift of the Eucharist is the locus of this spiritual fruitfulness in history. In one sense, the Holy Spirit himself is the ultimate gift that is bestowed as the fruit of Christ's death and resurrection. It is necessary for Jesus to depart in order for the Spirit to be given (John 16:7). It might seem that the Spirit comes "after" the death and resurrection of Christ to remind the church of his historical deeds and words, or to apply the merits of his saving work. In truth, the Spirit was present all along as co-accomplisher of the incarnate Son's saving work. Christ gives the whole of himself in the Eucharist precisely by giving us the Holy Spirit, who co-accomplishes Christ's eucharistic giving by distributing the spiritualized body and blood of the risen Christ, thereby gathering creation into the ecclesial body of Christ. The Holy Spirit is "after" or "beyond" the historical and bodily existence of Christ in the sense that he is continually unveiling and communicating the inexhaustible depths of the incarnate life of Christ. The eucharistic flesh and blood of Christ is inexhaustible because it contains and mediates what is best and most intimate in the Trinity—the reciprocal exchange of love between Father, Son, and Spirit:

> The Eucharist implies much more than that [Christ] merely stands before the Father as mediator in virtue of his acquired merits; likewise more than that he merely continues in an unbloody manner in heaven the "self-giving" he accomplishes in a bloody manner on earth. It ultimately means that the Father's act of self-giving by which, throughout all created space and time, he pours out the Son is the definitive revelation of the Trinitarian act itself in which the "Persons" are God's "relations," forms of absolute self-giving and loving fluidity.[23]

At this point we can return to the passage from Caldecott cited above:

> The celebration of the Mass . . . is an echo or symbol of a sacrifice that is eternally taking place in God. But the heavenly sacrament is not merely something that is being done by God: it *is* God. It is not done by the Holy Trinity: it *is* the Holy Trinity. The Father is always pouring himself out for the Son, the Son is eternally offering himself to the Father, and the Holy Spirit is the divine nature given and received—the "gift" that passes eternally between them.

---

23. Balthasar, *New Elucidations*, 118–19.

The mystery that Caldecott touches when he refers to the liturgy as a sacrament of the eternal exchange of love in God is that Christ's Eucharist does not simply disclose God's love for humanity; at a deeper level the Eucharist reveals and mediates the Father's eternal love for the Son and the Son's eternal love for the Father in the Spirit. God's very being is love, and in receiving this sacrament the creature is invited to share in this love of God for God.

Together with his mentor J. R. R. Tolkien, Caldecott reminds us that the Eucharist "is the one great thing to love on earth," because in loving this gift we are brought into communion with the innermost secret of God's own life and love. And in receiving this gift with Mary at the foot of the cross we are given fresh eyes to see and receive the radiance of God's beauty in all the forms of creation.

> Giftedness is the signature of God upon creation. But our being is not simply a gift to us; it is God's gift to himself. Created human nature is a gift that the Father gives to the Son, along with his divine nature. And it is a gift that the Son gives the Father, by being born as Man, dying on the Cross, and rising to new life. Creation is therefore gift both in relation to God, and in relation specifically to each of the Persons. Filled with the Holy Spirit in order to be given to the Father by the Son, it is transformed into the Son's Eucharist or "thanksgiving." The world indwelt by the Spirit is therefore now infinitely more than it was when it was created. It speaks not only with its own voice, but with the voice of the Son, who gives glory to his Father with this transformed creation.[24]

24. Caldecott, *Radiance of Being*, 181–82.

7

"Wisdom Hath Builded Herself a House" (Prov 9:1)

A Meditation on Mary as the Temple of God's Beauty[1*]

Adrian Walker

Vergine Madre, figlia del tuo figlio, / umile e alta più che creatura,
termine fisso d'etterno consiglio, / tu se' colei che l'umana natura /
nobilitasti sì, che 'l suo fattore /
non disdegnò di farsi sua fattura.[2]

I. The Beauty of God's House

The title chosen for this Festschrift in honor of Stratford Caldecott, *The Beauty of God's House*, admirably expresses an insight that informs his entire work, which is saturated with his vision of the cosmos as a house and temple of the divine beauty. The following pages are devoted to a meditation on the original archetype of this cosmic temple: the Holy Theotokos. But the Virgin Mother is the personal archetype of the cosmos only insofar as she is also the created "beginning" of *all* the Lord's "ways" (Prov 8:22), the divinely appointed pre-condition of the *oiko-nomia* governing the entire cosmic household from its origin.[3] Mary, then, is nothing less than the

1. For Léonie Caldecott. I would also like to thank the three companions of the Holzhofhäusle for their patience and encouragement.

2. "Virgin Mother, your Son's own child, humbler and higher than creature is, fixed end of eternal counsel, you are she who so ennobled human nature that its Creator saw no indignity in becoming the creature of what he himself had made" (Dante, *Paradiso*, XXXIII, 1–6). All translations mine, unless otherwise indicated.

3. The presupposition governing every statement touching Mary in what follows is

"morning rising" (Song 6:10), the undiminished splendor of the world's unmarred beginning—shining forth at the very point where the world's marring is turned to glorious "eucatastrophe" in Christ.[4] The inventor of the word *eucatastrophe*, J. R. R. Tolkien, might have been thinking of the Virgin's unique part in the radiant unity of beginning and end, creation and redemption, when he wrote to his friend Robert Murray, SJ, "I think I know exactly what you mean by the order of Grace; and of course by your references to Our Lady, upon which all my own small perception of beauty both in majesty and simplicity is founded."[5]

If Mary is the archetype of the cosmos, we should expect the cosmic economy to look (to the eyes of faith) like a prefiguration of, and preparation for, her mission as the *Virgo Mater*. As Hopkins puts it, "[a]ll things rising, all things sizing / Mary sees, sympathising / With that world of good, / Nature's motherhood."[6] Taking Hopkins' words to heart, I will devote most of the essay to exploring the analogical correspondence between plant, animal, and human generation, on the one hand, and the virginal motherhood of the *Dei genetrix*, on the other. Although this enterprise is chiefly theologi-

---

that her role as an enabling condition of the divine economy depends entirely on God's free, creative election of her for this task. It is God alone who gives himself Mary's "Yes" as the hypothetically necessary condition of his self-communication ad extra: "The eternal prius of God's Word of love veils itself in an impotence that grants the beloved space for a prius of his own: God's love for the world, the world that is his child, awakens love in the latter's heart. This is so true, in fact, that God's love can itself become the child of a Mother who bears it and awakens it to divine-human love. The divine Word awakens man's answering word by itself becoming an answering love that trustingly leaves the initiative in the world's hands" (Balthasar, *Glaubhaft ist nur Liebe*, 96). This passage shows that Balthasar's warning against the "cosmological" and "anthropological" reductions implies no repudiation of the *analogia entis*. Balthasar's concern is simply to make it clear that God becomes the primary instance of the analogy entirely by virtue of his own sovereignly free self-communication. But precisely because God's freedom comprehends the entire disitnction between absolute and relative, he can manifest his distinctive primacy from within the very relative priority of the creature: the handmaiden whose deepest humility lies in her consent to be the Mother of God.

4. Mary, the fruit and presupposition of the Redemption, is also the original idea according to which the world was first created. As Adrienne von Speyr puts it, Mary "has her place in the event of the world's creation, and she has this place in virtue of her role as 'co-redemptrix.' The idea of 'co-redemption' is 'older' than that of pre-redemption. The latter is a consequence of the former, a means to an end. Mary contains the idea of the perfect human being, the idea that God had in mind when he created the first man, so that in reality Mary is not the second Eve, but the first" (Speyr, *Maria in der Erlösung*, 9).

5. J. R. R. Tolkien, letter to Robert Murray, December 2, 1953. See http://www.americanidea.org/handouts/06240107.htm.

6. "May Magnificat," in Hopkins, *Poems of Gerard Manley Hopkins*, 42.

cal, it also requires philosophical reflection on the significance of generation within the cosmic economy. What, then, does the generative act reveal to philosophical reason about beauty's sway over the economy of nature? Can we say that this economy is for the sake of beauty, or must we ascribe to it some other, less noble end?[7]

In arguing for the first of these two options, I will be defending the metaphysical primacy of beauty against what Robert Spaemann calls "modern ontology," which "thinks of ends [*Zwecke*] only as tendencies to self-preservation, that is, to the preservation of what already exists."[8] Now, as Spaemann explains, this reconception of ends amounts to an "inversion of teleology"[9]: whereas Plato, Aristotle, or Aquinas thought that things seek to maintain themselves in being for the sake of participation in the beautiful, the proponents of the "modern ontology" claim to unmask what we call "beauty" as (at best) a function of the tendency to self-preservation.[10]

7. This talk of the "economy of nature" presupposes an analogy between *technê* and *physis* such that "[t]he ordering of the prior towards the posterior has a similar pattern in what is by art and what is by nature" (Aristotle, *Physics*, II, 8: 199a17–20). Nature, of course, remains the primary analogate: it is not nature that imitates art, but "art [that] imitates nature" (ibid., II, 2: 194a21–22), reproducing nature's activity of disposing matter for the instantiation of a definite eidos. Nevertheless, the analogy between art and nature also implies their dynamic interplay, or circumincession: "Each [of the two terms] is" therefore "for the sake of the other" (ibid., II, 8: 199a15). On the one hand, nature calls for the originality of art, which is why Aristotle can say that "in some cases [art] contributes to the accomplishment of what nature cannot work out for itself" (ibid., 199a16). On the other hand, art obeys the originality of nature, which, for all its "creativity," art cannot replace, but can only reveal in a secondary, though of course original, manner. Given this circumincession, substantial form itself is like an art that its possessor "imitates" by maintaining itself in the world according to that form: "If a house were one of the things that come to be by nature, it would come to be as it now does by art, whereas if the things existing by nature came to be not only by nature, but also by art, they would come to be just as it is in their nature to do now" (ibid., 199a12–15).

8. Spaemann, "Naturteleologie und Handlung," 45.

9. Ibid.

10. The moderns "inverted" teleology in part because they sought a universally acceptable basis for the (re)constitution of human society. They claimed to find this basis in the pure formality of the individual's self-relation, which, they thought, everyone could readily identify with, once it was purged of any heteronomous telic ordering. In order to achieve this purgation, then, the moderns inverted the natural relation between the good and desire. If in the natural order of things we desire to keep on being because (our) being is good, the moderns stipulated the inverse proposition: we call (our) being "good" because we desire to keep on having it. The modern inversion of teleology, then, is the thought experiment of re-imagining the good as the subjective epiphenomenon of irrational self-clinging. The real good is collapsed into the apparent good, while the apparent good is collapsed in turn into a pure function of blind self-assertion. But if being lacks any radiant appearing of the true good, it is equally empty

For them, the paradigm of reality, the measure of realism, is no longer the beautiful, but blind self-assertion: "Everything is 'struggle for existence,' and Socrates' admonition to consider 'whether the beautiful and the good may not be something other than merely granting or receiving physical safety' is shoved aside as a sentimental effusion. Even the state no longer serves the good life, but the guaranteeing of mere life."[11]

Spaemann contrasts modernity's inversion of teleology with Aristotle's insight that "self-preservation is simply the lowest form of the universal striving of finite being for participation in the eternal. The tendency to endure over time is a kind of imitation of what an otherwise unattainable identity with the eternal would be."[12] This passage contains an allusion to Aristotle's account of the end of generation in *De Anima* (II, 4, 415a26–415b7). In the next section of the essay, I use this text to make three related points: first, the chief *telos* of generation is not self-preservation, but participation in the divine beauty. Second, this participation enables the individual living being to (do something like) accept death in the very act of producing offspring. Third, the interweaving of generation and death sheds light on what self-preservation truly is: a moment within the interplay between individual and community, neither of which can be whole apart from the other. Taken together, these three points prepare the conclusion of the second section: participation in God's beautiful wholeness is the primary gesture of individual existence and of the entire economy of nature, without which nothing could have either a self or the wherewithal to preserve it.

The interweaving of generation and death is not merely a *misère*, but also a *grandeur*, an expression of nature's deepest identity as a manifestation of the divine beauty. Nevertheless, the complete fulfillment of this *telos* requires a change in the manner of generation, its final clarification in the light of God's ultimate self-gift. In the final section of the essay ("The House of God's Beauty"), which relies heavily on the Mariology of Nicholas Cabasilas, I argue that the *Virgo Mater* plays a crucial role in this transformation, helping Christ lift the unity of love and death out of the cycle of carnal generation and into the supra-sexual nuptials that he consummates with his Church on Calvary. This leads to the central insight of the third section: Mary's virginal motherhood is the end of generation, the eschatological fulfillment both of the creature's desire to "beget on the beautiful" and of the Creator's even deeper "desire" to receive himself back from that

---

of beauty as well, since the beautiful is just another name for that appearing.

11. Spaemann, "Natur," 28f.

12. Spaemann, "Naturteleologie und Handlung," 45f.

very begetting (*"figlia del tuo Figlio"*).[13] In light of this double fulfillment, I conclude with an evocation of Mary's identity as the archetypal "house" that "wisdom hath built herself" (Prov 9:1), indeed, as the personification of (created) wisdom itself.[14] In the *tota pulchra*, the cosmos is a natural prefiguration of the church, a temple of Trinitarian love whose beauty the Father and the Son give each other in their Holy Spirit before the very foundation of the world. "*Dominus possedit me in initio viarum suarum, antequam quidquam faceret a principio. Ab aeterno ordinata sum, et ex antiquis, antequam terra fieret.*"[15]

II. Unfailing Gift

The immediate context of Aristotle's account of the end of generation in *De Anima* (II, 4) is the discussion of the "nutritive soul"[16] that occupies the entirety of the chapter. According to Aristotle, the *threptikê psychê* is "the first and most common power of soul, thanks to which all [living] things have [their] being alive,"[17] and so their very being *tout court*.[18] At the same time, the nutritive soul contains a duality of operations, namely "genera-

13. Caldecott often asks, does God "gain" anything from the world? Caldecott unreservedly acknowledges God's beautiful freedom from need and envy, yet he draws a surprising consequence from this confession of divine impassibility: the Creator stands so blissfully above all created *passio* that he can enter into it personally without the slightest injury to his infinite Godhead. God's passionless passion is of course entirely voluntary, yet the divine choice to undergo it involves no deliberation or hesitation, but combines in a unique and simple gesture all the deliberate counsel of wisdom and all the ecstatic transport of violent love. Eternally at rest in the serene ecstasy of the Trinitarian embrace, God is free to conceive a passionate desire for his creature, though this desire remains the pure expression of his own perfection as everlasting gift.

14. Mary embodies the ideal of creaturehood, but the converse is also true: the ideal of creaturehood reflects something of her concrete, unique person (which, of course, is inseparable from that of her Son). As Adrienne von Speyr puts it, "It is absolutely certain that she will one day belong to heaven, and her place in heaven is already guaranteed when the heaven is first created. Moreover, her pre-redemption does not occur simply in the form of an expectation or idea, but in the form of a real factuality. It is a fact with real consequences. Such *concretissima* are familiar features of eternal life" (Speyr, *Maria in der Erlösung*, 9).

15. "The Lord possessed me in the beginning of his ways, before he did aught from the beginning. From eternity I was ordained, and from of old, before the earth was made" (Prov 8:22–23). These are the first words of the epistle for the feast of the Immaculate Conception in the extraordinary form of the Roman rite.

16. Aristotle, *De Anima*, II, 4: 415a23f.

17. Ibid., 415a24f.

18. "For living things, to be alive is what it is for them to be at all" (ibid., 415b13).

tion and the use of food."[19] Whereas the fundamental purpose of nutrition is to "conserve [the living thing's] substantial being [*ousian*],"[20] generation consists in its activity of "making another like itself."[21] Of these two works, however, it is generation that constitutes the "*telos*" of the nutritive soul,[22] and, by implication, of the tendency to conserve substantial being. Aristotle unfolds this implicit claim in *De Anima*, II, 4: 415a26–415b7, where he presents generation as the telic completion, the fully manifest truth, of conservation itself.[23]

For one of the most natural of works for living things (as many as are complete and not damaged, or not spontaneously generating) is to make another like itself—an animal an animal, a plant a plant—so as to partake so far as it is able in the eternal and divine. All things reach for this and for the sake of this do whatever they do according to nature ("for the sake of" being twofold: *for* what is aimed at and *for* what is benefitted). Since, then, it is unable to share in the eternal and divine by way of continuity, because perishable things do not admit of persisting as the same thing and one in number, each thing shares in the way in which it is able to partake (one more, another less). So it persists not as the same thing but as one like itself, not one in number but one in form.[24]

Note Aristotle's remark that all things act for the sake of God, not, of course, in order to benefit him, but in order to receive the benefit he imparts to them. Contrary to what is often said, Aristotle's God is a generously

19. Ibid., 415a26.

20. Ibid., 416b14.

21. Ibid., 416b24. The nutritive dimension of the soul "is productive of genesis, not the genesis of what nourishes itself, but the genesis of another like what nourishes itself. For its substantial being already exists, but nothing generates itself, but only conserves itself. Consequently this sort of principle of the soul is a power such as to conserve what has it as the kind of thing it is. For its part, food prepares it to be-at-work. This is why, deprived of food, it cannot be" (ibid., 416b15–20).

22. Ibid., 416b24.

23. *Telos* is not primarily a goal, but a completion of actuality, whose intrinsically desirable plenitude then provides the "for the sake of which": the *a priori* reference point that gives motion its coherence as a form of striving. An important consequence of this is that the *telos* never merely arrives at the end of movement, but is also present to it at the beginning. Indeed, if time is a "moving image of eternity," it is because the *telos* constantly shines down "from above," unceasingly appearing, withdrawing, and, in the same instant, pledging the renewal of its appearing, while matter reaches up "from below" to receive this same downward shining, whose threefold pattern it continuously bears out of its dark, fruitful womb: "Like a mother," matter "remains underneath as the co-cause with form in the production of what comes into being" (*Physics*, I, 9: 192a13–14).

24. Aristotle, *De Anima*, 54.

self-imparting efficient cause, who not only bestows being on his effects, but also gives them the gift of causality as well.[25] For their part, the *causae secundae* act chiefly in order to commune with the *causa prima* in its generous self-impartation to the world. By definition, this universal aspiration ("all things reach for this") must govern even the tendency to conserve substantial being. Since conservation primarily seeks to maintain *ousia* as a common good over the whole of time,[26] its complete meaning first becomes manifest in generation, which is the only one of the nutritive soul's works that fully displays its latent reference to the *bonum commune*. Placed within this context, conservation turns out to be a partial expression of a much larger and richer whole than the modern doctrine of self-preservation admits: the living thing's natural readiness to share in the intergenerational project of providing a "temporal eternity" to house God's unfailing gift of

25. Aristotle famously says (in Jaeger's version of the text) that God "moves [*kinei*] as an object of love [*erômenon*], while by means of a moved thing [*kinoumenô*] he moves the others" (Aristotle, *Metaphyiscs*, XII, 7: 1072b3–4). Since Aristotle explicitly says that God "*kinei*," i.e., moves in the *transitive* sense of the verb, the adverbial phrase "as an object of love" should not be read as a denial of his efficient causation, but as an account of the manner in which he exercises it. We could express the matter as follows. God's active communication of the divine energeia is the ontologically prior condition of the world's very being: "From a Principle of this sort, then, the universe and nature hangs down [*êrtêtai*]" (Aristotle, *Metaphysics*, XII, 7: 1072b13–14). There is thus never a time when the world hasn't already presupposed God's effective self-impartation. Nevertheless, because the world is not God, it cannot remain in the "already" of the divine self-gift without simultaneously "reaching out" to receive it anew from moment to moment. But this "reaching out" is not simply, or even primarily, an autonomous activity. It is first and foremost the *a priori* condition of non-divine being, which exists only in the form of "becoming-what-one-already-is"—a form, Aristotle is saying, for which God's effective causality is chiefly responsible, before (ontologically) any action or passion on the part of the world.

26. The expression "over the whole of time" recalls Aristotle's teaching on the so-called eternity of the world, which he justifies by arguing that, if the world suddenly came into being, there must have been a time, however brief, when it merely existed without existing as something definite and complete. Although Arisotle is certainly right to reject the idea of bare, unmarked existence, which contradicts the act-character of being, the Catholic dogma of "creation in time" implies no such contradiction. *Creatio passiva* does begin, Catholics hold, but in its beginning it is already complete *in principle*. Indeed, the task God assigns to the "first moment" is precisely to guarantee the "in principle completeness" of *creatio passiva*—and so to found the wholeness of time as an ever new, always coherent recapitulation of the unique experience of coming into being fresh from the Creator's hands. *Creatio passiva*, then, is like the execution of a musical score, whose completeness establishes the first note of the performance as a radical beginning, while distinguishing it from contextless noise meaninglessly clanging in the void. This beginning then continues to resound in ever fresh, yet always coherent, ways throughout the remainder of the piece, giving the players a chance to help make the performance a once-only event, as if they themselves were improvising the score as they go along.

being.[27] This readiness is the *leitmotif* of the three points I propose to treat in the remainder of this section: (1) the chief *telos* of generation is not self-preservation, but participation in divine beauty; (2) this participation enables the individual's implicit acceptance of death (or something analogous thereto) in the very joy of producing its offspring; (3) the interweaving of generation and death allows us to retrieve self-preservation as a moment within the interplay between individual and community.

1. The Primacy of Beauty

In a striking passage in *Metaphysics*, XII, 7, Aristotle says that God originates the world in virtue of his beautiful mode of being, which is his unfailing—and therefore "necessary"—harmony with his own perfection as the *actus purus*.[28] But if God's efficient causality is a revelation of his beautiful self-coherence, then this revelation must be equally beautiful in its turn. God cannot cause as the beautiful, in other words, unless he also causes in a manner worthy of the beauty that he is. Now, God's manner of causation owes its beauty above all to two interrelated manifestations of his beautiful self-coherence: the unhesitating promptitude and the unwavering reliability of his bestowal of being. For its part, the world proves its authenticity as God's proper effect by mirroring this beautiful interweaving of promptitude

---

27. I borrow this term from Charles Péguy (*Porche du mystère de la deuxième vertu*, 76). Here the poet speaks of man's responsibility "to assure (it's incredible), to assure [Christ's] eternal words a kind of second eternity beyond the one they have already, a temporal and carnal eternity, an eternity of flesh and blood, a nourishment, an eternity in the body, an earthly eternity." For Aristotle, living things have an analogous responsibility as secondary causes of their offspring. God's gift of life is unfailing, and unfailingly effective, but this very fact both enables and requires living things to prove its indefection by giving it a "second eternity" from below. Put another way, God's gift enables living things to (co)generate (cosmic) time as a "moving image of eternity," and thus as a spatiotemporal display of the unfailing promptitude of that very gift itself.

28. "It [i.e., the Unmoved Mover] is by necessity being, and insofar as [it is] by necessity [being] [it is] beautifully. It is thus [i.e., as beautiful] that it [i.e., the Unmoved Mover] is principle" (Aristotle, *Metaphysics*, XII, 7: 1072b10–11). The "necessity" that Aristotle ascribes to God here is the "impossibility of being otherwise than simply [himself]" (ibid., 1072b13). It is the twofold indefectibility thanks to which the *actus purus* is the eternally indefectible Good and enjoys an eternally indefectible harmony with it. Divine necessity, as Aristotle understands this term, thus includes the perfection of freedom, not in the sense of indetermination, but in the sense of the entirely self-determined completion of pure actuality—the true meaning of the phrase "thought thinking itself." For Aristotle, then, God is the transcendent archetype of what, in us, would be the beautiful congruence of natural form at the height of its completion and virtuous character at the height of its excellence.

and reliability on which its being depends.[29] "All things," then, "reach for" divine eternity, not primarily in order to immortalize themselves, but in order to con-form to the beauty of the unhesitating, unfailing gift that makes the world exist. We see a specific manifesation of this universal striving in the ready self-abandonment by which individual plants and animals die into the unbroken continuity of their *eidos*. Even man and wife embody this same cosmic *eros*. Indeed, they become its prime analogate when, losing themselves in the ecstasy of their union, they (implicitly) anticipate their eventual death, and so open themselves to the surprising gift of new life from God. This insight already anticipates the next point.

2. Generation, Death, and Participation in Beauty

If God displays his beautiful freedom from envy by unhesitatingly imparting his own eternal vitality to others,[30] living things reflect his unstinting self-impartation in the generative act, which allows them to rejoice in life's abundance ("as many as are complete") and communicate it to their offspring in the same beautifully indivisible gesture. Aristotle's definition of the generative act as the "production of another like oneself" highlights its character as a beautiful *analogon*,[31] a contracted representation, of God's

29. I borrow the term "proper effect" from Aquinas.

30. Aristotle affirms that "God possesses a life and duration that is continuous and eternal" (Aristotle, *Metaphyiscs*, XII, 7: 1072b29–30). Indeed, God's subsistent actuality is itself "a life that is best and eternal" (ibid., 1072b27–28). This latter text suggests that, in a certain sense, there is only one life: (divine) eternity. Granting this assumption, there are only two possibilities: either one is eternal life itself or one participates in it. Since God entirely exhausts the first possibility, only the second remains for non-divine things. If they are going to have life, then they have to share in the eternal life that God alone substantially is. This argument may help explain why Aristotle stresses "participation" in our text from *De Anima* II, 4. There is no contradiction between this emphasis on participation and Aristotle's "usual" doctrine of analogy. God's efficient causality, in fact, is the unfailing origination of an analogical community of *telê* of which he is at once the source, the *analogatum princeps*, and the transcendent common good— which, by the way, is why internal and external teleology cannot be separated, but are just two dimensions of the same internally differentiated cosmic manifestation of the divine generosity.

31. The analogy is more than an external resemblance, for the worldly analogue serves as a kind of "organ" of God's unfailing gift of being. Needless to say, God is not naturally united to the living thing (or even to the cosmos *in toto*) as the rational soul is naturally united to its body. The living being is not a "member" of God, but only an instrumental secondary cause of his unstinting self-impartation. Nevertheless, "as the whole soul is present in every part of the body whatsoever, in the same way the whole God is present in all things and in each thing" (Aquinas, *Summa Theologiae* [*ST*] I, q. 8, a. 2, ad 3).

unenvious self-gift: insofar as the generator produces an offspring that is "like itself," its begetting represents God's eternal persistence in being; insofar as the offspring it produces is an "other," a distinct "self," its begetting mirrors God's unfailing self-impartation. Needless to say, the likeness between the generative act and God's indefectible self-gift subsists only within a greater unlikeness between them, since the animate body cannot eternally persist "as the same thing but [only] as one like itself." Nevertheless, the living being's very readiness to let "one like itself" continue in its place, as the inheritor of its *ousia*, includes something like an (implicit) acceptance of death, which thereby becomes the seal of generation as a self-gift in imitation of God.[32] In his *Portal of the Mystery of Hope*, Charles Péguy presents a specifically human embodiment of this implicit attitude: the good father who does not regard his children as strangers to his *ousia*, but welcomes them as the rightful heirs destined to enjoy it in his place. Having already died into his paternal mission, Péguy suggests, such a man finds his proper self-regard not apart from, but together with, the habitual thought of

> his . . . children . . . Of whom he is the father before God . . . His
> . . . children who will succeed him and who will outlive him
> on the earth. Who will have his house and his lands. And if he
> does not have any house or land, they will at least have his tools.
> . . . And with his tools his children will inherit . . . what he has
> already given them . . . the force of his blood. For they have
> issued from his loins. . . . His . . . children will hold his place
> on the earth. When he will no longer be there. His place in the
> parish and his place in the forest. His place in the Church and
> his place in the household. His place in the town and his place
> in the vineyard. And on the plain and on the hillside and in

---

32. This consideration suggests a "theodical" reading of our text from *De Anima*, II, 4 as a response to the following problem. The unity of the cosmos consists in a universal "reaching for" divine eternity. But while the cosmic whole is imperishable, some of its parts, such as plants and animals, are not. How, then, can their appetite for divine eternity be satisfied, even for an instant, if they cannot persist forever as God does? Doesn't nature act unjustly in giving things that will fail to be an appetite for the kind of entity that can never fail to be? The answer to this objection, Aristotle says, is the generative act, which enables the living being to touch eternity in its very acceptance of death, which thereby becomes a seal of a self-gift that assimilates it to the "eternal and divine." Aristotle does not regard this transfiguration of ugly corruption into beautiful gift as an abolition of corruption *per se*, but only as its indirect transformation into a manifestation of the primacy of life, which it at first seemed to contradict. From this point of view, there is no need to ascribe to the Aristotelian "theodicy" I've just sketched a premature closure that would immunize it against the Paschal Mystery, by which Christ swallows up our corruption in his glory—leaving only his eucharistic "Yes," his radical gift "to the very end" (John 13:1), as the eternal, incorruptible fruit of his death.

the valley. His place in Christendom. . . . Because it's the places,
great God, that have to be held. And all of this must go on. . . .
He thinks tenderly of the time when he will no longer be and his
children will hold his place. On earth. Before God.[33]

3. Individual and Community

The peasant father whom Péguy portrays in this passage from the *Portal*
conceives of his identity entirely in terms of the place he occupies in the
universal order of things: "on earth" and "before God." Thinking of himself
simply as one in a long line of placeholders, he can regard even his death as
the last implication of a transmission of *ousia* that, in principle, was already
complete when he begot his first child (or even when he first entered upon
the married state). But the father's self-identification as a link in the chain
of generation is as much an act of realism as it is an act of generosity: how,
in fact, could one hope to identity oneself if one really were a bare particular, an abstract tautology isolated from any context larger than one's own
sheer individuality? In implicitly posing this question, Péguy underscores
one of the deepest lessons to be learned from Aristotle's account of generation: the continuity of my existence over time is the continuity of my sharing in a complete meaning, a beautiful wholeness, that I cannot possess in
isolation but only as part of a community that outlives me.[34] This retrieval

33. Péguy, *Porche du mystère de la deuxième vertu*, 27–30.
34. Unless the individual living being were naturally ordered to an ultimate wholeness comprehending each of its successive states of being, it would be reduced to a
heap of disjointed fragments lacking any intrinsic continuity or coherence over time.
Failing to constitute a proper *suppositum* of its own time, it would also lack the intrinsic
wherewithal to be a real "self" in the first place, so that any self-preservation we might
ascribe to it would be formally indistinguishable from its death (or its never having
been alive at all). "When the notion of finality falls, more than just the notion of causality falls with it. The notion of continued existence over time, and so of motion, falls
as well" (Spaemann, "Die Unvollendbarkeit," 122). Now, ultimate wholeness does not
belong to the individual in isolation from its species: individuals are wholes in their
own right precisely *because* they are parts of their species. "Part" is an analogical term,
which in this case does not indicate a piece or a fragment, but an individual possessing
the specific nature in its own right. We can thus fruitfully compare the relation between
individual and species to the relation between letter and alphabet. While the single letter is intelligible only as part of an alphabet, and a world without alphabets would also
be a world without letters, it is equally true that alphabets are inconceivable without
single letters, and each letter plays an indispensable role in constituting the whole of its
corresponding alphabet. Similarly, the living individual owes its very existence to the
pre-existing natural community of the species, outside of which it would make no more
sense than a letter detached from any corresponding alphabet, yet the species persists

of "self-preservation" as a moment within the interplay of individual and community implies no dissolution of substantial being into an impossible universal flux. Aristotle's point, in fact, is not that the individual lacks *ousia*, but that its *ousia* is never merely its private good, but is always a real *bonum commune*, a true universal subsisting (only) in nature's unbroken generative self-renewal. The individual stands *on* its own, to be sure, but it does so only while standing *for* the entire analogical community of beings.[35] To be is to represent[36]—within the universal exchange that is the world's "worlding," its status as the moving image of the unfailing divine (self)gift on which it depends:

> It is now time, then, to inquire in which way the nature of the whole has the good and best, either as something separate, existing just as itself on its own, or by reason of the order [within it]. Or is it in both ways, as in the case of an army? For the good [*to eu*] of the army is in its order and in its general. Indeed, it is principally the general, since he is not on account of the order, but the order is on account of him. Now, all things are set together in a certain order. They are not, however, ordered in the same way, but there are swimming things, and flying things, and growing things. But neither are things so constituted that

only insofar as its individual members produce their own replacements, thus assuring that its *eidos* never lacks a particular instance. In one and the same act, the individual submerges in the species-life—and (re)emerges as a representative of the species that comprehends it *aliquo modo* within the wholeness of its own distinct existence.

35. This representative "standing for" involves no absorption of the living thing's distinct individuality into a super-ordinate collective. Three points: (1) the living individual has to be a distinct whole in its own right, otherwise it cannot represent the form of the species, which is a principle of wholeness *ab intrinseco*. (2) This representation, however, is not a univocal affair, and some exemplars of the specific form will represent it more excellently than others. (3) As we rise in the the *scala naturae*, individual freedom plays a correspondingly larger role in determining the unequal quality of representation. This is why, at the height of the *scala*, particularly excellent individuals can represent the man's true vocation in opposition to the collective and in defiance of "public opinion"—as in the case of Socrates or the Old Testament prophets.

36. Every *ousia* is a unique *analogon* of the universal community of beings. In this sense, Aristotle's doctrine of analogical unity at least implicitly "grazes" the recognition of a positive, intrinsic infinity present in and above finite form. Compare this passage from Goethe: "In every living being, what we call parts are indivisible from the whole in such a form that they can be understood only in and with the same, and neither the parts can be applied as the measure of the whole nor the whole as the measure of the parts, and so . . . a limited living being takes part in infinity or, rather, it has something infinite in itself, if we do not prefer to say that we can never wholly grasp the concept of the existence and the perfection of the most limited living being, so that we must explain it by declaring it, just as much as the awesome whole in which all existences are comprehended, to be infinite" (Goethe, "Studie nach Spinoza," 4).

the one has nothing in relation to the other. The contrary is the case, since all things are set in order together in relation to one, but [it is] as in a household, [where] the free members have the least permission to do any random thing, but all or most of what they do follows a prescribed order, whereas the slaves and the beasts make but a small contribution to the common good, while much of what they do is at random. For nature is a source of this kind for each of them. I mean, for example, that all things necessarily end up decomposing. And the other things in which all commune in view of the whole are like this as well.[37]

III. The House of God's Beauty

If we compare the cosmos to a household, as Aristotle himself does in the passage I've just cited, we can say that its primary law, its ruling *oiko-nomia*, is beauty. In the great cosmic household, it is not necessity that measures beauty, but beauty that measures necessity.[38] This is why the chief end of generation has to be participation in the beautiful, and not compensation for death. Indeed, there is a sense in which death is not even possible outside of generation. It is only once I have "made another" who is "like myself" yet not myself, that I have someone to whom I can gladly entrust my place in the world's household. But this glad relinquishment is the *analogatum princeps* of death. In "making another like myself," then, I *give* myself my inevitable bodily dissolution—transformed in advance into an expression of "the one thing needful," that is, God's unfailing gift of being:

> This is why love is so closely related to death. He who begets says Yes to his own death—not just physiologically, but also, in some sense, spiritually. The man gives himself away to the woman, but

37. Aristotle, *Metaphysics*, XII, 10: 1075a11–25.

38. In God, beautiful necessity coincides with the freedom of being wholly himself, which is to say, the Good *simpliciter*. God's necessity, which measures all other forms of it, is "the impossibility of being otherwise than simply [himself]" (Aristotle, *Metaphysics*, XII, 7: 1072b13). For its part, non-divine entity, which is not simply the Good, always stands in need of something "without which [it cannot have its proper good or] well-being [*eu*]" (ibid., 1072b12). This necessary dependence exposes terrestrial bodies to the risk of a third kind of necessity, which involves "violence, because it is against a thing's inner impulse [*hormê*]" (ibid). Yet even though it enables violence, dependence on others for the realization of one's proper good is not against nature, but in accord with it. By weaving things into the fabric of a universal communion prior to their "choice," in fact, such dependence enables them to receive a proper share in God's beautiful necessity, his divine freedom from any invidious distinction between being and self-impartation.

the woman also gives herself away to the man; both pronounce their Yes to their own impermanence: The child not only must live, it must also outlive them. The father withdraws from the stage so that his son can take the place in the limelight that is due him as his father's heir. And yet where does the wave of life rise up more loftily than in the generative act? Where is life more conscious of its potency than in the pleasure of giving itself away? Mustn't we say that life is never more alive than when it gives itself up and dies over into the other? That it reaches its apex precisely when it realizes what it means to be a vessel whose contents are greater than the vessel itself?[39]

So far, I have been talking about death as the common end of all animate bodies, but it is now time to confront a problem that is uniquely bound up with the mortality of man. Although our earthly life inevitably comes to an end, we still have to take a position with respect to its inescapable finitude. The naturalness of our eventual demise is not just given *to* us, but must also be achieved *by* us. To be sure, the form of the generative act anticipates this achievement, implicitly elevating our coming bodily dissolution into a *telos* that crowns the beautiful form of our lives. And yet, our personal achievement of this task—which is in any case more a matter of self-surrender than of self-control—always remains partial and ambiguous. We can never make our death fully natural by our own power alone, if only because we are constrained to shape it within the limits of the *corruptio* overshadowing our present state of being.[40] Only Christ's supernatural victory over death can

39. Balthasar, *Homo Creatus Est*, 291. When a living being makes "another like oneself," it is performing an act analogous to a father's gladly imagining himself as a fond memory for his son. Such acceptance of one's demise (or analogous equivalent) from the standpoint of one's bodily fruit is the "form" of death. For its part, bodily dissolution is not death *tout court*, but only the "matter" of death. There can, of course, be no death without this matter, but, as Aristotle explains in another context, the necessity imposed by any material is only a hypothetical one, which presupposes ordination to the realization of some form, hence, to some *telos*. Necessity in the primary, "non-hypothetical," sense is nothing other than the absoluteness of the beautiful itself—here manifested in self-gift as the "form" of death. On the merely hypothetical necessity of the material, see Aristotle, *Physics*, II, 9: 200a10–14: "[W]hat explains why the saw is like this? The fact that it is meant to be something and for the sake of something. To be sure, this latter, i.e., what it [the saw] is for the sake of, cannot come into being unless [the saw] be of iron. Necessarily, then, there has to be a piece of iron if there is going to be a saw and its work. Which was just our point: The necessary exists by virtue of hypothesis, but not as a *telos*."

40. Balthasar holds that our earthly life is naturally finite. Even the gift of original justice, he thinks, need not have suppressed this natural finitude. It does not follow from this, however, that unfallen Adam was destined for corruption. On the contrary, Balthasar hints that the natural end of Adam's earthly existence would have coincided

fully naturalize it, because only his cross can perfectly disentangle the good finitude of the earthly body from its sin-darkened corruption.[41] Yet Christ cannot accomplish this work *for* us or *in* us without also accomplishing it *with* us as well. This insight underlies the explanation of the soteriological significance of Mary's Dormition that Nicholas Cabasilas offers us in the following passage from his homily on the Assumption:

> It was necessary, in fact, that her all-holy soul be loosed from her most sacred body. Now, as soon as her soul has been loosed, it is immediately attached to her Son's, like a second light cleaving to the first. But even her body, after having remained a little while on the earth, also departed along with it. It was necessary,

---

with his transition to (supernatural) incorruption. Nevertheless, while the *corruptio* overshadowing the end of our lives *pro statu isto* is a result of sin, our acceptance of death can still (imperfectly) reveal something of the truly natural, incorrupt end that God could have bestowed on an unfallen Adam: "[E]ven death includes a positive aspect that God, in his goodness, has built into his good creation. When the book of Wisdom assures us that God did not create death (Wis 1:13; 2:23–24; echoed in Rom 5:12), it is plain from the context that by 'death' it means the perdition of sinful man; the text considers physical and spiritual death as a concrete unity (Wis 1:12). But the finitude of living beings, which already characterizes sub-human nature, is not an evil for which man's sin could be blamed. Rather, this finitude displays the wisdom of the Creator, who has made man for the supernatural goal of 'incorruption' (Wis 2:23), a goal that man cannot attain except by totally giving himself over to his Creator. The creature's act of giving itself over is rooted in its being, and when it is performed consciously it is the most precious gift it can place in the hands of its Maker" (Balthasar, "Der Tod vom Leben verschlungen," in *Homo Creatus Est*, 190f.).

41. "Jesus's death, then, occupies a central place in his mission. Moreover, it differs from every other human death, which is not just a biological event, but is also concretely overshadowed by the punishment for sin. Both of these considerations give us a way of defending Anselm's soteriology. . . . [T]he pro nobis interiorly takes over sin's alienation from God, even though it does so in an act of obedient love. In this way, it effects a reconciliation that is likewise no mere exterior event, but passes through the interior liberation of the sinner from his sin, a liberation that opens to him, by the working of the gratia liberatrix, the possibility of reconciling himself in his turn to the God who is reconciled to him. . . . For the same reason, even the universal effect of Christ's death, its impact on the whole of humanity cannot be called 'generic' (universal does not mean generic). Although it touches all men, it does not reach them anonymously; it takes each person into account, so that each individual whom it touches must also respond to it in a personal fashion. We now see that the fruitfulness of Christ's enspirited body coincides with the fruitfulness of his person, and that this coincidence is possible only because his act of reconciliation has transformed biological death into the expression of the personal fullness of life that he is. The natural ('animal': 1 Cor 15:45) man, being finite, is subject to a death that his very coming into being makes an inevitable reality for him. This same death has now been robbed of its independence; it has become a moment within the fullness of personal life, so that, when the Church sings in its liturgy that 'by his death he has conquered death,' it is proclaiming the literal truth" (Balthasar, "Person, Geschlecht und Tod," in *Homo Creatus Est*, 128f.).

in fact, that she traverse all the paths her Son had traversed, and shine upon both the living and the dead, and complete the sanctification of nature in every respect, and only then receive back her fitting place.[42]

In this passage, Cabasilas presents the Dormition as the completion of the co-redemptive death that Mary undergoes at the foot the cross.[43] But the death she suffers on Calvary is also a birth, by which she (painfully) begets her Son in the souls of his "many brethren." These co-redemptive birth pangs, which Mary first experiences as she stands by her Son's cross, are themselves already implicit in her "Yes" to his incarnation. Her virginal maternity is thus a first step in God's transformation of carnal generation into a new and eternal nuptiality. Because she does not know carnal generation herself, she can help liberate the unity of love and death it contains into a higher form where it can finally display the whole of its (eucharistic) virtue: the supra-sexual, yet truly physical, union between Christ and his ecclesial Bride.[44] In Mary, the human species fulfills its natural unity by dying and rising with Christ into the *communio personarum* of the church.[45]

42. Ibid., 221.

43. Cabasilas develops his Mariology—one of the greatest in the history of the church—in three "homilies" edited by Martin Jugie, in the early 1920s: *Homélies mariales byzantines*, in R. Graffin—F. Nau, Patrologia Orientalis, 16. The titles of the three homilies are as follows: *Sermo in Nativitatem Deiparae*; *Sermo in Annunciationem Deiparae*; *Sermo in Assumptionem Deiparae*. I cite as follows: homily title (in English), (Jugie's) section, Greek column number (in brackets), line number(s). Cabasilas, *Homily on the Assumption of the God-bearer*, 10, [391], lnn. 1–8.

44. Cabasilas affirms Mary's co-redemptive role when, for instance, he writes that "she was her Son's ally in the struggle for my salvation" (Cabasilas, *Homily on the Assumption of the God-bearer*, 11, [389], lnn. 21–22). After having dwelt at length on the pains of this "struggle," Cabasilas adds that "she had to commune in every respect with the Son's providence in our regard. And just as she imparted a share in flesh and blood to him, and just as, in return, she received a share in his graces, in the same way she also received a share in all his pains and his grief. And he, bound on the cross, received the lance in his side, but her heart was pierced by a sword, as the most divine Simeon had prophesied" (ibid., 12, lnn. 19–26). Note, finally, the intimate connection between Mary's co-redemptive suffering and her Assumption: Mary was "the first to be conformed by way of likeness with the death of the Savior" and so "participated before all others in the Resurrection" (ibid., 12, [390], lnn. 31–33).

45. Mary co-creates the state of consecrated virginity, which also helps guarantee the sacramentality of Christian marriage. Balthasar underscores this interpenetration of virginity and marriage in light of their common participation in the Eucharist: "[W]hat we have . . . said about a man's becoming Christian in Baptism applies in a very particular manner to his entering upon a human marriage, which, even looked at from a purely worldly point of view, already involves acceptance of the [following] . . . paradox . . . as a form of life: 'eternal fidelity' within the limits of an inevitable temporality. Paul very consciously places this paradox within the encompassing framework of the Covenant

The Theotokos, then, is the "end of generation," because her virginal motherhood superabundantly fulfills the whole natural tendency both of generation and of matter[46]—into the new eon where "they no longer marry or are given in marriage, but are like the angels of God in heaven" (Matt 22:30). In the *Virgo Mater*, the creature becomes the undying fruit of its own death with Christ,[47] and so attains the end for which it was first brought into

---

that, in its New Testament form, has now become a marital alliance between Christ and his Church, which, released from him as Head, is at the same time his body, which Paul is able to affirm thanks to a flashback to the book of Genesis (Eve's creation from Adam's side). . . . [A]ll purely 'biological' sexual desire and emission of seed are taken up into the total act of complete personal self-gift. True, what the man gives over to the woman in sexual intercourse is only a tiny part of himself, which, looked at from the outside, retains all its 'animality' and is incapable of overcoming the physical distance between the spouses' bodies. Yet this mere part becomes the pure expression of an event whose possibility depends on Christ's Eucharist: a total mutual interpenetration that includes the biological, while going far beyond it" (Balthasar, "Person, Geschlecht und Tod," in *Homo Creatus Est*, 129f.).

46. The natural *unio* of the species includes a certain unity of being and love, nature and person that finds its complete meaning in the supernatural *communio* of the church. Although the passage from natural *unio* to supernatural *communio* requires death and resurrection with Christ, this radical *caesura* establishes a relation between the human species and the Catholic Church that is comparable to that existing between the literal and spiritual senses of Scripture. On the one hand, ecclesial communion is founded upon specific union, just as the spiritual sense is founded on the literal. On the other hand, specific union is a prefiguration of the church whose fully manifest truth comes to light only in ecclesial communion (insofar as it is a sacrament of the eschatological presence of God "all in all"). The creation of this relation belongs in a special (but not exclusive) way to the Holy Spirit, who personifies the eternally accomplished unity of being and love, nature and person in the Trinity.

47. In *Summa contra Gentiles* III, ch. 22, Aquinas shows that "the end of generation as a whole is the human soul, to which matter tends as its ultimate form. For the elements are for the sake of mixed bodies, while these are for the sake of living things. Among these, moreover, plants are for the sake of animals, while animals are for the sake of man. Man, then, is the end of the whole of generation." Similarly, just as man is the end of sub-human generation, Christ is the end of human generation. To be sure, the hypostatic union is primarily the result of a gratuitous, supernatural divine self-communication, but the *telos* of this self-impartation also includes a fulfillment of the whole natural tendency of generation. This is why the virginal conception is supernatural in its *manner*, but fully natural in its *substance*. Indeed, there is a sense in which it is the first fully natural conception, as if the true "mother of all the living" were not the Old Eve, but the New.

being.[48] Indeed, Mary is herself the choice "fruit of creatures,"[49] the radiant *telos* of the creation,[50] whose unfading wholeness reveals the ultimate beauty that God has destined for his beloved handiwork. As "our life, our sweetness, and our hope," Mary assures us in her own glorified body that the world is a temple, a cosmic sanctuary whose purpose is not "vanity," as inverse teleology tacitly assumes,[51] but the inhabitation of God's own incorruptible glory: "Since it was impossible for the creation to rise up from corruption so long as the children of God had not attained their liberty, the Virgin provided the ransom for its purchase: Him who was the first-born from the dead."[52]

48. "For since in all things the fruit is that which returns nature to its begetter through the accepted cessation of existence and [in so doing] reveals it new from its very origin, who remade men? What is the source of the new creation? Who changed this universe?" (Cabasilas, *Homily on the Assumption of the God-bearer*, 3, [379], lnn. 12–15). Cabasilas's answer is Christ—to whom we owe also the Virgin Mary.

49. Mary embodies a singular, superabundant completeness that is at once her unique privilege and the common good of the universe, the fullness of grace and the finest bloom of nature, the redemption of creation and the achievement of its original purpose, the pre-condition of the world's existence and the purifying recapitulation of its long agony.

50. Cabasilas, *Homily on the Assumption of the God-bearer*, 3, [379], lnn 9–10.

51. "Indeed, we do well to proclaim the blessed [Mary] as the reason why human beings endure in existence and even exist in the first place. But even this is not enough. For even the heaven, and the earth, and the sun, and this entire cosmos received their well-being and their being at all on account of the Blessed Virgin, like a tree does on account of its fruit. But if we call the tree 'good' on account of the fruit, and the man who rejoices in the tree has in fact praised the fruit, who is unaware that the whole dignity, and grace, and adornment of beings . . . befits the Virgin alone? It is legitimate to say, then, that the judgment God pronounced concerning these things when he said they were good [*kala*], indeed, surpassingly good, was a praise of the Virgin" (ibid., 2, [378], ln. 39–[379], ln. 8).

52. In *ST* I–II, q. 85, a. 6, Thomas asks whether death is natural or a penalty for sin. His answer is complex. "Incorruption," he says, "is more natural to man than it is to other corruptible things," inasmuch as the human soul is "not altogether subject to bodily matter, like other forms, but rather has an immaterial operation of its own [*propriam*]." Nevertheless, "man is naturally corruptible, if by 'nature' we mean matter left to itself [*sibi relictae*]." "At the moment of man's creation," however, God, "filled up this lack in nature [*supplevit defectum naturae*]" with the gift of original justice, which gave "the body a certain incorruptibility" it otherwise would not have had. "And in this sense," Aquinas continues, "it is said that 'God did not make death' and that death is a penalty for sin," in that sin caused God to leave our bodily matter to its own tendency to dissolution. In one respect, then, the discrepancy between our innate longing for immortality and the resources of the cosmos to fulfill it is natural: even "universal nature," the administratrix of the cosmic economy, cannot provide us with incorruptibility, though it "would choose an incorruptible matter [for the human body] if it could." In another respect, however, it is our sin that first introduces us to the experience of this discrepancy—in the form of a disillusioning "vanity" (Rom 8:20). Thanks to our sin, we

Now, Mary's identity as the *telos* of creation implies her full presence to its *archê*—in the form of an immaculate "Yes" that in some sense accompanies her very genesis.[53] "Simultaneously with her coming-into-being in the way of nature [*hama tô phynai*]," Cabasilas writes, Mary "was already starting to build a resting-place for the one who was able to save. She was preparing the only house for God that was truly adequate to him."[54] The simultaneous fruit of nature and of grace,[55] the *Immaculata* is as indivisibly

---

meet matter "left to itself," and are thus tempted to imagine the "self" chiefly in terms of matter's exposure to corruption. It is then but a short step from this image of selfhood to the inversion of teleology, which sees (temporary) resistence to corruption as the only possible *naturally given* sense of individual existence.

53. The eschatological completeness of Christ's redemptive act is so entirely the precondition of Mary's existence that she can enter into the world, not as a sinner still in need of the Redemption, but as the unfallen (New) Eve, and so as the creaturely co-condition of the world's salvation: "She alone made a truce with God before the common reconciliations. Or, rather, at no time did she in any way need truces, since from the very beginning she stood firm as the leader in the chorus of God's friends" (Cabasilas, *Homily on the Assumption of the God-bearer*, 3, [368], lnn. 17–20). Cabasilas immediately adds, however, that "she became all these things for her fellow human beings" (ibid., ln. 21). Thanks to her sinlessness *ab initio*, in fact, Mary represents the whole of man, who in her gives himself as an unspoiled gift to the Word—who then creates from this self-gift the all-pure human will by whose free obedience he redeems the world: "And having taught and persuaded her in this fashion, God acquires her as his Mother, and borrows flesh from someone who knows and wills [what is happening], so that, just as he was conceived voluntarily, in the same way she, too, might conceive voluntarily and, at the same time, willingly become Mother by the voluntary motion of her own counsel. Now, the main reason why this happened was to enable her to do more than merely contribute to the economy, or to be deployed in its service as an instrument moved by an alien hand. She was to offer her very self, and become a co-worker with God of his providence for the human race, so as to become a partaker and sharer with him of his generosity in its regard. But there was another reason too: just as the Savior himself was not man and the Son of Man merely by reason of the flesh alone, but also had a soul, and mind, and volition, and whatever else belonged to man, in the same way all this happened that he might obtain a perfect Mother who served his begetting, not only with the nature of her body alone, but also with her mind, and her volition, and everything she possessed, and the Virgin might be Mother in both body and soul, and she might offer the entire man, whole and unspoilt, for the ineffable birth-giving" (ibid., 5, [370], lnn. 22–41). As this passage suggests, the doctrine of the Immaculate Conception is an implication of the the dyothelite orthodoxy defended by Maximus the Confessor.

54. Ibid., 3, [369], lnn. 6–9.

55. "What happens to the other saints after their release from the body, namely, their immobile possession of virtue and the good, happened to the Virgin even before she put off the body" (ibid., 9, [388], lnn. 24–27). This immobility in the good is primarily the effect of grace, since no creature can be impeccable *ex puris naturalibus*, but it also manifests the beautiful originality of her own freely obedient nature: "By the radiant bloom that she drew from within herself, she demonstrated the beauty of the common nature and drew to herself the Impassible, and he was man on account of

unique in her own order as the Incarnate Word is in his.[56] Although she is of course not God, the Virgin Mother nonetheless manifests the divine originality in the medium of a creaturely obedience that, in its own way, is every bit as original as God's own self-gift: "By the creature's 'Yes' [*phônê*], the Creator himself is created."[57] Indeed, the originality of Mary's God-bearing reveals the creaturely face of what, following Bulgakov, Caldecott calls "*Sophia*"[58]: the convertibility of being and love whose archetypal (hyper)form is God's own triune infinity, in which substance and donation are always already one:[59]

the Virgin" (ibid., 2, [368], lnn. 11–13). Compare the opening lines of Adrienne von Speyr's *Magd des Herrn*: "As a sheaf is gathered together in the middle and unfolds at either end, in the same way Mary's life is gathered together in her 'Yes.' It is from this 'Yes' that her life receives its sense and its shape and unfolds itself towards the past and towards the future" (7).

56. "Clearly, then, [God] didn't choose as his Mother the best of the human beings existing at the time, but the best *simpliciter* [*haplôs*]. Nor [did he choose] someone who suited him better than the entire human race, but someone who suited him so thoroughly in every respect [*dia pantôn*] that it would befit him to have her as his Mother" (Cabasilas, *Homily on the Annunciation of the God-bearer*, 8, [374], lnn. 27–31).

57. Ibid., 8, [376], ln. 31. This understanding of Mary's divine maternity as (under grace) the highest expression of nature's originality illumines, it seems to me, the analogy between art and nature that Aristotle already noted in the *Physics*. Now, this analogy is itself part of a larger whole: the analogy between the "made" and the "begotten." Indeed, he himself defines generation as the "*making* of another like oneself." But the analogy between the made and the begotten is not exhausted within the confines of the world, since it presupposes an even more fundamental analogical correspondence between the made creature and the begotten Son. Just as the Father generates the Son in a unity of natural emanation and personal self-gift, the Son is both the uncreated *Imago* of the Father's generative self-giving and the living "art" by which the Father expresses his self-giving towards creation. Now, the unity of natural emanation and personal self-gift in the paternal *generatio activa* is sealed by the Son's participation in the production of the Holy Spirit. By the same token, the Spirit plays an irreducible role in fully revealing the Son's identity: *ad intra* as the consubstantial expression of the Father's self-giving; *ad extra* as the *uncreated* source, model, and end of the creatures whose innate originality constitutes them as analogues of the Only-begotten. But the Holy Spirit elevates this *ad extra* revelation to its highest expression in Mary's act of generating the very God who made her. Doesn't this suggest that her virginal conception *de Spiritu Sancto* is the *creaturely* source, model, and end of the analogy between the made and the begotten, and so between art and nature?

58. Caldecott offers a Catholic retrieval of the Russian sophiological tradition in his new book, *The Radiance of Being*, 250–75.

59. On the substantial identity of divine unity and triune hyperform, see Augustine, *De Trinitate*, VI, 10, 12: "For in that [uncreated] Trinity there is the supreme origin of all things, and the most perfect beauty, and the most blessed delight. This is why those three appear as mutually determined and, at the same time, are infinite in themselves." Compare Maximus the Confessor's account of the one divinity as both unlimited and orderly in *Ambigua ad Thomam*, I (PG 91: 1032B): "We worship a sole cause that is not

I have said that the act of being is an act of giving, an act of knowing, an act of love. It is Trinitarian. The same cluster of metaphors illuminates the nature of created being, the dynamic relationship to God, which is intrinsic to all existing things. Giftedness is the signature of God upon creation. But our being is not simply a gift to us; it is God's gift to himself. Created human nature is a gift that the Father gives to the Son, along with his divine nature. And it is a gift that the Son gives the Father, by being born as Man, dying on the Cross, and rising to new life. Creation is therefore gift both in relation to God, and in relation specifically to each of the Persons. Filled with the Holy Spirit in order to be given to the Father by the Son, it is transformed into the Son's Eucharist or "thanksgiving." The world indwelt by the Spirit is therefore now infinitely more than it was when it was created. It speaks not only with its own voice, but with the voice of the Son, who gives glory to his Father with this transformed creation.[60]

"Wisdom hath builded herself a house" (Prov 9:1). To be sure, the "wisdom" whose "tabernacling" (John 1:14) Solomon foresees is above all the Father's Uncreated Word, who (together with the Holy Spirit he co-spirates) assures the beautiful coherence both of the intra-Trinitarian unity of being and love and of the divine plan to communicate this unity *ad extra*. Nevertheless, the "wisdom" the prophet beholds also includes an ancillary *sapientia creata*, whom the triune God freely gives to himself as the creaturely origin of his entire, beautifully coherent plan.[61] Yet rather than

---

stingy, as if it were limited to one person, but that is also not disorderly, as if it were poured out indefinitely. No, the sole cause we worship is the one constituted by the Triad naturally co-equal in honor: Father, Son, and Holy Spirit, whose wealth is their natural coinherence and the one effulgence of their splendid glory. The divinity, then, is not poured out beyond these riches, lest we should have to introduce a throng of gods, nor, on the other hand, is it restricted within them, lest we should have to condemn the divinity of penury." Note Maximus's insistence that the one divinity is coextensively both monad and triad at the same time: "The Triad is truly a monad, for it is as such that it exists, and the Monad is truly a triad, for it is as such that it subsists, since there is just one divinity both existing monadically and subsisting triadically" (ibid., C).

60. Caldecott, *Radiance of Being*, 181f.

61. Mary's life unfolds in the unfailing coinherence of her Immaculate Conception, her "Yes" to Annunciation and cross, and her Assumption into Heaven. The indivisible unity of these three moments is a permanent created condition of the indivisible unity of Christ's own "theandric" person. For the same reason, it is also a permanent created condition of Christ's act of "recapitulating of all things" (Eph 1:10). As the New Eve, Mary is the New Adam's "co-recapitulator," who helps him gather up creation, redemption, and eschatological glorification into an "economy for the fullness of time" (Eph 1:10), a single mighty display of the "manifold wisdom of God" (Eph 3:10). It is surely

stressing her own originality as the created "beginning of [the Lord's] ways" (Prov 8:22), the Virgin Mother prefers to "delight" (v. 31) in the originality of the creation itself. "Playing over the whole earth" (ibid.), she enters into creation's common joy in the beauty of being, a joy she makes her own in a gesture whose simplicity almost seems to belie the name that properly belongs to it: "recapitulation." And yet it was precisely this simple gesture of recapitulation—along with the total "Yes" of which it is a part—for whose sake God first conceived the cosmic household and its ("proto-ecclesial") economy of beautiful communion. "Created wisdom" is a universal principle, then, because it is first a singular creature: the unspoiled maiden from Nazareth upon whose simplicity (if I may tweak the line from Tolkien) God first founded all his ideas of majesty "from of old" (Prov 8:23). The beauty of her face, radiant with the light springing up from the unfathomable abyss of her humility, was God's first "glimpse" of the complete, living Idea of what Hopkins aptly called the "dearest freshness deep down things"[62]: the originality that marks *esse creatum* (the unrecognized soul of Aristotle's *physis*) as the "proper effect" of the God whom the Holy Spirit lets be ever-new gift in himself.[63]

---

not accidental that each of the three defining moments of Mary's life corresponds particularly to one of the three defining moments of the divine *oikonomia*: her Immaculate Conception to the creation, her twofold "Yes" to the Incarnation, and her Assumption to eschatological glorification.

62. "God's Grandeur," in Hopkins, *Poems of Gerard Manley Hopkins*, 66.

63. John Paul II hints at the connection between created being as gift and the gift-character of God's inner life in the following text: "In his own inner life, God 'is charity,' an essential love common to the three persons. Considered as a personal property, love is the Holy Spirit, inasmuch as he is the Spirit of both the Father and the Son. This is why, as uncreated love-gift, the Spirit 'searches the depths of God.' It can be said that in the Holy Spirit the inner life of the triune God is sheer gift, the mutual exchange of love among the divine persons, and that through the Holy Spirit God 'ek-sists' in the mode of gift. The Holy Spirit is the personal expression of this donation, or, as we might say, of this being-as-love. He is love in person, gift in person, and he gives the notion of the person that superabundance of truth, that ineffable deepening of insight, which comes only through the Revelation of personhood in God. At the same time, insofar as he is consubstantial in divinity with the Father and the Son, the Holy Spirit is love and (uncreated) gift, the living foundation, as it were, from which flows down the whole largesse of gift given to creatures (created gift): the gift of existence given to all things by creation, the gift of grace bestowed on man by the economy of salvation. As the Apostle Paul has written, 'the charity of God has been poured out in our hearts by the Holy Spirit who has been given to us'" (*Dominum et Vivificantem*, 10).

8

Health and Hope

Michael Cameron

Et dixit, qui sedebat super throno: "Ecce nova facio omnia.
. . . Ego sum Alpha et Omega, principium et finis. Ego sitienti dabo
de fonte aquae vivae gratis. Qui vicerit, hereditabit haec, et ero illi
Deus, et ille erit mihi filius."

—REVELATION 21:5–7

Tolkien understood that words and language can really express the
beauty of what is unveiled in Being, and that, through the beauty of
an imagined world, one can open the reader once more to wonder at the
miracle of Being, to joy at the beauty and goodness of what appears therein,
and to astonishment over the event of its simply being there. By showing
that existence can be imagined otherwise, mythopoeic art helps liberate the
mind from the straitjacket of a presumed necessity in the things that are,
and invites us to look at things afresh, as proceeding from a free and sovereign creative imagination. Tolkien also knew that each mythic tale is itself
such an event, a sub-creative participation in the epiphany, an effoliation
of reality with its own beauty and truth, causing joy and wonder, capable
of leading those with eyes to see to a deeper appreciation of the mysterious
radiant glory of reality. In this sense he knew fairy tales can come true and
so spent the best part of his life writing one.

The Lord of the Rings attains such lofty artistic peaks, as is attested by
its universal reception. Like the Athelas plant, the book has a wholesome
virtue. We breathe an air of "living freshness" from its leaves as we read,
and all at once are walking in "dewy mornings of unshadowed sun in some
land of which the fair world in Spring is itself but a fleeting memory."[1] Let

---

1. Tolkien, *Lord of the Rings*, 865, book 5, chapter 8: The Houses of Healing.

us journey for a while in this wholesome air and explore something of the sense of health and hope it contains.

For Tolkien these are central themes and are bound up with his primary sources of inspiration in writing the book. Among these latter was his love for his wife and family; included were the friendships that bound him to the Tea Club and Barrovian Society. The members of the TCBS shared a delight in the beauty of language, but were parted early in death. And lastly, his sense of time and place informed the writing, a living and local sense of tree, hill, and history. Spousal love and its fruits then, and the sundering doom of every human life, and memory, the inheritance of every soul, gathered to the present in the concrete conditions of life and language. It is in connection with these sources of inspiration that we may most fruitfully explore the themes of health and hope in *The Lord of the Rings*. Let us begin in Minas Tirith, where, during the great battle of the Pelennor fields, these themes come to the fore.

Faramir and Éowyn are dying when Aragorn enters his city in the garb of a ranger and comes to the houses of healing. Faramir has been pierced by a poisoned dart. He is exhausted, weighed down by grief, and haunted by the Black Breath, a shadow of despair. He burns with a fever, while Éowyn, in the next room, is fading away, grey and cold after battle with the Witch-King. Her shield arm is broken and her sword arm paralyzed. They lie both in an evil slumber.

Faramir had kept his hope, unlike Boromir his brother, who fell into despair, and with it into corruption and the desire for power. But now his hope is sorely tried and appears thin like a mere thread tying him still to the world. He is a man of noble quality, intelligent and fair in his dealings with others, valiant as a man of war. Something of the air of Númenor still surrounds him. He does not seek the power of domination and made no attempt to take the ring from Frodo. The history of Gondor is alive in him and he holds dear the memory of the glory of the city of the kings, yearning for its renewal. But, though a true knight, his eagerness for his father's affirmation led him to a foolhardy obedience, which almost cost his life. With his final rash excursion against the forces of Mordor a shadow was already creeping across the hope in his heart.

Éowyn had lived in patience, suffering the long, slow humiliation of Wormtongue's contempt for the house of Eorl, and his leering infatuation with her. At heart, she is a woman of courage and gentleness, but indignation and a sense of futility had begun to grow. She had begun to long, if not for a renewal of the courtesy and hospitality of the king's hall, then for a new life, one of more honor and beauty. Her yearning took shape with the coming of Gandalf and his three companions to Edoras and it was mixed with admiration of Aragorn. She would be a queen in a house of honor and renown. But her mood led her to mistake his pity and refusal for a condescending pride and she turned to vainglory and a search for honorable death in battle.

The lore-master of Gondor and his assistants have been at work already before the arrival of Aragorn. Faramir's wound has been cleaned and leeches used to assuage the fever. Éowyn's broken arm has been set with due skill. They still had some skill in Minas Tirith even at the end of the Third Age to guide and augment the healing power, which inheres in the living body. Unfortunately, with the concentration on learning they had lost something of their old wisdom, as Gandalf complains. They had forgotten the healing virtue of Athelas.

What they had retained of the craft of the Númenóreans had its origin from the elves. Having the greater faculty for aesthetic perception the elves saw more beauty, and in proportion their medicinal craft was higher and more complete. Elrond is the master healer who alone could save Frodo from the Morgul blade. Being the son of Eärendil, and a stargazer, his craft is still informed by the light of Valinor. His heart and mind are moved and instructed by a beauty in which art is yet undivorced from reason, and knowledge undivided from love.

When he comes to the houses of healing, Aragorn brings wisdom out of Númenor to complete the craft of the lore-master, but he also comes as a king with healing hands. The scent of Athelas will invigorate the hearts of all present. And, more than that, his material presence, communicated by touch, is itself a powerful remedy. Tolkien comes closest here to the portrayal of a religious act in *The Lord of the Rings*. In Númenor the role of priest and king were identified in the same person and Aragorn here embodies that idea.

Aragorn places his hand upon Faramir's brow and his ears are opened to the calling of his name. With intense struggle Faramir is wrested from the bonds of a listless wandering. At this moment, Athelas, through the sense of smell, evokes in Faramir the memory of the glory of Númenor. This ancient beauty is recollected in the moment when Faramir recognizes the king in love and knowledge. When Sam had first spoken of Aragorn on the paths of Ithilien, Faramir had believed the ranger's claim to the crown would require adequate proof and demonstration. In the event, Faramir is compelled to recognition by the very presence of all he had hoped for and held dear in memory.

The elves had always had a special talent for memory and it was their particular sorrow to treasure the beauty of a passing world even in view of its final passing away. With the estrangement of the two Kindred, men lost much even of what memory they kept for themselves. In Faramir something of the old friendship with the elves remains, and with it a participation in their keeping of ancient memory. In Faramir's healing, Athelas gathers to the present all the beauty of this memory in the presence of the king. He understands in this moment that all worldly beauty in its passing proceeds in the present from a beauty immemorial, and believes that nothing will be lost of all that he has loved in Middle-Earth. Here, in Aragorn, is the authentic prefiguration of the incarnation of Ilúvatar in Tolkien's works of fantasy. Aragorn's answer to Faramir's response of loving obedience is "awake . . . be ready for my return,"[2] remain in my hope.

Éowyn's healing begins in the same way as Faramir's. The sense of a new beginning given her is accentuated by the scent of Athelas, like an "air wholly fresh . . . and young, as if . . . newmade."[3] However, she does not wake to see Aragorn, but her brother Eomer. Her body is healing but she has not yet found her hope. She remains unwillingly in Minas Tirith and has no desire for healing.

Faramir's love for Éowyn begins with pity, a pity of kinship and close to love.[4] "You and I have both passed under the wing of the shadow and the same hand drew us back."[5] This sense of common destiny, in which his love begins to grow, allows her also to heal and begin to hope, because the hope in which he remains—that of all the Captains of the West—is rooted in pity. It is the pity of Bilbo and of Frodo for Gollum, pity that recognizes kinship and a common experience of brokenness, and that refuses to pass judgment on another. If hope were rooted in the strength of men the quest would have failed. It is a pity that does not pass judgment, but spares life, which leads at last to the ring's destruction.

In a letter to C. S. Lewis, Tolkien describes the state of Christian marriage as "total human health."[6] At the stroke of doom, when time halts for an eternal moment, Faramir and Éowyn attain this state in principle as they clasp hands upon the walls of Minas Tirith. It is attained as hope in the form of a corporeal vigor in Faramir to whom Éowyn clings and draws close, despite what reason might conclude from the sight of the great shadow rising before them. All at once, Faramir understands the meaning of his dream of the ineluctable wave, and the temptation to despair at the loss so soon of

2. Tolkien, *Lord of the Rings*, 866.

3. Ibid., 868.

4. Finrod describes the two kinds of pity; see Tolkien and Tolkien, "Athrabeth Finrod ah Andreth," 324.

5. Tolkien, *Lord of the Rings*, 965, Book 6, chapter 5: The Steward and the King.

6. Tolkien, *Letters*, 60 (letter 49).

the love he has found is met by a hope and joy in heart and limb "which no reason can deny."[7] Éowyn shares this hope and joy of Faramir.

For Éowyn, however, it is not yet full grown. It is threatened still by her misunderstanding of Aragorn's pity for her. She still perceives it as the condescending pride of one who marks a difference in fortune, that he should ride to battle and glory and she should not. Only with Faramir's declaration of unconditional love, a love that would still be operative even were she to achieve the ends of her vainglorious desire for honor and renown, is she freed from the lingering source of that desire in indignation and resentment. She confirms her love for Faramir and is fully healed. At last, they have been "made whole"[8] together, and wait in good health and hope for the return of the king.

On the Pelennor fields Faramir meets Aragorn, returning in triumph out of Mordor, and asks leave to surrender his stewardship. It is an act of the utmost poverty, putting himself and his hopes for a future life with Éowyn at the disposal of the king. He does what his father and brother were unable to do: give back to the king what is his very own. He thinks that in giving up the stewardship he will be displaced by the king. But, as it happens, Aragorn both elevates him to the status of royalty and declares that he should keep the title of steward.

Some weeks later, during the celebrations in Edoras, what was attained in principle at the stroke of doom, the "total human health" of spousal love, is brought to completion in the betrothal of Éowyn and Faramir. Éowyn's broken frame is restored and full strength has returned to her right arm. There is gentleness in her recognition of Aragorn as liege-lord and healer, and with it she attains completion of bodily healing. Her aspirations for elevation to royalty are fulfilled even in giving them up as she and the Prince of Ithilien are plighted in troth. We have seen that health is not complete unless hope is present, a hope for always more life and fruitfulness. Being made whole again in Christian marriage, then, does not mean a closed ring of self-sufficiency and satisfaction, like the ring of Sauron, but as with the wedding ring of Éowyn and Faramir there is a jewel set in the circumference, breaking the closed circle, and keeping married love open to ever new possibilities.

In the fullness of health Faramir and Éowyn live out their lives and love in the Garden of Gondor, among the hills of Emyn Arnen, dwelling always in sight of the king's city. There the trees grow with joy and every living thing is nurtured by the healing hand of Éowyn. Faramir will order the

---

7. Tolkien, *Lord of Rings*, 963.

8. Ibid., 868.

land and the waterways. They live as stewards, giving back in perpetuity to the king what is his very own, in a fullness of possession born out of a spirit of poverty. This principle of fullness and poverty as the form of their lives, in which health is completed by the hope of always more fruitfulness in the land of Ithilien, culminates in the sundering of man and wife in death. In the end, everything must be given up, even that which is held most dear, in an experience of the utmost poverty, before one can enter into the fullness of life in Arda Remade.

Tolkien portrays this final transition of health and hope through death into eternity not in the love of Éowyn and Faramir but in a spousal relation of a different order. He could not find a way to include the love story of Aragorn and Arwen in the main body of the text of *The Lord of the Rings* because there are aspects of it that transcend the story. It almost seems greater than the whole story itself. Their love started before the adventure begins and comes to its completion only after the tale is brought to its conclusion.

Aragorn begins as a lowly ranger, growing to a lordly figure upon his entrance into Gondor. In the houses of healing he is a Christlike figure entering in humble guise into his own realm to heal. With his marriage to Arwen all his hopes are fulfilled and he appears as a king triumphant, and with his death that same hope that Faramir enacted at the stroke of doom is brought to its highest expression. Aragorn receives the gift of Ilúvatar of his own free will, even though it means leaving behind everything he has hoped for and holds dear. The fullness of poverty is expressed in the giving up even of Arwen his beloved spouse.

The marriage of beauty and sorrow in the tale of their parting strikes one like a blow, which takes the breath away. There is great sorrow for the spouses with the decline of life to memory and in the sundering of their shared lives, but no hint of despair as hope in its essence is revealed at last as unconditional trust in Ilúvatar. In death a great beauty is unveiled in Aragorn and through him a glimmer of the glory of Arda Remade. This is his gift to Arwen in their parting, the fundamental affirmation of that which was the principle of their union and the wellspring of their fruitfulness upon earth, and with it great beauty, resplendent from beyond the circles of the world, the intimation of a final common destiny, glory undimmed and life eternal.

Arwen must remain in this trust and hope of glory, looking forward to a life of even greater freedom, loosed from the circles of the world, where the memories of earthly things are gathered in an eternal present and are even *more* than what they are upon earth, until at last she too may choose death willingly under the golden boughs of Cerin Amroth. But although Tolkien portrays death as the final transition of health and hope, death is not the final word. Already in the houses of healing, he prefigures, in the healing of Éowyn and Faramir, an immediate participation, even in Arda Marred, in the life of Arda Remade.

The houses themselves convey a sense of the church, wherein are gathered those loyal to the king, by allegiance or friendship, "of all dwellings the most blessed"[9] as Éowyn will describe them later. It is perhaps one of the true inspirations of the film version of *The Lord of the Rings* that the voice of Arwen fills them with a beautiful melody. Tolkien did after all allow that music might be added to the mythology. Arwen is a Marian presence there, present as a mediator of healing, pleading for those who are ill. Aragorn comes to the houses in humble guise to heal. As the king who heals by touch and presence he represents our Lord, the incarnate King of heaven, who, especially in the Blessed Sacrament, heals the world from within by touch and presence.

In this way, we find the Eucharist at the heart of Tolkien's conception of health and hope in *The Lord of the Rings*:

> The one great thing to love on earth . . . there you will find romance, glory, honor, fidelity, and the true way of all your loves upon earth, and more than that: Death: by the divine paradox, that which ends life, and demands the surrender of all, and yet by the taste (or foretaste) of which alone can what you seek in your earthly relationships (love, faithfulness, joy) be maintained, or take on that complexion of reality, of eternal endurance, which every man's heart desires.[10]

Ultimately, then, the healing of Éowyn and Faramir takes place in an ecclesial-like context in which the beauty of scent and melody open them in wonder to receive healing and wholeness with joy from the hands of the king. It is an image of the fullness of eternal health and hope brought to us in the Blessed Sacrament, our being re-made whole in the risen Christ. And to such fullness we are opened and most surely led by Our Lady, the epitome of beauty in the order of grace, upon which is founded all Tolkien's "perception of beauty both in majesty and simplicity."[11]

The beauty of *The Lord of the Rings*, an ancient beauty recollected in the present, which opens us in wonder to the mysterious radiant glory of reality, has its foundation in the beauty of Our Lady, which opens us to recognize, in the radiant glory of Our Lord's sacramental presence in the world, the manifestation of God's love for each and all, come to heal and

9. Ibid., 965.
10. Tolkien, *Letters*, 53 (letter 43).
11. Ibid., 172 (letter 142).

make us whole again. Arwen's melodic presence in the houses of healing recalls the beauty of Our Lady in majesty as queen of heaven and bride of the
Lamb at the heart of the church. But, Tolkien chooses to accentuate there
the beauty of Our Lady in simplicity. For it is the scent of Athelas leaves
that keenly calls to mind the beauty of her simple presence in the church as
handmaid of the Lord, the King of heaven's own mythic foil with which he
first adorned his tree of tales.

> *Et Spiritus, et sponsa dicunt: "Veni!" Et qui audit, dicat: "Veni!"*
> *Et qui sitit, veniat; et qui vult, accipiat aquam vitae, gratis.*
> (Rev 22:17)

9

Stratford Caldecott

Ecology on One's Knees

Mary Taylor

I. Ecology and the Imagination

Stratford Caldecott is best known for profound work primarily focused on a Catholic vision of reality: on writers like Tolkien and Chesterton; the Christian mysteries; liturgy and the sacraments; interreligious dialogue; and the transcendentals Beauty, Truth, and Goodness as the foundation of education. One might think that anything he wrote on ecology was merely marginal, peripheral to his other writings.

One would be mistaken. Nothing is peripheral; in fact one might say that everything is central, and that his writings on ecology constitute a microcosm of his entire opus. For what Dante says of God's creation—*ogni parte ad ogni parte splende*,[1] each part radiates with its own splendor (received as a gift from a greater light) which it then reflects back to all others—is true of Caldecott's own work as well. To turn from most academic writing on ecology to Caldecott's is to enter a world of beauty, enchantment, and surprise, where ecology touches upon everything else—theology, mathematics, biology, ethics, physics, music, liturgy—converging and emerging, a dance done with grace and courtesy, ancient truths striking us with new force and freshness.

Caldecott does not have abstract environmental or ecological theories, any more than the apostles had Christologies; they, and he, encountered Christ, and everything springs from this concrete event. For Dante, a single glance from a little Florentine girl in the street pierced his heart and set him

---

1. Dante, *Inferno*, Canto VII, 75. The whole is an inexhaustible "ever-greater," not a "totality" that can be encompassed by the human mind.

on a trajectory that brought him all the way to the throne of God. Caldecott's ecological reflections are rooted in the wonder and delight the human person experiences in the face of the sheer, amazing *being* and *beauty* of particular people and natural things. Those reflections grow through art and a true and contemplative science, and they do not stop until they flower into the metaphysics of a creation that is embraced within eternity and vibrant in the mystery of love. The unity to which all creation is called—"a center, which like all centers is smaller than the whole but encompasses and projects everything else"[2]—is the summing up of all things in Christ.[3] All of nature is shaped by this *telos*.

The wholeness in Christ may elude us at first: "The more diverse and varied are the productions of nature, the more seemingly distinct from human life and from each other, the more exotic and bizarre, the more nature reveals herself as fragmentary."[4] But that which is fragmentary cries out for something greater, if only by highlighting its absence: "The modern discovery of ecological interdependence is itself only a pointer towards the mystical whole to which all creatures belong."[5] Dante, in his final beatific vision, is struck by the revelation of the wholeness of the created order: "In its depths I saw ingathered, bound by love in a single volume, that which is dispersed in leaves throughout the universe."[6] For Caldecott as well, the book, the "single volume" bound by love, is an especially fruitful cosmic analogy: "The universe as observed by the naked eye is a book of symbols waiting to be read; it is an act of self-expression by God, a theophany imbued throughout with the intelligibility of the divine Logos."[7] Each of those symbols "is a kind of gestalt, in which a universal meaning can be glimpsed. . . . The world is transformed into a radiant book to be read with eyes sensitive to spiritual light."[8]

It is the poetic imagination, the poetic consciousness, which allows us to encounter and "read," by the "spiritual light" of Love, the great manuscript that is the created order, and in the process to re-enchant the desacralized world.[9] Caldecott does not issue a call to be poetic "rather than"

2. Caldecott, "Creation as a Call to Holiness," 167.

3. Eph 1:10.

4. Caldecott, "Creation as a Call to Holiness," 167.

5. Ibid.

6. Dante, *Paradiso* Canto XXXIII, 85–87. Bonaventure: "From all we have said, we may gather that the created world is a kind of book reflecting, representing, and describing its maker, the Trinity" (*Breviloquium* 2.12, 230).

7. Caldecott, "The Science of the Real."

8. Caldecott, *Beauty for Truth's Sake*, 48.

9. Ibid., 49.

discursive; the poetic imagination is not the modern imagination of feelings alone, but what we might call the analogical imagination in accord with the intellect as a path to truth.[10] He likes to tell the story of Pythagoras, who discovered the laws of harmony by walking by a blacksmith shop. Stopping to investigate what we would call the empirical causes of the different tones he heard, he invented the scientific method at the same time that he laid the foundations for Western music.[11] Pythagoras represents that original unity between mathematics and art, reason and faith, science and religion, and for Caldecott the problems of our culture, including ecological ones, are the result of the loss of that unity, a fissure between a more intuitive knowledge and a "modern," scientific one, which left both as anemic simulacra of what each could be were their inner relationship not artificially severed.

Recovering an "original unity" does not mean merging into one that which we have learned to see as dualistic opposites; it is the univocal imagination that privileges absolute unity, as the equivocal imagination privileges absolute difference. The poetic, contemplative, analogical imagination "marries"—connects through similarity while respecting the difference, in a mutual conditioning—the poles it encounters, marriage being the paradigmatic unity that depends on distinction rather than dissolving it. The ultimate form of this spousal union is Christ in whose Incarnation the divine and the human meet. For Caldecott, this will mean that there is no final *resolution* of the brokenness, the "dis-ease," of the ecological crisis through technology or social science alone; instead, it is the unity with God in the Trinity that "is achieved through man (humanity), [which] ultimately enfolds and transforms the entire cosmos."[12] It is through Christ that *reconciliation* with nature is possible. These words of John Paul II are often quoted by Caldecott and might serve as a précis of what underlies his ecological vision:

---

10. Caldecott says "poetic imagination" depends on analogy; the language of the equivocal, univocal, and analogical imagination, to which he would be sympathetic, is borrowed from Fr. William F. Lynch, *Christ and Apollo: The Dimensions of the Literary Imagination*. Also see D. C. Schindler: "The imagination is, if not the center of the human being, then nevertheless that without which there can be no center, for it marks the point of convergence at which the soul and body meet; it is the place where faith in the incarnate God becomes itself incarnate and therefore truly becomes faith. . . . Far more than a mere faculty, the Christian imagination is a way of life, and this is because we might say it represents the point of intersection between Christianity and the world. In this case, a starved imagination represents a crisis indeed" ("Truth and the Christian Imagination," 522).

11. Caldecott, "Creation and the University," 5. See also Caldecott, *Beauty for Truth's Sake*, 91.

12. Caldecott, "Creation as a Call to Holiness," 161.

The Incarnation of God the Son signifies the taking up into unity
with God not only of human nature, but in this human nature,
in a sense, of everything that is "flesh": the whole of humanity,
the entire visible and material world. The Incarnation, then, also
has a cosmic significance, a cosmic dimension. The "first-born
of all creation," becoming incarnate in the individual humanity
of Christ, unites himself in some way with the entire reality of
man, which is also "flesh"—and in this reality with all "flesh,"
with the whole of creation.[13]

For Caldecott's ecology, then, there is certainly no fixation on immediate technical solutions, but neither is there a flight from the immediate
problem into abstraction. The part and the whole interpenetrate. He does
not ignore population growth, climate change, or deforestation, but sees
them in the light of the tensions of existence between grace and nature, the
infinite and finite, ontology and history, and more deeply in the primary experience of wonder in the presence of the great gift of Being, of amazement
at beauty as an ontological truth, and ultimately in Christ. The Christian
analogical imagination, in harmony with the will and intellect, is the means
through which creation can be restored and redeemed:

When Adam fell from grace, the whole creation was somehow
dis-graced, or put out of joint. The healing of the world therefore cannot be envisaged without a reordering and a healing of
the inner world of the imagination, intelligence, and will. This
insight is easy to relate to the modern study of ecology and to
the broader development of a more holistic worldview in postmodern science.[14]

It is the imagination that enables us to look beyond the facts at the sur-
faces of things to the form, imagination "that interprets, that gives meaning
to the world, by 'joining the dots,' discovering the otherwise invisible connections between things, events, qualities."[15] What we call the "ecological
crisis," despite its many proximate causes, is not so much a problem to be
solved by recycling or remediation—though they must be dealt with—but is
ultimately rooted in a failure of the imagination.

In the second part of this paper we will look at Caldecott's evaluation
of the "First Trajectory" and "Second Trajectory" of views:[16] the utilitarian

13. John Paul II, *Dominum et Vivificantem*, §50.

14. Caldecott, *Beauty for Truth's Sake*, 108.

15. Caldecott, *Beauty in the World*, 122.

16. In a blog post titled "A Deeper Ecology," Caldecott refers to M. Taylor's use
of "trajectories" as "a new paradigm for considering the ecological question." Taylor

environmentalism derived from modernity and the holistic and postmodern responses to it. In the third part we will consider a "Third Trajectory," a Trinitarian, Christocentric cosmology. The fourth continues with Caldecott's "spiritual anthropology": the *imago Dei*, the person as microcosm and mediator of the created order, and the call to holiness as the inner link between "saving the earth" and "salvation."[17] The fifth part is the concluding section.

II. First and Second Trajectories: Modern Environmentalism and Responses

Responses to the ecological crisis, the call to "save the earth" or "preserve the environment," are often motivated by fear of loss:

> That the loss of species will denude the earth of colorful interest and variety; that the loss of forests will lead to climactic and atmospheric changes endangering health; that overproduction will lead to impoverishment of arable lands and even to desertification; that pollution will kill the rivers and poison the air and land.[18]

There is nothing wrong with this; it is a profoundly human response. The suffering, fear, or sadness experienced when facing a debased environment is the disclosure of a brokenness that calls to mind the truth of our interrelationship with nature, with each other, and with God. But as Caldecott says, that fear tends to be reactive, looking first to immediate technical solutions, even though they may bring new problems without getting at the true source of the original issue:

> The secular mentality responds to our state of decay and suffering by trying to overcome this weakness through technology.

borrows the term from Pope Benedict XVI, who (in *Spe Salvi*, 17) speaks of a "programmatic vision" based on "science and praxis," with faith dualistically displaced to the level of "purely private and otherworldly affairs" and replaced with a Baconian "faith in progress," as "the trajectory of modern times." Modernity, then, is the "First Trajectory." The "Second Trajectory" includes various responses to the First; the term is not meant to reduce radically diverse schools of thought to one, but it is simply a way to categorize those that *through their own self-description* deliberately set themselves in opposition to the dualism, utilitarianism, and reductionism of modernity. Pope Benedict calls for a "new trajectory," discussed later as the Third Trajectory, in *Caritas in Veritate*. See M. Taylor, "A Deeper Ecology."

17. Caldecott, "Creation as a Call to Holiness," 165–67.

18. Schmitz, *Recovery of Wonder*, 118.

But technology employed without an understanding of the world's relation to God always tends to makes the situation worse. Using technology, we try to anticipate the "glorious liberty of the children of God," through medicine, drugs, surrogates and avatars. But if we rely on technology to save the world, we end by reducing the world to a machine.[19]

How did we get to the state in which our hope seems to lie primarily in technology, a hallmark of what one might call the First Trajectory of responses? It began with a paradigm shift. The cosmos was once seen as alive with light and life, radiant with the True, the Beautiful, and the Good, imbued with meaning and value and an intelligibility that could be known truly, though not exhaustively, by the mind. Persons were made in the image and likeness of the God from whose hand came the gift of the created order, and despite the ever-present reality of human sin, they found their places in communities that were constituent of their very being.

The genealogy of modernity from late medieval nominalism has been elucidated, as Caldecott points out, by many others from many perspectives—Catholic, Orthodox, Marxist, and feminist[20]—and there is little need to review its reductionism, dualism, and isolated individualism here nor its "will to power" in the Scientific Revolution's goal of mastering nature. For the purposes of this discussion of the person's relation to natural entities, what is important is that it meant the elimination of "the 'vertical' or 'interior' dimension of reality—the dimension of metaphysical form, final causality and divine providence, and with that the last remaining possibility of a contemplative science."[21] Believing everything can ultimately be captured in its net, this *via moderna* is a triumph of the univocal imagination, which makes of unity an absolute by abstracting and externalizing every part's relation to the whole; every relation is, then, merely mechanical. This flattened and truncated worldview has resulted in today's "natural resource managerialism," a utilitarian stance toward the environment in which human beings (themselves reduced to machine- or computer-like entities) are extrinsically related to a natural world that is instrumentalized for their use and over which they have power to shape to their own often arbitrary ends.

No one writes as beautifully as Caldecott does on what he calls above "contemplative science"; he does not attack science *itself*. Even understood at the most basic technological level, technical environmental fixes—the

19. Caldecott, "At Home in the Cosmos" (2012), 111–12.
20. E.g., Romano Guardini, Louis Dupré, Alisdair MacIntyre, Charles Taylor, Carolyn Merchant, and many more.
21. Caldecott, "The Science of the Real."

remediation of contaminated soil, for example—are achievements that have their place. But, he asks, at what cost? "In a society where efficiency and material productivity are the supreme values, and everything is measured, in the end nothing is truly understood, and no one is loved. . . . Nothing is given; instead, things are bought and sold. There are no covenants, only contracts"[22]—that is, only utility, not love.

A different response to the fear of loss (of species, of forests, etc.) followed the truncated rationalism, the mechanism and utilitarianism of First Trajectory environmentalism. It saw additional losses—of community, relationship, and enchantment—and rejected much of the First Trajectory's reductionism. It also looked to a wider ethics that would encompass not only animals but even the land itself.[23] This Second Trajectory[24] naturally turned to *holism*, a holism sometimes purely material while at other times taking the quasi-mystical form of seeing the earth as a single organism, "Gaia." "Deep ecology" proposed a "bio-centrism" or "eco-centrism" to replace a hierarchy that supposedly privileged "anthropo-centrism" (itself an ambiguous term). In all its forms, and perhaps most consciously and deliberately in "emergentism," it eschewed the transcendent-immanent divide by *equating* transcendence and immanence—a "horizontal transcendence."[25] The difficulty with the rejection of hierarchy and transcendence, says Caldecott, is that even most Christian ecology, such as Christian ecofeminism, along with the "deep ecology" literature that runs alongside it, does not "grasp the paradoxical fullness of the mainstream tradition":

> God is not merely immanent (like a soul within a body), nor merely transcendent (like a Deist watchmaker). He is both, and immanent precisely because He is transcendent, and therefore

22. "A covenant is a mutual commitment that creates a unity of persons so close that it amounts to membership of a family. This is what distinguishes it from a legal contract, which may outwardly resemble it. In a contract, each side agrees to do a certain thing, and once those promises are discharged, the contract ceases. When a covenant is made, on the other hand, a gift of self is exchanged. In other words, each person places his or her own soul in the other's power. This is a much deeper, more powerful relationship" (Caldecott, *Catholic Social Teaching*, 36). Covenants and contracts are not mutually exclusive; contracts of utility may find their place within a larger covenantal relationship.

23. Aldo Leopold's "The Land Ethic," published in *A Sand County Almanac* a year after his 1948 death, was foundational: "The land ethic simply enlarges the boundaries of the community to include soils, waters, plants, and animals, or collectively: the land" (171).

24. See note 43, in which Pope Benedict refers to mistaken views of nature, such as seeing it as untouchable.

25. See, for example, Goodenough and Deacon, "The Sacred Emergence of Nature."

impossible to circumscribe or limit. As for hierarchy, there is a paradox here which even Dionysius the Areopagite preserved, in his enthusiasm for ranks of angels "ascending and descending on the Son of man" (John 1:51): the different "levels" of creation are ways not of separating creatures from God but of connecting them, and above all a way of manifesting the beauty and grace of God in an ordered cosmos.[26]

The new term, *ecology*, began to be preferred, and Caldecott too sees the term *environment* as misleading, implying as it does an Enlightenment-inspired dualism, "an opposition between humanity (or whichever species is under discussion) and its surroundings, reducing the rest of nature to a kind of backdrop—and at worst to a complex set of raw materials and mechanical forces."[27] *Ecology* attempts to overcome the fragmentation. Its Greek root meaning refers to the "logic" of ordering one's home, one's household:

> This original meaning is also what lies behind the use of the word to describe one of the newest of the sciences. The science of ecology treats the whole earth as the "home" of humankind, and studies the ordering of this, our natural environment. What it reveals above all—and what makes it so fascinating—is the complex interconnectedness of all living processes on the planet.[28]

But at the other end of the spectrum of reaction against First Trajectory environmentalism, many postmodern ecologists saw in deep ecology and the drive to holism a combination of naïveté and univocity that was merely the mirror image of the position they tried to refute. They opted instead for equivocity and the tensions of ambiguity. Currently, some reject the term *ecological*, with its emphasis on "logos"—meaning pattern, reason—in favor of *ecotonal*, from *oikos* (dwelling) and *tonus* (tension).[29] Among their intentions are the rescuing of the beauty of the particular, the importance of the body, the sensuousness of the flesh, in a word, the reality of the finite within historical horizons. There is much that is beautiful and true and good here, especially when they reject a totalizing rationalization of reality, and champion intersubjectivity and local solutions.

---

26. Caldecott, "Lost in the Forest?"

27. Caldecott, *Beauty for Truth's Sake*, 105.

28. Caldecott, *Catholic Social Teaching*, 44.

29. Coles, "Ecotones and Environmental Ethics." Also, some postmodern ecologists writers use the language of "reconciliation," "agape," "generosity," "caritas" and other terms borrowed from Catholicism, but emptied of their Catholic content.

Yet they miss the mark. Not only does their equivocal imagination reject meaning—logos—abandoning it in favor of ambiguous tensions (any meaning is merely provisional and fleeting *local* meaning); the person, whom Caldecott (and Catholicism) sees as central,[30] is as lost here, dissolved into the congeries of social forces, as he is when reduced to another transitory node in the web, or just another bioform.[31] Caldecott is one of the great explicators of the recognition by John Paul II and Benedict XVI that ecological issues cannot be set in opposition to persons and the "life" issues related to them, but are profoundly interwoven; "human ecology," Caldecott says, "is inseparable from environmental ecology, because respect for nature must include respect for ourselves, for our sexuality, and for human life in all its stages and manifestations."[32] That "radiant book" Caldecott calls us to read is indeed, in Dante's words, a "single volume bound by love"; as Pope Benedict XVI says in a passage often quoted by Caldecott,

> The book of nature is one and indivisible: it takes in not only the environment but also life, sexuality, marriage, the family, social relations: in a word, integral human development. Our duties towards the environment are linked to our duties towards the human person, considered in himself and in relation to others. It would be wrong to uphold one set of duties while trampling on the other.[33]

Despite his criticisms, Caldecott finds much to be said for these attempts, however incomplete, to protect and preserve either unity or difference. The very thing that postmodern theorists reject—a flight from finitude, limitation, history—is precisely what the Incarnation overcomes and is the only true way to overcome. That God would take on human form *within history* means that the limitation and finitude of created beings are great goods,

30. There are many schools of personalism that see the person as free, not determined; as relational, not merely individual; and as of central importance, not reduced to equivalence with other entities. The distinctive Catholic form is based on love, and sees that "the inner structure of love is revealed as Trinitarian. In any complete act of love the self of the lover is simultaneously given, received, and shared. To be united with another through love is not to lose one's distinctive identity but to be confirmed in it" (Caldecott, *Beauty in the World*, 33).

31. Holists see entities only as processes, temporary phenomenal constructs in an endless flow. In these philosophies of identity, as Benedict XVI says, the boundaries between persons, and between persons and the natural world, "are absorbed, are revealed as provisional" (*Truth and Tolerance*, 34). Those who reject holism have their own forms of nominalism that deny the integrity of persons and the things of nature; see especially David Bentley Hart, *The Beauty of the Infinite*, for cogent counterarguments.

32. Caldecott, "At Home in the Cosmos" (2010), 5.

33. Benedict XVI, *Caritatis in Veritate*, §51.

not things to be escaped. At the same time, sacramental theology reveals that because all creatures, constituted in relation to God and gifted at every moment with the act of existence, are open interiorly to infinite mystery,[34] they are endless epiphanies of meaning and not merely ambiguous tensions or temporary crystallizations.

While Caldecott sees that all things have their own separate integrity, he perhaps writes most sympathetically on those who long for unity. A great convergence of forces, from the Romantics to the "gentle empiricism" of Goethe to phenomenology to the "participatory physics" that followed Heisenberg, meant that rather than seeing other living things as resources ready to hand, one sees that all things are interdependent and that the world is "more than a mechanism, more than the sum of its parts."[35] He is certainly, in a sense, a holist—"every gesture we make, every breath we take, every mouthful we eat, every sight we see connects us to the entire fabric of creation, on which we depend, and which we affect in our turn"[36]—though his holism will involve a deeper ontology than the Second Trajectory provides. Before turning to Caldecott's vision, there is one last point to be made.

Though Caldecott's Christian ecology has much in common with these responses to First Trajectory environmentalism,[37] much if not most recent ecological thinking has *blamed* Christianity for ecological degradation. Lynn White's 1967 "The Historical Roots of Our Ecological Crisis,"[38] a staple within anthologies of environmental essays, was the seminal paper that set the agenda for later debates in environmental philosophy and ethics. It traced the ecological crisis to the biblical creation story, to Christianity's supposed belief in "perpetual progress," and to its contrast with a paganism that sees nature as divine. Christianity, White said, "established a dualism of man and nature," insisting that "it is God's will that man exploit nature for his proper ends."[39] This opened the door for later theorists to claim that Christians focused on "anthropocentrism," leaving natural entities with no intrinsic value. In response to White, Caldecott agreed with those who said that "the exploitative mentality we have seen develop in recent centuries is not rooted in Christianity at all, but arises from a gross misunderstanding."[40] The "dominion" of Genesis is not domination but

34. Caldecott, "Theology of Gift," 5.
35. Caldecott, *Beauty for Truth's Sake*, 105.
36. Caldecott, "Christian Ecology."
37. Especially with eco-phenomenology.
38. White, "Historical Roots."
39. Ibid., 1205.
40. Caldecott, "Lost in the Forest."

stewardship, as Caldecott and other writers have eloquently explained. The absolute separation of nature and grace, with its "two-story" transcendent, eternal Above and its transitory Below, is derived, even if wrongly, from a neo-scholasticism that perhaps tried too hard to preserve God's freedom at the expense of ending up closer to dualism, or even to Gnosticism. The oppositions between biocentric and anthropocentric as well as between intrinsic value and instrumental value descend from the dualisms of the Enlightenment, not Christianity. Both the notion that Christianity demands "perpetual progress" to the extent of "using up" the created world and the notion that paganism can reveal to us a kind of divine immanence in nature while Christianity gives us only a distant, absolute dictator ruling over a de-sacralized and inert universe are antithetical to Catholic teaching. The former derives from the Baconian drive to control nature, and the latter from a misunderstanding of the doctrine of Creation, so important to Caldecott's ecological and cosmological vision, to which we now turn.

III. The Third Trajectory: A Trinitarian Cosmology

To borrow from C. S. Lewis, one of Caldecott's favorite authors, the Second Trajectory's deep ecology knows the "deep magic" of relationality, but it only goes as far back as "the dawn of Time"[41]—it is still entirely immanent. Since time itself is created, one must look "into the stillness and the darkness before time dawned" in order to discern "a magic deeper still,"[42] not as a flight from time into an abstract eternity, but as the fullness and flowering of time. Holism is right that we are related to everything else, but that is not simply because we share the same space, because we are physically or chemically or biologically made of the same "stuff" or because, true though it may be, we are profoundly interdependent in a material or social sense. Caldecott is one of the seminal thinkers of a Third Trajectory of thinking, echoing Pope Benedict XVI's call for a "new trajectory"[43] that is a rediscovery of the ontology of relation understood through love[44] and rooted in a proper understanding of creation.

41. Lewis, *The Lion, the Witch, and the Wardrobe*, 147.

42. Ibid., 178.

43. Benedict XVI, *Caritas in Veritate*, 53. Benedict XVI is referring to a deeper view of the category of relation as it relates to the development of peoples, but he also speaks of going beyond two mistaken views of nature, in which we see nature either as an "untouchable taboo" (as some pantheists and holists do) or "abusing it" (as the technical domination of Baconian science does). Ibid., 48.

44. The relation between ontology and love is that Being is revealed as "love made concrete." Caldecott, *Beauty in the World*, 148–49.

The deeper ontological truth of creaturely being is to be found in the Trinity, says Caldecott; the Trinity is the "hermeneutical key," the key that opens every lock, including the doctrine of creation.[45] What is it about the Trinity that enables it to do this? First, the Trinity is where unity and diversity, union and distinction, similarity and difference, find their source and summit, not as dry metaphysical terms but as the living reality of Love.

> The unity-in-distinction of the Trinity is the basis for an analogy that runs right through creation as a kind of watermark: the analogy of "spousal" union between subject and object, self and other. The life of love revealed in Christ promises to each of us no mere absorption into the Beloved, but our own integrity and fulfillment in the very measure we give ourselves away.[46]

That "give ourselves away" leads to the second point: a theology of creation as gift. Caldecott embraces the understanding of the Persons of the Trinity not merely as substances, but as substantial relations of love, the giving and receiving of love between the Persons which overflows so that every creature receives its being and its life as a gift: "Creation is an act of the Trinity, and existence is a participation in the Trinity—a participation in the Trinitarian act of giving, receiving, and being given."[47] God as self-giving love is at the heart of the mystery of creation and is the archetypal model, as both the formal and final cause, of all relationships in the created order.[48]

> The metaphysics and theology of gift thus restores a dimension to nature long since stripped away by Nominalism and its successors. It re-establishes the priority of relationship over object, of person over thing, and therefore a sense of natural interiority, of true metaphysical depth, and the wonder that is the root of philosophy.[49]

Here, contemplative science, the fruit of the poetic and contemplative imagination, is returned. Cartesian dualism lacked the imaginative dimension entirely, and the dualistic divisions of First Trajectory environmentalism

---

45. Caldecott, "Theology of Gift," 2. And note that there is no "impersonal Absolute" above or prior to the Trinity; there is no unified essence *behind* the Trinity from which the Persons proceed. Yet there are not three Gods, but one: "Each Person in himself . . . is indistinguishable from the Godhead as such. . . . Each Person is centered or grounded not in himself but in the other. . . . The 'Godhead beyond God' is (evangelical) love." Caldecott, "Trinity and Creation," 707.

46. Caldecott, "The Science of the Real."

47. Caldecott, "Theology of Gift," 5.

48. Caldecott, "Marian Dimension of Existence," 284.

49. Caldecott, "Theology of Gift," 5.

are not overcome by privileging one over the other in antagonistic opposition between persons and nature. On the other hand, the univocity and equivocity of the Second Trajectory responses do not go far enough. The beings of the world are not unified only by biology or physics, as the many holists would have it, nor do they exist side by side in an uneasy, agonistic truce, as many postmoderns would have it. Instead,

> The world . . . is a community of creatures, open to a destiny which transcends them all. Each and every creature is an expression of the loving attention of God. Each reflects in a unique way some aspect of the infinity where each becomes eternal. Through participation in Christ, the creation dies, but it also rises, a new heaven and a new earth; and in that new earth there is a holy city which is also a garden, "coming down from God out of heaven, prepared as a bride adorned for her husband."[50]

The contemplative, poetic imagination unveils the truth that persons and the things of nature, like faith and reason, the world and God, or subject and object, are poles, distinct realities that nonetheless are united, as in a marriage. The "new trajectory" Benedict XVI asked for points, then, to an ontological relationality of love. Created beings—both persons and the things of nature—have a triadic structure, a relation from, toward, and in God, making all creatures our ontological siblings. To discern the traces of the Trinity in creation is an ancient Christian intuition: the "distinctive insight" of the church fathers, especially Athanasius, the Cappadocians, and Maximus the Confessor, was "to identify all being—even stones and stars—in the light of the Trinity as essentially rooted in the relational and personal."[51] And Caldecott refers us back to Aquinas, who said that every creature carries the trace of Trinity "(1) in being created as an individual, (2) in having a form, and (3) in being related to other things."[52] This is the "radiant wholeness which accompanies the creature like a star, reflecting within the particular limits of creaturehood the inexhaustibility of the divine goodness as always more."[53]

That "more" is more than one could ever descry through the univocal imagination or the equivocal imagination alone. All of creation, as a gift of the Trinity, is ordered towards the Incarnation and reconciliation in Christ in whom all the metaphysical fractures are healed without either being absorbed into the other. We are able to grasp something of this great mystery

50. Caldecott, "Creation as a Call to Holiness," 167.
51. Caldecott, *All Things Made New*, 27.
52. Ibid., 36 (referencing the *Summa Theologica* [*ST*] I, q.45, a.7).
53. Caldecott, "Theology of Gift," 5.

through analogy, which links seemingly different and even seemingly ir-reconcilable things with one another across the created and uncreated order and which is "at the foundation of poetry, theology, and science."[54] The po-etic imagination depends on interplay of likeness and difference that is the heart of analogy, a "marriage of the particular and the universal in the eye of the heart."[55]

That this should be the heart of Caldecott's ecological vision should not be a surprise. The sense that the world "comes fresh from God's hand and that its natural qualities express aspects of his beauty"[56] must be reawakened if ecology is to be anything more than a tug-of-war between technical crisis management and those who fault the policies of such management for the crisis; between a "shallow ecology" that tries to save nature by applying bu-reaucratic and technocratic remedies and a "deep ecology" that wants to "let it be"; and between totalizing theories that try to capture all meaning and those from whom all meaning escapes.

We turn now to Caldecott's anthropology, in which the acting per-son, through the integration of ethics with spirituality and cosmology, is revealed as the link between ecology and redemption; for the person, "the stewardship of creation is nothing less than the service of Christ."[57]

IV. The Third Trajectory: The *imago Dei* and the Call to Holiness

What is ecology, in the light of a Trinitarian, Christocentric cosmology? It is not simply a "subject"; it is a practice, a way, a discipline. Like all disciplines, it has its own integrity, and like all disciplines it cannot be fully understood without "the human person who is the subject and in a sense the object of all these disciplines."[58]

Returning again and again to Romans 8:19 ("For the creation waits with eager longing for the revealing of the sons of God"[59]), Caldecott in-

54. Caldecott, *Beauty in the World*, 151.

55. Caldecott, *Beauty for Truth's Sake*, 47 (and see 46–48).

56. Caldecott, "Trinity and Society," 541. In this article Caldecott reminds us of the need for the poetic imagination: "Paradoxically, perhaps, it is in the imaginary worlds of Narnia and Middle-Earth that this sense may be regained. Both Lewis and Tolkien possess a strong sense of the natural and mysterious beauty of the earth, of its animals and plants, its weathers and seasons, its wide spaces—and the even wider field of the stars above. These things are lovingly described by them in a way that can enable us to look with fresh eyes at the real world around us" (542).

57. Caldecott, "At Home in the Cosmos" (2012), 119.

58. Caldecott, "Creation and the University," 8.

59. And continuing in 8:20–23: "For the creation was subjected to futility, not of its

terprets it in light of the person as "microcosm"—a term used by medieval thinkers—a "little cosmos" reflecting God's beauty and "containing all the elements of nature, and faculties or powers corresponding to both animals and angels."[60] Pope John Paul II gave new life to the notion of man as microcosm as an image of God—the *imago Dei* [61]—as well as a compact representation of the ordered cosmos. Affirming the bond between persons and the rest of creation, John Paul II, says Caldecott,

> sought to recall us to our original mission as stewards and priests of nature, receiving the creation from God's hand, cultivating it or making it fruitful, and giving it back to him in sacrificial worship. . . . Man was intended to be the mediator of creation, the one in whom all things connect, through whom all things are reconciled, the image of the invisible God (Col. 1:15–20). This high calling is fulfilled in Christ, the new Adam, into whom we are baptized when we receive the Holy Spirit.[62]

Thus, as did Maximus the Confessor, Caldecott linked the status of microcosm with the role of mediator—"Adam's role in the cosmos is a priestly and mediatory one"[63]—and what follows from seeing the person as both microcosm and mediator, says Caldecott, is that ecological disorder in the macrocosm is in a very real sense "*our fault*, being a reflection or projection of our own interior dis-ease,"[64] our own alienation from God. As John Paul II said, sin, the refusal to submit to God, destroys the person's internal balance with detrimental effects: "Wounded in this way, man almost inevitably causes damage to the fabric of his relationship with others and with the created world."[65]

---

own will but by the will of him who subjected it in hope; because the creation itself will be set free from its bondage to decay and obtain the glorious liberty of the children of God. We know that the whole creation has been groaning in travail together until now; and not only the creation, but we ourselves, who have the first fruits of the Spirit, groan inwardly as we wait for adoption as sons, the redemption of our bodies."

60. Caldecott, "At Home in the Cosmos" (2012), 107.

61. There is nothing dualistic about this: "human bodiliness participates in the *imago Dei*. If the soul, created in God's image, forms matter to constitute the human body, then the human person as a whole is the bearer of the divine image in a spiritual as well as a bodily dimension." International Theological Commission, "Communion and Stewardship," §31.

62. Caldecott, "At Home in the Cosmos" (2012), 108.

63. Ibid., 107.

64. Caldecott, *Beauty for Truth's Sake*, 108.

65. John Paul II, *Reconciliation and Penance*, §15.

The person may be a "micro-cosmos," an image reflecting the whole within the part, but, says Caldecott,

> Even the animals and stones can claim as much. Every created thing is made in the "image" of God, in the sense that it forms an *analogy*. But a true "likeness" is something more than analogy. To be in the likeness of God something must participate in the dynamic relationship of Son to Father and Father to Son in the Holy Spirit. The realization of this likeness to God, which is the final perfection of our nature, depends on the use we make of our freedom with the help of grace.[66]

Something more, involving the person's freedom, is necessary for the reconciliation and redemption of creation. The Second Trajectory ecologists, as we have pointed out, saw the need to turn to ethics; the insight that there is a connection between morality and the well-being of nature goes as far back as the Hebrew Scriptures:

> There is no faithfulness or kindness, and no knowledge of God in the land; there is swearing, lying, killing, stealing, and committing adultery; they break all bounds and murder follows murder. Therefore the land mourns, and all who dwell within it languish, and also the beasts of the field, and the birds of the air; and even the fish of the sea are taken away.[67]

Likeness to God and participation in the life of the Trinity will certainly encompass upright action. Ethical thinking in ecological circles, though, has tended to focus on "rights," not only of nature, but even of inanimate natural objects and landscapes. Caldecott points out that it is difficult to develop "an adequate moral theory based on rights alone that can address the need to conserve natural resources and biodiversity,"[68] not least because rights require concomitant responsibilities. Nor is extrinsic moralism—the ubiquitous "ecological police" lecturing one on recycling or what car to drive—the answer. Ecological damage, he says, is clearly more the result of vices like human greed and selfishness; more important than "codifying a list of rights belonging to nature or to animals, and then legislating to enforce them, [is] to become the kind of people who are never cruel to animals or needlessly destructive."[69] Putting the emphasis back on the cardinal

---

66. Caldecott, "Creation as a Call to Holiness," 166.

67. Hos 4:1–3.

68. Caldecott, *Beauty for Truth's Sake*, 108.

69. Caldecott, "At Home in the Cosmos" (2012), 119.

virtues of prudence, justice, temperance, and fortitude, he says, would lay the foundation "for a way of life that would be truly sustainable over time."[70]

Holiness calls us through and then beyond the cardinal virtues to the theological virtues of faith, hope, and love, which then re-invigorate the cardinal virtues. Love is the form of all the virtues and faith the necessary path; in his ecological discussions Caldecott turns to hope. Tolkien gave the Elves two words for "hope"—first, *Amdir* ("looking up") or optimism. Caldecott says, "The assumption that the ecological crisis can be solved, that big corporations can be persuaded to change their ways, these fall under the heading of Amdir."[71] Yet Amdir isn't enough: "The fact is that we can struggle for a better world, we can fight for the trees and animals and defend the coral reefs, but optimism or Amdir alone cannot sustain us."[72] Tolkien's second word is *Estel* ("trust"), the hope that stems from natural trust in the being of things. It gives, says Caldecott, a certain sense of detachment, but atheists are deprived of even this natural piety. And so "many environmentalists are falling into despair . . . without 'the greater hope' that Christianity offers, environmentalism will end in fanaticism."[73] That greater hope, which Tolkien *expresses* but does not explicitly speak *about*, is not a hope in some pie-in-the-sky afterlife, which could act as an excuse for inaction, but a hope in "the present and in the eternity to which the present is inseparably connected."[74]

The "revealing of the sons of God" of Romans 8 fleshes out to mean that "the children of God are revealed in a life of holiness."[75] Borrowing a phrase from Hans Urs von Balthasar and Benedict XVI, the person, living a life of faith, hope, and love, finds his fulfillment in the "cosmic liturgy."[76] The

70. Caldecott, *Beauty for Truth's Sake*, 108–9.

71. Caldecott, "At Home in the Cosmos" (2012), 110.

72. Ibid.

73. Caldecott, "At Home in the Cosmos" (2010), 11–12.

74. Caldecott points to a fragmentary prophecy in Tolkien's "Debate of Finrod and Andreth" that makes it plausible for the Incarnation to "make sense" as a future possibility in the pre-Christian *Lord of the Rings*. "Estel, then, means trust in God," he concludes ("The Lord and Lady of the Rings").

75. Caldecott, "At Home in the Cosmos" (2012), 119.

76. Caldecott has often referred to John Paul II's statement that the church needs to breathe with "two lungs," incorporating the Eastern church's liturgical and iconographic cosmic vision. He refers to Pope Benedict XVI's adoption of Hans Urs von Balthasar's expression "cosmic liturgy" to characterize Maximus the Confessor: "Jesus, the one Saviour of the world, is always at the centre of this solemn 'liturgy' . . . Jesus Christ is the reference point that gives light to all other values. This was the conclusion of the great Confessor's witness. And it is in this way, ultimately, that Christ indicates that the cosmos must become a liturgy, the glory of God, and that worship is the beginning of

difference, says Caldecott, between a universe and a cosmos "is not morality so much as prayer,"[77] which overflows with thanksgiving, *eucharistia*, the liturgy of the church:

> The true liturgy and Eucharist begin where philosophy begins, in amazement and gratitude, in praise for the sheer existence of so much beauty, so much actuality. Forests and mountains, deserts and stars, animals, plants and insects are here and gone in a day, and their existence is fraught with sorrow, but God made them. In our obscure desire to unite ourselves with the Giver, to find the source and thank him, somehow, for the community of being, we begin to recall the reason we were made, and to play our part in the redemption of the world.[78]

Caldecott says that "the heart and core of this cosmos-made Church is the Virgin Mary."[79] The discussion of the person as microcosm and mediator, helping to redeem, through the call to holiness, the creation waiting in eager longing for the revealing of the sons of men, is incomplete without Mary and her "yes" to God, and the "yes" we must all embrace in order to "play our part in the redemption of the world."[80] Caldecott quotes David L. Schindler approvingly in a passage he himself might have written:

> The whole world, in and through the church, is destined for a transfiguring espousal with Jesus Christ. . . . This marriage is understood in the radical and comprehensive sense as a Eucharistic exchange intended to leave not even the smallest particle of the cosmos unwed. The terms of the offer of marriage are established by Trinitarian and Christic love, and the marriage is made actual only through the Marian fiat.[81]

V. Conclusion

After all this one might ask, "Doesn't this just amount to a general enthusiasm? Where are the practical considerations?" Benedict XVI said, "The Church does not have technical solutions to offer" but rather is open to the

---

true transformation, of the true renewal of the world."

77. Caldecott, "At Home in the Cosmos"(2012), 107.

78. Ibid., 119–20.

79. Caldecott. "Cosmology," 313.

80. Caldecott, "At Home in the Cosmos," 120.

81. Schindler, *Heart of the World, Center of the Church*, 21–23, quoted in Caldecott, "The Marian Dimension of Existence."

truth found in any branch of knowledge, unifying its separate fragments, and mediating it "within the constantly changing life-patterns of the society of peoples and nations."[82] Caldecott has written about Third World debt and population growth, about industrial pollutants and genetic exploitation; turning to his writing on natural law, economics, distributism, and development, one can find a wealth of connections to day-to-day environmental issues which all could benefit from his insights: "I find that environmentalists are often acting on instinct," he says, "and tend to be unaware of the coherent philosophical support that they could find in Catholic social teaching, based on natural-law principles such as the common good, the equal dignity of all persons, solidarity, and subsidiarity."[83] Yet the point of this study is that his contribution is unique. It goes beyond policy specifics, beyond illuminating Catholic philosophy and social teaching, however brilliantly he does those things. In the end, it even goes beyond the rescue of the analogical, poetic, Christian, contemplative imagination to that which contemplation beholds and is enraptured by: not the ambiguous tension, *tonus*, of "ecotonality," but the *logos* of ecology named in the Gospel of John: Jesus Christ, the Word (*Logos*) of God.

For Dante, looking more deeply in the "single volume bound by love," the beatific vision resolves into the *imago Dei*, the face of Christ. For Caledcott as well, in the vision of "the Radiance of Being"[84] all things are sacramentally embraced into that Face: "To be created is to be made in the image of the Son. Even stones and stars, plants and animals, fungi and viruses are aspects and fragments of that image. . . . The *whole*, too, is an image: the cosmos is not merely an assembly of individuals but a unity that itself receives existence from God and reflects his beauty."[85]

---

82. Benedict XVI, *Caritas in Veritate*, 9. And see the International Theological Commission document titled "Communion and Stewardship," §78: "We must note that theology will not be able to provide us with a technical recipe for the resolution of the ecological crisis, but . . . it can help us to see our natural environment as God sees it, as the space of personal communion in which human beings, created in the image of God, must seek communion with one another and the final perfection of the visible universe."

83. Caldecott, "Session V."

84. This is the title of Caldecott's 2013 Angelico Press book. "Reality is dazzling, it is full of radiance, the radiance of beauty. And yet our capacity to respond . . . requires something of us. It requires us to resonate with that mystery, so that there is something in us that resembles it, something connatural with it. That capacity, that depth is opened within us by the experience of love, in the moment when we understand ourselves to possess a meaning and destiny of our own. Until that moment we have no way to connect with the beauty that we see" (Caldecott, "Creation and the University," 19).

85. Caldecott, "Creation as a Call to Holiness," 165.

This vision of the radiance of Being, of a cosmos "transfigured, eternalized, perfected *in its living integrity*, which includes all that is good in the creatures that currently adorn it,"[86] passing through the refining fire of Christ's death and resurrection, "marries" the most current ecological, cosmological, and theological thinking, and at the same time is a *ressourcement* of the ancient Christian view:

> They may not have had (or needed) the term "ecology," but the ancient writers were deeply aware of the interrelatedness of the natural world, and of man as the focus or nexus of that world. . . . [It is] a profound insight which remains valid, and the present ecological crisis could only have developed in a world that has forgotten it, or forgotten to live by it.[87]

Something Caldecott said of the great saint of ecology, Saint Francis, applies to him as well (though he would vigorously protest the comparison!). He said that Francis "is not the end-point, but rather a pointer, a signpost towards the great reconciliation of Christians in one and the same calling. That can only be achieved by the following of Christ in the flesh, through death to resurrection, bringing with us the whole of creation."[88] To borrow a phrase from one of Caldecott's favorite authors, Hans Urs von Balthasar, Caldcott's ecology is ecology "on one's knees," for

> the cosmos itself is not complete until the image of the Trinity is perfected in the world by the self-offering of creation to the Father, in the Son, through the Spirit, accomplished through man. The ultimate perfection of creation is achieved through Christ, microcosm and mediator, in whom alone, through the Church that is his extended Body, the universe as a whole is personalized. . . . Until it is subsumed into the love of God through being offered in the eternal sacrifice of the Son to the Father in the divine Liturgy, the cosmos can have only a shadowy existence. But within the Liturgy it is brought within the Trinity, where all of reality is eternally present in glory.[89]

86. Caldecott, *Catholic Social Teaching*, 47.
87. Caldecott, *Beauty for Truth's Sake*, 107.
88. Caldecott, "Creation and the University," 13.
89. Caldecott, "Creation as a Call to Holiness," 166–67.

10

Beyond the Binary Logic of Market-Plus-State

A Sane Social Order for the Global Liberal Age

David L. Schindler

In his discussion of the historical background to modern economics, twentieth-century English economist R. H. Tawney (d. 1962) says that medieval thinkers embraced two fundamental assumptions: "that economic interests are subordinate to the real business of life, which is salvation, and that economic conduct is one aspect of personal conduct, upon which, as on other parts of it, the rules of morality are binding."[1] The idea of founding

> a science of society upon the assumption that the appetite for economic gain is a constant and measurable force, to be accepted, like other natural forces, as an inevitable and self-evident *datum*, would have appeared to the medieval thinker as hardly less irrational or less immoral than to make the premise of social philosophy the unrestrained operation of such necessary human attributes as pugnacity or the sexual instinct.[2]

According to Tawney, some of his contemporaries think that the twentieth century, with "its attempts to fix fair wages and fair prices" and to establish various other controls, appears to have affinity with the medievals' rejection of "the uncharitable covetousness of the usurer and the engrosser" (speculator). Acknowledging some affinity, Tawney nevertheless says it is superficial. To claim significant similarity "is to do less than justice to precisely those elements in medieval thought which were most characteristic."[3] The significance of the medieval contribution, according

1. Tawney, *Religion and the Rise of Capitalism*, 31.
2. Ibid., 31–32.
3. Ibid., 61.

to Tawney, consists "not in its particular theories as to prices and interest, . . . but in its insistence that society is a spiritual organism, not an economic machine, and that economic activity, which is one subordinate element within a vast and complex unity, requires to be controlled . . . by reference to the moral ends for which it supplies the material means."[4] Indeed, for the medievals, a doctrine that takes economic interests to be "the servant, not the master, of civilization, may reasonably be regarded as among the . . . truisms which are a permanent element in any sane philosophy." Regarding the difference between premodern and modern economics, then, in sum, Tawney insists that it is scarcely "an unmixed gain to substitute [modernity's] criterion of economic expediency, so easily interpreted in terms of quantity and mass, for the conception of a rule of life superior to individual desires and temporary exigencies, which was what the medieval theorist meant by 'natural law.'"[5]

Of course, in rendering this summary judgment, Professor Tawney scarcely overlooks the fact that criticisms are warranted regarding medieval economic practices. Critics and eulogists are both right, he says.[6] It is important "to insist on the prevalence of avarice and greed in high places [in the Middle Ages]." Nevertheless, "it is not less important to observe that [the medievals] called these vices by their right names, and had not learned to persuade themselves that greed was enterprise and avarice economy."[7] Indeed, "whatever emphasis may be laid—and emphasis can hardly be too strong—upon the gulf between theory and practice [in the medieval period] . . . the endeavor to draw the most commonplace of human activities and the least tractable of human appetites within the all-embracing circle of a universal system still glows through it all with a certain tarnished splendor."[8] Regarding premodern in relation to modern economics, Tawney thus argues, in a word, that what is most significant are the premises upon which medieval theory is based, rather than "the specific contributions of medieval writers to the technique of economic theory."[9]

To prepare us for the following argument, it will be helpful to specify some of these premises. I will do so in terms of the Thomistic philosophical tradition, drawing on a little-known mid-twentieth-century book by George Speltz titled *The Importance of Rural Life according to the Philosophy*

4. Ibid.
5. Ibid., 62.
6. Ibid., 60.
7. Ibid., 61.
8. Ibid., 60.
9. Ibid., 31.

of St. Thomas Aquinas: A Study in Economic Philosophy.[10] Following the brief sketch of medieval theory, we will see, with the help of Stratford Caldecott, that the central premise of subordinating the political and economic to the natural and personal remains in play throughout the development of Catholic social doctrine and is itself developed in the anthropological view articulated in Benedict XVI's *Caritas in veritate.*[11] Looking critically at the binary model of market-plus-state that characterizes modern liberal society, my paper will propose this anthropological truth realized in the order of love as the "third" reality that will resolve the market-state dialectic.

I.

(1) According to Aquinas, the human being is a political and social animal ordered to cooperation with others for the attainment of the "good life." The good life involves acting in a virtuous manner and having a sufficiency of bodily goods. The end of virtuous living is final beatitude with God after death.[12] Aquinas thus—unlike the Stoics, for example—understands bodily goods as true goods because of his idea of the body-soul relation.[13] He distinguishes material goods in terms of those that are strictly needed for the health of the body (*bonum corporis*) and those that are not strictly needed and thus fall into the class of external goods (*bonum exterius*). Bodily goods are considered higher than external goods such as "riches" (*divitiae*) since the former are of their very nature limited, and essential for the practice of virtue.[14] Speltz writes,

10. Speltz, *The Importance of Rural Life according to the Philosophy of St. Thomas Aquinas.* Speltz became auxiliary bishop of Winona, Minnesota, in 1963 and attended the last three sessions of the Second Vatican Council. Paul VI appointed him bishop of St. Cloud in 1968, and he served as president of the National Catholic Rural Life Conference from 1970 to 1972. He was one of five bishops responsible for the background writing of the National Conference of Catholic Bishops' letter "Economic Justice for All: Pastoral Letter on Catholic Social Teaching and the U.S. Economy." See "Former Bishop George Speltz Leaves Behind Lengthy Legacy," *Saint Mary's Magazine*, Spring 2004, 39. I am indebted to James Stanley for this information.

11. Papal encyclicals will be cited throughout using the following abbreviations: Leo XIII, *Rerum Novarum* (1891) = RN; Pius XI, *Quadragesimo Anno* (1931) = QA; Paul VI, *Populorum Progressio* (1967) = PP, *Humanae Vitae* (1968) = HV; John Paul II, *Laborem Exercens* (1981) = LE, *Sollicitudo Rei Socialis* (1987) = SRS, *Centesimus Annus* (1991) = CA, *Evangelium Vitae* (1995) = EV; Benedict XVI, *Caritas in Veritate* (2009) = CV. The numbers in citations of these documents refer to paragraph numbers.

12. Speltz, *Importance of Rural Life*, 1 n. 1.

13. Ibid., 2.

14. Ibid., 4–5; cf. Aquinas, *Commentary on Aristotle's Politics*, 1.8 (hereafter cited

Since riches are sought for their power to procure other things rather than for the direct satisfaction of some bodily need, they easily come to be desired inordinately. Of those who are given to this inordinate desiring Aristotle writes that they, not knowing how to live well, think that enjoyments must be had in excess. For this they need an excess of riches.[15]

Such persons, for Aquinas, fail to realize that "riches are the least among human goods—less than the goods of the body, less than the goods of the soul, less than the divine good."[16]

(2) Because of this scale of values, Aquinas "gives an eminent place in the hierarchy of human activities to the life of the husbandman, whose work is ordered to the procuring of bodily goods for the immediate use of the household."[17] Accordingly, Aquinas also gives an eminent place to the agrarian way of life, while warning against the practice of trading. Traders, in other words, are more likely to fall into the practice of seeking to amass external goods, directing themselves "to the unnatural and limitless end of amassing money, ever more money."[18] Hence Aquinas says, "The perfect city will make a moderate use of merchants."[19]

(3) Speltz says that Aquinas's philosophy presupposes the centrality of the family as well as the then contemporary institutions such as the manor and the guild. *Oeconomica*, or household management, regulates affairs of the family in an orderly manner; bound up with *oeconomica* is "the natural wealth-getting of the husbandman which . . . belongs to household management."[20] The family "is a true cell of society,[21] a true regulator of production and consumption."[22] The manorial group, made up of member families, "provided a further check upon man's quest for external goods."[23]

as *In Polit.*).

15. Speltz, *Importance of Rural Life*, 5–6.

16. Aquinas, *In Polit.* 1.8, quoted in Speltz, *Importance of Rural Life*, 6.

17. Aquinas, *In Polit.* 1.8, quoted in Speltz, *Importance of Rural Life*, 6.

18. Speltz, *Importance of Rural Life*, 7.

19. *De regimine principium* 2.3 (hereafter cited in text as *De reg. princ.*), quoted in Speltz, *Importance of Rural Life*, 7.

20. Speltz, *Importance of Rural Life*, 9.

21. In ibid., 10 n. 30, Speltz gives a useful list of Thomistic references on this point: "Cf. *S.T.*, Ia–IIae, q. 104, art. 4, c; *In Polit.*, I, 2; *S.T.*, Ia–IIae, q. 90, art. 3, ad 3; IIa–IIae, q. 50, art. 3."

22. Speltz, *Importance of Rural Life*, 10. His footnote 31 is helpful with regard to this "production and consumption": "Cf. *In Polit.*, I, 8; *S.T.*, Ia–IIae, q. 20, art. 4, c."

23. Speltz, *Importance of Rural Life*, 10.

Its member families cooperated in the production and processing of natural wealth,[24] as also in the practice of the basic trades; for example, grazing land and equipment were used in common.[25] By reason of this functional organization a greater abundance and variety of goods was made available to the members of the manor. Yet such was the organization of the manor that this more extensive production and traffic in goods did not easily become inordinate. The production on the manor was directed to the needs of a particular manorial group, united by reason of community of place and function. For this reason it was naturally regulated by a limited end.

Aquinas approves of this organization because it "helped to maintain a true scale of values."[26]

(4) Further, it was important for Aquinas that the various social groups had a relative self-sufficiency. Human beings "must cooperate as a family group, as a village group, as a city group, and finally as a provincial group, if they are to attain the good life in full measure."[27] Though each of these groups had a relative self-sufficiency proper to itself, complete self-sufficiency presupposed an integration of all of them and thus was found only at the provincial level. Aquinas, then, emphasizes the perfection of self-sufficiency, but it is important to see that at each level the self-sufficiency already has community built into it. Speltz points out that "the rule of self-sufficiency is a rule of good order": each group is to perform the functions "for which nature has prepared it. It is part of good order that the smaller group should not be weakened by having its natural functions removed, and that the larger group should not be over-burdened by its taking over functions not proper to its wider and higher level of common enterprise."[28] Regarding private property, Speltz says that it is for Aquinas in accord with the natural law, but that it is nevertheless not a matter of absolute right: "Private property may not be separated from the social trust or moral stewardship which are bound up in the divine plan with it."[29]

---

24. For a discussion of the difference between natural and unnatural wealth-getting in the views of Thomas and Aristotle, see Speltz, *Importance of Rural Life*, 76–84, 171–72. Cf. also in this connection Speltz's comments on the importance of the growth of a money economy: 43, 126, 150, 167.

25. Speltz discusses the nature of this cooperation and the sense in which it was free in *Importance of Rural Life*, 32–49.

26. Ibid., 10.

27. Ibid., 11; Aquinas, *De reg. princ.* 1.1.

28. Speltz, *Importance of Rural Life*, 12–13.

29. Ibid., 14.

(5) Speltz emphasizes Aquinas's affirmation of the dignity of manual labor, citing Pius XI's *Quadragesimo anno* regarding labor in the modern factory: "Bodily labor, which was decreed by Providence for the good of man's body and soul . . . has everywhere been changed into an instrument of strange perversion: for dead matter leaves the factory ennobled and transformed, where men are corrupted and degraded."[30] Speltz says that it is easy to understand this judgment in Thomistic terms:

> According to a Thomistic principle of metaphysics and psychology when man acts, he acts as a person; such is the union of all his component parts and faculties under the rational soul. In all his acts, such as the act of one's hand in labor, the person acts; not merely the bodily member. Consequently, the manual labor of a man is more than the repeated physical movements of the members of his body. Manual labor is performed by the person who is endowed with intellect and will. Herein is its dignity. Granted a worthy end, [such labor] retains its dignity as long as it involves the functioning of the intellect and the will. It loses it when, like to the activity of the brute which is determined *ad unum*, it allows no opportunity for the intellect to point out possible variations in procedure or for the will to choose among these possibilities. The work of the husbandman is dignified if judged by these standards. Moreover it is noble in its purpose, namely, to provide for the necessities of life. St. Thomas calls the work of husbanding the fruits of nature "praiseworthy" [*In Polit.* 1.8]. The husbandman uses his rational faculties to direct the organic and non-organic forces of nature to the production of new things.[31]

For the foregoing reasons, Aquinas "may be said to favor the life of the people living on the land."[32]

(6) In the final chapter of his book, Speltz ponders the meaning of an agrarian policy consistent with Thomistic principles. To begin, he emphasizes with Pius XII that "the scope of every social life remains identical, sacred, and obligatory: it is the development of the personal values of man as the

30. Pius XI, *QA* 135, quoted in Speltz, *Importance of Rural Life*, 15–16.

31. Speltz, *Importance of Rural Life*, 16–17. Regarding the last sentence, see Aquinas, *Summa contra Gentiles* III, ch. 21 (hereafter cited as *Cont. Gent.*).

32. Speltz, *Importance of Rural Life*, 17. For a detailed discussion of the Thomistic understanding of domestic and occupational order, and the realization of this order in the agrarian practice of Aquinas's time, see ibid., ch. 4.

image of God."[33] The purpose of society, according to Saint Thomas, is to bring human beings "through virtuous living to the possession of God."[34] Among the moral virtues, the virtue of religion is thus preeminent.[35] Particularly suited to the acquisition of this virtue,

> the life of the husbandman is one of close cooperation with, and constant dependence upon, God. . . . It will be natural to the husbandman to recognize God as the Lord of all creation, and thence to bind himself to Him through the virtue of religion. . . . Not only is rural life of itself suitable to man's personal religious development, but the stability of rural institutions—the family and the community—that will come with a sound agrarian policy, will also favor the development of religious institutions and corporate worship.[36]

(7) Furthermore, the age of technical progress with its development of machines, while displacing persons from the land, has not fostered the increase in leisure it promised. Those displaced tend on the contrary to "become engaged mainly in manufacturing, in the service industries, and in clerical work."[37] The tendency is toward more production based on mechanical efficiency, in contrast to the tendency of a sound agrarian order toward the human values with which that order is intrinsically bound. Indeed, Speltz quotes Tawney's *The Acquisitive Society*: "All economic activity [tends to become] equally estimable, whether it is subordinated to a social purpose or not."[38] This is so, at root, because with increasing reliance on the machine and on the associated factory work, there comes a loss of leisure *in* work itself—the work that makes up the substance of a person's life. In this connection, Speltz takes note of the "poverty of spiritual values" that often exists in the modern "trend toward urbanization" attendant upon "scientific, mechanical, and industrial progress."[39]

In summarizing the Thomistic-era philosophy of the state and the domestic order, Speltz cites the words of Christopher Dawson: "The base of the social

33. Pius XII, "Christmas Message of 1942," quoted in Speltz, *Importance of Rural Life*, 132.

34. Speltz, *Importance of Rural Life*, 132; *De reg. princ.* 1.14.

35. Speltz, *Importance of Rural Life*, 132; cf. *ST* II–II, q. 81, a. 6, c.: "Religio praeeminet inter alias virtutes morales."

36. Speltz, *Importance of Rural Life*, 133.

37. Ibid., 136.

38. Tawney, *Acquisitive Society*, 33, quoted in Speltz, *Importance of Rural Life*, 136.

39. Speltz, *Importance of Rural Life*, 137–38.

edifice was constituted by the family as the primary social and economic unity. Beneath and upholding politics—the Law of the city—there was economics—the Law of the household."[40] It is this link between the law of the city and the law of the household, with the presupposition of the household's need for an appropriate amount of land, that Speltz most wishes to defend. He says that "rural life was . . . important in St. Thomas' philosophy because of its contribution to the good order of the economic, social, and political life of the State."[41] Speltz cites *QA*, which points with regret to the fact that this order is wanting today: "The highly developed social life which once flourished in a variety of prosperous institutions organically linked with each other, has been overthrown and all but ruined, leaving thus virtually only individuals and the State."[42] Speltz insists, then, that although there can be no question simply of rejecting the complexity of modern economic life with its vast technological developments, we must nevertheless work to restore the teleology indicative of medieval economics: "Unless teleological principles, operating through autonomous groups within the State, give order to our highly complicated economics, the State will find itself overburdened in trying to supply by legal control what is wanting in natural control."[43] Speltz concludes that the "philosophy of Aquinas, which is an agrarian-decentralist philosophy, is of a nature to rebuild these autonomous groups—the family on the land, the rural community and the city-country unit—and it is valid today."[44]

---

40. Dawson, *Judgment of the Nations*, 189, quoted in Speltz, *Importance of Rural Life*, 139. For a profound study of how the organic social-economic relations characteristic of ancient-premodern society were transformed by the "self-regulating market" mechanisms of modern liberalism, see Polanyi, *The Great Transformation*. Polanyi, one of the most significant social-economic theorists of the twentieth century, focuses above all on the notion of "embeddedness"—the idea that the economy is not autonomous and that market principles need to be subordinated to social relations, religion, and politics. Polanyi's own proposed solution, however, appeals in the end mostly to the state to perform the necessary limiting function vis-à-vis the market—that is, rather than to the religious and social-familial communities that would *limit* the market first through the interior habits of virtue and organic relations. It is the priority of these latter communities that I wish to argue is the key principle affirmed continuously, albeit with development, in Catholic social teaching.

41. Speltz, *Importance of Rural Life*, 172.

42. Pius XI, *QA* 78, quoted in Speltz, *Importance of Rural Life*, 172–73.

43. Speltz, *Importance of Rural Life*, 173.

44. Ibid., 178.

II.

Many readers will recognize the affinity of Speltz's and Tawney's principles with the Distributist or Personalist approach to economics espoused by G. K. Chesterton, Dorothy Day, and others in the early twentieth century, an approach taken up more recently by Stratford Caldecott in his reflections on the theological dimensions of Catholic social teaching. The present essay argues that the principles of economic theory adduced by Tawney and Speltz in the name of Aquinas and the medieval period, and indeed expressed in Distributism, are still valid. The principles continue to undergird the social-economic teaching of Paul VI, John Paul II, and Benedict XVI as developed in light of the Second Vatican Council. Key to this continuity is Benedict's rejection of the "binary logic of market-plus-state,"[45] which echoes Pius XI's rejection of a social order reduced to the power of individuals, on the one hand, and the state, on the other.

Caldecott draws out this continuity within development as ably as anyone in the English-speaking world. Thus, a look at Caldecott's writing on Distributism and its foundation in both the family and local, organic, and religious communities will help us relate the medieval premises outlined above to recent papal teaching considered in more detail. Caldecott's discussion of Distributism is central to his work and shows the breadth and depth of Distributist principles as carried forward in the recent teaching of John Paul II and Benedict XVI.[46] The key to Distributism, says Caldecott, lies in its conviction that the main ill besetting "advanced" industrial societies is "'the decay of personality. The remedy is the revival of personal property.'"[47] Hence Caldecott explains, "With Chesterton, [Belloc] believed that, prior to the Reformation and despite the defects of the feudal system, the English had lived in what was, in effect, a Distributist society. Through the enclosure of common land and the appropriation and exploitation of monastic property by the Tudors this society was destroyed, and the ground prepared for the development of modern capitalism during the Industrial Revolution." In a sense, one might say that Capitalism was built on, or at least presupposed, "the destruction of that particular synthesis of contemplation and action that lay at the heart of feudal civilization."[48] The Distributists affirmed "the medieval guild system as a way of regulating production and ensuring qual-

45. Benedict XVI, *CV* 39.

46. Caldecott, "Beyond Left and Right" (hereafter cited as "Beyond"); "Trinity and Society" (hereafter cited as "Trinity"); "To the Editor: On the Distribution of Property," (hereafter cited as "Distribution").

47. Gill, *Holy Tradition of Working*, 158, quoted in Caldecott, "Trinity."

48. Caldecott, "Trinity."

ity. . . . Although they were in favor of what is now called 'subsidiarity,' and against government interference wherever possible," they were not hesitant about

> appealing to the government for help in getting Distributism started, by encouraging education in handicrafts or farming, and the development of a less centralized market system for distributing produce. They advocated special legislation to shelter the small, and differential taxation to handicap the large. . . . Such measures might seem to work against freedom—but the Distributists argued that they were intended only to hamper the freedom of the few who wished to destroy the independence of the many.
>
> The widespread distribution of shares in big business enterprises . . . was regarded by the Distributists as a very imperfect way of realizing economic freedom, for the control exercised by a shareholder in a privatized industry is "distant, indirect and largely impersonal."[49]

In a word, Distributism "was imbued with a strong sense of the value of place, of environment, and of cultural diversity," and it placed a high premium on "personal loyalty, honesty, and family life." The key to what Distributism took to be a balanced economy was "the wide distribution of personal property throughout society."[50]

"In America, around the middle of [the twentieth] century," says Caldecott, "the Catholic Worker movement led by Dorothy Day and Peter Maurin (influenced by the distributists as well as by the French personalists)[51] developed from a very similar inspiration."[52] Caldecott cites Day: "We are

49. Ibid. Caldecott notes that elements of Chesterton's vision appear to reemerge in works like E. F. Schumacher's *Small is Beautiful* (1973) and Jane Jacobs' *Cities and the Wealth of Nations* (1984).

50. Caldecott, "Beyond," 381.

51. For a discussion of Emmanuel Mounier and Personalism and their influence on Dorothy Day and Peter Maurin, see Zwick and Zwick, *Catholic Worker Movement*, 97–115. See, for example, the discussion of Mounier's creative notion of private property (106); his idea of eternity as *beyond* time and not simply *after* time, thus underscoring the relevance of the beyond *in the here and now of history* (112); and his conviction that "modern Christianity is dangerously allied to capitalist and bourgeois Liberalism" (105). This book by the Zwicks, founders of Casa Juan Diego, the Houston Catholic Worker house, is an especially clear and profound study of the vision undergirding the work of Day and Maurin. See also Day, *On Pilgrimage*. Regarding Mounier, see, e.g., his *Personalist Manifesto*. Since the key principles of both Chesterton's Distributism and Mounier's Personalism were integrated in the vision of Day and Maurin, and indeed also, we may say, of Caldecott, I will sometimes use the term "Personalist-Distributism."

52. Caldecott, "Beyond," 381.

working for the Communitarian revolution to oppose both the rugged individualism of the capitalist era, and the collectivism of the Communist revolution."[53]

Caldecott acknowledges that "there is much about distributism and personalism that appears to be outdated."[54] Indeed, he even suggests that "we may wish to avoid the term 'Distributism,'" and also that of the "'third way,' with all its complicated associations."[55] Nonetheless, he insists that "some revised and updated form of these is emerging as the new political 'paradigm in waiting.'"[56] Many people today "appeal to sustainability and diversity, reciprocity and responsibility, solidarity and subsidiarity; but these ideals cohere only within a religious understanding of human persons, and arguably within a trinitarian understanding."[57]

The key to the new paradigm, then, lies in an adequate anthropology. This anthropology, which alone can sustain any new political paradigm, can

53. Ibid. As Chesterton puts it in the opening paragraph of *The Outline of Sanity*, which contains the essential principles of Distributism: "A pickpocket is obviously a champion of private enterprise. But it would perhaps be an exaggeration to say that a pickpocket is a champion of private property. The point about Capitalism and Commercialism . . . is that they have really preached the extension of business rather than the preservation of belongings; and have at best tried to disguise the pickpocket with some of the virtues of the pirate. The point about Communism is that it only reforms the pickpocket by forbidding pockets" (25). Twentieth-century Colombian scholar Nicolás Gómez Dávila expresses the matter in a similar vein: "In one system the legal ownership of the means of production lies with an individual, whereas it lies with a collective in the other, but this is a specific difference that does not alter the generic identity between them. . . . The point is precisely that communism and capitalism transform the human spirit in one and the same direction. . . . True, capitalism engenders an industrial, urban, and herd-like civilization; it produces a type of man who is separated from the essential routine of things, incapable of experiencing his work as a possibility of perfection and a requirement of reason, totally addicted to the desire for his own convenience, always eager to interpret things in their worst light in order to avoid the discomfort of yearning to imitate a nobility he cannot bear the idea of meeting, and, finally, surrendered to the mercy of all the demons inhabiting the collective spirit. Nevertheless, the obsolete rhetoric of communism—which gulls minds capable of distrusting bourgeois propaganda—cannot hide from us the terrible fact that one abominable universe is going to be replaced by the same abominable universe. *Ce mort saisit ce vif.* . . . What difference does it make who is going to own the factory if the factory is going to remain open?" (*Notas*, 62–63).

54. Caldecott, "Beyond," 381.

55. Caldecott, "A Distributist Manifesto?" para. 9.

56. Caldecott, "Beyond," 381. Regarding the often repeated charge that Distributism is dead, we recall the famous statement of Day: "The very fact that people are always burying distributism is evidence of the fact that it is not dead as a solution. . . . It is an issue that won't be buried, because distributism is a system conformable to the need of man and his nature" (cited in Zwick and Zwick, *Catholic Worker Movement*, 173).

57. Caldecott, "Beyond," 381.

be found in the principles of Distributism and Personalism. Caldecott explains: "The legislation that defines a market is always governed by many assumptions about human beings and society. Those that govern our present world economic system were largely formed during the Reformation, the Enlightenment and the Industrial Revolution."[58] Hence, the market created by liberalism is scarcely "neutral." It needs to be examined both philosophically and theologically. For Chesterton, "the 'coming peril' opposed by Distributism was something 'vast and vague,' 'something of which capitalism and collectivism are only economic by-products.' It was that spirit which refuses recognition and respect to the Creator and to the natural boundaries of created being, the spirit that has no gratitude, or ability to pray. This is the spirit that does not *receive* the world—and its own existence—as a gift, but wants merely to *take*."[59] Our liberal culture has "placed [*formless*] freedom *rather than love* in the supreme position, and the logic of this choice will, in time, affect everything."[60] "The point of speaking . . . about a *civilization of love* or a *culture of life* is simply this: if we wish to preserve our freedom, we must subordinate freedom to love."[61] In response to these problems, Caldecott insists, in light of the principles of Distributism—as indeed these principles are reflected and developed in recent papal teaching—that we must hold up "an alternative way of life" to liberal society, and seek to encode the "alternative spiritual logic" embodied in this life.[62] With John Paul II, he insists that "a family policy must be the basis and driving force of all social policies." We must "rethink labor, urban, residential, and social service policies" to foster the integrity of family life and the defense of life.[63]

In a 1990 article recalling the principles of Distributism, Caldecott elaborates on the distribution of property and the importance of the family.[64] Regarding the right to private property, Caldecott cites Leo XIII's *Rerum Novarum* (1891):

> The fact that God gave the whole human race the earth to use and enjoy cannot . . . serve as an objection against private possessions. For God is said to have given the earth to mankind in common, not because he intended indiscriminate ownership of

58. Ibid., 383.

59. Ibid., 384.

60. Ibid., 385.

61. Ibid., 385–86.

62. Ibid., 386.

63. John Paul II, *EV* 90, quoted in Caldecott, "Beyond," 387.

64. Caldecott, "Distribution" (see n. 16). Caldecott wrote this short "letter" after John Paul II's *Sollicitudo rei socialis* but before *Centesimus annus*.

it by all, but because he assigned no part to anyone in ownership, leaving the limits of private possessions to be fixed by the
industry of men and the institutions of peoples.[65]

Leo quotes Saint Thomas: "Man ought not regard external goods as
his own, but as common so that, in fact, a person should readily share them
when he sees others in need."[66] Finally, "John Paul II synthesizes this tradition in *Laborem Exercens* (1981) with his statement that 'the right to private
property is subordinated to the right to common use.'"[67] Noting a development in Catholic social teaching since *Rerum Novarum*, Caldecott asks
what clues we can find regarding this teaching's future direction. Given the
collapse of Communism, he says, attention has shifted to questions regarding the various forms of Capitalism. "What will be the Church's attitude to
the free market?"[68] He writes further, "In *Sollicitudo rei socialis* [1987], John
Paul II . . . emphasize[s] that 'the Church's social doctrine *is not* a "third
way" between *liberal capitalism* and *Marxist collectivism*,' because it exists
not on the level of ideology but rather of . . . theology."[69] Nevertheless, according to Caldecott, the encyclical's claim that "'the goods of this world
are *originally meant for all*' must have profound implications for the way we
structure our societies."[70] This claim is not a matter merely of eschatology,
as though any reference to a common use of goods had relevance only for
the next life. Such an interpretation, says Caldecott, overlooks the "tenor of
papal teaching on the virtue of 'solidarity.'"[71]

65. Leo XIII, *RN* 8, quoted in Caldecott, "Distribution," 628.

66. Leo XIII, *RN* 36, quoted in Caldecott, "Distribution," 628.

67. Caldecott, "Distribution," 628; John Paul II, *LE* 14.

68. Caldecott, "Distribution," 629.

69. Ibid.; *SRS* 41; cf. *CA* 56. Pertinent to the question of whether a "third way" is or
is not permitted or fostered in recent papal social teaching, Caldecott cites in his "Love
in Truth" (see n. 33) the following texts from John Paul II:

> The Church has no models to present; models that are real and effective can
> only arise within the framework of different historical situations, through
> the efforts of all those who responsibly confront concrete problems in all
> their social, political and cultural aspects, as these interact with each other.
> For such a task the Church offers her social teaching as an indispensable and
> ideal orientation . . . towards the common good. (*CA* 43)

> Since it is not an ideology, the Christian faith does not presume to imprison
> changing socio-political realities in a rigid schema, and it recognizes that
> human life is realized in history in conditions that are diverse and imperfect.
> (*CA* 46)

70. Caldecott, "Distribution," 629; John Paul II, *SRS* 42.

71. Caldecott, "Distribution," 629.

Caldecott then sketches an argument of his own that recalls Distributist principles. The argument begins with the notions of love and gift indicated in the gospel and expressed in the Trinitarian reality of God. Because the Trinity itself in a sense "is a society," "one could say . . . that social doctrine belongs at the very center of theology."[72] Now, "the closest analogy [in nature and] on earth to this loving exchange [among the Persons of the Trinity] is found in marriage."[73]

> The community of marriage becomes the foundation of human society in general. Re-reading Genesis with the help of *Laborem Exercens*, we can discern the reasons for giving such weight to the family in Catholic social teaching. Nature is entrusted to humanity as a whole, summed up in the first human couple. As humanity multiplies, the land passes into individual hands, but always by way of the family, and always under God. God gives the land to his people in a series of covenants. . . . The Covenant always involves a mutual giving of self to create a new community (or renew an old one).[74]

Caldecott concludes, "The vow by which the spouses give themselves to each other under God is what constitutes them as a community, and it gives them the right to own property sufficient to sustain themselves and their children."[75]

Here, Caldecott makes the explicit transition to Distributism. "The covenant of marriage gives a *family* the right to what the Distributists called a smallholding. Defined as that minimum property (of whatever kind) on which a family can sustain itself, the smallholding is to the family what the common earth is to humanity." Recognizing such a right, emphasizes Caldecott, "would change the nature of our society." To grant property to families as such instead of to the individual person "would be an admission that human beings are persons whose very existence is relational."[76] Elsewhere, Caldecott indicates what he takes to be five main points of John Paul II regarding the family's role in building the culture of life that is at the heart of any adequate social order.[77]

72. Ibid.

73. Ibid.

74. Ibid., 629–30.

75. Ibid.

76. Ibid., 630.

77. Caldecott, "Family at the Heart of a Culture of Life" (hereafter cited as "Family").

First, the family is a "sanctuary of life," "the place where human life may be most easily understood as *gift*," not made but given.[78] Caldecott cites Chesterton's famous passage in *Heretics*: "The supreme adventure is being born. . . . Our father and mother . . . lie in wait for us and leap out on us, like brigands from a bush. Our uncle is a surprise. Our aunt is, in the beautiful common expression, a bolt from the blue. When we step into the family, by the act of being born, we . . . step into a world which is incalculable, into a world that we have not made."[79] "To respect life as *given*," says Caldecott, is to relinquish "the desire to manipulate others for our own ends"; it is "to respect [life's] mystery, and the mystery of otherness and freedom."[80]

The second crucial role of the family lies in the field of *education*. "Through education, culture—whether it be a culture of life or a culture of death—is passed on, transmitted and developed. The family gives birth to culture."[81]

Third, being born into a family involves being born into a *society*, and this lays "the foundations for social activity in general." The sacramental form of the family "as a covenant of self-giving love can and should influence the entire political and economic sphere in which it is embedded," showing the need, for example, for what the church terms a "politics of solidarity," or again an "economy of communion."[82] Caldecott reminds us here of John Paul II's statement that "*through the family passes the primary current of the civilization of love*, which finds therein its 'social foundations.'"[83]

Fourth, the "family is a place where the force of *eros* can be . . . transformed with the help of grace, and directed to the service of life rather than death." Caldecott states, "It is an empirical fact that such a process of transformation does take place in the most seemingly ordinary of households—albeit often through the experience of great suffering."[84]

Finally, "a Christian family exists to give birth to Christ—to give birth to saints." "It is saints alone who can truly transform society and create a 'civilization of love.' This indispensable role of the family . . . depends on *prayer*."[85]

78. Ibid., 96.

79. Chesterton, *Heretics*, cited in Caldecott, "Family," 96.

80. Caldecott, "Family," 96.

81. Ibid., 97.

82. Ibid., 97–98.

83. John Paul II, *Letter to Families* 15, quoted in Caldecott, "Family," 98.

84. Caldecott, "Family," 98–99.

85. Ibid., 99.

Received as gift and realized in prayer, the root of human relationship lies in our dependence on our Creator, and its structure is ultimately given in the divine Trinity itself, whose image human beings reflect. The market economy for this reason, Caldecott says, must be compelled to take into account the rights of families—especially poor families—to property in accord with these principles.[86]

III.

Caldecott's understanding of the family's role at the base of a Distributist vision of the social-economic order allows us to relate the medieval premises discussed above, by way of a consistent anthropology, to the recent social-economic teaching of the church. I begin consideration of this recent teaching by recalling *Quadregesimo Anno*'s judgment regarding the reduction of the social-economic order of the time to an order constituted by individuals, on the one hand, and the state, on the other. Pius XI attributes this reduction to the loss of intermediate, organically structured institutions. His judgment is echoed in what Benedict XVI terms the binary logic of market-plus-state. *Caritas in Veritate* notes John Paul II's reference in *Centesimus Annus* (1991) to "the need for a system with three subjects: the *market*, the *State*, and *civil society*."[87] "The economy in the global era," says Benedict, "seems to privilege the . . . logic . . . of contractual exchange, but directly or indirectly it also demonstrates its need for the other two: political logic, and the logic of the unconditional gift."[88] John Paul II, according to Benedict, "saw civil society as the most natural setting for an *economy of gratuitousness* and fraternity, but *did not mean to deny it a place in the other two settings*."[89] If the market and the State "each . . . exercise a monopoly over its respective area of influence . . . much is lost: solidarity in relations between citizens, participation and adherence, actions of gratuitousness, all of which stand in contrast with *giving for the sake of having or possessing* [*dare ad habendum*] (the logic of exchange) and *giving out of a sense of duty* [*dare ex officio*] (the logic of public obligation, imposed by State law)."[90] *Caritas in Veritate* thus

---

86. Cf. ibid., 98. For a profound reflection on the centrality of the family in the life of culture—regarding one's sense of the body, of place, of holiness or reverence for life and for death, of habitation, of time and eternity, of craftsmanship, of gratitude, of creative fidelity and hope, and of the threat to these brought about by the industrial revolution, see Marcel, "The Mystery of the Family."

87. Benedict XVI, *CV* 38; cf. John Paul II, *CA* 49.

88. Benedict XVI, *CV* 37.

89. Ibid., 38; emphasis added.

90. Ibid., 39. I have slightly modified the Vatican's English translation of *Caritas in*

says that "the exclusively binary model of market-plus-State is corrosive of society."[91] Again, the "hegemony of the binary model of market-plus-State has accustomed us to think only in terms of the private business leader of a capitalistic bent on the one hand, and the State administrator [*procuratore*] on the other."[92] In reality, business has to be understood in a more comprehensive way that involves thinking of a "meta-economic kind." "Business activity has a human significance," which is "prior to its professional one" and "present in all work, understood as a personal action, an '*actus personae*.'"[93] *Caritas in Veritate*'s point here recalls Paul VI's judgment in *Populorum Progressio* (1967) that the church's social doctrine aims at integral human development. This judgment implies two truths: "that *the whole Church, in all her being and acting—when she proclaims, when she celebrates, when she performs works of charity—is engaged in promoting integral human development*," and "that *authentic human development concerns the whole of the person in every single dimension*."[94] For the church, the social question is thus a "radically anthropological question."[95]

In a more practical vein, according to Caldecott, Benedict "advocates sustainable and holistic development that takes account of all the dimensions of the human person and remains open to the transcendent. In chapter 4 [of *Caritas in Veritate*] he examines several threats to the integrity of human development": "the proliferation of rights detached from duties," due to the abstraction of rights from their rootedness "in the nature and authentic needs of the person"; the "impoverishment of sexuality and the imposition of materialistic ideas and policies with regard to the family"; "the excessive centralization of certain development programs, which take little account of the need for subsidiary and effective local management"; and the need to take account of "the enormous range of duties that arise from our relationship to the environment" that are "bound up with our relationship to the poor and toward future generations." These duties derive from recognition that "nature is a gift of the Creator containing an inbuilt order." This order demands respect also "for human life, sexuality, and the family—'the book of nature is one and indivisible.'"[96]

Veritate here and elsewhere in my citations.

91. Ibid.
92. Ibid., 41.
93. Ibid.
94. Ibid., 11.
95. Ibid., 75.
96. Caldecott, "*Caritas in veritate* and 'Integral Human Development,'" 183; *CV*, 51.

Regarding globalization in this light, then, *Caritas in Veritate* insists that we need "to *promote a person-based and community-oriented cultural process of world-wide integration that is open to transcendence.*" Only in this way will it be possible "to *steer the globalization of humanity in relational terms, in terms of communion and the sharing of goods.*"[97]

Now, the free-market critics of *Caritas in Veritate* themselves insist on the central importance of the institutions of society for securing the proper functioning of the political and economic orders. Indeed, one of these critics, Michael Novak, is often (not wrongly) associated with what *Centesimus Annus* highlights as the need for three subjects within the social system of a country—that is, not just state and market, but also civil society. However, interpretations of *Centesimus Annus* have differed precisely over *the sense in which* the logic proper to civil society—to familial, religious, and local-intermediate institutions—is to be understood *in relation to* the logic of the economy and the state. The problem concerns whether economic conduct *as such* is understood to be *bound from within* to the rules and virtues of morality—that is, to the teleological end of the human being. The problem concerns how economic interests are embedded in social relations characteristic of household, religion, and local-organic institutions. *Caritas in Veritate* recalls John Paul II's insistence in *Centesimus Annus* that, following deep changes in former Soviet bloc countries, we need "a comprehensive new plan for development, not only in those countries, but also in the West and in those parts of the world that [are] in the process of evolving." *Caritas in Veritate* states that this development "has been achieved only in part, and it is still a real duty that needs to be discharged."[98] The encyclical makes clear what this implies: we must understand "not only that traditional principles of social ethics like transparency, honesty and responsibility cannot be ignored or attenuated, but also that in *commercial relationships* the *principle of gratuitousness* and the logic of gift as an expression of fraternity can and must *find their place within normal economic activity.*"[99]

Benedict argues that it is just this integration of the logic of gift into the logic of the economy and indeed also of the state that lies at the heart of the development called for in *Centesimus Annus. Caritas in Veritate*, in other words, means precisely to correct the interpretation of *Centesimus Annus* that would fail to subordinate the profit seeking of business-economic activity to the end of the human person as such. Such subordination, which would affect from within the ordering of business activity, is

---

97. Benedict XVI, *CV* 42.

98. Ibid., 23.

99. Ibid., 36.

entailed by *Centesimus Annus*' call for an "authentic theology of integral human liberation."[100] "Economic life must be understood as a multi-layered phenomenon: in every one of these layers, to varying degrees and in ways specifically suited to each, the aspect of fraternal reciprocity must be present. In the global era, economic activity cannot prescind from gratuitousness, which fosters and disseminates solidarity and responsibility for justice and the common good among the different economic players."[101] Further, "solidarity is first and foremost a sense of responsibility on the part of everyone with regard to everyone, and it cannot therefore be merely delegated to the State. While in the past it was possible to argue that justice had to come first and gratuitousness could follow afterwards, as a complement, today it is clear that without gratuitousness, there can be no justice in the first place."[102]

By emphasizing *Centesimus Annus*' rejection of a binary free-market-plus-state logic, *Caritas in Veritate* recalls the issues raised by Tawney and Speltz. Benedict's encyclical thereby, *eo ipso*, forces the question of an alternative logic, and thus of what is often called a "third way." As indicated above, controversy continues regarding this supposed "third way" beyond the alternatives of capitalist economics and state-socialist politics.[103] The Distributists believe that such a "third way" is indeed problematic if conceived simply as another economic system. The problem is avoided, however, if, in seeking to go beyond the binary logic of market-plus-state, and thus to transcend the conventional alternatives of market freedom (capitalism) and state power (socialism), we mean merely to insist that the logic of the

100. John Paul II, *CA* 26; see also Caldecott, "Theological Dimensions of Human Liberation," and Congregation for the Doctrine of the Faith (CDF), *Instruction on Christian Freedom and Liberation*. This "new" theology of liberation, says Caldecott, demands a proper notion of freedom. For John Paul II, such a notion of freedom is linked with the renewal of Mariology that his pontificate emphasized. Jesus is the source of human freedom, but Mary at his side "is the most perfect image of freedom and of the liberation of humanity and of the universe" (CDF, *Christian Freedom*, 97, cited in Caldecott, "Human Liberation," 227–28, and in John Paul II, *Redemptoris Mater*, 37). Key for an authentic theology of liberation, furthermore, is the notion of freedom as liberation from sin. It is only when this is seen that we are able rightly to understand poverty, such that we can "see through the veneer of economic prosperity to the spiritual poverty within, the profound alienation of those who sell their labor as a commodity, and of those ensnared in the web of false needs created by consumerism" ("Human Liberation," 227; cf. *CA* 41).

101. Benedict XVI, *CV* 38.

102. Ibid.

103. See, for example, George Weigel's criticism of *Caritas in Veritate*, wherein he suggests that, while *Centesimus Annus* had "jettisoned the idea of a 'Catholic third way,'" Benedict's encyclical now apparently pulls back from this rejection. Weigel, "*Caritas in Veritate* in Gold and Red." All subsequent references to Weigel are taken from this article.

market and the state must be integrated into, hence informed by, an *anthropological logic* adequate to the human person. Benedict reminds us that

> fidelity to man requires *fidelity to the truth*, which alone is the *guarantee of freedom* (cf. Jn 8:32) and of *the possibility of integral human development* [*humanum omnibus ex partibus progressum praestare potest*]. . . . This mission of truth is something that the Church can never renounce. Her social doctrine is a particular dimension of this proclamation: it is a service to the truth which sets us free.[104]

In connection with the church's mission of mediating truth "within the . . . life-patterns of . . . society," Benedict states further that Paul VI's encyclical *Humanae Vitae* (1968) and his apostolic exhortation *Evangelii Nuntiandi* (1976) are "highly important for delineating the *fully human meaning of the development that the Church proposes.*"[105] Benedict then elaborates:

> The Encyclical *Humanae Vitae* emphasizes both the unitive and the procreative meaning of sexuality, thereby locating at the foundation of society the married couple, man and woman. . . . This is not a question of purely individual morality: *Humanae Vitae* indicates the *strong links between life ethics and social ethics,* ushering in a new area of magisterial teaching that has gradually been articulated (*auctum*) in a series of documents, most recently John Paul II's Encyclical *Evangelium Vitae*. The Church forcefully [*fermiter*] maintains this link between life ethics and social ethics.[106]

Citing *Evangelii Nuntiandi*, Benedict recalls that

> "between evangelization and human advancement—development and liberation—there are in fact profound links"[107]: on the basis of this insight, Paul VI clearly presented the relationship between the proclamation of Christ and the advancement of the individual in society. *Testimony to Christ's charity, through works of justice, peace and development, is part and parcel of evangelization,* because Jesus Christ, who loves us, is concerned with the whole person.[108]

---

104. Benedict XVI, *CV* 9.
105. Ibid., 15.
106. Ibid.
107. Paul VI, *Evangelii Nuntiandi* 31.
108. Benedict XVI, *CV* 15.

Further, Benedict takes up this emphasis on the whole person in connection with the Christian vocation to true development:

> *The Gospel is fundamental for development*, because in the Gospel, Christ, "in the very revelation of the mystery of the Father and of his love, fully reveals humanity to itself."[109] Taught by her Lord, the Church examines the signs of the times and interprets them, offering the world "what she possesses as her characteristic attribute: a global vision of man and of the human race". . . . The truth of development consists in its completeness: if it does not involve the whole man and every man, it is not true development. This is the central message of *Populorum Progressio*, valid for today and for all time. Integral human development on the natural plane, as a response to a vocation from God the Creator, demands self-fulfillment in a "transcendent humanism which gives [to man] his greatest possible perfection: this is the highest goal of personal development."[110] The Christian vocation to this development therefore applies to both the natural plane and the supernatural plane; which is why, "when God is eclipsed, our ability to recognize the natural order, purpose and the 'good' begins to wane."[111]

It is in light of *Caritas in Veritate*, including its interpretation of Paul VI and John Paul II, that we see the "third reality" meant properly to inform integral human development: the *anthropological reality* expressed in the truth of the human person as constituted relationally, or within community.[112] This original communal reality can be summed up in several principles. (1) The person discovers himself most basically in relation to God the Creator, and it is this fact of creation that establishes *Caritas in Veritate*'s central category of *gift*. (2) The Creator gives the gift of creation through the "primary vital cell" of human community, which is the "family founded on marriage between a man and a woman."[113] The human being, in other words, is a *being-with*, first in this spousal sense. (3) Furthermore, the marital unity between a man and a woman involves bodily union between them coincident with the soul-body unity of each, and thus intrinsic openness to life. (4) Finally, in light of the radicality of the relation originating in God as Creator, we see that cosmic community includes not only all hu-

109. *Gaudium et Spes* 22.

110. Paul VI, *PP* 14, 16.

111. Benedict XVI, *Address to Young People at Bangaroo*, July 17, 2008; cf. *CV* 18.

112. See Caldecott, "Caritas." For an outline of *Caritas in Veritate*'s teaching, see Caldecott, "Love in Truth."

113. Benedict XVI, *CV* 44.

man beings (though especially and most properly these), but also all the physical-biological beings that make up the natural environment. Benedict states in this connection that "*nature expresses a design of love and truth. . . .* [It] speaks to us of the Creator (cf. Rom. 1:20) and his love for humanity. It is destined to be 'recapitulated' in Christ at the end of time (cf. Eph. 1:9–10; Col. 1:19–20). Thus it too is a 'vocation.'" Nature is given to us "as a gift of the Creator who has given it an inbuilt order, enabling man to draw from it the principles needed in order 'to till and keep it' (Gen. 2:15)."[114]

The integral human development called for in Catholic social teaching thus includes the promotion of community in an all-embracing sense. But this catholic sense of community bears a definite order. The order begins and ends with God; it is centered especially in human persons, and then in natural-cosmic entities, all of these understood most basically as *creatures*, hence as *gifts of the Creator*. The family is the primary mediator of God's gift of creation and is characterized by an openness to the co-creation of new life that is inseparable from care for the gift of nature.

Community in the sense indicated here of course opens to a vast number of different and ever-larger communities and social institutions—up to the state rightly understood as a "community of communities."[115] It is crucial to keep in mind, however, that the integrity of all worldly communities presupposes and depends on the order first given in creation. Therefore communities or institutions characterized most obviously by voluntary (i.e., "fraternal") reciprocity are understood properly only as ordered in light of that community defined most basically by relation to God through a life-giving spousal union of man and woman. As we have seen, the integral human development that is the end of Catholic social doctrine "concerns the whole of the person in every single dimension."[116] "If it does not involve the whole man and every man, it is not true development."[117] The point, then, is that this true human development is fully realized only insofar as it passes through and is formed by community with God mediated by the family that is lived with integrity—lived with the whole of one's self in relation to the whole of God in service to the whole of other persons, in a way that is respectful of the whole truth, goodness, and beauty of every cosmic entity.

Caldecott's comments on technology in connection with the church's social teaching bring into relief the fragmentation of this wholeness in

114. Ibid., 48.

115. Dorothy Day, citing Martin Buber; see Zwick and Zwick, *Catholic Worker Movement*, 173.

116. Benedict XVI, *CV* 11.

117. Ibid., 18.

community wrought by the logic of modernity. In contrast to the medieval agrarian social structure, a technological society "will require of Catholics a more radical (and dangerous) stance than the one they have generally taken so far."[118] Reflection on what may be called the historical periods of "'modernity' and 'postmodernity,'" says Caldecott, shows "the need for a more profound cultural critique to be incorporated into the social teaching of the Church."[119] Though indicating a significant shift from modernity, postmodernity remains in essence "a continuation and intensification of the 'logic' of modernity."[120]

At the time of *Rerum Novarum*, which may be recognized as the church's first formal expression of a social doctrine, the church could presuppose a different cultural framework: "a community still to some extent rooted through an agricultural economy in the natural environment, and a common belief in the dignity of human nature, the same in all human beings."[121] That is, the vestiges of premodern civilization enabled her "to appeal to the natural moral law and attack specific injustices." Now that the logic of modernity has finally eroded even these vestiges, however, the church has "to give a whole new religious inspiration to the culture." This, says Caldecott, explains "why Pope John Paul II made the 'new evangelization' the theme of his pontificate, and why his social encyclicals have to be read . . . as a part of a wider cultural critique"[122]—hence, for example, his encyclicals *Veritatis Splendor*, *Evangelium Vitae*, and *Fides et Ratio*. Caldecott sums up:

> Whereas the target of *Rerum Novarum* had to be the injustices brought about by industrial capitalism (and the socialist reaction to capitalism by then taking shape), the target of the new cultural critique must be—in addition to these specific injustices—something much more subtle and pervasive: our consumerist, technologically driven way of life, the logic that expresses itself in this way of life, and the spiritual disorder that lies behind it.[123]

What we need, then, is to understand properly the logic of modernity that has radicalized in the last century. Caldecott emphasizes that "the lifestyle of the affluent West" still generates "specific inequalities of wealth

118. Caldecott, "New Sins," 489.

119. Ibid.

120. Ibid., 491.

121. Ibid., 493.

122. Ibid.

123. Ibid.

and patterns of exploitation across the planet," and these "need to be de-
nounced and opposed, just as before."[124] The "'lifestyle' of postmodernity,
however, has lifted a mask and revealed the 'death of God' and the reduction
of knowledge to power that lies at the core of the modern project. . . . In
the medieval civilization (for all its faults) work, art, study, and political
life were all perceived as belonging to a religiously based . . . order" and
consequently were "oriented towards the divine, even if society was divided
as to how this orientation was to be expressed."[125] In modernity, on the contrary, such orientation is no longer acknowledged in a public way, or, if it
is, then only in a "purely conventional" way, "emptied of real content." The
injustice of modernity, Caldecott insists, is "against not only the image of
God in man but God himself." In asserting this, Caldecott insists that he is
not making "a plea for a return to an older sacral society"; medieval society
was itself marked "by deep flaws and problems of its own." The point, rather,
is that in the contemporary situation, the victim of injustice has become the
very "sense of the integrity of the world as a gift of God formed by divine
wisdom."[126]

　　Caldecott's claim certainly seems radical. But that is just the point:
social development and human liberation, rightly understood in terms of
Catholic teaching, cannot prescind from the gratuitousness that takes its
first form within community in the original and radical sense indicated
above. *Caritas in Veritate* insists, *"Everything has its origin in God's love,
everything is shaped by it, everything is directed towards it."*[127] This love,
which is the principle of the micro-relationships of family, friends, and
small groups, is meant to be the principle also of the macro-relationships
proper to the social, economic, and political order. Authentic interpreters of
Catholic social thought will recognize that the economy and the state cannot avoid responsibility for protecting and supporting the communities that
provide the first home for this love. This is the burden of the call to sanctity
that comprehends *"Caritas in veritate in re sociali*: the proclamation of the
truth of Christ's love in society."[128]

---

124. Ibid.
125. Ibid.
126. Ibid., 494.
127. Benedict XVI, *CV* 2.
128. Ibid., 5.

IV.

The critics of *Caritas in Veritate* on both the right and the left, in the name respectively of the market and the state, overlook or explicitly resist the need for just this integrated logic of love that is demanded by the Christian vocation to development.[129] With this logic in mind, we now return to the question indicated in the title of the present essay and raised by *Caritas in Veritate*: how do we overcome the "hegemony of the binary model of market-plus-State"?[130] Responding to this concern, Benedict puts forward the principle of "gratuitousness" and "reciprocal gift."[131] Centering his response in the love revealed by God in Jesus Christ, and thus linking his argument with the theology of the Trinity, the pope calls for "*a deeper critical evaluation of the category of relation.*"[132] *Caritas in Veritate* thus looks to the deepest roots of an authentic Christian anthropology in its effort to show a direction beyond the market-plus-state logic that currently dominates global society. We have seen Caldecott's development of Benedict's anthropology of love, which presupposes and unfolds into a distinctive sense of human *community*. The significance of this development comes into especially sharp relief when placed in the light of the dominant alternative views on the Catholic right and the Catholic left regarding the church's social doctrine. I conclude by discussing examples of these alternative views.

First, from the right, there is the American Catholic writer George Weigel, who finds *Caritas in Veritate* "simply incomprehensible" when it calls for an "openness, in a world context, to forms of economic activity marked by quotas of gratuitousness and communion." Weigel criticizes the fact that the encyclical seems to be more "about the redistribution of wealth than about wealth-creation." He likewise criticizes the encyclical's call for the creation of a "'world political authority'" to ensure integral human development. Weigel says that these features of the encyclical may be due to the cardinals and others working at the Pontifical Council for Justice and Peace instead of to Benedict himself. He suggests that readers may therefore want to mark out in red and gold the passages of the encyclical that indicate the editorial hand respectively of the cardinals and the pope, and he presumably means thereby to recommend acceptance of the authoritative teaching of *Caritas in Veritate* on the basis of this proposed redaction. Finally, directly pertinent to our question, Weigel suggests that, while *Centesimus Annus*

129. For a discussion of these critics, see my "Anthropological Vision of *Caritas in veritate*," especially 431–41.

130. Benedict XVI, *CV* 41; see also 38, 39.

131. Ibid., 39.

132. Ibid., 53.

had "jettisoned the idea of a 'Catholic third way,'" Benedict's encyclical apparently is open to this idea. Indeed, Weigel asks in sum whether there are now two social-doctrine traditions, one reaching from Leo XIII's *Rerum Novarum* to *Centesimus Annus*, the other from *Populorum Progressio* to *Caritas in Veritate*.[133]

The second example, from the Catholic left, is provided in the so-called Dayton Declaration, "On All of Our Shoulders: A Catholic Call to Protect the Endangered Common Good."[134] The signatories of this document are responding to a certain reading of the free market and, in this context, say they write out of concern "for our nation and for the integrity of the teachings of the Roman Catholic Church." They write "to hold up aspects of the Church's social doctrine that are profoundly relevant to the challenges our nation faces at this moment in history, yet are in danger of being ignored." The obligation to the "stewardship of common good" proper to Catholic social teaching is fulfilled in myriad ways, "but indispensibly [sic] among them, through the policies of our government." "America," the Declaration says, "is at a tipping point where the traditional commitment of our government to protecting and advancing the common good is in very real danger of being dismantled for generations. Members of the 'Tea Party,' libertarians, Ayn Rand followers and other proponents of small government have brought libertarian views of government into the mainstream; legitimating forms of social indifference."

Now, the Declaration says that some Catholics "invoke 'prudence' to argue that since bishops are not competent to judge the details of policy proposals, there is no properly 'Catholic' problem with [candidate Paul Ryan's] policies." Noting the challenge of Christian prudence as expressed in *Caritas in Veritate*, the Declaration recalls *Caritas in Veritate*'s central principle: "The truth of Christian love must animate all dimensions of society. *Caritas* is more than a generic inspiration, if love is *truth*, it must give specific form to our actions." Prudence therefore also involves "consideration of the full range of options available and an honest assessment of the outcome of policy proposals."

---

133. All quotations from George Weigel, "*Caritas in Veritate* in Red and Gold."

134. "On All of Our Shoulders: A Catholic Call to Protect the Endangered Common Good," October 9, 2012, http://www.onourshoulders.org/ (hereafter cited as "Declaration"). This document was signed by over 150 American Catholic theologians, and other Catholic academics and ministers, in response to issues raised leading up to the November 2012 American presidential election. The Declaration is particularly concerned with the policies of Catholic Republican candidate for vice president, Congressman Paul Ryan, as these policies are linked expressly with the individualist vision of twentieth-century author Ayn Rand (and her well-known novel *Atlas Shrugged*).

After presenting five main principles of Catholic social doctrine, "On All of Our Shoulders" concludes thus: "We live at [a] time when the social indifference of libertarian thought is achieving broad cultural legitimacy and political power. . . . Ours is a moment that demands the fullness of the Church's teachings as few others have. To be truly prophetic, the Church—bishops, clergy and lay faithful—must proclaim the fullness of its message to all parties, movements, and powers."

While I will momentarily consider each of the five points in more detail, my contention regarding the alternative approaches illustrated by Weigel and the Declaration is that both are shaped by the binary logic of market-plus-state characteristic of our global social order.[135] Indeed, I believe both approaches miss the *anthropological soul* of Catholic social teaching—the soul from which *Caritas in Veritate* means to break open and transform this reductive binary logic. Weigel collapses Benedict's call for gratuitousness prematurely into a political call for an expansion of state authority. Accordingly, and not surprisingly, he finds Benedict's teaching in *Caritas in Veritate* "incomprehensible" in terms of its neglect of the free market's creative forces. The Declaration, in its turn, seeking to avoid the individualism of the liberal—or what it terms "libertarian"—market, cites the Catholic principle of the common good, all the while emphasizing precipitously the role of government power in securing this good. To be sure, both Weigel and the authors of the Declaration are clear that there is more to Catholic social teaching than the realities of market and state: there are local-civil institutions that must be protected in accord with the principle of subsidiarity. The problem is that neither of the two approaches comes to terms with what Benedict XVI (following Paul VI and John Paul II) signals as the need for the *integration* of an anthropology of love into economic and political institutions; that is, neither takes adequate account of the nature and spirit of the communities *given by nature*, which alone can generate and sustain the life-patterns and virtues proper to an anthropology of love. Therefore, neither approach succeeds in correcting the logic of the market or the state internally through the dynamic for love and reciprocal self-gift—the gift for which "the human being is made" and which "expresses and makes present his transcendent dimension."[136]

135. More attention is given in this paper to the Declaration than to Weigel's work because, while Weigel's implied acceptance of this binary logic is more obviously apparent, the Declaration's intention to stay the market forces that Weigel means to uphold renders its acceptance of the same binary logic more difficult to perceive.

136. Benedict XVI, *CV* 34.

My contention is that these dominant approaches continue to assume, albeit from opposing directions, the binary logic of market-plus-state characteristic of the *"anthropo-logic" of Anglo-American liberalism*.

Liberalism has of course had a much broader and deeper influence on America than has Ayn Rand, however much the latter shares liberalism's individualist presuppositions. At the heart of the liberal tradition stands the individual person who is originally abstracted from any inherent social relations (cf. John Locke). The freedom of such an individual is essentially freedom of choice, a freedom structured first "negatively" in relation to (any possible intrusive activity on the part of) others. Liberal *economic* freedom is ordered toward profit, and likewise demands above all protection from intrusive activity arising from other individuals' free pursuit of profit. From this negatively protected free exercise of choice flows the wealth necessary—if not sufficient—for human happiness. The "more" required for human happiness in a qualitative sense is not the proper concern of liberal economics. The liberal political or governmental order, in turn, understands its essential task also negatively, that is, as a matter of protecting individual citizens from intrusive or harmful activity by others, and thereby securing "public order." This task is thus understood to be "coercive" in nature rather than "pedagogical"—that is, not concerned intrinsically with communicating what is truly good to citizens through the mediation of families and local communities organically tied to families, as was the case in ancient-classical, Christian statecraft.[137] What I mean to highlight here is simply that

137. Regarding the terms *public order* and *coercive*, cf. the statement by John Courtney Murray: "The public order is that limited segment of the common good which is committed to the state to be protected and maintained by the coercive force that is available to the state—the force of law and of administrative or police action" (Murray, "This Matter of Religious Freedom," 40). Murray argues that the idea of a primarily pedagogical state (or what he understands as the "paternal" or "ethical" state) has been replaced in recent (especially post-John XXIII and post-Vatican II) Catholic social teaching with that of a primarily coercive state, with a corresponding shift away from the idea of common good to that of public order. In response to his argument and in light of the present paper, let me record three important points: first, recent Catholic social teaching as articulated especially in *Caritas in Veritate* demands some *positive integration of a definite sense of community into the proper concerns of state-political power*. Second, no state, including the liberal state, can avoid the implied endorsement of a particular kind of community to the exclusion of other kinds. Not even the liberal state, in other words, despite its hallmark insistence to the contrary, can avoid sanctioning its own definite vision regarding the human person in relation to God, other persons, and the whole of nature. In short, there is no government that does not, however unwittingly, imply a pedagogy regarding the nature, dignity, and destiny of the human being. Regarding this claim, see my "Repressive Logic of Liberal Rights" and "Freedom, Truth, and Human Dignity." Cf. also here the statement in the *Catechism of the Catholic Church*: "Every institution is inspired, at least implicitly, by a vision of

neither liberal economics nor the liberal state is of its inner logic concerned with human good, or love (virtue, teleology, a logic of gratuitousness, and the reciprocal gift of self), that is, with the logic of the human person in his or her naturally given community with God in and through the family. Neither liberal economics nor the liberal state is adequately concerned with fostering the communities wherein love originates and is most properly formed. Whatever importance love or genuine community may have in terms of "private" institutions, this importance can be acknowledged only by way of an influence *per accidens*, operative only extrinsically, with respect to the "public" liberal economic or political orders. Love, in other words, can constitute no "third" anthropological reality understood to *shape from within* the freedom of the economy or the power of the state.

The "public" logic of liberal economics and politics thus remains of its essence binary, leaving us with negative individual freedom, on the one hand, over against coercive state power, on the other. This opposition between individual freedom and state coercion is reproduced in the opposition between the liberal market's negative freedom and the liberal state's exclusively coercive power, a power designed to correct market freedom by containing its excessive exercise in pursuit of profit. State power becomes proportionately more extensive as market entities tend of their inner liberal logic to aggrandize and indeed monopolize their economic power. The state's political power, however, exercised modestly *or* extensively, remains in any case devoted of its inner logic to the *external* control of misused (economic) freedom, and so far to managerial skill and technical "expertise"—to programs, policies, and regulations that are of their essence coercive. As

---

man and his destiny, from which it derives the point of reference for its judgment, its hierarchy of values, its line of conduct" (no. 2244). Third, the dominant readings of conciliar and post-conciliar papal social-political teaching with respect to the (liberal) state and the church-state question have failed almost uniformly to take into account the implications of the *communio* ecclesiology central to the council. That is, insofar as such readings argue against any direct positive influence of the church on the state, the church is conceived invariably in terms of the institutional-Petrine church, as distinct from the church in its lay-Marian meaning as the communion of saints. To be sure, the communion of saints is ordered intrinsically to the Petrine church (cf. CDF, "Letter to the Bishops," 1992). However, the present paper's call (in the name of *Caritas in Veritate*) for the influence of Catholic social teaching on the state is to be understood as a call answered properly by the "saints" in their living out of community in the world— and by the church as the community of saints in the world. Overlooking the distinction between the institutional-Petrine church and the lay-Marian church, the dominant liberal reading of Catholic political teaching assumes (wrongly) that any influencing of the state toward the end or good of man will involve undue intrusiveness with respect to individual freedom and dignity. For a discussion of the relevance of *communio* ecclesiology for this dominant liberal reading of the distinction between church (or religion) and state, see my *Ordering Love*, 65–132, especially 111–24.

coercive, liberal state power is by definition not aimed properly at foster-ing or positively enabling any transformation, or *genuinely inner* limitation, of (economic) freedom through virtue or acts of gratuitousness—that is, through the familial-local communities that are the primary home of these.

Neither Weigel nor the Declaration denies the importance of gratu-itousness, gratitude, the reciprocal gift of self, love, or indeed the originally given communities of family and religion in which these realities are born and properly sustained. On the contrary, what Weigel resists is the effort to make these realities *internally* operative in market institutions. His resis-tance, that is, indicates the very sort of extrinsicism that *Caritas in Veritate* explicitly calls into question (cf. 38, 39, 41). Weigel's response to *Caritas in Veritate* is to read its criticism of extrinsicism precipitously, simply as a call for an expansion of state power. In its turn, the Declaration insists that love as a matter of truth "must give specific form to our actions"; but it then expresses this most immediately and basically in terms of state power. To be sure, the manifesto-like character of the Declaration entails the necessity of leaving unsaid much that is important. The relevant point, however, is that the Declaration frames its proposals in terms of those principles of Catholic social teaching that it judges "to be the most in danger of being ignored or distorted in contemporary public debate." The Declaration acknowledges that "the dignity and sanctity of human life from conception to natural death" is "chief" among the principles of Catholic social doctrine. But it then insists that, while this fundamental principle "is far from adequately implemented in our laws," "there is little or no confusion about the Church's teaching on this matter"; and that the Declaration may therefore omit this "chief" principle from the Declaration's list of principles without implying any illegitimate priority of the latter over the former. My argument, however, concerns *the precise sense* in which "the dignity and sanctity of human life from conception to natural death," on the one hand, and the demand for so-cial justice, on the other, need to be seen *in their mutual relation*, in terms of what *Caritas in Veritate* terms "*integral human development.*"[138] According to *Caritas in Veritate*, the Catholic social principle most fundamentally in danger of being ignored or distorted in the current cultural situation is that of *the reciprocal self-giving and God-centered love and community* character-istic of integral human development. It is this social principle that therefore needs above all to be integrated into any appeal to government policies that would be consistent with Catholic social teaching—and thereby sufficient to distinguish a genuinely Catholic from a liberal appeal to government policy

---

138. The full title of *Caritas in Veritate* in English is "Integral Human Development in Charity and Truth." The expression recurs in paras. 4, 8, 9, 11, 17, 18, 29, 30, 34, 44, 48, 51, 55, 62, 67, 74, and 77.

as a means of redressing social-personal injustice. The Declaration fails to qualify its appeal to government policy adequately with respect to just this integration that indeed "is most in danger of being ignored or distorted in the contemporary public debate." In the very weighting it gives to government policy, the Declaration tends on the contrary, *eo ipso*, to reinforce the logic of the liberal state in the latter's characteristic marginalization of familial, religious, and local-organic communities as primary social agents.

The Declaration, in other words, despite—or indeed *within*—its opposition to Weigel's (or Ryan's) free market, *completes the arc of the very anthropology of liberalism that drives that market, albeit now in the form of liberalism's coercive state power.* I conclude by showing how the problem manifests itself in the Declaration's five principles.

The first principle emphasizes that the "human person is social not individual," linking this view with the human imaging of God in his reality as "one God in three Persons."[139] The Declaration emphasizes in this light that "we are all really responsible for all."[140] This principle is, of course, true. The point, however, is that the *responsibility of all for all* entailed by Catholic social teaching carries a definite *order* or *form* and indeed *spirit*, which are indicated in the particular sense of *community, reciprocal gift of self,* and *acts of gratuitousness* emphasized in *Caritas in Veritate.* Specifically, then, given the burden of *Caritas in Veritate* in light of present cultural circumstances, what is essential is that the Declaration qualify the role of government power, relative at once to liberalism's coercive understanding of that role and to familial-local communities' understanding of their own role in relation to government power. The sense in which such qualification would affect the nature of state policy in ensuring the responsibility of all for all will become more apparent in the discussion of the remaining principles.

The second principle of the Declaration states that in Catholic social teaching "government has an essential role to play in . . . promoting the common good." Further, the church "considers government to be as 'necessary' for human nature as the family." This is true. But it creates a serious complication for the Declaration's own proposal. On the ancient, or classical Christian, view, the state to be sure is natural: it has its proper reality as *an extension of the prior familial and local communities,* indeed, as "a community of communities." Within this context, the ancient-medieval state of course has a purpose that reaches beyond familial-local communities; but this purpose is essentially subordinate to the end of the person whose reality

---

139. Declaration, quoting John Paul II, *SRS* 40. All quotations concerning the Declaration's principles are taken from the text of the Declaration (see n. 132).

140. John Paul II, *SRS* 38.

is first realized in these communities and ordered to community with God. The power of the state, in other words, is meant *to foster the prior "power" of the person in his or her originally constituted community*; even as the power of the state will then, as the extension of this personal-communitarian "power," necessarily accomplish things that cannot be rightly accomplished in abstraction from the state.[141] It is within familial-local community ordered to God that the "integral development" of the relational-social person is properly realized: that the love and virtues characteristic of the person as relationally constituted are formed. Indeed, it is just the absence of this love and these virtues that becomes manifest in the personal vices that solidify into the structural sin characteristic of the liberal market.[142] This "structural sin" to be sure will require policies of control via the coercive power of the state. The point is not that state intervention may not be necessary, but only that the state, on the view required by authentic Catholic social teaching, needs to be clear about the priority of love and self-gift and about the *particular communities* that best sustain such love. Any rightly conceived "solidarity" that the state would promote via its policies must be mediated and given its form as far as possible *through* these communities.[143]

Regarding the role of government power, then, the Declaration needs to clarify its conception of the common good in relation to the respective anthropologies of *Caritas in Veritate*, on the one hand, and of the liberal tradition, on the other. Acceptance of the former anthropology would

141. Let me emphasize: my argument here in no way implies that the state itself should act *specifically* as a family or religious community. The point is simply that the state rightly understood needs somehow, in principle, to acknowledge and foster the human and religious relationality whose order is structured into human nature already in the act of creation.

142. Cf. *SRS* and CDF, *Christian Freedom*.

143. It seems to me helpful in this context to recall Dorothy Day's well-known—and controversial—emphasis on "anarchism" as an antidote to both the individualism of the right and the "statism" of the "left." Day says that the term *anarchist* is "deliberately and repeatedly used [in *The Catholic Worker*] in order to awaken our readers to the necessity of combating the 'all-encroaching state,' as our Bishops have termed it, and to shock serious students into looking into the possibility of another society, an order made up of associations, guilds, unions, communes, parishes—voluntary associations of men, on regional vs. national lines, where there is a possibility of liberty and responsibility for all men" (quoted in Zwick and Zwick, *Catholic Worker Movement*, 158). Day's anarchism is perhaps best understood—paradoxically—as a "communitarian anarchism": as an approach to political life, that is, which emphasizes simultaneously *both* community, though *not first* that organized via state power (*an-arche*), *and* individual freedom, though only as ordered *in and toward community*. Rightly understood, the idea expressed in Day's "communitarian anarchism" may thus suggest a good starting place for dialogue between right and left—for the kind of dialogue invited by the argument of *Caritas in Veritate*.

require clearly stating the government's concern for the person *as relationally constituted in familial-local community and open to God*, all in light of a renewed recognition of the state's bearing some positive pedagogy regarding the nature of that good. Failure to qualify the role of government power in terms of the person so constituted would, on the contrary and by the very fact of this failure, imply acceptance of the liberal reduction of the "common good" to a "public order" that presupposes a society made up of individual agents to whom justice is administered only in an external manner. Such a failure would indeed imply a reduction of the common good to *external-material goods*, as distinct from any *interior-spiritual good*, thus undermining the primacy of the person as rightly understood in light of the order and ends of familial-religious community.

In its third principle, the Declaration states that "the doctrine of subsidiarity both limits government and demands that it act when local communities cannot solve problems on their own." This doctrine thus has both a negative function—limiting overreach by the government—and a positive function—calling for governmental action "when problems cannot be solved on the local level." The Declaration cites Ryan's budget plan (tied by Ryan to the anti-government views of Ayn Rand) as a crucial policy issue in response to which this positive function is called for. Such a plan, says the Declaration, "will radically reduce the size of government and consequently cut funding for private and religious safety net providers such as Catholic Charities who depend upon federal grants and contracts for much of their funding. This fails the positive obligation under subsidiarity to render needed assistance."

Now, adequate commentary on the Declaration's references to subsidiarity would require us to enter into policy details in a way not possible in the present forum. It must suffice simply to recall Catholic social teaching's ordering principles apropos of subsidiarity (as defended in the present essay). In this light, my contention is that the state's primary purpose with respect to subsidiarity rightly conceived is to permit and protect the integrity of familial, local, and religious communities. Such protection to be sure entails the state's favoring definite kinds of tax policies. But the question regarding direct funding of these communities by the state is more ambiguous. In fact, the state's protection of such communities in the integrity of their beliefs and practices might entail exclusion, or in any case substantial limitation, of direct funding, that is, insofar as such funding risks involving the state precipitously in delimiting or controlling these beliefs and practices. In a word, the primary question apropos of subsidiarity rightly understood is whether the state's funding of (or any other policy affecting) organizations like Catholic Charities involves any threat of restricting the latter's embrace of the fullness of Catholic social doctrine, in service to integral human development. The question of government support in the form of direct funding emerges properly only as a function of this prior question.

My purpose here, then, is not to question in principle direct state funding of local or religious communities; neither is it to impugn the Declaration's reference to the funding of Catholic Charities as an example of subsidiarity. My purpose is simply to recall that the unique contribution of Catholic social teaching lies in its integration of local, God-centered community into justice as ordinarily conceived in liberal societies and to emphasize in this light that a rightly understood subsidiarity demands recognition above all of just this integration of local, God-centered community into the administration of justice. What I am suggesting, then, is simply that the Declaration's comments regarding the principle of subsidiarity leave insufficiently qualified what must be the primary concern of any such principle as conceived in *Caritas in Veritate*: that the state act toward the familial and religious communities within its legal purview—irrespective of whether these communities do or do not receive direct funding—in a manner that protects the integrity of these communities *in the unity of their religious-and-social mission*.[144]

144. Examples of institutions that need to be especially emphasized in light of the principle of subsidiarity rightly understood, then, are smaller communities that receive no direct government aid, such as the Little Sisters of the Poor and their homes for the care of the elderly, houses of hospitality like Casa Juan Diego in Houston, Catholic families, and local Catholic schools. Does a given government policy enable these institutions to integrate their "social" work with their explicitly religious purpose? With respect to Catholic families: does a given state policy permit these families the integrity of the exercise of their right to educate their children—a right recognized by the church as a primary right? With respect to Catholic schools: do state policies permit these schools to teach with integrity the Catholic understanding of marriage and family? Furthermore, it seems to me instructive, in pondering this question of the state and subsidiarity, to consider the example of Catholic universities in the debate regarding the *mandatum*, or "mandate," for theologians to teach in such universities demanded in 1990 by John Paul II's apostolic constitution *Ex corde Ecclesiae*. Presidents of at least two major Catholic universities objected to this mandate on grounds that, by implying the subordination of inquiry to an authority external to the university, the mandate risked violating the integrity of inquiry that should characterize the university. These presidents, however, in registering such objections, did so without taking note of the ways in which the university is already beholden to forces external to the university, that is, in forms including government-funded research; the influence of corporations and industry; the demands on the curriculum made by graduate professional schools in law, medicine, and technological science; and the demands made by the culture generally with regard to credentialing for careers. Indeed, the same limitation seems to me to characterize the "Land-O'Lakes" statement made by Catholic university presidents in 1967. I refer to this example of Catholic universities vis-à-vis the perceived threat to their integrity simply to take note of the apparent disproportion between the presidents'

The fourth principle speaks of the "preferential option for the poor," insisting with the United States Conference of Catholic Bishops that the needs of the hungry and the poor come first. The fifth principle states that "whatever the threat of government power, any adequate response to our challenges must address the facts of economic power as well." The fifth principle also cites *Caritas in Veritate*'s statement that "grave imbalances are produced when economic action, conceived merely as an engine for wealth creation, is detached from political action, conceived as a means for pursuing justice through redistribution."[145]

The concerns expressed in these statements are important. But the Declaration emphasizes problems of poverty, hunger, and wealth here in their obvious sense, that is, as problems simply of the physical poverty, hunger, and wealth of the sort that government in liberal societies seeks to redress.

Catholic social teaching keeps reminding us that what the most vulnerable persons in society need above all is the human love that is open to the divine love revealed by God in Jesus Christ—*which love includes of its essence provision of clothing, food, and sufficient material property and possessions.* This is scarcely a niggling qualifier. Feeding and clothing the poor *cannot be separated from loving* the poor and *remaining present with* them—all the while allowing for government action that would enable and facilitate this sort of presence.

In this light, we recall the Personalist-Distributism brought richly and comprehensively into focus by the writings of Caldecott. Catholic social

---

fear of losing subsidiarity due to restriction by external control from the church, on the one hand, and from the state, corporations, etc., on the other. It is helpful in this context to recall Dorothy Day's frequent reference to "the irony of so many people granting unquestioning obedience to what she called Holy Mother the State while criticizing the idea of the leadership of Holy Mother the Church" (Zwick and Zwick, *Catholic Worker Movement*, 171). Or we might say, in the spirit of Day: the Catholic presidents and academics who objected to the mandate seemed more fearful that the university would operate *ex corde ecclesiae* than *ex corde imperii*. What I have in mind here, then, regarding the Catholic university's securing of the integrity of reason vis-à-vis its (possible) instrumentalization by—by virtue of subordination to—the external demands coming from the state, the professions, corporations, and the like, can be indicated in terms of features of intelligence such as the following: Benedict XVI's idea of reason as open to the *logos* of love, in his "Faith, Reason, and the University"; Marcel's sense of presence as articulated, for example, in "The Mystery of the Family"; Josef Pieper's reflections on interiority in *Living the Truth*, 5–105; and Michael Polanyi's notion of knowledge as "indwelling" in *The Tacit Dimension*. Cf. also in this connection my *Ordering Love*, 383–429. I should emphasize here that acceptance of the mandate in and of itself scarcely resolves the intrinsic problems regarding the nature of intelligence indicated in these examples.

145. Benedict XVI, *CV* 36.

teaching as understood by the Distributists understands poverty and hunger and wealth most basically in terms of the *meaning of love* as revealed in Christ and embodied especially in communities rooted in the family and the church. Chesterton, Day, and Maurin all recognized that God is a social good, that meaninglessness is the deepest form of poverty, and that "social work" takes place at the intersection of time and eternity. They understood that wealth consists most fundamentally in the quality of one's relationships to those with whom relation is given intrinsically in the act of creation. They lived the truth articulated by Mother Teresa when the latter insisted that her "social work" involved at root being a contemplative at the heart of the world. They understood that the meaning of poverty and neediness has to be placed most fundamentally within the spirit of the Beatitudes, of Matthew 25, and of Mary's Magnificat.[146]

The upshot of the foregoing, then, in sum, is that the negative economic freedom of individuals is not answered first or most properly by a coercive state power that redresses quantitatively conceived poverty and hunger via the technically conceived methods of state government.[147] The banalities of (Paul Ryan's) Republican Party, in other words, are not adequately answered by the banalities of (Barack Obama's) Democratic Party.

Let me emphasize, then, that the burden of my criticism is not at all that the Declaration means to deny the principles enunciated in the name of *Caritas in Veritate* and Personalist-Distributism. The criticism bears rather on the Declaration's abstraction from such principles in its characterization of the social principles it judges "to be the most in danger of being ignored or distorted in contemporary public debate."

The Declaration, in sum, focuses on the importance of government policy in redressing social-economic problems, setting itself against the backdrop of the individualist, anti-government approach represented by Paul Ryan. In so doing, however, the Declaration falls into the trap of the binary logic of market-plus-state that *Caritas in Veritate* urges us to avoid. According to *Caritas in Veritate*, the Catholic social principle most in danger

146. The call to sanctity was understood by Day and Maurin to provide the essential form and spirit of their work. On this see, for example, Zwick and Zwick, *Catholic Worker Movement*, 235–49 (and passim). For a wonderfully concrete sense of the "ordinariness" of sanctity in the spirit of Day, cf. Zwick and Zwick, *Mercy Without Borders*, 253–62.

147. Cf. Marcel: "The modern State, all of whose organs have been successively overdeveloped, will tend finally to kill everything which it claims to sanction or foster in the human being, for it is beyond its power either to give life or to reveal it and recognize it" ("Mystery of the Family," 94–95). We can rightly appeal to such a (modern-liberal) state, then, only proportionately to its being transformed in the manner indicated in *Caritas in Veritate* (as conceived in the foregoing argument).

of being ignored or distorted in the current cultural situation is that of God-centered love, gratuitousness, and reciprocal self-giving. What is needed today above all is a renewed sense of the anthropological truth of the human person as constituted communionally with other persons, and indeed with all creatures, in relation to the Creator through the family. It is just this communion-based anthropological truth that, according to Benedict XVI, indicates the "third" reality meant to transform the dominant binary logic of liberal-free-market-plus-liberal-state. My argument, in the name of the tradition of Catholic social doctrine as developed by Paul VI, John Paul II, and Benedict XVI, and interpreted in light of Personalist-Distributism and the writings of Stratford Caldecott, has been that the Declaration stresses the importance of state policies while failing to take adequate note of this anthropological "third" reality meant to order the state (and the market) from within, via its transformation of the whole person and every single person.

The Declaration so far leaves intact the very binary logic that contemporary Catholic social doctrine rightly understood has set out to overcome.

V.

The most likely objection to my argument is that it is not the purpose of the economy or polity *as such* to concern itself with the nature of *community*. But that is just the burden of Benedict XVI's argument in *Caritas in Veritate*. The economy and the state *as such* exist only *qua actualized in* human persons.[148] And these persons, insists *Caritas in Veritate*, are intended by nature and by grace to seek to integrate economic and political order with the logic of reciprocal self-gift that alone suffices to move us beyond the dominant binary structure. Once this is seen, we can make the proper inference regarding what should be the priorities of rightly conceived economic and political order—to protect the integrity and foster the growth of those communities in which habits of reciprocal self-giving are first formed.

It is here, again, that the work of Caldecott stands out clearly. Caldecott unfolds the *theological anthropology* indicative of the continuity-within-development of the church's social teaching from its origins in the gospel, through the Middle Ages, to its "new" articulations in the twentieth and twenty-first centuries. Indeed, we are now able to see how right Caldecott is to suggest that we need "to consider the possibility that Catholic social

---

148. Benedict XVI, *CV* 36.

principles might imply a more radical departure from current economic orthodoxy than any nation has yet attempted."[149]

This reference to the radicality of Catholic social principles leads, in conclusion, to what seems to me the single most fundamental, or indeed most conventionally "reasonable," objection to my argument, namely, that a sense of community rooted in acts of gratuitousness and reciprocal gift of self is nowhere to be found in the global-liberal social order. Proposals like Benedict XVI's, in other words—which Caldecott shows entail significant transformation of present-day education, science, and technology—are thus claimed to be simply not possible; indeed, they seem utopian. As a former colleague of mine would say, such a claim is not only true, it is obviously true. The argument it implies, nonetheless, is in the first instance irrelevant: it begs the very burden of social teaching as conceived by the church. The issue raised by the objection, in other words, is that of "realism"—of a Christian prudence that would attempt only what is possible, taking into account the concrete circumstances prevalent in our given cultural situation. Now, the demand indicated by the appeal to prudence is, of course, in principle legitimate. Christians need to recognize that the only "city" that can fully realize integral human development is the "heavenly city," the eschatological community of saints. Indeed, any effort completely to realize this integral human development within the present historical order would necessarily involve reliance on ever more extensive—to the point of totalitarian—political control. An appeal to the virtue of prudence is therefore essential in the face of the call for gift-centered communities that would shape the "public" economic-political order.

The simple but basic burden of my argument, however, is that the prudence to be properly recommended must be informed by *genuinely Christian* as distinct from *liberal* premises. Catholic social doctrine and liberalism, in other words, operate with different senses of what is realistic or really works, or again regarding what is possible or merely ideal. What liberal societies typically take to be merely *ideal* needs to be understood, from the point of view of the gospel or a genuine Christian philosophy, to have roots *in reality* itself. Ideals, in other words, in their truest sense, are tied to the *teleological ends* given with nature as created by God. Ideals are *ends* that, as fundamentally *gifts* given by God, become at once *tasks* to be realized by man in response to God. Ideals as thus indissoluble from these ends given with nature—a nature that is open from the beginning to the further, final end revealed by God in Jesus Christ—are not only *not unreal*, but are also what we *need and desire most from within the depths of our*

---

149. Caldecott, "Trinity," par. 1, "Some Alternatives."

hearts and minds. On an understanding that is properly both scriptural-theological and anthropological, we cannot both *be* (real) and *not need and want to realize (ever-more fully) the gift* of being—our *being as gift*—that most defines our *reality in the world*.

Catholic social teaching as enunciated by Benedict XVI in *Caritas in Veritate*, then, does not demand that the community of reciprocal self-gift rooted ultimately in the Trinitarian love of God be somehow "coerced" prematurely into existence via the forceful mechanisms of government that would limit market freedom (ever more extensively)—though of course government policies ordered in light of human community rightly conceived are both legitimate and necessary. The crucial point, rather, is that Christians themselves must seek to integrate this love into whatever activity they engage, including economic and political activity. Christians must engage this activity prudently, *but with a prudence that is informed by the premises not of liberal economics or the liberal state, but of that very love itself*. Such a rightly conceived prudence, furthermore, does not in the first instance expect success, in the liberal sense of success. As has rightly been said, "success is not a name of God."[150] On the contrary, a genuinely Christian prudence—which indeed is consistent with an ancient Greek understanding of prudence—is interiorly open to suffering, and in any case is not surprised when suffering comes.[151] Ancient and medieval Christians, pondering the life of Jesus and the early saints, recognized that suffering—witness unto death, *martyrion*—is indeed a "normal" state for Christians in society. Suffering, in other words, is to be expected in any genuinely "realistic" Christian participation in any human society, and acknowledgment of this fact must be incorporated within any genuinely Christian appeal to prudence. Only in more recent times have Christians come to believe otherwise—to believe, for example, that they can participate in liberal social institutions, as they could not in pre-Christian or pagan institutions, with the reasonable expectation of success except insofar as these liberal institutions behave morally inconsistently with respect to their proper liberal logic. Benedict's social doctrine, with its integral human development, shows that this is not true: Christianity bears an *anthropology* fraught with a dynamic logic of recipro-

150. Hans Urs von Balthasar referencing Martin Buber in the former's *Razing the Bastions*, 46.

151. Cf. Joseph Ratzinger's discussion of how Plato deals with the question of what is likely to be the just man's position in this world. Plato says the "just man will be scourged . . . and at last, after all manner of suffering, will be crucified" (*Republic* 2.361e–362a). Ratzinger points out, in light of this text, that even in the non-Christian, when justice is lived, "something is sensed of that revelation of man which comes to pass on the Cross" (Ratzinger, *Introduction to Christianity*, 293).

cal self-gift, and this anthropology of gift *eo ipso* unsettles and re-orders the inner logic of liberal social order, right and left. Only if Christians have understood this have they understood the fullness of Catholic teaching as envisioned in *Caritas in Veritate*. Only if they have understood this are they justified in terming their approach to contemporary economic-political reality "prophetic."[152]

It is in light of the foregoing, in sum, that we can see why *Caritas in Veritate* insists that the question of development today *"has become a radically anthropological question"*; why this *"question of development is closely bound up with our understanding of the human soul"*; and why "only a humanism open to the Absolute can guide us in the promotion and building of forms of social life—structures, institutions, culture and *ethos*."[153]

In this light we can see finally, with Caldecott, why a social doctrine conceived in terms of such principles demands a radical, but precisely not "unrealistic," response to liberalism's binary logic of market-plus-state that presently dominates global culture.

152. Often linked with questions regarding prudence, utopianism, and "real" versus "ideal" as discussed in the foregoing paragraphs, is the question regarding short-term versus long-term approaches to cultural problems, in which the short-term is typically understood to be the more practically effective approach. However, it is only in light of the true end of human existence—whose full realization can occur only in the life that follows death and which realization entails suffering along the way—that one can have a right conception of short-term prudence in the first place. Without the long-term informing the short-term, the logic that chooses the short-term becomes effectively *the only long-term approach*. The point, then, is that short-term prudence is rightly conceived from a Christian perspective only insofar as it is informed by a christological sense of time as open to eternity.

153. Benedict XVI, *CV* 75, 76, 78.

11

The Politics of the Soul[1]

John Milbank

For Stratford Caldecott, in profound gratitude for his life's work

The politics that we practice today is a politics without the soul. I want to argue that it is thereby a perverse politics, an anti-politics, and even, in the end, an impossible politics. If we are to survive as recognizably human, we need to return to a politics of the soul, albeit in a new guise.

What do I mean by a politics of the soul? More fundamentally, what do I mean by the soul? Very simply, "soul" is the medium in which we dwell as human beings. There is no other space in which we could humanly live. As the possessors of souls, we are able to move our bodies, whose parts are coherently held together in a pattern that can itself be described as soul. A soulful reality is a shape deemed "living" by virtue of its capacity to reposition and reshape itself within its environment. Such a reality is also aware of other souls who inhabit the same psychic space and within this space it is also aware of other, non-psychic realities. Thus Aristotle declared that the soul is not only "the form" of the animal body but is also "in a manner all things." In the case of human beings, at least, souls are also capable of thought, or of consciously reflecting on all that they are aware of. They also have the capacity for freedom, through which they can move their own psychic motions or thoughts, themselves.

Because conscious thought and freedom seems redundant from the point of view of nature—its necessities and blind spontaneities—and because they cannot be adequately explained in materialist terms, many cultures, religions, and philosophies have argued that the core of the soul can exist apart from the body and that it must be derived from and governed by a higher and invisible spiritual power that directs all of reality.

---

1. Milbank, "The Politics of the Soul."

Today of course such perfectly rational views would be nonetheless widely contested. More widely still they would be held to belong to the sphere of private opinion and private debate. Affirmation of the soul would not be seen as very relevant for public affairs and certainly not as the basis upon which public affairs should be organized. Surely that is not feasible, given the extent of our disagreements over metaphysical matters? Is it not self-evident that we need to base our political, economic, and even most social arrangements on principles that are metaphysically neutral, on procedural norms that are fair to all and to many competing perspectives?

That notion lies at the heart of our contemporary liberal assumptions. But I would like to argue that they are not really metaphysically neutral and that in the end they lean inevitably towards materialism. If that is the case, and if one believes in the reality of soul, then liberalism is not humanism because it tends to deny the ontological space in which we can alone operate in a truly human fashion. In doing so it has to appeal to a sub-human or a post-human space in a way that is becoming increasingly manifest.

So I will claim that where one does not base the social and political order on the reality of the soul, then in the end one is on a path that will either undo itself or finally undo humanity. But initially, just what does it mean to speak of a politics of the soul? The clearest reference point here is Plato. In the *Gorgias* he defines the "art of government," that is to say the political art, as that which ensures the good health of the soul in the way that medicine ensures the good health of the body.[2] From our modern point of view this is thoroughly confusing. For Plato appears to say that politics is identical with psychology—something supremely public and collective identical with something supremely private and individual. His reason for doing so is that he thinks that there can only be a specific art of human governance, a political art, if there is such a thing as a psychic reality. For otherwise, if human beings were only physical, they could adequately be governed by medicine. It follows in consequence that governance has a problematically dual application: politics must be psychological, because people must be freely and consciously encouraged towards the good life; they cannot just be manipulated. On the other hand, psychology must be political, since the soul should not be ruled by the body, but by an authority superior to its own nature—the authority of the good, the true, and the beautiful, which Plato took to be objective spiritual realities.

In Plato's consideration of psychopolitics, however, there is always a problem. Which comes first, the political soul or the psychic city? The problem arises because Plato rightly thought that our will and desires are only

2. Plato, *Gorgias*, 464b.

moved by the scope of our intellectual vision. Thus we always will the good, but are too often deluded by false simulations of the genuine good. Yet in that case, how can the lost and deluded individual really reform himself? He needs help in the shape of a teacher, a community, and finally a good *polis* or city. But because governance applies also to the individual, good cities can only be built by good men whom Plato took to be religiously inspired philosophers. We seem to be trapped in such a vicious circle that Plato often suggests only the intervention of divine inspiration and providential luck—as in the case of the daemonically guided Socrates himself—indeed a kind of "grace," can undo.[3] A genuinely human, virtuous life depends on the periodic irruption of extraordinary individual charisms, however we may account for this.

In another way also, Plato insisted on the crucial place of the religious dimension. For him good governance, right order, does not just mean the superiority of the soul over the body, whether for the individual or for the city, though it does indeed involve that. More fundamentally he places in parallel the diseased body and the diseased soul, or alternatively the healthy body and the healthy soul. As his program for the education of the guardian class in the *Republic* well shows, he is primarily concerned with our integral wellbeing as embodied souls, or soul-informed bodies. In the case of the body, good government means the control of the body by psychic wisdom, which will advise you to listen to your doctor rather than to the blandishments of the archaic equivalent of TV cooks.[4] Since there is nothing human higher than the soul, does this mean that psychic self-control is the highest private political art?

But this is the idea that Plato is perhaps most anxious of all to refute.[5] For if self-government means merely self-control, then why may this not be exercised simply in terms of improving one's own power and corporeal contentment? Understood in this fashion, the rule of the soul could be merely the conscious and manipulative, suavely urban augmentation of military strength and pride, which we know can subdue our spontaneous and baser passions for the sake of the pursuit of glory. And this is just what the sophists, according to Plato, took psychic governance to be: a self-disciplined, relentlessly cunning deployment of words whereby one could manipulate others to one's own ends. For this perspective, the pursuit of political rule is naturally undertaken for the augmentation of one's own pleasure and satisfaction.

3. See in particular Plato, *Meno*, 99b–100c.

4. Plato, *Gorgias*, 465a–e.

5. See here primarily the entire argument of the *Republic*.

This aim would seem to bend the political back into the psychic, albeit in a monstrously narcissistic variant: the ruler rules in order to be himself a pure individual, free from all constraint. However, Plato's claim is that in reality sophistry tends to remove the psychic from the political sphere. This is because, for the sophists, as for the historian Thucydides, we must split reality between nature or *physis*, on the one hand, and law or *nomos*, on the other. Nature and culture have nothing to do with each other, because nature is inexorable and meaningless, inciting blind passions, while culture, shaped by law, is entirely willful, conventional, and artificial.[6] This ensures that individual expressions of soul in artifice are just conscious manifestations of a blind will to power, as it were, vagaries of nature, rather than revelations of natural order. And in seeking power in the city they have to try to incite and manipulate all sorts of other blind and egotistic human passions. In this way, ironically, through the highest exercise of a refined and cynical artifice—that has today reached a new pitch in contemporary advertising and celebrity culture—they encourage the invasion of the civic realm of *nomos* by ever-greater manifestations of pre-human *physis* which we can never hope to command. One gets, precisely, "the urban jungle."

Plato's refusal of this picture is actually in harmony with the archaic wisdom of most human societies. For they do not generally divide nature from culture, but think of nature as itself including many animal cultures and of human culture as itself a natural manifestation. In Platonic terms this means that the realm of the *psyche*, though higher than the material, is still fully a part of nature. It is for this reason that he thinks that political life cannot be accounted for in terms of anything pre-political—for example, as we would now tend to think, anything evolutionary. As he puts it in *The Laws:* "habits, customs, will, calculation, right opinion, diligence and memory will be prior creations to material length, breadth, depth and strength, if (as is true) soul is prior to matter."[7] Notice here again the mix of public things like "habit and custom" with private things like "diligence and memory" as equally belonging to the psychic sphere.

It follows for Plato, as perhaps for most pre-modern human beings, that if human culture cannot be reduced to pre-human nature, and yet is itself fully in continuity with that nature, that it must be guided by a power and by standards higher than itself. The sophists denied this, but thereby they effectively denied the integral reality of the human, since they split the psychic sphere between the invading ravages of egoistic nature on the one hand and the arbitrary contrivances of the human will on the other. The

6. See Sahlins, *Western Illusion*.

7. Plato, *Laws*, 896c–d.

latter, if guided by no given and natural, but also higher, power can inherently know no bounds—a circumstance which must eventually encourage the creation of a post-human superman.

It then follows that there can be no art of politics, defined as an exercise of justice, irreducible to either natural necessity or an individual will to power, if the soul that rules itself or other souls is not guided by the transcendent reality of the true, good, and beautiful. In practical terms this means that the just ruler does not *merely* ensure that the social realities of brute force and material need are kept in their spatial places by reason (for this risks reducing reason itself to a subtler kind of coercive power), but rather that he continuously tries to ensure through *time* and on differently arising occasions that these subordinate things and all different things are harmoniously and proportionately blended in such a way as to participate in the transcendent *kalon* which is both goodness and beauty. To do this is to exercise intuitive and non-technical *phronesis,* a capacity somewhat akin to the Daoist virtue of "inaction" and one which, of course, Aristotle learned the importance of—as of so much else—from his master Plato to whom he remained largely faithful.[8]

For Plato, then, it is clear that the reality and irreducibility of the soul cannot be disconnected from the transcendent realm, which he understood to be the realm of the gods and the forms, even though he did not think one can entirely prove the reality of this realm, but must resort to the language of myth and the practice of ritual in order to experience its reality.[9]

Now modern people might find themselves happy with the idea that religious beliefs can keep alive in individuals a sense of the objective reality of the Good and of the irreducibility of human conscience and freedom. They would not tend to see the religious dimension as anything that need be publicly affirmed—and indeed would be all too conscious of the dangers attendant upon doing so. However, from a Platonic perspective this would be entirely illogical. Why? Because, as we have seen, the psychic is for Plato as much the shared sea in which we swim as it is a kind of vital saltwater bubble inside ourselves. If the guidance of the soul depends upon its vision of transcendence, then this is needed as much in public as in private, precisely because the good person requires the training by the good city every bit as much as the good city can only be shaped by good people.

One can here usefully say a little more about the fundamental Platonic *aporia* as to which comes first, city or soul? As I have already indicated,

---

8. For the central role of *phronesis* in Plato, see again the *Republic*. It is even arguable that *phronesis* has a broader scope in Plato than in Aristotle—being less reducible to an internal "spatial" balance between reason and the passions.

9. See Pickstock, *After Writing*, 3–46.

Plato tends to resolve it by invoking a divine act that interrupts the vicious cycle. However, this is not for him a *deus ex machina* insofar as occasional inspiration is linked to the poetic recitation of good myths that can benignly "charm" the soul, and to the practice of religious liturgy and sacrifice.[10] It is indeed liturgical practice which for Plato tends to mediate the private and the public—in ritual we are most privately before the gods and yet most of all with others in our shared human predicament.[11] This was best realized by the theurgic Platonists like Iamblichus and Proclus who insisted against Plotinus on the "complete descent" of the human soul into the body and equivalently on the way contemplative ascent has to be matched by a divine descent towards human beings of the gods in ritual and magical practices.[12] (It was, of course, in the tradition of theurgic neoplatonism that the co-founder of *Temenos*, Kathleen Raine, most of all stood, in succession to her hero, Thomas Taylor, the late eighteenth-century first translator of the complete Platonic corpus, and of the neoplatonists Iamblichus and Proclus, along with works of Aristotle [whom he rightly read as a Platonist] into English.[13])

The theurgists tended to suggest, beyond Plato, that the philosopher-ruler did not risk contamination by political engagement, precisely because the rituals of the city were crucial for his own education.[14] Thus the wise man requires a combination of peaceful theoretical reflection with political engagement. This view informed their support of a mixed constitution blending monarchy and aristocracy with democracy—and it also accentuated the elements of populism in Plato, which one can too easily ignore. Whereas the sophists sought democratically to manipulate and alter popular opinion, Plato often appeals to this opinion in its perennial and generally unalterable character—especially with respect to morals and religion—*against* the advocates of democracy, which he took to mean merely that we should be ruled by prevailing fashions.[15] Equally he exalts in the *Gorgias* the art of humble artisans over and above the political arts of rhetoric.[16]

10. See, for example, *Laws*, 887d.

11. See the *Laws* in general.

12. See Shaw, *Theurgy and the Soul*.

13. Raine and Harper, *Thomas Taylor*.

14. See O'Meara, *Platonopolis*.

15. For example, *Gorgias* 489a–b. Addressing the young sophist Callicles: "Do the majority believe or do they not that equal shares, not unequal, are right, and that it is baser to do wrong than to suffer wrong?" Socrates then goes on to argue that this witness of the *vox populi* suggests that such beliefs are founded in *physis* and not just *nomos*.

16. Ibid., 511a–513a.

This more balanced view of what shapes human wisdom, however, entirely depends upon the idea that the life of the city—our psychic life in common—is already guided through shared habits and customs and rituals by the realm of the gods, as Plato had himself already indicated in *The Laws*. By noting this, one can, I think, go on to suggest that the new sense in Plato of a universal good lying beyond the insight of any one given culture relates *both* to a new validation of a social rebel like Socrates, who might see further than his own time and place, *and* to the idea that within a community there needs to be another spiritual, mystical community—which need not be an elite one—in order that the often brutal processes of politics may submit to something higher than themselves.

But why should not the critical jolt of the individual conscience be enough here? I would argue that it is not enough precisely because the main reality of all human association, including political association, *is itself psychic*.[17] In other words it is to do with friendship, as both Plato and Aristotle taught; it is to do with benevolent generosity as they taught in common with Confucius in the Far East. It is to do with a reciprocal sharing of all that it is good. Only secondarily is it about organizing the distribution of material goods and about designing laws, which are always somewhat arbitrary, yet should reflect as far as possible non-arbitrary justice.

Now one crucial way to remind politics and politicians of this truth is to specifically identify a socially inward spiritual community to which politics is finally answerable—a community whose seeking of harmonious relationship with humans, animals, plants, gods, and God is in excess of either material need or coercive law. Hence Plato already spoke of a city of the philosophers; in the case of Buddhist civilizations we have the phenomenon of the *Sangha;* in the case of Islam (so much at times philosophically influenced by Plato) of the *Umma*. Ancient Israel had her tribe of Levites, and most dramatically, in the case of Christianity, one has the phenomenon of *the church*. Most dramatically, because here the separation from the political state and yet the political centrality and inclusivity of the spiritual community was taken the furthest of all.

17. One can add here that the modern assumption that individual conscience is a sort of locked box within which it is impossible to know to any degree how it is to be someone else can be questioned. For if the psychic is real as a spiritual space then there is no reason why other minds should not enter my psychic space, or rather why we should not meet in a shared psychic space wherein, indeed, gestures and words allow us to some degree to experience what it is to be the other. After all, we only experience even ourselves through the reflex experience of how we are registered by other things and people. There is a profound link here between what Charles Taylor has called the desired buffering of the modern self from invasion by unseen spiritual forces with its buffering against invasion by other human spirits.

Here I think one can argue that while Confucius indeed grasped the universality of the ethical, he could not so far disentangle it from the customary as to arrive at the sense of the validity of individual rebellion, nor the need for a spiritual and higher "politics within politics." Meanwhile, the original Hindu impulse (later much modified, as we can see by the extraordinary ethical witness of Mahatma Gandhi) could at times amount to a kind of higher spiritual sophistry in the name of an amoral monism, for which the individual soul achieves most power and most magical influence precisely by indifferently removing itself from the community and from normal earthly aims.

Perhaps I am gently suggesting here that Kathleen Raine's vision was more specifically Western than she realized. In any case, there would seem to be something singular in the early Western simultaneous discovery of the transcendent Good, the priority of the individual person, and the need for a spiritual community. Another and arguably more consummate version of this is conveyed by the Hebrew Scriptures and then by the New Testament. And yet this discovery of the universal and of the individual did not originally break with the primordial human sense of the continuity of nature with culture, nor of the need of the individual for human relationship and succor by family, friends, and community.

I think today what our politics needs is a revival of the archaically Western vision in a new form. It needs this rather than the fearful combination of Western libertarianism with an Eastern technologism of the spirit, collectivist autocracy, and temptation to spiritual nihilism that could be arising in Asia and parts of Europe. And it needs it rather than the lamentably disenchanted and voluntarist transcendence increasingly advocated by (especially Sunni) Islam to the relegation of its profound mystical legacy. But above all it needs it rather than our modern liberal political legacy since the seventeenth century.

Why should this be so? Surely this liberal legacy has further released individual freedom and our respect for the individual? Surely it has increased true spiritual community in the form of a spirit of diversity and Feuerbachian recognition of the otherness of the other, whereby we are less likely to confuse our own preferences with transcendent norms?

Now I think that one can candidly admit that those things have proved true up to a point. At first the exaltation of negative freedom of choice helped sweep away many rigid restrictions, hierarchies, and mistrust of difference that have eventually seemed without justification even for their often Christian instigators. However, in the long run liberalism seems to swallow itself and to reveal that, as a mode of sophistry, it erodes the very political field it claims to save. This self-swallowing turns out to mean that eventually liberalism is exposed as tautologous and as only applying to itself, thereby revealing nothing of the deeper truths about human association.

Let me explain what I mean in three instances, going backwards from postmodern liberalism through modernist liberalism to original, early modern liberalism. Postmodern liberalism advocated deconstruction whereby one reveals the arbitrariness of any construct and the way that "higher" values are only revealed by their complicity with contrasting "lower" ones. This very simple exercise, of course, proved for a time eminently marketable and made many a career. However, its validity depends wholly on the assumption that every artificial construct is merely arbitrary and that the co-dependence of higher and lower somehow disproves the inherently hierarchical nature of their relation. But of course, only liberalism itself makes this assumption about human constructs: they are the result of contractual agreement and so forth, since there can be no consensus about objective values. Thus liberalism imagines it can deconstruct the non-liberal—the religious, the customary, the deferential—but in reality all that liberalism can deconstruct are the works of liberalism itself. And this tends to deconstruct liberalism *tout court* as being always the operator of the deconstructible. Of course the postmodernists knew this—but even when exposing the inconsistencies of liberalism, they could not exit from the liberal logic upon which even that exercise of skepticism depended.

The second and modernist self-swallowing of liberalism concerns the law of diminishing returns on marginal utilities as expounded by neoclassical economics from the late nineteenth century onwards. The problem is that, as with deconstruction, this law only applies to the products of liberal choice itself. Trivial material goods or things which are merely the election of my passing fancy (which is all that liberalism and neoclassical economics can recognize in terms of valid desire) are subject to the reverse lure of boredom and lose their significance and so lose economic value over time. But that is not true of symbolically valuable objects like your grandmother's ring or of relational goods, whether enjoyed along with other people or other natural realities. I can constantly find more, or more to treasure in a person or a beloved landscape. And a non-liberal economy could realistically express, even through the various modes of exchange—through contract, price, salary, profit, and interest—our often mutual appreciation of such things, since human disagreement is just not as absolute as metropolitan liberals like to fantasize.

However, if liberalism encourages an economy based on our boredom with shallow things, inciting us to want always more, then liberalism itself is of diminishing utility. At first it unleashed a thousand blossoms of creativity, but in the long term it undermines creative impulses to produce the genuinely valuable, and it equally undermines the trust upon which all economic interventions and exchanges ultimately depend. We have recently seen all too well how an entirely amoral market is actually a dysfunctional market.

In the third place, liberalism has now swallowed its own early modern origins, as Jean-Claude Michéa has argued.[18] These had overwhelmingly to do with an abandonment of the politics of the soul. The process (as Michéa fails to mention) had begun well back into the Middle Ages but was certainly consummated in the seventeenth century. It arose to a large degree because agreement concerning the transcendent Good started to be associated with conflict and warfare. Yet in the face of an increasing exigency for peace at any price, Thomas Hobbes and others oddly assumed a hyperbolic violence, a war of all against all as the natural human condition. They did so in part because they thought (and unsurprisingly, after the all too many wars of religion) that disagreements regarding the nature of the Good were not subject to rational arbitration.

But this exposes to view a remarkable *chiasmus*. While Christianity believed that reality was originally and at heart peaceful, and only violent because of the irruption of sin, and yet in practice had often encouraged warfare, liberalism exactly reverses this. In the name of reducing conflict, liberalism thought that reality was inherently agonistic and humans naturally egotistic and prone to conflict. For this reason seventeenth-century liberalism totally rejected Renaissance humanism with its high view of the psychic dignity of man. Here it often assumed the legacy—as with Adam Smith—of Calvinist and Jansenist doctrines of total depravity.[19]

Liberalism, then, is most fundamentally a pessimism. It tries to invent what Michéa calls *l'empire du moindre mal* on the perverse basis of the worst human tendencies. Even when Jean-Jacques Rousseau reversed Hobbes and proclaimed the isolated, natural subject wholly innocent, his Genevan inheritance still resonated in his view that society always corrupts through a contagion of mimetic violence. Today we tend to have in consequence a combination of "right-wing" Hobbesian liberalism in economics with "left-wing" Rousseauian liberalism in culture. Though the two appear in media

18. Michéa, *The Realm of Lesser Evil.*

19. In detailing the horrors committed in the name of liberalism—slavery, imperialist exploitation, abuse of workers—Losurdo (*Liberalism: A Counter-History*) tries to blame these on the alien influence of a "providentialist" political economy which saw governmental intervention in the social and economic sphere as impious: both the earlier Burke and Tocqueville at every stage used such arguments. But this is not the distortion of liberalism by ancient theology, but the influence of a new (largely Jansenist) theology that is part of the very constitutive fabric of liberalism itself. See Latouche, *L'Invention de l'économie,* 117–64.

politics to be at odds, this is a charade to prevent us from seeing that no democratic debate actually exists: nearly all of us are economically right, culturally left, but liberal either way and in secret collusion.

How, though, does liberalism think order can arise from amorality or even from vice? In two ways, which are really but one: by the invisible hand of the market and of civil society, which coordinates perfectly separate and isolatable private desires, or by the visible hand of government. But in either case—and nearly always the two processes are combined—human relationship is sidestepped, and we are mediated behind our backs by an act of instrumentalist and rationalistic manipulation. This is always carried out in the name of pure, abstract "growth"—ether in collective wealth or collective power.

Yet in the long run, if all human interaction is bypassed, we start to lose the skill for it. We trust only ourselves and no others, and certainly not the government. Neither does the government trust us: thus one gets the pursuit of private profits whose ease of gaining is to do with the fact that they merely transfer and do not grow real wealth; thus one also gets an increasing number of posh criminals who calculate that they can flout the social contract and get away with it; thus again one gets increasingly criminalized politicians who bleed the system for their own private interests.

In this way liberalism more and more produces the war of all against all that was its own presupposition. But this does not thereby prove that presupposition, because it is only the practice of liberalism that has produced the circumstances it originally merely assumed. For despite the many wars over truth—and are they not more noble than liberal wars over money, and less terrible than the wars of power that have been instigated by nihilists who have taken liberal logic to its limits?—human culture could never have arisen without practices of trust: of gratuitous gift, counter-giving, and gratuitous giving again which anthropologists have long known form the main bond of all human societies. In this sense "society," as socialists and anarchists argued against the liberals, is indeed more fundamental than either law or contract, either politics or economics.

Therefore in all three ways we can see how liberalism is self-eaten by its own mean and sordid declarations, however well intentioned. Thereby it has devoured itself in a fourth way that corresponds to its second, eigthteenth-century phase of liberalism as political economy. Only liberalism is subject to its own fantasized government by the hidden hand, because only in the case of liberalism do private actions have no public intentionality upon which a wider public intention could be constructed that is in continuity with the first actions, even if they never envisaged this upshot—just as the shapers of the Anglo-Saxon *moot* never envisaged the modern Houses of

Parliament. But where there can be no such continuity, as in the case of liberal principles applied to itself, then the hidden hand works to produce a yet worse chaos out of a perverse attempt to distill, from chaos, order.

At the heart of these four self-swallowings lies the refusal of the reality of the soul and so of the political sphere as such, properly understood. For with liberalism, the realm of the psychic and of the psychopolitical is corroded from two opposite directions, echoing the sophistic division between *physis* and *nomos*. On the one hand everything human is declared only natural—we are a bunch of greedy apes with bigger brains. On the other hand, everything human is declared entirely artificial, just stuff that we have made up. This is true of seventeeth-century "New Science" also—it was alternatively seen as the new and literal truth of nature, equivalent to the knowledge of God himself (e.g., by Galileo Galilei), and as "merely" the pragmatic truth of technological control, telling us nothing about how deep nature "really is" at all (e.g., by Marin Mersenne).[20]

In this way liberalism tends to make the human vanish in two directions—archaically in the face of the tide of prehuman nature and futuristically as we can today see more clearly in favor of a "posthuman" project that can hopefully subordinate human egotism and the unpredictabilities of desire to a cybernetic future that will augment the liberal "peace of a sort" into an absolute but absolutely eerie, biotechnical tranquility.

Moreover, these two opposite directions by no means mystically coincide—except, perhaps, at the never-to-be-reached utopian point when experts would have willed away their own will in favor of a sheerly "natural" cybernetic determinism. But before that point liberalism always imposes upon us entirely contradictory imperatives, which negatively reveal the *unreality of trying to deny, abolish, or ignore the soul.*

Thus liberalism declares, as we have seen, that all is natural and yet all is artificial, because it cannot admit that we are supposed to be cultural, that nature most fully reveals herself in the human experience of love for nature, for other humans, and for the divine. This duality further plays itself out in the contradictory demand that all sacrifice their liberty to the needs of growth, and yet that the "rights" of all to assert their negative liberty and material comfort against this need are equally absolute; in the view that we must submit to inexorable economic necessities, and yet that economic processes are the ultimate expression of human freedom; in the demand that we work all the time, and yet equally relax and consume all the time; in the view that all our significant actions impinge on the freedom of others and so must mostly be criminalized and exposed to public ridicule in the name

---

20. See Latour, *We Have Never Been Modern.*

of "transparency," while equally we enjoy a right of absolute privacy to do what we like so long as it is (supposedly) done only to ourselves. This despite the fact that any damage we did truly to ourselves and our own soul would render us the most dangerous of citizens—as a recent British example shows all too well. Whoever loses his own soul, cannot in fact gain even the world, because thereby he has helped destroy the human world also.

These polarities tend further to coagulate in deeper ones of "male versus female," "human industry versus natural environment," and "rational ego versus the unconscious."[21] In all three cases we have to endure the social and psychological damage of a seemingly unmediable tension, which ruins our personal relationships, our integration of culture with nature, and our ability to relate dreams and imaginings to our everyday public lives. Yet in all three cases also we fail to see that exaggeration in either direction (for example, the simultaneous modernist adulation of both pure public functionalism and purely subjective fantasy) is precluding the possibility of a harmonious balance of the sexes, powers, and forces around an integration that must necessarily be psychic in kind.

Of course, we need sometimes to work and sometimes to play: to discern what is more physically or more spiritually caused; to expose some things and keep others hidden; sometimes to put the community first and sometimes the individual; to criminalize some things and leave other wrongs to the force of shame and social disapproval. But the point is that, without the vision of the transcendently good, we have no prudential or non-active way to make these discernments, and proportionately to *distribute* different "rights," and so liberalism is involved in an increasingly hysterical shuttle between the various sets of poles, which are always variants on the archpoles of *physis* and *nomos*. Above all, it tends to encourage the foolish view that anything not against the law is acceptable, while endlessly criminalizing (as did New Labor in the United Kingdom) minor offenses and utterances.

For this reason liberalism is now not just the enemy of politics, of high culture, folk culture, and human flourishing, but also the enemy of freedom itself and of true civil liberties which are rooted in a discernment of justice and in respect for the reality of the individual soul and of the superiority of the spiritual community lying freely beyond the law and beyond economic calculation.

It is for these reasons that we must, I think, recover, in the wake of Kathleen Raine, the spirit of the archaic West. Yet this does not mean restoring unjustifiable hierachies, inequalities, and prejudices that liberalism rightly swept away. After all, Christianity had already democratized

---

21. See Clarke, "Afterword: Wolfram's Parzival."

Platonism with its ultra-theurgic message of a God who reached down to be born in a manger and with its more open yet more extreme mysteries of water, bread, and wine. The higher wisdom had now become an elevation of just that ordinary and yet unfathomable love or reciprocity known to all human cultures.

In the course of the nineteenth century, various socialisms, co-operative movements, and finally Catholic and much Anglican social teaching started to realize these more egalitarian implications of Christianity, not in the name of the liberal left or of Enlightenment, but precisely in criticism of its egoistic pessimism.

They appealed indeed, as Michéa argues, to what George Orwell called "common human decency," which Michéa equates with the practice of gift exchange or of reciprocity. However, one can question Michéa's view that this can so readily be a secular vision. For we now know more clearly than did Marcel Mauss that gift exchange was always a cycle involving nature and the gods as well as human beings. If gifts could be bonds, then that was because they were sacred symbols. The problem indeed is that this tends to involve many different visions of the nature of "goods" that are exchanged, which are only symbolically valued goods because they participate in an eternal Good, which different cultures might perceive differently.

Therefore liberalism was not wrong to see a problem of conflict as arising from these competing visions, and a general secular gift exchange, it might be argued, is but another illusory universalism (to rival that of liberal egoism). Yet the price paid by liberalism for the refusal of the politics of the soul remains too high—in venturing a drastic cure, it finally threatens to kill the human patient.

What can be suggested here instead is that Christianity has already universalized gift exchange. To a considerable degree, its symbolic enclosures have been gradually deserted in favor of abstract and relatively secularizing structures of law and contract. However, notions of divine grace arising in both Greek and biblical thought permitted a sense of universality also to be construed in terms of generosity. God gives to all and we owe a return of gratitude to God, which includes practices of liberality towards and between creatures.[22] The consequent internalization of the duty to give did not as yet usually involve an exclusive confinement of the "true gift" to a unilateral gesture independent of any hope of return, even if the latter begins to be thought of as superior within the Stoic thought of the Roman sage Seneca.

---

22. See Tarot, "Rèperes pour une histoire de la naissance de la grace."

On the whole, however, early Christian thought did not favor the purism of the unilateral in this manner. Supremely, the Christian *ecclesia* was conceived and enacted by Paul, in ways that echo other emphases in Seneca, as a cosmopolitan practice of reciprocity beyond law and contract. The goods exchanged here shared in and were validated by a symbolic gift that was nothing other than one fully generous and sacrificial human being who was thereby deemed divine. In this way the *aporia* of intimate but exclusively symbolic gift *versus* universal but impersonal norm was resolved in terms of the universality of the *yet more absolutely particular*—as Hegel and more recently Alain Badiou have helped us see. This particular has further proliferated through all the equally "particular" styles of the Christian legacy, which have nonetheless shown a Catholic capacity to be receptive to the multifarious insights of other human traditions.

But whether or not my reasoning in this instance seems acceptable, I do not see how we can sustain the genuine Western legacy unless we revive, more democratically, its archaic idiom. This is required, I think, both in order to sustain the absolutely incomparable value of the person and of relational reciprocity in free association. We need both the mysticism of the individual soul and the spiritual and liturgical community of souls, in whatever sense. For our true human equality resides in the upper register of the shared psychic and not in the lower register of matter, which is the realm only of the unconscious and occultly striving or desiring, and so in neither case of the communal. Whenever equality has tried to speak in the name of our lowest shared attribute, a fantasized and grim purpose has been ideologically attributed to the innocent simplicity of matter—whether of racial preference, class preference, or economic growth for the sake of it. The option of "disenchanted immanence" has failed us dismally.

Instead, I have been advocating a more democratized version of "enchanted transcendence," which sees all worldly realities, including cultural ones, as symbolizing something higher and hidden. This perspective respects both nature as beyond the human and yet the higher place of many degrees of flora and fauna, with humanity at the top, within that nature itself. Allowing that our psychic culture belongs to *physis* allows us also to develop a humanistic ecology that yet avoids a triumphalism about the human ability to control the natural world.

This perspective is also to be preferred to the "disenchanted transcendence" of Jansenism and Unitarian Newtonianism that drove so much of the Enlightenment—where the creation does not symbolize an arbitrary God, but is rather his plaything. Fallen human beings are then encouraged like their maker to dominate nature, even though they cannot be trusted to relate to one another but must rather bend to this deity's providential cunning that distills a simulacrum of the political out of psychic disorder.

But enchanted transcendence is furthermore to be preferred to the enchanted immanence or pantheism of the pre-Romantic Goethe and other "radical enlightenment" Spinozists, or more recently of Heidegger. For while this perspective allows us to wonder at the irreducible enigma of nature (and rightly argues that we can better understand the causes of the natural world by religiously or poetically contemplating its upshots than by dissecting its mechanisms), it denies the reality of personal forces behind nature and so denies the sanctity of our own interpersonal life.

Katheleen Raine was so much more perceptive than most university academics in realizing that fully fledged early Romantics—like Blake, Shelley, Wordsworth, and Coleridge with their German contemporaries Novalis, Hölderlin, and Freidrich Schlegel or their French ones Joseph Joubert, Chateaubriand, Maine de Biran, and the young Victor Hugo—for all their idiosyncratic, diverse, and periodic modes of political radicalism, actually refused this impersonal pantheism just as much as they refused the cult of "Nobodaddy," or the worship of monstrous willfulness. Instead, they sought to reenchant transcendence and thereby recover the archaic Western wisdom in a more culturally dispersed, imaginatively mediated, and feeling-imbued idiom that could unite nobly esoteric teaching with openly popular appreciation.

12

The New Atheism and Christian Cosmology

Aidan Nichols

Preamble

Stratford Caldecott has been an indefatigable apostle for the faith, with countless initiatives to his credit for its furtherance in culture. And in his own writing, the theme of cosmology has been perhaps the most prominent. I hope, therefore, that my own great debt to him, as publisher, publicist, and friend, will be not remitted but registered by the contribution that follows.

Who Are the New Atheists?

Atheists come and go in various centuries. The phrase "The New Atheism" denotes principally a group of writers who emerged in America and Britain from 2004 onwards, along with their supporters and epigones. They are sometimes known, with apologies to Saint John the Divine, as "The Four Horsemen": Sam Harris, author of *The End of Faith: Religion, Terror, and the Future of Reason*;[1] Richard Dawkins, author of *The God Delusion*;[2] Daniel C. Dennett, author of *Breaking the Spell: Religion as a Natural Phenomenon*;[3] and Christopher Hitchens, author of *God Is Not Great: The Case against Religion*.[4] In themselves, public disputes about the existence of God—and atheism is normally defined as the denial of divine existence—are not, of course, something new. Thus in the 1960s, for example, there was already a debate about the so-called death of God. The April 8, 1966, issue of *Time*

---

1. Harris, *The End of Faith*.
2. Dawkins, *The God Delusion*.
3. Dennett, *Breaking the Spell*.
4. Hitchens, *God Is Not Great*.

magazine, for instance, had as its cover, against a black background, the words in red letters "Is God Dead?" And it will not escape Catholic clergy interested in knowing what went wrong in the post-Conciliar epoch in the West that this issue appeared only nine months after the conclusion of the Second Vatican Council. Further back, in the years immediately following the Second World War, the vogue for Existentialist Humanism in continental Europe produced its own discussion of the desirability or otherwise of recognizing the existence of God, and notably as to whether divine planning was compatible with human freedom. Most famously of all, nineteenth-century natural science, via the Darwinian theory of evolution, stimulated a renewal of philosophical materialism among the educated elite, to which G. K. Chesterton made his own inimitable response in his critical essays published in the reign of Edward VII: *Heretics* and *Orthodoxy*. The New Atheism of today is closest to the last of these, the Darwin effect, not least because it is led more by scientists than by philosophers. As we shall see, it is in one respect a rerun of mid-Victorian debates, which is why the name of Darwin crops up with such predictable regularity.

There is, however, one, if not only one, clear difference that separates it from the historical Charles Darwin, and indeed from such late Victorian adherents of Darwinism as the Cambridge philosopher Henry Sidgwick. Whereas the latter (Darwin, Sidgwick, and others) were fearful for the future of culture—or, as they would have said, civilization—once it became plain that there was no God to support traditional morality (for by what sanction could the masses now be bidden to be good?), the New Atheists who are our contemporaries consider their own atheism to be, on the contrary, a liberation of authentic morality and hence a boon for the future of culture. In this, they resemble such postwar European Existentialists as Jean-Paul Sartre, though their reason for regarding atheism as a necessary condition of genuine humanism is very different from his. For Sartre, it is only if there is no God who has laid down the essence of human nature in advance that human beings are free to define the shape of their own existence as they decide, and to Sartre's eyes it is in such free decision that the heart of morality consists. For the New Atheists, by contrast, scientific enlightenment, by eliminating religion, will sweep away the principal current threat to the flourishing of the human species, which to their mind is not, as it was to Sartre, lack of existential commitment but religion itself.

Where Does the New Atheism Come From?

It is widely credited that the emergence of the New Atheism is related to the events formulaically described as "9/11": the destruction by militant Muslims of New York's landmark Twin Towers. A central and distinctive thesis of the New Atheism runs: Religion is murderous. While, to be sure, only extreme religion commits atrocities, moderate religion, say New Atheists, is also dangerous because it provides cover for extreme religion and prepares the way for it. This is the principal theme in Harris's *The End of Faith*, and it is prominent in both Dawkins' *The God Delusion* and Hitchens' *God Is Not Great*, the title of which is of course a parody of the daily announcement of the Islamic profession of faith from the minaret. The enormous sales of these books in the United States, a society where a large majority of people are nominal theists of Christian tradition, is thus partly to be explained by Islamophobia, but Islamophobia extended (so it may be suggested) into fear of hard-line evangelicalism. Just as Muslim militants attacked the Twin Towers, so evangelical militants have attacked abortion clinics, and to conventional liberals no great moral divide separates these two examples of terrorist acts. In the case of Richard Dawkins, the bogey-role played by evangelicalism among the American-based writers (who include a second Englishman, Christopher Hitchens) is assigned, rather, to the Catholic Church. This is curious, given the highly minoritarian status of Catholic Christianity in England, but it probably reflects an awareness that Catholics form the backbone of the anti-abortion movement, itself deemed a threat to humane coexistence (of adults, presumably). Dawkins began to develop an aggressively atheistic agenda long before 9/11—in the 1980s, in fact.[5] Without focusing on the issue of terrorism, his atheist apologetics manages to include, nonetheless, the claim that religion is not only epistemologically ungrounded but tends ineluctably to the generation of moral evil.

What Is the Impact of the New Atheists?

The New Atheism appears to have had a degree of success in its attempts to persuade people that even mild religion has the capacity to breed extremist attitudes—for which latter thesis there is some empirical evidence in the way that in America evangelical Protestantism has grown recently at the expense of mainline Protestantism (just as, it may be said, orthodox Catholicism in the same period has grown—albeit not demographically to the same extent—at the expense of liberal Catholicism in that country).

5. McGrath, *Dawkins' God*, 8–9.

Enthusiastic religiosity alarms secular-minded people (as perhaps it alarms some national conferences of bishops!). Were one to think merely politically about these matters, there could be some wisdom in restraining such enthusiasm if it is true that, as David Ramsay Steele, author of *Atheism Explained: From Folly to Philosophy*, declares, "Bold and explicit atheism is generally a response to bold and explicit religiosity."[6]

Steele believes that atheism is on a winning streak in American culture today. What are the trends in the United States that he has in mind? This is an important question for us on the British side of the Atlantic as well. The Catholic Church in America is too important to the English-speaking world, owing not least to its publishing houses and journals and to the exemplary character of a number of its bishops and seminaries, for us in Albion to face its decline with equanimity. Likewise, the example of American society is crucial more widely for rebutting the so-called secularization thesis, according to which the more prosperous and educated a society becomes the less religious does it turn out.

The trends involved are often expressed statistically. Overall, as protagonists of the New Atheism like to point out, the category of Americans who disavow any religious label has increased steadily over a number of years. Their number has now hit 16 percent of the population at large, and, somewhat worryingly, that figure rises to 25 percent for those aged between eighteen and twenty-nine.[7] In itself, however, this trend is too long-standing to be attributable to the New Atheism, and doubtless has a number of triggers. It may be worth adding that the decline of the Catholic population in the United States (as likewise here in England) is masked by ongoing Catholic immigration. The Pew Research Center's Forum on Religion and Public Life, in its "United States Religious Landscape Survey," suggests that, at the end of the first decade of the twenty-first century a third of native-born American Catholics have disaffiliated from the church, around half of whom have joined no other religious body. Nearly all the other half of this constituency have become Protestants: some two-thirds are converts to evangelicalism, while one-third have started attending the mainline Protestant denominations—Presbyterianism, Methodism, Episcopalianism, and Lutheranism.[8]

Arguably there are few lessons for church policy to be learned from the statistics of conversions to Protestantism, since the likely reasons why people have left the Catholic Church for, alternatively, evangelical and mainline

---

6. Steele, "Is God Coming or Going?" 11.

7. Ibid.

8. As noted in Reese, "The Hidden Exodus."

bodies, cancel each other out: we are not strict enough, confessionally and morally, for potential evangelicals; we are too strict for potential mainliners. The remedy here, as everywhere, is better catechesis, better liturgy, better preaching, and more focused or at least attentive pastoral care. There may, however, be particular lessons to be learned from those who disaffiliate and join no other Christian body, since these statistics will surely include some people influenced in recent years by the New Atheism. Rebutting the New Atheism is, then, worthwhile, and not just in America.

What Do the New Atheists Have to Say?

The writings of the Four Horsemen of Atheism cover too wide a number of topics to be dealt with in a single presentation (there are several book-length responses to Richard Dawkins, the only English-based member of their company, such as those by the Oxford professor Alister McGrath, a biochemist turned theologian, and, in briefer compass but more comprehensively, by the English Dominican Thomas Crean).[9] But a principal common thread in their writings is the case to be made against theism from the side of natural science, and especially from the standpoint of the life sciences.

The natural sciences, thanks to their practical as well as theoretical achievements, understandably enjoy great prestige in our culture, not least in the shape of medical technology and information technology, the two main ways where they impinge on ordinary life. Yet, as an Irish writer has remarked, the increasing abstraction of scientific theories means that these sciences exercise "much less influence on the prevailing image of the world in the general culture of our times than they did in the preceding centuries."[10] That may seem a surprising claim, but I believe it is true. Too many concepts in modern science seem to violate common sense: I have in mind, for example, the notion of string theory for which the entire universe is made up of tiny vibrating strings, or the postulate of the so-called M-theory that our universe is merely one of many, none of the others being, however, accessible by experiment. Both of these notions are prominent in Stephen Hawking's 2010 book *The Grand Design*, in which he declared his own atheism explicitly for the first time.[11]

In terms of dislodging science from its position of cultural dominance it is perhaps just as well that the vast majority of people who read of them

9. McGrath, *Dawkins' God*; see also Crean, *A Catholic Replies to Professor Dawkins*.

10. Cáoimh, "Roman Catholicism," 148.

11. Hawking and Mlodinow, *The Grand Design*.

find these cutting-edge scientific theories inherently implausible. It partly makes up for the unfortunate fact that in recent centuries in England, and thus in Anglo-America, the predominant form philosophical enquiry has taken has been either empiricism or analytical philosophy. I call their salience "unfortunate" because in themselves these philosophical movements are not well placed to challenge the hegemony of natural science: empiricism owing to its tendency to morph into positivism, which is another name for scientism—regarding natural scientific methods as the only methods of human enquiry likely to produce worthwhile results; and analytical philosophy because it has often defined its own task as furnishing the underlying logic for scientific formulations. Such philosophical traditions produce a bias towards accepting the science-centeredness New Atheists typically espouse.

Rebutting the New Atheism's Critique

Fortunately, however, the empiricist bias of our culture has one redeeming feature, and this is its respect for historical facts. Here to my mind is where a critique of the scientism of the New Atheists could appropriately begin. The New Atheists assume that the Judaeo-Christian tradition has been constantly, not to say consistently, at loggerheads with natural science. The historical evidence fails to support this thesis. So far as the English-language discussion goes, aside from a couple of late nineteenth- or early twentieth-century histories of the interrelation of science by positivist writers, it seems correct to say that no substantial contributors to this subject have ever before taken this unrelievedly bleak view of the relations of religion and science. Even leaving aside those scholars who argue that, without the doctrine of creation understood through the lens of Christian metaphysics, modern science could never have emerged in the sixteenth and seventeenth centuries (I am thinking of such writers as the Hungarian Benedictine Stanley Jaki and the Oxford physicist Peter Hodgson),[12] it is a commonplace to say that in the general history of the relations of Western science and Western religion the case of Galileo is outstanding for proving the exception to the rule.[13]

The Galileo case is notoriously complex (non-standard discussions hold that, for instance, the papal objection was really to his atomic theory, which, in the manner of its expression, entailed difficulties for the eucharistic conversion understood as transubstantiation, or that, alternatively, Galileo was censured for seeking to prove a novel physical theory from scripture).

12. Jaki, *The Origin of Science*; see also Hodgson, *Christianity and Science*.
13. McMullin, *The Church and Galileo*; Numbers, *Galileo Goes to Jail*.

But assuming that the standard accounts are correct, namely, that the charge against him was teaching the demonstrable character of heliocentrism, then Peter Harrison, an Australian Protestant, who until recently held the Andreas Idrios Chair of Science and Religion at Oxford, writes helpfully,

> In the case of Galileo, the Catholic Church was not opposing science per se. On the contrary, it was using its considerable authority to endorse what was then the consensus of the scientific community. This course of action may have been imprudent, and it offends modern sensibilities. But it does not betray any intrinsic antipathy towards science on the part of the Roman Church.[14]

It was owing to the embarrassment caused by the Galileo case that not only Catholic but also Anglican and other Christian spokesmen were cautious, in the mid-nineteenth century, when faced with the challenge of Darwinism.[15] The celebrated debate in Oxford between Thomas Huxley and Bishop Samuel Wilberforce of which a purely legendary account entered popular consciousness in the Victorian period, so far from being a slapstick, knock-about affair between a sage of science and an outraged ecclesiastic, was actually a high-level discussion of the scientific counterevidence to Darwin's thesis. Like many nineteenth-century clerics in the Church of England, and indeed, for that matter, like Darwin himself, Wilberforce was a self-taught naturalist.

Such scientific counterevidence (which may be brought forward either to dispute evolutionary transformism as such or to criticize a particular version of such transformism) remains of great importance when Darwin's thesis is reductively interpreted, as it was at Huxley's hands where random mutation leading to the survival of the fittest figured as evolution's only motor. This reductionist unilateralism returned with the Neo-Darwinians of the 1930s, and now today it is back once more with the New Atheists. When we are considering Darwinism of this kind, it is not irrelevant to note some of its wider ambiguities. I have in mind the social philosopher Herbert Spencer's inferences from Huxley's popularized Darwinism (to which Darwin himself was not, it seems, altogether resistant[16]). Historians of the modern period often regard Spencer's "Social Darwinism" as fostering militarism or at the least sharpening international antagonism, notably between the British and German empires, in the years preceding the First World War.

14. Harrison, "Introduction," 5.

15. Artigas, Glick, and Martinez, *Negotiating Darwin*; Moore, *Post-Darwinian Controversies*.

16. Weikart, "Recently Discovered Darwin Letter."

It certainly helped popularize eugenics, new technologies for weeding out weak examples of the species, especially in Germany.[17]

This, so it would seem, is the essential background in America to the rise of creationism, an outright rejection of any form of evolutionism, since the principal motivation of leading creationists, who included William Jennings Bryan, a three-time Democratic Party presidential nominee, was not so much the defense of a literal reading of Genesis for its own sake as it was the assertion of the equality of all members of the human species as children of Adam.

In the eyes of a number of commentators, the New Atheists are fundamentalist Darwinists who adhere (so to speak) less to the Darwin of history than to the Charles of faith. Darwin himself wrote, in the sixth edition of *On the Origin of Species,*

> As my conclusions have lately been much misrepresented, and it has been stated that I attribute the modification of species exclusively to natural selection, I may be permitted to remark that in the first edition of this work, and subsequently, I placed in a most conspicuous position—namely, at the close of the Introduction—the following words. "I am convinced that natural selection has been the main, but not the exclusive, means of modification." This has been of no avail. Great is the power of steady misrepresentation.[18]

Such simplification did not cease when, in the 1930s, the Darwinian theory was married with Mendelian genetics with a view to showing how variations in organisms occur, and are passed on, through chromosomes—what Mendel called "inheritance particles." (Darwin knew variations produced characteristics that were heritable, but not *how* they were heritable.) Such synthesizing of Darwinian natural selection with genetics was subsequently repeated in the second half of the twentieth century, this time with the new genetics, which were "new" because they now investigated the chemical composition of chromosomes—an area opened up by the work of James Watson and Francis Crick in their discovery of the double helix: the shape or form of DNA (the molecule that contains the genetic code) and RNA (the molecule that carries out the instructions of DNA in the making of proteins).

The version of the theory of evolution found in, especially, Daniel Dennett and Richard Dawkins maintains the same unilateral character that Darwin himself criticized in Huxley and others. Dennett remarks

17. Weikart, *From Darwin to Hitler.*
18. Darwin, *On the Origin of Species,* 395.

sweepingly that the idea of natural selection "unifies all of biology and the history of our planet into a single grand story."[19] But for Gabriel Dover, who holds the chair of genetics at the University of Leicester, writing apropos of the selfsame strategy adopted by Dennett's English counterpart, Richard Dawkins, acceptance of this maxim commits its supporters to a "global explanation for the evolution of complex adaptations in all life forms, wholly in terms of 'for the good of the genes'"[20] by means of a monocausal theory that is simplistic and (therefore) ultimately unconvincing.

In *Dear Mr. Darwin: Letters on the Evolution of Life and Human Nature*, Dover proposes instead a variety of causes for novelty in biological function. Among these causes, natural selection of optimal adaptations to current environment is only one. Alongside natural selection and adaptation must be placed, firstly, what Dover calls "neutral drift"—non-advantageous mutation spread by sexual reproduction—and "exaptation"—the subsequent evolutionary validation of neutral drift by later changes in the environment, as well as, secondly, "molecular drive" entailing "adoption" or "molecular co-evolution"—which is where a "molecularly driven" change in a population allows that population, on average, to adopt a component of its existing environment not previously accessible to it (thus, for example, when centipedes develop legs they are able to enter new habitats away from predators).[21] The palaeontologist Stephen Jay Gould adds that also needed for the full evolutionary story are such one-off events as meteorite storms whose impact on earth may have been the single chief cause for the disappearance of the dinosaurs and the emergence from their shadow of the mammals.

These more recent arguments about the factors operative in the story of evolution supplement other objections raised since the days of Darwin's earliest critics, objections that constitute difficulties for the theory of evolution as such. These would include the relative absence of intermediate forms in the fossil record; the long-term stability of most species; the exuberance, surpassing utility for survival, in such matters as the coloration of butterfly wings; the damaging nature of most mutations in animal life; and (perhaps especially) the interdependence of organs or characteristics that would have to appear simultaneously if they are to grant an evolutionary advantage. The difficulty of seeing how the interdependence of functioning parts in the cell itself could have appeared gradually was, it seems, the problem which prompted the conversion to some form of theism of the British academic

19. Dennett, *Darwin's Dangerous Idea*, cited in Caldecott, "Theories of Evolution," 5.

20. Dover, *Dear Mr. Darwin*, 51.

21. Ibid., 42.

sometimes called the most celebrated atheistic philosopher of the English-speaking world, the late Anthony Flew.

Design as Fine-Tuning and Human Origins

Let us assume, then, that certain members of the scientific community are right to reject a monocausal account of the development of species. In that case, insofar as there has been a process of evolution in the story of life forms on this planet (and, for the reasons just given, some, with understandable caution, would prefer to affirm only what one French writer has called a "strong bond between all living things"),[22] one should (accordingly) speak of a fine-tuning of the factors involved in the development of the species which make up the ecological setting of man.

Just so, a very different kind of scientist—the astrophysicists concerned with the origins of the universe—have often spoken of the fine-tuning of factors enabling the Big Bang or primal singularity (generally dated fourteen billion years BC) to issue in galaxies made up of solar systems with planets, some of which are capable of sustaining living organisms. Indeed, some supporters of galactic fine-tuning argue that the universe had to have the kind of dimensions it has for it to be likely that our sort of life would emerge, since the factors involved are so numerous and delicately balanced that nothing smaller will do. This is the so-called anthropic cosmological principle.[23]

If we apply this same idea to the emergence of higher animals, the question then naturally arises, should such fine-tuning be called "design"? The Canadian philosopher Charles Taylor has something to say on this subject. What Taylor calls "ideological Darwinians" put forward what he terms

> the dogmatic negative claim that the ultimate account of how evolution works, if we ever attain it, will make no reference to design in any shape or form. Design must purely figure among the *explanada* [the things that are to be explained], never among the *explananda* [the things that do the explaining], of evolutionary theory. [Such ideological Darwinians] face off against "creationists," who wish to deny altogether the descent of species, at least as far as humans are concerned. The locus of intra-cosmic mystery here which most people feel who aren't in the grip of

22. Blignières, "Un regard thomiste sur l'Evolution," 63.
23. Barrow and Tipler, *The Anthropic Cosmological Principle.*

either ideology, viz. how it is that somehow design emerges in a universe of contingency, is rigorously banned by both sides.[24]

While eschewing creationism, then, Taylor seeks to distance himself from those who disdain all concept of design in the cosmos. May it be suggested that fine-tuning—both in the development of species on earth as much as in the emergence of the wider galactic universe—is the crucial embodiment of design?

In effect, to maintain as much constitutes a *new sort of design argument*. We have been through this kind of shift before. The early modern design argument, as found in the age of Newton, was already something different from the medieval arguments from end-directedness—from teleology. The medieval arguments, as in Saint Thomas's fifth way, simply pointed to the overall orderliness of the world. Either agency is *for* something, or it is quite unintelligible. The early modern design argument, whose most distinguished supporter was Isaac Newton himself, went further because, to quote from Taylor again, that argument "hoped to fathom God's Providence in its own terms," which the medievals had not ventured to do.[25] Seventeenth- and eighteenth-century natural philosophers sought to show how the universe had been shaped to conduce to the welfare of God's creatures, and notably to the welfare of human beings, seen as lords of creation. Design as fine-tuning, when considered in the context of the evolution of species, is neither of the medieval kind nor of the early modern variety. Instead, it concentrates exclusively on a single phenomenon: the conspiring together of a variety of mechanisms and events in the emergence of the inhabitants of the planet as we know them.

If this is what we should understand by the phrase "intelligent design," then the latter is not (as has been alleged) dependent on the positing of gaps in scientific knowledge that one day may be filled naturalistically. On the contrary, accepting evolution as a hypothesis—*datum non* (entirely) *concessum*—this argument for fine-tuning concerns the dovetailing of factors in evolution that scientific knowledge already entertains.

Taylor might well agree—so far. Yet he overlooks a doctrinal point that no intellectually responsible Catholic Christian should ignore. The Catholic Church has a long-standing doctrinal tradition, expressed most recently in Pius XII's 1950 encyclical *Humani generis*, for which the human soul is directly created by God, and cannot be regarded, therefore, as simply derivative from prior configurations of animal life. There is a sense in which Catholic Christians are *inevitably* creationists—albeit on this single point.

24. Taylor, *Secular Age*, 331.
25. Ibid., 343.

We cannot accept that the moral and spiritual life of humanity belongs to an unbroken continuum in the biosphere. Here there really is, we hold, a gap that science cannot fill. It is not primarily a gap in an explanation, but an ontological gap, a gap in reality. However, this ontological gap between the human soul and all other known life does itself *require* an explanation.

What is remarkable here is that the new genetics and that other growth point in the natural scientific study of the human being, the neuroscience of the brain, appear to have reached a point where, so some would argue, these sciences need to recognize the qualitative difference represented by the advent of *homo sapiens*. In his *Why Us? How Science Rediscovered the Mystery of Ourselves*, the scientific commentator James Le Fanu describes how, on the eve of the new millennium, high hopes were raised for two massive international scientific projects: the mapping by geneticists of the human genome, and the scanning by neuroscientists of the structure of the brain. These two projects initially entailed a prediction by scientists that the mystery of man's distinctiveness in the cosmos would shortly be solved. The Human Genome Project should have involved demonstrating how particular arrangements of genes in human beings account for their difference from other primates or, for that matter, from mice or mushrooms. The other project, called "The Decade of the Brain," should have enabled us to understand how particular sets of neurons in the brain correspond to the various kinds of perception and thinking that we hold to be distinctively human— there being no available evidence that other animals do crosswords or compose music comparable to Mozart's. According to Le Fanu, both projects egregiously failed, in the sense that they produced results that shed no light on the truly big questions about man. The discovery in the Genome Project that we share 98.5 percent of our genes with chimpanzees (55 percent with the house fly, 35 percent with bananas) meant that, genetically speaking, there was nothing to account for, for instance, human powers of reason and imagination or the human faculty of language. As one historian of science put it, the Genome Project proved to be

> one of those rare and wonderful moments when success teaches us humility. . . . We lulled ourselves into believing that in discovering the basis for genetic information we had found "the secret of life"; we were confident that if we could only decode the message in the sequence of chemicals, we would understand the "program" that makes an organism what it is. But now there is at least a tacit acknowledgment of how large that gap between genetic "information" and biological meaning really is.[26]

26. Keller, *Making Sense of Life*, 16. See also Chandebois, *Pour en finir avec le darwinisme*.

Similarly, in the Decade of the Brain, exhaustive scanning of the brain shows each separate task not only lighting up the immediately relevant part of the brain but, in Le Fanu's words, "generating a blizzard of electrical activity across vast networks of millions of neurons,"[27] such that, for instance, thinking about a particular word or enunciating a particular word seems to activate brain activity virtually in its entirety. This was not what was expected. As John Maddox, the editor of the flagship scientific journal *Nature*, noted at the close of the Decade of the Brain, "We seem as far from understanding the brain as we were a century ago. Nobody understands how decisions are made or how imagination is set free."[28] Or to put it another way, the realization is dawning that one can know all that appears to be knowable about the structure of the brain and still know nothing about the mind (or, as some of us still prefer to say, the *soul*).

A Christian Cosmology

Evidently, natural science is seeking to answer questions that lie outside its proper domain. A Christian cosmology, resourced from both revelation and the wisdom tradition of metaphysics, may be better able to answer them. In terms of the doctrine of creation, we can speak of God thinking the entire order and dynamism of the universe from the moment of its origin, so as to allow the progressive deployment of its latent powers. Augustine of Hippo already had remarkable intuitions about the progressive deployment of the virtualities of created nature, especially in his *De Trinitate* and the *De Genesi ad litteram*. In the former of those treatises, he wrote, "Certainly, all that we see has been created originally and fundamentally, *originaliter ac primordialiter*, in a kind of web of elements, *in quadam textura elementorum*."[29]

At the same time, the doctrine of creation, which asserts the radical dependence of the world on God for its being, also entails the openness of the world to God at all points. A Christian cosmology will accept the possibility of special divine agency within the cosmic process: and in the case of the emergence of man this is verified by the theological anthropology of the church. Although divine imagehood extends to the human body—for man is a body-soul composite—that imagehood has its seat in the human soul, which is itself the sign of our personal character, our inherent potential for hypostatic relatedness to each other in a communion of loving knowledge, which mirrors that of the Holy Trinity. This is not a feature of the cosmos

27. Le Fanu, *Why Us?*, 17.
28. Maddox, "Unexpected Science to Come."
29. Augustine, *De Trinitate*, 9.9, 16.

that could have emerged from below, yet it required an adjustment in human brain size to be feasible in a physical context. The size of the actual human brain is quite disproportionate to the needs of a hunter-gatherer population, such as, for natural anthropology the first human beings were. Our kind of brain is in that context evolutionarily disadvantageous, for it multiplies the energy needs of the body and creates especial problems for obstetrics in childbirth.

I would like to mention here the often forgotten co-discoverer of natural selection, Alfred Russel Wallace, whose 1858 letter to Darwin on variations from types, written from his fieldwork camp in the Moluccas, spurred Darwin to rush out in 1859 the publication of *On the Origin of Species* for fear of being scooped. In Wallace's judgment, natural selection would by itself have prevented the emergence of human-type intelligence since the latter was not, he considered, a useful adaptation to environment. This led Wallace to invoke as explanation what he called an "Overruling Intelligence," his name for God.[30] I find it noteworthy that for his own mature notion of guided evolution, set out in his 1910 synthesis *The World of Life*, Wallace revived a doctrine of angels as teleologically directive powers ensuring the calibration of factors in evolution and their convergence on a kind of being (namely, ourselves) who could both understand, and at the same time, aesthetically delight in, the living world.[31] That Wallace was not an orthodox Christian, perhaps not a Christian at all, makes it the more interesting that he sought to access this now marginalized theme of Christian cosmology.[32]

A Christian cosmology will not of course confine itself to the Overruling Intelligence and the possible mediating role of the angels in cosmic becoming. Writing to the Colossians, Saint Paul already warned against allowing speculation about the cosmic powers to displace interest in the mystery of Christ. A Christian cosmology will affirm the more primary mediation of the world's creation by the pre-existent Logos, who, as the expression of the Father's mind, is the ultimate source of the intelligibility that science explores. It will also affirm the destiny of the world as the world's taking up into the latreutic act whereby the Word incarnate gives glory to

30. Smith, *Alfred Russel Wallace*, 34, 31.

31. Flannery, *Alfred Russel Wallace's Theory*, 17. What Wallace has to say is consonant with Saint Thomas Aquinas's teaching that God governs inferior things through superior ones—not because he is lacking in his own power but, on the contrary, from the abundance of his goodness, by which he allows creatures to share in the causality that constitutes his nature as the First Cause Uncaused (Aquinas, *Summa Theologiae* I, q. 22, a. 3). The First Cause gives *being*; secondary causes determine it.

32. Mongrain, "Eyes of Reason," 193.

the Father through healing and elevating the human species by his cross and resurrection, sending forth on redeemed humanity the Spirit of them both, the consummator of the cosmos, with implications for the wider universe that we find already laid out by Saint Paul in the Letter to the Romans for the wider universe: "the whole creation groaning in travail together until now" (Rom 8:22), but then it will be "set free from its bondage to decay and obtain the glorious liberty of the children of God" (v. 21).

Man as the child of God clothed in Jesus Christ, our Archetype and redemptive Re-fashioner, within an ecology eschatologically transformed by the Spirit—that is our sure and certain hope for the world.[33]

---

33. For a magnificent evocation, based on twentieth-century Eastern Orthodox writers, see Theokritoff, "Embodied Word."

13

Many Mansions in My Father's House

A Qur'anic Interpretation

Reza Shah-Kazemi

For each We have appointed from you a Law and a Way. And had God willed, He could have made you one community. But in order that He might try you by that which He hath given you [He hath made you as you are]. So vie with one another in good works. Unto God ye will all return, and He will inform you of that wherein ye differed.

—QUR'AN 5:48[1]

This part[2] of verse 5:48 is often given as a proof-text for upholding the principle that religious diversity, far from being the result of purely human contingencies, is a divinely willed phenomenon and is therefore to be accepted and respected as such. It should also be seen as one of the key verses of the Qur'an in which the metaphysical principle of unity in diversity (*al-wahda fi'l-kathra*), and its converse, diversity in unity, is intimated. It also articulates the theodicy underlying the phenomenon of religious diversity, a phenomenon that might be seen as implied in the words of Christ: "In my Father's House are many mansions" (John 14:2).[3] Seen from a Qur'anic perspective, this idea of diversity subsisting within or contained by the unity

---

1. The translations given here are based on the now classic translation of Muhammad Marmaduke Pickthall, with certain modifications.

2. The latter part, that is; the beginning of the verse will be cited below.

3. It is interesting and important to note that, according to the immensely influential Sufi master, the Shaykh al-'Alawī, the Arabic word for Father, *Ab*, is a Name of God, precisely because Jesus referred to God thus: "Verily I go unto my Father and your Father" (John 20:17). See Lings, *Sufi Saint of the Twentieth Century*, 150.

of the divine reality goes to the very heart of the Islamic principle of *tawhīd*, which does not simply mean "unity," or the affirmation and declaration of unity, but rather "unification" or "integration." At the highest level, the unification in question pertains to our conception of God: since, objectively, there is no divinity but God, so, subjectively, our conception of that reality must be shorn of any alterity—either numerical or ontological. We must realize that God's oneness transcends both numerical unity and ontological plurality. There is indeed but a single divine Essence, but that Essence comprises infinite perfections, whence the panoply of divine names and qualities. The "House" of God's essence is beautiful, and within this House are "many mansions" of beauty: the infinitude of his most beautiful qualities. God is beautiful (*jamīl*), the Prophet tells us, and he loves beauty (*jamāl*);[4] hence, the names designating his qualities must likewise be not just beautiful, but supremely beautiful: "Unto Him belong the most beautiful Names [*al-asmā' al-husnā*]—so call Him by them" (7:180).

This diversity within unity can be seen on various levels, beginning with the divine, the scriptural, and the religious, and extending to the existential and the human reflections of the one and only reality: "We shall show them Our signs[5] on the horizons [around them] and in their own souls, until it be clear to them that It is the Truth. Doth it not suffice that thy Lord encompasseth all things?" (41:53–54).

From a Qur'anic point of view, the plurality of religions is not the result of fallible human "cognitive responses" to the ineffable Absolute—as one kind of pluralism, that expounded by John Hick, would have us believe;[6] rather, in the light of 5:48 and kindred verses, the plurality of religious forms is a mysterious and inspiring expression of the infallible will and unfathomable wisdom of God. That wisdom is unique—"There is no new thing under the Sun" (Eccl 1:9)—but its expression through different religious forms varies. Verse 5:48 clearly establishes the fact that each religious community has its own (formal) law and its own (spiritual) path, and that the reason for diversifying these laws and ways is for God to test the different communities, using as a standard "that which he hath given" each of these

---

4. This is a strongly authenticated saying, found in various collections; see for example *Sahīh Muslim*, vol. 1, *Encyclopaedia of Hadith*, 53, saying no. 275. The saying is also found in the collections of al-Tirmidhī and Ahmad b. Hanbal.

5. The word here is *āyāt*, plural of *āya*, which also means "verse," as of scripture.

6. For Hick's influential but flawed attempt to delineate a philosophy of religious pluralism, see his *God and the Universe of Faiths*. See, for a good critique of this perspective, D'Costa, "The Impossibility of a Pluralist View of Religions," and my *Other in the Light of the One*, 249–66, in which Hick's pluralism is contrasted with Seyyed Hossein Nasr's universalism.

communities. One recalls here the parable of the talents in the Gospel (Matt 25:14–30).

The specific rites and rituals, legal and ethical codes, principles of thought and culture, comprised within each religious form, correspond precisely to the needs of the different communities addressed by the revelation. For the messenger bearing the revelation is always sent conveying the message in "the language of his folk" (14:4). This message is identical in its essence, however varied be the forms assumed by it, and however different be the languages by which it is articulated:

- "And We sent no messenger before thee but We inspired him [saying]: There is no God save Me, so worship Me" (21:25).

- "Naught is said unto thee [Muhammad] but what was said unto the messengers before thee" (41:43).

- "Say: I am nothing new among the messengers" (46:9).

Another important expression of the unity of the message, despite the variety of outward forms it assumes, is given in the following verses, which come closest of all to defining the Muslim *credo* (closest, that is, after the double testimony of faith: "No god but God; Muhammad is the Messenger of God"): "The messenger believeth in that which hath been revealed unto him from his Lord, and [so do] the believers. Every one believeth in God and His angels and His scriptures and His messengers—we make no distinction between any of His messengers" (2:285). This refusal to distinguish between the Messengers, as regards the fundamentals of their message, is echoed in several other verses. For example:

> Say: We believe in God and that which is revealed unto us, and that which is revealed unto Abraham and Ishmael and Isaac and Jacob and the tribes, and that which was given unto Moses and Jesus and the prophets from their Lord. We make no distinction between any of them, and unto Him we have submitted. (3:84)

Just as the essence of the message is universal, comprising all the forms by which it is enclothed and delivered to the different communities, likewise, the result of heeding the message—salvation—is of necessity universal. Salvation is to be regarded not as the exclusive prerogative of any single community, but as the reward of grace bestowed upon the soul that sincerely submits to God in accordance with the *Law* and the *Way* prescribed by God. Indeed, one of the most impressive expressions of the metaphysical or supra-confessional scope of the Qur'anic perspective is the way in which it defines access to salvation in terms of intrinsic faith rather than extrinsic religious affiliation:

Truly those who believe, and the Jews, and the Christians, and the Sabeans[7]—whoever believeth in God and the Last Day and performeth virtuous deeds—surely their reward is with their Lord, and no fear shall come upon them, neither shall they grieve. (2:62)

Here, the list of religious believers according to denomination is abruptly cut short by the universal principle which all outward religious forms are supposed to signify and help to realize: belief in the Absolute and accountability to the Absolute, on the one hand, and virtuous action, on the other. There are thus many celestial gardens in the Paradise of "my Father's House." In light of 2:62 and other such verses, it is not surprising that, when asked the question, "'Which religion is most beloved by God?' the Prophet did not refer to any particular religion. Instead, he answered: 'The generously tolerant faith proper to primordial (Abrahamic) monotheism [*al-ḥanīfiyya al-samḥa*].'"[8] In other words, he points allusively to a key spiritual quality which should be infused into the soul by religion as such; the implication is that whichever religion is most successful in producing this trait becomes "the most beloved" religion to God. This close identification of generosity and tolerance with the very substance of monotheistic faith might also be seen as a comment on 49:13, which informs us of the very *raison d'être* of diversity on the human plane:

O mankind, We have created you male and female, and We have made you into tribes and nations in order that you might come to know one another. Truly, in the sight of God, the most honored of you is the most pious of you. (49:13)[9]

The hierarchy within humanity is based on intrinsic piety, not on such extrinsic factors as gender, tribe, nation, race or religion—such distinctions

---

7. The identity of the Sabeans is somewhat contested in the sources, but those "Sabeans" with whom the Muslims came into contact historically constituted a community centred in Harrān, which claimed to trace its origin back to the Prophet Enoch (in Islamic terms, Idrīs), "who is also regarded in the Islamic world as the founder of the sciences of the heavens and of philosophy, and who is identified by some with Hermes Trismegistus. The Sabaeans possessed a remarkable knowledge of astronomy, astrology and mathematics; their doctrines were in many respects similar to those of the Pythagoreans." Nasr, *Science and Civilization in Islam*, 31. See also McAuliffe, "Exegetical Identification of the Sābi'ūn."

8. Khan, *Saḥīḥ al-Bukhārī*, 34 (translation modified). This rather wordy translation of two Arabic words is difficult to avoid; the word *ḥanīf* means not just one who unerringly "inclines" towards the truth of the one God, but is personified in the Qur'an by Abraham, who thus stands for the original, or primordial monotheist par excellence.

9. See for discussion my *Spirit of Tolerance in Islam*.

being governed by the principle of mutual knowledge, and this principle, in turn, deriving its spiritual value from the piety such knowledge is supposed to foster. To return to 5:48: "so vie with one another in good works," the best of works being those that lead to love and knowledge of God. Still with 5:48, let us take careful note of the way in which the verse begins, for this statement of the relationship between the Qur'anic revelation and all previous scriptural revelations reinforces a fundamental aspect of the principle of diversity within unity: "Unto thee We have revealed the Scripture [al-kitāb] with Truth [that it may be] a confirmer of all Scripture [al-kitāb] that came before it, and a protector thereof" (5:48). Here, the key term is al-kitāb, "the Book" or "the Scripture": previously, we read about kutub, "books" or "scriptures," and that it is incumbent on all Muslims to believe in all the "books" revealed by God (2:285). Now, we see that these outwardly diverse books are in fact one in essence. Similarly, with regard to the messengers of God: they are outwardly distinct, but the Muslim is to say with regard to them, "We make no distinction between any of His Messengers," as noted in the same verse, 2:285. Not only are there many religions in "my Father's House," but there are also many scriptures, many prophets—and also, as the following verses reveal, many names of God and many temples of God. According to the exegetical tradition, these verses were the first to be revealed in relation to the legitimacy of warfare in Islam:

> Permission [to fight] is given to those who are being fought against, for they have been wronged, and surely God is able to give them victory; those who have been expelled from their homes unjustly, only because they said: Our Lord is God. Had God not driven back some by means of others, monasteries, churches, synagogues and mosques—wherein the name of God is oft-invoked—would assuredly have been destroyed. (22:39–40)

Not only is self-defense given as the primary justification for fighting, but also the oneness of the quintessential Name of God is alluded to in the diverse liturgical languages in which it is oft-invoked, in the various temples of worship which the Muslim is enjoined to defend. "Self"-defense is thus defense of all true believers, of whatever denomination; it is one and the same Name of God that is invoked in their temples, whatever be the particular language in which it is expressed. So it is not just the name Allāh, and the mosques where this Name is invoked, that the Muslim is bound to defend as sacrosanct; rather, there are many divine names, many liturgies, and many temples of worship in "my Father's House."

However, it might appear that, in certain verses, the Qur'an falls short of the universalism expressed in those we have cited above; for example, when we are told, "Whoso seeketh a religion other than Islam, it will not be accepted from him, and he will be a loser in the Hereafter" (3:85). Indeed, several traditional commentators hold that this verse abrogates 2:62—a notable exception, however, being Tabari, who maintains, with irrefutable logic, that God does not abrogate his promises.[10] It is only legal stipulations that are subject to abrogation: 2:62 cannot be abrogated because "in respect of the bestowal of reward for virtuous action with faith, God has not singled out some of His creatures as opposed to others."[11]

One way of resolving the apparent contradiction between the two verses, 2:62 and 3:85, is to focus on the literal (which is also the universal) meaning of the word *islām*: that which is unacceptable to God is any religion *other than islām* in the sense of "submission" to those religions—those specific Laws and Ways revealed by God and stressed in 5:48. Anyone seeking, in other words, a man-made religion will be *a loser in the Hereafter*. Again we return to the principle of a unique essence "housing" diverse forms: the religious phenomenon *per se* is an expression of unity in diversity, and diversity in unity:

> He hath ordained for you of the religion that which He commended unto Noah, and that which We reveal to thee [Muhammad], and that which We commended unto Abraham and Moses and Jesus, saying: Establish the religion, and be not divided therein. (42:13)

Establish *the* religion, not *a* religion: this pertains to the core of the message which is immutable and indivisible—*be not divided therein*. This message is imparted to the different prophets, of whom the Qur'an has named some, but not all. As the Qur'an itself mentions the fact that it has *not* mentioned all the prophets, the scope of the phenomenon of prophethood and revelation is expanded in an indefinite manner beyond the confines of Semitic monotheism: "Verily We sent messengers before thee; among them are those about whom We have told thee, and those about whom We have not told thee" (40:78). Indeed, there is no community on earth that has not

10. In his commentary on II: 106—"We abrogate no verse, nor do We cause it to be forgotten, but that We bring one better than it or like it"—Tabari writes, "Thus, God transforms the lawful into the unlawful, and the unlawful into the lawful, and the permitted into the forbidden, and the forbidden into the permitted. This only pertains to such issues as commands and prohibitions, proscriptions and generalizations, withholding and granting authorization. But as for reports, they cannot abrogate nor be abrogated" (*Jāmi' al-bayān*, 546).

11. Tabari, *Jāmi' al-bayān*, 373.

been the recipient of a divine message: "For every community [*umma*] there is a messenger" (10:47). It can therefore be argued that these and other such verses allow the spiritually sensitive Muslim to include within the sphere of divinely revealed religion even those traditions that (apparently) do not accept the phenomenon of divine revelation, such as Buddhism.[12] In this connection, the following verse is a kind of touchstone of authenticity: "If they believe in something like that which ye believe, then they are rightly guided" (2:137).

When confronted by an alien religion, the following questions will be asked: How "similar" is this religion to that which has been revealed by God through the Qur'an? How "similar" is it to the religion of "primordial nature" (*al-fitra*)?[13] What is the degree of similarity, and how is one to gauge it? This entire domain is left open-ended, so there can be no dogmatic foreclosure in the face of alien religions; rather, it is for each individual to answer the question about what counts as something "like" (*mithl*), doing so according to the data available on the religion, on the one hand, and on the basis of one's own resources of intellectual discernment, moral sensibility, and spiritual contemplativity, on the other.

This interpretation of the meaning of Islam is strengthened when one takes into account the Qur'anic censure of what one might call religious "chauvinism"—the narcissistic notion that only "my" religion saves, and all other religions are devoid of salvific power. Certain groups among the People of the Book encountered by the Muslims appear to have made this sort of claim about their own faith, whence the following important rebuttal:

> And they say: None entereth paradise unless he be a Jew or a Christian. These are their vain desires. Say: Bring your proof if ye are truthful. Nay, but whosoever submitteth his purpose to God, and he is virtuous, his reward is with his Lord. No fear shall come upon them, neither shall they grieve. (2:111–112)

The Muslim is told here not to respond to the baseless exclusivism of the People of the Book by upholding an equally unseemly and illogical exclusivism in turn; rather, the Muslim is told to reply with a principle, not a prejudice: the principle of *islām* as submission—"whosoever submitteth [*aslama*] his purpose to God"—not the prejudice of Islam, conceived as

12. See my *Common Ground between Islam and Buddhism*.

13. See 30:30. This religion of the fitra is referred to by the Prophet in a strongly authenticated saying as being that in accordance with which every baby is born; its parents then superimpose upon this immutable "spiritual constitution" a subsequent and relatively superficial religious identity.

one particular confession among others, formal affiliation to which, alone, opens up the gates of Paradise.

Islam itself can thus be regarded, in the light of *tawhīd*, as a principle of oneness or integration: oneness of the divine message, of human submission, of ultimate salvation. This oneness, however, is displayed in diverse forms, and herein lies one of the most important messages of Islam for devout and intelligent believers within all faiths, that is, for those who devoutly believe in God and in the normativity of their own religion and whose intelligence cannot deny the validity—at whatever degree—of religions other than their own. The Qur'anic perspective on the diversity of religious phenomena and the unity of their common substance helps one avoid the two great pitfalls of our times, as far as religious belief is concerned: corrosive relativism, on the one hand, and explosive fanaticism, on the other. For the Qur'an provides us with a spiritual, God-given (and not artificial, man-made) means of resolving outwardly diverse religious forms within a single transcendent essence; it does so, moreover, without detriment to the uniqueness and irreducibility of each of the forms thus subsumed within that essence: *for each We have appointed a Law and a Path* (emphasis added). God could have made us one religious community, but he made us as we are: diverse communities, all of which are nonetheless rooted in the one Truth. Oneness of essence is maintained without any descent into reductionism, and diversity is maintained without any descent into relativism.[14]

In this universally conceived Islam, therefore, the essence of the message is identical, while the forms taken by the message and delivered by the messengers are diverse and different, indeed, mutually exclusive. This formal differentiation is most clearly marked in the rites that each religious community is to practice: "Unto each community We have given sacred rites [*mansakan*] which they are to perform; so let them not dispute with thee about the matter, but summon them unto thy Lord" (22:67). The Lord is one, the rites he has revealed, many: there are many rites performed in "my Father's House."

There are many faces of God in "my Father's House." On the one hand, the Muslim is told specifically to turn in prayer to the Ka'ba at Mecca: "Turn thy face toward the Sacred Mosque, and ye [O Muslims], wheresoever ye may be, turn your faces [when ye pray] toward it" (2:144). And yet, on the other, the believers are told that "wherever ye turn, there is the Face of God" (2:115). One notices a paradoxical combination between ubiquity and specificity: the Face of God is everywhere, but the Muslims have been charged to

14. See Schuon, *The Transcendent Unity of Religions*, for a metaphysical exposition of this point of view; see also his excellent essay, "The Contradiction of Relativism."

turn their faces to him only in a particular direction. The ritual orientations ordained by God are means of establishing spiritual trajectories aimed at the unique Reality, and yet one must follow one set of such rites exclusively, in order to comply with the will and the wisdom of God in establishing a particular Way. The resolution of the apparent contradiction between one God and many religious beliefs and rituals is poetically expressed in the following verse:

> And in the earth are neighbouring tracts, and gardens of vines, and fields sown, and palms in pairs, and palms single, *watered with one water*. And we have made some of them to excel others in fruit. Surely herein are signs for a people who use their intelligence. (13:4; emphasis added)

The "water" of God is one and only, and yet the fruits to which it gives rise are multiple. The One is visible through the many, and the root of the many is discernible in the One. This vision of oneness does not require being blind to multiplicity and pretending that it is only an illusion—that the One alone is "real." Nor is the One to be regarded as a conceptual abstraction in the face of the concrete, manifest "reality" of the multiple. Rather, the multiple phenomena are to be grasped as so many projections or manifestations of oneness, each phenomenon being unique, by virtue of the source of its projection; and yet, each phenomenon is rendered transparent by the unitive vision that sees the face of God everywhere, according to 2:115 (cited above). From this perspective, one sees through the aspect of multiplicity to the real unity that each phenomenon replicates in its own way—to the oneness which gives it all its reality and without which it is reduced to nothingness. To see the One in the many is thus to see the Infinite through the very prism of the finite, the Absolute through the forms of the relative. Conversely, to see the many in the One is to intuit the roots of all phenomena within their celestial archetypes: all the "fruits" watered on earth are seeded by their celestial archetypes on high:

> Each time they are given sustenance [*ruziqū*] from the fruits thereof [from the gardens of Paradise] they say: this is verily what we were given as sustenance [*ruziqnā*] before [on earth]; and they were given something similar to it. (2:25)

There are infinite celestial fruits in "my Father's House," for "verily He giveth sustenance [*yarzuqu*] to whom He will beyond all measure" (3:37).[15]

---

15. This is the response given by the Blessed Virgin to the question of Zacharias when he asked her how she received fruits (out of season, according the commentators). See also 2:212 and 24:38 where this phrase is repeated almost verbatim.

It is from these paradisal archetypes that all positive phenomena descend to earth: "There is no thing but that its store-houses are with Us, and We do not send it down but in a known measure" (15:21). According to a divine saying, one of the cornerstones of Sufi doctrine: "I was a hidden treasure, and I loved to be known, so I created the world." Here, the hidden treasure can symbolize the Father's House, and the mansions, the worlds that manifest the hidden treasure. For the divine Abode, by virtue of encompassing all the archetypes of Paradise, comprises within itself all the terrestrial manifestations of those archetypes. All positive phenomena are thus reintegrated within their unique source. From this point of view, the whole of creation is "encompassed" by the divine reality, in accordance with the import of the divine Name, al-Muḥīt, "He who encompasses": nothing can be situated in a dimension outside of the one and only Reality. "Doth it not suffice that thy Lord encompasseth all things?" (41:54). All things in existence are indeed within "mansions" that are encompassed by "my Father's House."

One might add here: there are many degrees, modes, and aspects in the Paradise of "my Father's House." In the Qur'an, Paradise is multifaceted: in the chapter titled "The All-Compassionate,"[16] there is mention of two pairs of Paradise each with its own particular modes of celestial delight symbolized by different fruits, garments, etc. Moreover, the very notion of a heavenly House comprising diverse "rooms" is explicitly mentioned in other verses of the Qur'an. For example: "As for those who are ever conscious of their Lord, they shall have [in the Hereafter] mansions [ghuraf, pl. of ghurfa] raised upon mansions, beneath which rivers flow" (39:20). The idea evoked here, and in many other verses, is a plurality of degrees within Paradise, together with a sense of spiritual journeying through these degrees: "You verily shall journey on from plane to plane" (84:19).

Just as God remains absolutely One despite the infinitely varied forms of his Self-Disclosure, so mankind remains one despite the multiple religious worlds into which it is divided, for God made man in his own image. It is thus that the Qur'an says that "the creation and resurrection of you all is but as a single soul" (31:28). And also: "If anyone kills a single soul . . . it is as if he had killed all mankind; and if anyone saves a single soul, it is as if he had saved all mankind" (5:32). Ultimately, all souls are to be found in "my Father's House."

On all four levels—the divine, the religious, the existential, and the human—unity of essence is enriched, not compromised, by diversity of expression, and diversity of expression enhances, rather than contradicts, the orientation towards unity. The "Father's House" is made all the more

16. al-Raḥmān (ch. 55)..

glorious by the infinite diversity of the mansions it contains: *ad majorem Dei gloriam*. Each of these mansions can be understood as a perfection inwardly comprised within the undifferentiated, infinite perfection of God. Just as the perfections are one with all others in their inner infinitude, becoming multiple only when projected into finite existence, so this uniqueness is itself reflected in the very midst of the diversity of the cosmos in the fact that there is no repetition in manifestation: each manifestation is new, unique, and thus original in the sense that it bears testimony to the uniqueness of its origin. But because this origin is infinite, it is infinitely varied and diverse in its manifestations: we thus have a uniqueness, which kaleidoscopically displays diversity, and a diversity which unfailingly reproduces uniqueness. Diversity is thus integral to unity, and unity is perpetually affirmed in diversity.

To conclude: despite the fact that all paths lead to the one and only summit, it is necessary to follow one particular path up the mountain; to shift continuously from one path to another is to engage in what might be called "bad manners" on the plane of spiritual propriety, that is, in Arabic terms, showing bad *adab* towards God. Since God has established the particularity and uniqueness of each of the religious paths, it is not for us to reduce one to another or mix one with another—both reductionism and syncretism are to be avoided if the character of one's submission to the divine is to be sincere. The practice of the rites is, in and of itself, efficacious, but the fullness of the grace embedded within the rites is realized in the measure of one's sincerity in performing them; and this sincerity in turn is expressed not only by virtuous intent, but also by respect for the formal integrity of these rites, thus, for their irreplaceable God-given form and their irreducible uniqueness. Sincerity in this domain is also expressed by self-effacement before the God-given holiness of the rites, these theurgic means by which saving grace reaches out to us. These graces are both salvific in the hereafter and sanctifying in the here-below; it is perhaps for this reason that the Qur'an refers to the saints, the "friends of God" in this world, in precisely the same terms as the saved in the Hereafter. As we saw earlier, at 2:62, the saved of all the various traditions are described as follows: "No fear shall come upon them, neither shall they grieve." As for the saints,

> Verily the friends of God are those on whom fear cometh not, nor do they grieve: Those who believe and are ever-mindful of God; theirs are good tidings in the life of the world and in the Hereafter—there is no changing the Words of God—that is the Supreme Triumph. (10:62–64)

Jesus is referred to as a "Word of God," as well as "a Spirit from Him" (*kalimatuhu . . . wa rūhun minhu*; 4:171). One might therefore regard the "Words of God" as being another way of referring to the "friends of God" in the above passage, for Jesus is the "friend of God," the saint, par excellence. All the saints can thus be seen as revelatory words of sanctified and sanctifying glory, uttered by the divine truth, and thus as holy mansions within the Father's House of infinite majesty and beauty: "Sanctify them through thy Truth: Thy Word is Truth" (John 17:17).

14

What Is the Place of the Nude in Sacred Art?

David Clayton

In his writing on the human person and art, John Paul II created a renewed interest in the nude in art in general, and in sacred art in particular. His call for artists to represent the human form "naked without shame" (Gen 2:25) has given many artists the inspiration to paint nude figures in service of the church. This article compares the writings of the pope on this matter with the traditions of the church to try to assess how artists ought to respond. The conclusion I draw is that far from representing a new Catholic permissiveness (as some have interpreted), he is reaffirming a very traditional line. While the arguments I make can be extended to other disciplines, the most obvious being sculpture, this discussion considers predominantly painting.

In 1984 the cleaning and restoration of the frescoes of the Sistine Chapel in the Vatican began in a process that was to take ten years. It was unveiled on April 8, 1994, in the presence of Pope John Paul II. The cleaning process was so aggressive that it removed not only the wax and soot that had accumulated as a result of centuries of candle smoke, but also some of the wall painting itself—including loin cloths and fig leaves added by artists after Michelangelo. These additions had been placed there on the instruction of later popes who were less tolerant of nudity than Julius II, who commissioned the original work. Much has been made of the restoration process. Firstly, some were concerned that not only had later paintwork been removed but also some of the original done by Michelangelo. As a result, they said, restorers had to add new color and when they did so, they did a poor job. Consequently, the newly cleaned chapel had an artificial, almost electric brightness to it that did not correspond to what the original would have looked like. For my part I cannot comment on that, for I do not know how it looked originally. I will say that regardless of its authenticity, I prefer the cleaner, brighter, new version to the dirty one of 1984.

In regard to the loincloths and fig leaves, the controversy was all the greater because, it was said, John Paul II had directly asked for these to be removed in order to reveal the human bodies in full nudity, his intention being that it would become a pictorial representation of his theology of the body. This, it was suggested, put him at odds with the fathers of the Council of Trent (which "banned nudity in church") and especially Pius IV, who ordered the first cover-up in the 1560s immediately following the council. This controversy seems to me to have been, to some extent, manufactured. First of all, I cannot find any mention of a ban on nudity in the Council of Trent. It does specify that "all lasciviousness be avoided, so that images shall not be painted and adorned with a seductive charm."[1] This is not the same as saying that all nudity is banned, but rather that there should be prudential judgment as to whether or not a figure, nude or clothed, is lascivious. As a result of the council, it is true the judgment of what was appropriate did change and Pius IV ordered that *some* figures were to be amended. In the following centuries, subsequent popes ordered additions. If the restorers were indeed following John Paul II's directions, then we can conclude that his judgment matched precisely that of Pius IV after the council: those amendments made at his instruction in the 1560s were left intact, and only those added by later popes were removed. Furthermore, it is worth noting that the main figures that John Paul II focuses on in his homily, Adam and Eve, have never been covered up at any stage as far as I can ascertain. So the central focus of his discussion was not on newly revealed figures.

Regardless of the accuracy of any of this, we can say for certain that in April 1994, as all assembled and looked up at the newly cleaned chapel ceiling and walls, there were some figures that were nude and others that were not. This is the Sistine Chapel that John Paul II was referring to in his remarks: it is this current view that is important in this discussion.

What Sort of Nudity Are We Referring To?

In talking of nakedness and nudity in art what are we talking about? At one level, nudity is very easy to define: someone is nude if they have no clothes on. However, it is not as simple as this, for the image is distinct from what it portrays. It is possible to have a picture of someone who has no clothes on and whose sexual organs are hidden by carefully positioned tree boughs, for example, and these are generally not so contentious. Also, in consideration of what is appropriate in sacred art, the discussion invariably opens

---

1. *The Canons and Decrees of the Council of Trent*, Session 25, On the Invocation, Veneration and Relics of Saints, and on Sacred Images.

out into discussions of degrees of nakedness. Sometimes, in my experience, it extends to consideration of paintings of the Blessed Virgin breastfeeding the baby Jesus with nipple clearly visible; or of small children and babies who are naked—perhaps Our Lord and Saint John the Baptist as boys; and even the common paintings of Christ on the cross (wearing a loincloth). Although it would clearly be very easy to paint such images in an inappropriate way, I would say that generally these are not images that are likely to cause problems if done well and that most would expect a good artist to be able to do this.

If, however, the breasts of our Lady were revealed but she was not feeding our Lord, I think more people might object and the risk of an inappropriate image would be much greater. This indicates that while what we see is important, there is more to this than considering *only* what we see. There is a story of a judge on a trial in which a publisher was being prosecuted for publishing obscene material, in the early 1960s when the laws were much stricter than they are now. As I heard the tale, in the trial it very quickly became apparent that attempts to define pornography simply in terms of what parts of the body could be seen or were referred to in print would not be adequate. The publisher's lawyer pointed to the fact that there was a tradition of the nude in art and this meant that any nudity should be allowed. The judge was not inclined to accept the argument and remarked that while he couldn't say what pornography was, he knew it when he saw it. This immediately made him the subject of ridicule in the press as out of touch; but in fact there is more sense to this than he was given credit for. So much of what makes imagery objectionable is not what is seen, but the way it is portrayed and how we, the viewers, are disposed to see it. This makes it very hard to define precisely what is good and what is bad, and we are faced with the same sort of discussion here. The context and the artistic style affect our judgment as much as the content, and for this reason the same subject can be lascivious—to use the word of the council—in the hands of one artist, but perfectly decent in the hands of another.

If we wanted to reduce the risk of inappropriate imagery to the minimum, we could easily stipulate that only fully-clothed figures are painted. The reason that we do not do this is that it is not only permissible at certain times to have naked forms, but it is also actually desirable. In the painting of Adam and Eve in paradise, for example, their nakedness is essential to the understanding of the situation. As an extension of the description of our first parents in the book of Genesis, and following John Paul II, the discussion here considers particularly what is necessary to reveal human sexuality in an ordered way—naked without shame. In doing so, therefore, it focuses almost exclusively on consideration of artistic style—*how* a subject is painted—rather than the fine considerations of content, on the assumption that potentially all those aspects of the human body that reveal human sexuality are visible. We can assume, therefore, that if we find a style of painting in which complete nakedness (in which the sexual organs are visible) can be presented in an ordered and dignified way, we will have found a way also to tackle these other, less risky, images as well.

So what criteria did John Paul II use to make the judgment as to what is appropriate in regard to the human figure? We get some idea from his homily made on that day in the Sistine Chapel. In referring to the paintings, he said,

> It seems that Michelangelo, in his own way, allowed himself to be guided by the evocative words of the book of Genesis, which, as regards the creation of the human being, male and female, reveals: "The man and his wife were both naked, yet they felt no shame" (Gen 2:25). *The Sistine Chapel* is precisely—if one may say so—*the sanctuary of the theology of the human body.* In witnessing to the beauty of man created by God as male and female, it also expresses in a certain way, the hope of a world transfigured, the world inaugurated by the Risen Christ, and even before by Christ on Mount Tabor. We know that the Transfiguration is one of the main sources of Eastern devotion; it is an eloquent book for mystics, just as for St. Francis Christ crucified contemplated on the mountain of La Verna was an open book.
>
> *If we are dazzled as we contemplate the Last Judgement by its splendor and its terror,* admiring on the one hand the glorified bodies and on the other those condemned to eternal damnation, we understand too that the whole composition is deeply penetrated by a unique light and by a single artistic logic: *the light and the logic of faith that the Church proclaims, confessing:* "We believe in one God . . . maker of heaven and earth, of all things seen and unseen." On the basis of this logic in the context of the light that comes from God, the human body also keeps its splendor and its dignity. If it is removed from this dimension, it becomes in some way an object, which depreciates very easily, since only before the eyes of God can the human body remain naked and unclothed, and keep its splendor and its beauty intact.[2]

Some commentators have interpreted the pope's statement as strong validation for nudity in art, and as a result many artists have embarked enthusiastically on programs of paintings of nudes. I have seen paintings

---

2. Homily of His Holiness John Paul II, April 8, 1994, 6.

and sculptures of figures in carefully contrived poses and striking gestures made in all sincerity and which are presented as the art of the theology of the body.

Some of this is good, in my opinion; however, my sense is that many have misinterpreted the pope's words: in fact he is not giving artists quite the license that they are claiming. In order to attempt to understand fully what he is saying, let us consider first what shapes the form of the artistic traditions of the church and compare this with the reflections of the Holy Father on the subject.

The Three Traditions of Figurative Liturgical Art

In his book *The Spirit of the Liturgy* Pope Benedict XVI identifies three established traditions of authentically Catholic art, which are distinguishable from one another stylistically. These are the iconographic tradition, which we tend to associate today with the Eastern Church (although in fact there are many Western styles); the Gothic, which was a Western form that dominated in the period from approximately the mid-twelfth century to the High Renaissance; and the baroque ("at its best"), which is the form that flowered in the seventeenth century before degenerating in the next century under the influence of the Enlightenment (along with much of the wider culture).[3]

The thing that forms the style of these different types of art is the way in which they reveal or emphasize different aspects of humanity. Each communicates both visible and invisible truths. To take a simple example, man has a body and a soul and both must be indicated by the artist. As the soul is invisible, this presents particular problems to the painter or sculptor. It calls on the artist partially to abstract, that is, to deviate from strict visual appearances so this abstraction (literally, a "drawing out") suggests otherwise hidden truths. It takes great skill to do this. (We shall discuss how it is done in regard to each tradition in a moment.) We are very used to this idea in another context—in cartoons and animation (I am talking here of a cartoon in the Walt Disney sense, not in the older sense of a preparatory drawing for a painting). Every cartoonist portrays a human figure but exaggerates features in order to communicate a caricature. When this is done well, we understand instinctively, whether we approve or not, just what the artist is trying to communicate. The artist cannot deviate too far from actual

---

3. See Martin, *Baroque*. The definition of the baroque as the art of western Europe of the seventeenth century is given here by John Rupert Martin, the great authority on this artistic style.

physical appearances, though, for if he did we wouldn't know what we were looking at.

It may surprise some people to learn that exactly the same considerations must apply in Christian art. Every Christian representation must be a balance between naturalism and idealism. The first transmits what we can see, and the second transmits what we can't. The difference between the political satirist and the Christian artist is that while the cartoonist portrays the person in a narrow way, emphasizing only a few aspects of character, the Christian artist who is seeking to paint sacred art must seek to reveal the full beauty of the human person. This is a sterner test. He must ennoble by revealing the fullness of humanity—demonstrating that we are the greatest and most beautiful of God's creatures. If he swings too far in the direction of either idealism or naturalism, then his picture will overemphasize one aspect at the expense of the other and in extreme cases even transmit heresy (as some distorted figures of modern art do). Given that the style that sets the standard for Christians is liturgical art—that intended as art for worship and prayer—which can affect profoundly those who see it, it is vital that a Christian artist work hard to get it right.

As with so much, tradition is a guide. The stylization of each of the traditions of liturgical art of the church was worked out painstakingly by fruitful dialogue amongst many people. Without much, if any, direction from a central authority on the specifics (although very broadly laid out general principles have been given, for example, by ecumenical councils), a coherent order emerges out of personal communication and interaction among the liturgists, theologians, and philosophers of the church and artists and patrons. What fuels the engine of this process is the beauty of the work of each artist who produces something new. His complete work is seen by others, and if they are impressed they look to work in a similar vein, perhaps improving on what he has done. If there is change it is driven by the need of the current community for something hitherto unseen in art, not by the personal tastes of the artist. The power of the beauty and conformity to truth of these traditions is evidenced by the extraordinary way in which they dominated the art of their period even spilling out into the wider culture and become the stylistic models of the secular art of the period.

Until we reach the final day we cannot assume that we have heard the final word (or perhaps I should say "seen the final picture") in artistic style. There are always some individuals whose work sits outside these traditions that nevertheless have, in personal and unique ways, reflected the truth and beauty of the Word, and this will continue in the future. Also, there is room for the development of new traditions. It is always possible that one will produce work with a characteristic style that speaks so powerfully to its age that it sets the trend for other artists in one's time and into the future. Writing in 1947, Pius XII even considered the possibility of modern art contributing, but he laid down conditions: that its stylistic elements were created in order to meet a particular need of the time and that it avoided the error of excessive naturalism (he calls it "realism") or idealism (he uses the word "symbolism"). In fact, I suggest that in practice his criteria rule out most modern art—most wouldn't pass the test! He expressed it in *Mediator Dei* as follows: "Recent works of art which lend themselves to the materials of modern composition, should not be universally despised and rejected through prejudice. Modern art should be given free scope in the due and reverent service of the church and the sacred rites, provided that they preserve the correct balance between styles tending neither to extreme realism or to excessive 'symbolism' and that the needs of the Christian community are taken into consideration rather than the particular taste or talent of the individual artist."[4]

The Basis of the Different Styles of Authentic Liturgical Art

Those who have read John Paul II's *Theology of the Body* will be aware that there are different stages of human existence. First, there is man before the fall, Original Man, characterized by Adam and Eve, who were "naked without shame" and enjoyed an innocence that comes from purity and complete reliance upon God. Second, there is Historical Man, mankind after the fall, experiencing the fear and resentment that results from a dislocation in relationship with each other and with God. Though not as good as man ought to be, Historical Man is still good and has the potential for sanctity. We are all historical men and women. Third, there is Eschatological Man. This is the destiny that God intended for each of us. In this stage, if we cooperate with grace, we fulfill our human purpose as saints, partaking of the divine nature in heaven in communion with the Trinity in a perfect exchange of love and in perfect and perpetual bliss.

We can look at these traditions in the light of this. The iconographic tradition[5] reveals Eschatological Man. Inspired especially, as John Paul II said in his homily, on the description of the glorified Christ in the transfiguration in which the saints in heaven participate. All stylistic features are formed by the desire to communicate the reality of man in heaven. For example, the figures have halos, representing the uncreated light shining

4. Pius XII, *Mediator Dei*, 195.

5. This includes all the local variations that are consistent with the iconographic prototype, for example, Celtic, Carolingian, Ottonian, and Romanesque art in the West.

out of the glorified body, and for similar reasons there are no cast shadows (which would result from external light sources). Consistent also with the communication of the heavenly realm, which is outside space (as well as time), the icon deliberately reduces the illusion of depth as far as possible with optical devices such as reverse perspective. The figures live, so to speak, in the plane of the painting.

The baroque tradition reveals Historical Man who is different and accordingly has a very different style from the iconographic. Examples of painters of the baroque are Velazquez, Georges de La Tour, Zurbarán, Van Dyck, Rubens, Guido Reni, and Ribera. In contrast with the iconographic style, the baroque deliberately sets out to create an illusion of space using devices such as perspective and shows deep cast shadow from external light sources.

Because its presence is heightened in a fallen world, shadow has become a symbol of evil and suffering. Shadow has been a symbol of evil and suffering since long before the baroque period. The ancient Office of Tenebrae (which means shadows and darkness), for example, symbolizes just this in the dark days, as it were, of the Triduum. In baroque art the shadowy depths are exaggerated to make this point. However, the Christian message is not one of despair. Just as Easter Sunday follows Good Friday, hope due to Christ the redeemer is always with us even in the darkest periods, so within the painting the shadow is always contrasted with bright light, which represents the light that overcomes the darkness.

The baroque style is far more naturalistic than the iconographic style but it is not simply a representation of visual appearances. The artist varies the color content, the sharpness of edges, and the contrast in order to draw our eyes to the important parts of the figure and the painting in accordance with the natural hierarchy of being. Furthermore, the skillful use of these devices ensures that man is given a dignity and a beauty worthy of someone created by God. While always the art of fallen, Historical Man, the baroque nevertheless emphasizes man's potential for sanctity, which is created in us, and the need for God's grace to realize it. It is the art of suffering and hope. Because the style of the baroque period is more naturalistic than other forms of sacred art, the idealization is more subtly applied and less apparent, but it is there all the same.

Baroque art should be clearly distinguished from the academic art of the nineteenth century (and figures such as Ingres or Bouguereau). This is a heightened naturalism detached from a genuinely Christian understanding of the human person (even if some of the artists of this period were believers). The way in which the artist deviates from visual appearances is different from that of the earlier form driven by a different understanding of man. As a result it became either sterile and cold or else sentimental and saccharine.[6] Much of what formed twentieth-century modern art was an overreaction to nineteenth-century academic art. Although the artists themselves thought they were reacting to Christian tradition, they were in fact reacting, aesthetically at least, against a lesser, sterile version of it.

The Gothic is the third Catholic figurative tradition. This appears to oscillate between the styles of Eschatological and Historical Man. Historically it is a transitional form between the two, derived from the Western iconographic forms that preceded it, such as the Romanesque, and anticipating the baroque, which postdated it (it lasted from approximately the mid-twelfth century up to the sixteenth century). It might be thought of as the art of pilgrimage. The stylistic elements point both to heaven and to a fallen world. It reflects the fact that although we can never fully make that transformation to Eschatological Man in this world, there is nevertheless a continuum between the two states along which we can make progress through the transforming process of participation in the sacramental life of the church in the here and now. Even in this life we are not stuck, immobile in a life occupying the shadowy depths thinking only of our potential for sanctity—we can start the transition to sanctity right now and experience Christian joy. Like the spires of the Gothic churches, Gothic art reaches up to heaven, but at the same time it is firmly planted on earth. To illustrate the point we can consider the work of the late-Gothic artist Fra Angelico. He used elements of both the visual vocabulary of the increased naturalism and cast shadow that were developing around him, such as perspective and shadow (which we see in his most famous Annunciation, for example), and at other times used the iconographic prototype of uncreated light and "flatness"—for example, when portraying heavenly scenes such as the crowning of the Virgin. His selection depended upon the theological point he wanted to communicate.

Why Not the High Renaissance?

Some may be surprised that the High Renaissance does not appear in the list (and neither do the mannerist styles that followed it in the sixteenth century). In terms of artistic style, the High Renaissance represents a break from the Gothic, which precedes it, and a period of transition that culminates in the development of the baroque sometime later.

---

6. See Martin, *Baroque*. The point that there is a contrast between nineteenth-century art and the baroque is also made by Benedict XVI in *The Spirit of the Liturgy*.

It is a radical change in the way that artists were trained that formed the High Renaissance and caused the break with the Gothic. All traditional art training involves (in varying degrees) both the copying of works of great masters and the direct observation of nature. In the training of any artist, the influence that affects the style in which he ultimately paints is the art with which he is most familiar. So someone who wants to draw superheroes in the style of Spiderman should go to life-drawing classes and copy as many figures from Marvel comics as he can. In the Gothic period, the level of observation of nature increased strongly, but the stylistic substrate onto which this heightened naturalism was fused was the Romanesque, which is a variant of the iconographic. For this reason there is no clear break between the Gothic and the iconographic in terms of style; one is a slightly "naturalized" version of the other, the level of naturalism gradually increasing over time.

When we come to the High Renaissance and the period of the sixteenth century, however, there was a clear dislocation in style. This was because artists no longer looked to Romanesque or Gothic masters for their inspiration, but to the ancient Greek and Roman sculptures that surrounded them in Italy and were being excavated at the time. As it was in an early, developmental stage, the period of the sixteenth century is characterized not so much by a coherent tradition as it is by dominant, individualistic but brilliant figures such as Leonardo, Michelangelo, Raphael, and Titian, each drawing his own inspiration and varying in style. Gradually, the contributions of these and other masters were assessed and a coherent tradition integrating theology and form developed out of their work. Much of the synthesis was driven by a response to the Council of Trent (which closed in 1564) as part of the Catholic Counter Reformation. This is what became the baroque of the seventeenth century.

What about the Art of Original Man?

I am not aware of a tradition that manifests Original Man in the way that Eschatological Man and Historical Man are represented. In thinking about what it might look like, I began by talking to theologians and reading the church fathers who describe the appearance of Adam and Eve in paradise (such as Ephrem the Syrian in his *Hymns on Paradise*). This suggests to me that in many ways the bodily appearance of Original Man is very similar to Eschatological Man, shining with an uncreated light. One person who has written about this more recently is the twentieth-century theologian Eric Peterson. He wrote about it not as theology of the body, but rather in a theology of clothes in a short article titled "The Theology of Dress."[7] He points out that Original Man did not need to wear clothes because he was, so to speak, clothed in glory. This glory did not dazzle and hide, but rather it revealed his sexuality in a way that was appropriate to the person. The body radiated brightly with a light that communicated the truth of the whole person; this could be seen and apprehended by those around him fully because in their purity their ability to do so was perfect. After the fall stripped man of this glory, Historical Man is naked in a way that Original Man was not. Not only is the light that radiates the full truth of his being dimmed, but because the observers who look at him are impure too, they are less able to apprehend whatever aspect of the truth that is transmitted. The result is that we only perceive man in a diminished form, less beautiful. We often think of clothes as covering up things that should not be revealed. But in fact when we see Historical Man naked, the problem is not that we see too much, but rather that we see too little. Clothes are necessary, but not as something that hides the human state; rather they fulfill a function of a temporary and partial completion of it. They make up for what was lost in the fall. Their purpose is not to hide sexuality, but to reveal it in an ordered and dignified way. It is a natural appreciation of this fact, I suggest, that leads to most societies (until the present day) choosing feminine and masculine styles of clothing. When a woman, for example, wears elegant and graceful feminine clothing, it communicates to others around her in an ordered way that she is a woman. For Historical Man, it seems, the way to reveal sexuality in an ordered way is to wear clothes.

Michelangelo and the Icon— Two Possible Models for Original Man?

Elsewhere in his address in 1994, John Paul II praised the work of Michelangelo as revealing man and woman, "naked without shame" (Gen 2:25). This is a clear reference to his portrayal of Adam and Eve. What is he seeing in Michelangelo's work that leads him to think that style is appropriate to the subject matter? There may be a number of things, but two come to mind. First is that John Paul II feels that Michelangelo's figures shine with a light that originates from God. As we have said, the traditional picture of Original Man is one that is clothed in glory, which is shining with uncreated light. The Holy Father made the connection between this and the uncreated light

---

7. Reproduced in *Communio* by Erik Peterson, who died in 1960. I am grateful to Stratford Caldecott for making me aware of this article when I was talking about this topic with him.

of Eschatological Man, which we see in the glorified Christ on Mount Tabor. Indeed, he draws our attention to the similarity in appearance of Original Man and Eschatological Man in reality, and therefore to the appropriateness of artists using a similar approach in portraying each: "The whole composition is deeply penetrated by a unique light and single artistic logic. . . . On the basis of this logic in the context of the light that comes from God, the human body keeps its splendor and dignity."[8]

This suggests that the iconographic form would also be suitable for the portrayal of both Original Man and Historical Man, and John Paul II says as much. (I would add that early Gothic art also has that quality of light and might also be suitable.) A second reason for the pope's interest, I suggest, is the correspondence of Michelangelo's work to Greek classical sculpture. Michelangelo is not unusual amongst the artists of his time in copying Greek and Roman statues and allowing this to influence his style. In fact, pretty much all artists did so from the High Renaissance to the beginning of the twentieth century. What is unusual is the degree to which he allows the Greek ideal to influence his own style. If one looks, for example, at the facial features of his work the similarity between them and those of the earlier period are striking. Most others (a possible exception being Raphael) sought a far greater degree of naturalism. In his *Theology of the Body* John Paul II cites Greek classical art as a model for portraying human nakedness in an ordered way. He talks of the need of artists to go beyond what the senses perceive ("suprasensual") and through this heightened idealization to reveal invisible truths:

> In the course of various epochs from antiquity down—and especially in the great period of classical Greek art—there are works of art whose subject is the human body in its nakedness, the contemplation of which allows one to concentrate in some way on the whole truth of the man, on the dignity and beauty— even "suprasensual" beauty—of his masculinity and femininity. These works bear within themselves in a hidden way, as it were, an element of sublimation that leads the viewer through the body to the whole mystery of man. In contact with such works, we do not feel pushed by their content toward "looking to desire," as the Sermon on the Mount puts it; in some way we learn the spousal meaning of the body, which corresponds to and provides the measure of "purity of heart."[9]

---

8. Homily of His Holiness John Paul II, April 8, 1994, 6.

9. John Paul II, *Man and Woman He Created Them*, 376.

As mentioned, in his Sistine Chapel homily he remarks also on how the iconographic tradition has a stylization that portrays the light of the glorified body. Interestingly, John Paul II is not the first to make the connection between the Greek classical sculpture as a model of the glorified body and to then draw parallels with icons. Pavel Florensky was a respected and highly influential commentator on icons who did the same. He was a Russian Orthodox priest who in the early twentieth century contributed significantly to the development of a theology of icons during this period. What makes this all the more interesting is that he was generally extremely negative about Western forms (unfairly, I would say—he did not acknowledge the baroque or Gothic as authentic forms, for example), yet he did see something in Greek classical art. Despite the fact that they are very different in many ways (not least, as a genre of three-dimensional sculptures and the other of two-dimensional paintings), he notices that both convey the human form in an idealized way that through partial abstraction is a move towards a truer picture: "Russian iconography of the fourteenth and fifteenth centuries is the perfection of imagery achieved, an equal of which or even a similar to which the history of world's art does not know and to which, in a certain sense, only Greek sculpture can be juxtaposed—likewise an incarnation of spiritual images and likewise, after a luminous elevation, corrupted by rationalism and sensuality."[10]

A Summary: John Paul II's Position on the Nude in Art in Sacred Art

I suggest that John Paul II's position could be summarized as follows: the portrayal of nudity in art is desirable, even for sacred art in churches, if it is portraying Original Man, that is, the human person naked without shame and revealing human sexuality as gift, or the glorified figures of saints in heaven. In practice this means a highly idealized portrayal that would show a glorified body, shining with the light of God. He suggests two possible forms that seem appropriate therefore: the traditional iconographic style which, although portraying Eschatological Man, is a model formed around the portrayal of glorified man and so might be considered appropriate for Original Man as well, or some visual form based upon classical Greek

10. Florensky, "Iconostasis": "Русская иконопись XIV-XV веков есть достигнутое совершенство изобразительности, равного которому или даже подобного не знает история всемирного искусства и с которым в известном смысле можно сопоставлять только греческую скульптуру—тоже воплощение духовных образов и тоже, после светлого подъема, разложенную рационализмом и чувственностью."

sculpture. As an example of the second he points us to the highly personal interpretation of Michelangelo as seen in the art of the Sistine Chapel.

At the same time, the Holy Father is very clear that naturalistic styles representing Historical Man are very likely to be inappropriate. In his homily in the chapel John Paul II said, "On the basis of this logic in the context of the light that comes from God, the human body also keeps its splendor and its dignity. If it is removed from this dimension, it becomes in some way an object, which depreciates very easily, since *only before the eyes of God* can the human body remain naked and unclothed, and keep its splendor and its beauty intact."[11]

He is referring here to naturalistic styles that are based upon a close adherence to faithful representation of man as he appears to the observer in this life. These are to be rejected because such strict adherence to visual appearance ignores invisible truths about man and therefore does not reveal the whole truth. He makes this point strongly in his *Theology of the Body*:

> It is not possible to agree on this point with the representatives of so-called naturalism who appeal to the right to "everything that is human" in works of art and in the products of artistic reproduction, and who claim that in this way they act in the name of the realistic truth about man. It is precisely this truth about man—the whole truth about man—that requires us to consider the sense of the intimacy of the body and the consistency of the gift connected with the masculinity and femininity of the body itself, which reflects the mystery of man proper to the inner structure of the person. We must consider this truth about man also in the artistic order if we want to speak of a full realism.[12]

One might argue that there is no more a justification for nude images of Historical Man to be seen by the public than there is for living, breathing people themselves to be nude in public. If the image portrays Historical Man accurately, those who will be seeing it will also be fallen, that is, impure people who cannot see as God sees. Taking this into account, the artist should use the same device for revealing human sexuality that each of us does in real life, that is, he should put some clothes on the figure. The consideration of who is to look at the painting should never be forgotten, we are told: "What we have called 'ethos of the image' cannot be considered in abstraction from the correlative component, which one would have to call 'ethos of seeing.' The whole process of communication is contained between these two components, regardless of the vastness of the circles described

11. Homily of His Holiness John Paul II, 8 April, 1994, 6; emphasis added.

12. John Paul II, *Man and Woman He Created Them*, 372.

by this communication, which in this case is always 'social.'"[13] The situations where we see each other, historical men and women, appropriately naked in real life are highly personal relationships, such as between spouses or between a doctor and a patient—this is the "social" dimension that the pope refers to above. A piece of artwork is, almost by definition, for broader consumption and it therefore reduces those who are made privy to such a relationship to the status of voyeur.

All of this reinforces the point that the artist today who wishes to respond to the pope's call would be most certain in doing so by employing iconographic or gothic styles, or one based on classical Greek sculpture. Styles that are more naturalistic than these and have a much greater correspondence to physical appearances are most likely inappropriate.

The Response of Artists Today

Most of the Catholic artists that I am aware of who are responding to the call of the pope are working either in individualistic modern styles that sit outside tradition,[14] or in the highly naturalistic style of nineteenth-century academic art. This latter style, in my opinion, comes under the category referred to by John Paul II of a form of naturalism based upon a claim to "the right to 'everything that is human'"[15] and is inappropriate. Those interested in understanding their working ethos and how it is manifested in their art, including many nudes, should visit the website of the Art Renewal Center.[16]

The method by which style of painting is taught is called the "academic" method. Given that, in my experience, many people, including Catholic artists, contrary to this see this style as an appropriate way to represent the nude, it is worth examining it in greater detail to consider the validity of this hypothesis.

The Academic Method

The academic method of drawing and painting (and sculpture) developed in the art schools that were established and took hold in the sixteenth and seventeenth centuries and then dominated until the end of the nineteenth

13. Ibid., 377.

14. And therefore it is difficult to generalize, except to say that their style seems to indicate that they are unacquainted with the detail of what John Paul II said.

15. John Paul II, *Man and Woman He Created Them*, 372.

16. See www.artrenewal.org.

century. It is called "academic" because the most successful early schools had the word *academy* in their names—it was done deliberately to evoke an image of the culture of classical Greece by making a connection with Plato's academy (although Plato's school was not an art school). They taught a systematic method of observation and drawing which, it is said today, originated with Leonardo and Michelangelo. This method has remained largely the same right up to the present day, although by the nineteenth century it had become detached from its Christian ethos. In the nineteenth century the schools were either large institutions, which still called themselves academies, or else small workshops; in France the latter were called *ateliers* (literally, "workshops") and were run by working artists. While there were some differences between their teaching styles, both taught what was essentially the academic method.

Under the influence of the impressionists initially, and then of modernism, pretty much all the academies and ateliers of Europe had closed by the beginning of the twentieth century, and the schools that replaced them did not teach drawing so rigorously. This began the decline in artistic skill that is so characteristic of the twentieth century. This is because although the impressionists were themselves highly skilled and academically trained artists, they eschewed tradition and refused to teach it to the next generation of artists. So clean was the break in tradition that resulted that the academic method might have died altogether if it had not been for a few individuals who persisted in using it and teaching it despite the adverse opinions of most of the art world.

The most well known of these is Robert Ives Gammell, who died in 1981. Ives Gammell grew up in New England, where it took perhaps twenty years longer than in Europe for the academic schools to close. He learned the method at the school in the Boston Museum of Fine Arts in the period leading up to the First World War. He doggedly continued to paint and later to teach this method until the time of his death. Some of the people taught by him late in his life in the 1970s, when he was in his eighties, started to set up their own schools, with his help and guidance—I know of one in Minnesota, two in Florence, Italy, and one in Manchester, New Hampshire. Over the years, students who have emerged from the Ives Gammell line have established more schools, mostly small independent studios, as the academic method slowly reestablishes itself. While not all the schools that exist now come from this (I have heard of Russian schools that persisted, and one in Australia), a large proportion of the schools in the United States and Western Europe do. The method and ethos transmitted in nearly all the schools that exist today tends to be one that is based upon nineteenth-century classical naturalism, which they refer to as "realism." They use this term because they believe that their brand of extreme naturalism portrays reality. As we have discussed, from the Christian point of view, to call this nineteenth-century art realism is a misnomer, for such extreme naturalism does not portray the full reality of the person, limited as it is by an overemphasis on visual appearances.

If one reads the philosophy that typifies so many of these schools today (one may find examples on the Art Renewal Center [ARC] website, referred to above), it says explicitly that it is promoting an art that manifests the values of the Enlightenment which are contrary to those of the Christianity. While the differences in style between these and the baroque are subtle, they are critical.[17]

The ethos that drives these modern schools is first a desire to be a continuation of the flawed nineteenth-century form, and second a reaction against the misguided heightened abstraction of modern art. Because of this they emphasize a correspondence to physical appearances all the more strongly than their forebears of one hundred years ago. If the abstract art of the twentieth century is reflecting an overemphasis of the soul at the expense of the body—to the degree it claims to portray or reflect aspects of the soul, for example, human emotions and feelings separated from the body—this modern academic art overemphasizes the body at the expense of the soul. The two forms are more closely connected than they imagine, for each is the corollary of the other, two sides of a coin that represent the error of a philosophical dualism that separates body and soul in the description of man.

In the end, the test of the value of art is what it looks like. Readers should make up their own minds. When I look at the figures and especially the nudes displayed on the ARC website, the vast majority are, to my eye, charged with eroticism and do not transmit the full dignity of the human person. There is no accounting for whom God may choose to inspire, and who is able respond to that inspiration, of course, but we can say that to the degree that these works conform to the ethos they profess they are contrary to Christian tradition and to what John Paul II stipulated as appropriate for the portrayal of the human person.

---

17. I am often asked where a Christian who is seeking to work in the traditional way of the baroque might go to train. Despite the drawbacks I have mentioned, I unhesitatingly respond that they should go to any of these ateliers, for they will learn great artistic skill. Provided that they are aware of the differences of forms of nineteenth- and seventeenth-century academic art and the atelier encourages (rather than simply tolerates) the attendance of those with faith and the ultimate aim of modifying what they learn to the seventeenth-century style, then this will work. One such place is the Ingbretson Studio in Manchester, New Hampshire.

The Problem of the Nude Model

One of the great difficulties of the academic method, especially as it is taught today in regard to the portrayal of the human figure, is, it seems to me, the insistence of training through the drawing of nude models. When I was learning at one such atelier in Florence, the basic training consisted of the drawing of plaster casts of sculpture of the human figure (some of it classical Greek work) in the morning and figure drawing, which meant the nude, in the afternoon.

Drawing the nude figure has become such an accepted part of art training that it is rarely questioned by any art student or teacher today, even by devout Christians. If anyone does question it, they are usually met with incredulity. When I was a student in an atelier, while I was never wholly comfortable with the experience of drawing nudes, I never questioned that it was necessary if I wanted to be a good artist, and so viewed it as a necessary evil. It was not until I began teaching art in a conservative Catholic liberal arts college that I started to consider this in any depth. I anticipated that many students and even more parents would object to nude drawing and painting. In order to be able to justify what seemed to me to be an indispensable part of any serious art student's training, I set out to find arguments to defend the practice that were likely to convince skeptical parents. In fact, while I do not claim to have settled the matter definitely, to my surprise, the more I looked into it, the more it seemed to me that it was problematic.

The problem relates to the etiquette of the studio and the objectification of the model. Any students who have taken a life-drawing class will be aware of the strict etiquette that is usually applied: the model always dresses or undresses behind a screen; once naked, conversation with the model by students is strongly discouraged (in the studio where I studied, it was a strict rule that only the teacher was allowed to do so); and nobody other than teacher and students was allowed in the studio.

It is not a Christian ethos that is driving this etiquette; very few are students of Christian anthropology, or even Christian. However, they are nevertheless naturally aware of the fact that if this is done in a casual way, it becomes very undignified and uncomfortable for model and artists alike. Furthermore, if they did not observe this etiquette, they would have a great deal of trouble recruiting any models for their studio, for the models would not want to come back. This is demonstrated by the fact that I have very occasionally been involved with groups elsewhere that were lax in their application of this. It was noticeable how uncomfortable the model became and how embarrassed most felt if, for example, one of the students began to engage the model in a conversation, even about the weather.

This natural discomfort arises certainly, one suggests, from the temptation to lust, but it seems to me that it is more than that. Putting the sexual attraction aside, there is, it seems, an undignified imbalance in this scenario where one person is unclothed while the other is clothed. Curiosity alone tempts one to be a voyeur intruding into another's personal space, visually lapping up personal details of the body that would otherwise be hidden.

The etiquette of the studio does serve to remove the sexual element from the equation, but it does so by eliminating other aspects of the personal relationship between artist and model. Thus it heightens the objectification of the person, if not sexually, in other ways. As a result, the artist feels that he is looking not at a person, but at a nude, a form, a body. This seems to be supported by how those involved will describe the experience: most I have spoken to tell me that the sexual element is removed because they are so engrossed in studying the shapes in order to draw them that they are not thinking about the person to whom the form belongs. This highlights the inherent problem with studying the nude in this scenario. The etiquette replaces one form of objectification with another. This objectification is always bad, regardless of what type, for a lack of love and respect for the person has contributed greatly to the breakdown of society and the culture of death.

There is another reason I am skeptical about the claim that this etiquette removes the temptation altogether. Temptation in this scenario arises from a stimulation of the passions. This cannot be controlled, for the passions are involuntary. Given this, I wonder how many can truthfully claim that their concentration level is so consistently high that they are wholly able to resist temptation when it occurs. Certainly I cannot.

In defending figure drawing, some draw parallels with other situations where disrobing is acceptable, especially that of doctor and patient. To my mind there is a crucial difference. The relationship between doctor and patient is an inherently personal one. No patient wants to be viewed by a doctor as a body to be treated for malfunctions, and any doctor who claimed that he wasn't interested in the whole person would not be a good doctor. It is the properly ordered gift and reception of charity that defines the personal aspect in this relationship and that makes disrobing acceptable. This is what is lacking in the artist-model relationship, I suggest.

Is there any way around this? Perhaps. I have heard a variety of alternative approaches suggested that might allow for an appropriate nakedness in the art studio. One might suggest that the answer is for the artist and model to be in a natural personal relationship with each other. This, however, does raise the question as to the appropriateness of third parties seeing drawings that a man makes of his wife. This is not unknown.

Another possibility might be for artists to draw only those to whom they have no sexual attraction, which would generally mean men draw men and women draw women and then engage with them personally. This might work if carefully handled. I was told that this is how Michelangelo always and Raphael (sometimes) used male models, even when the final painting was of a woman. Another solution used by Michelangelo was to draw dead bodies (which can be legitimately objectified). I am not aware of any proposal to do the same in the art schools of today.

Given all of these difficulties, we should ask ourselves, is it really necessary to have nude models? If it is not, then we needn't face the problem. I deal next with the most commonly given arguments in support of the idea that the drawing and painting of the nude in the academic method is necessary.

1. *Drawing the nude is necessary in the training of the artist, even for painting clothed figures, because of the need to understand the anatomy of the body.* It is a common assumption that in order to paint the human form, even a clothed figure, one needs to understand the anatomy of the human body, but this is not necessarily so. While it is true that some traditional methods adopt this approach, there are others that do not. Many of the great artists of the baroque period, for example, did not train in painting nudes—Velázquez and the artists of the Spanish school of the seventeenth centur,y for example, were not allowed to do so because of the influence of the church in Spain. My training in Florence was based on Velázquez's method (although unlike Velázquez, we did study the nude). I did not focus on human anatomy—consideration of the underlying muscle and bone structures, for example—at all. We had critiques every day when studying, and never once was I asked to consider the anatomy of the body I was drawing. Always the focus *visually* was on an abstract consideration of tone, color, and shape. This means that it makes no difference to the technique of observation if I am painting a figure, clothed or unclothed, or a still life or a landscape. This is *not* to say, when painting, for example, a portrait or figure (clothed), that the good artist does not at some level think about all *invisible* aspects of the person that he is trying to communicate and then abstract slightly from what is seen in order to do so.

2. *It is part of the tradition; the nudes of the Renaissance and the baroque are some of the greatest works of art ever painted.* In response to this I would say that while it was true that the nude became part of the tradition,

it did not become so to the degree that some now suggest. Also, it is a matter of opinion that these nudes are great, and one that has not been uniformly accepted since they were painted.

Prior to the High Renaissance the nude was never given the elevated status in the canon of imagery that it was to develop later. Generally, nudity did appear when the narrative demanded it, such as Adam and Eve in paradise, or the baptism in the Jordan. We see images of these figures in the medieval Book of Hours, for example. However, the images were highly idealized and painted in the iconographic or Gothic styles. These shone with the light of God and did not focus on the sexual organs in any detail—sometimes this aspect was so downplayed that they appear absent or smoothed over, as in a tailor's dummy. Artists did not train or study nude models systematically as they learned their craft, and one feels (and here I am speculating) that when portraying these figures they are relying on their memories of having seen nudity in ordinary personal relationships—in the family, in spouses or in parents when they were children. I have never heard of icon painters training by studying the nude, for example, but it is common to consider the structure of the human body with reference to what we know from our ordinary experiences.

The inclusion of the study of the nude figure did not become common in the Christian tradition until the High Renaissance and the baroque, but even then it was not universally accepted or without controversy. One of the most famous of these, Titian's *Venus of Urbino*, is generally accepted to have been made intentionally erotic. It was precisely to avoid this that the Spanish court during the seventeenth century did not allow the nude figure (as mentioned). There is one famous nude, the *Rokeby Venus*, painted by Velázquez—it was painted while he was visiting Italy.

It was in the nineteenth century that it seems to have become an unquestioned standard in the training of the academic method, and this was, as we have said, in the academies that no longer connected what they did with a Christian ethos. So it seems, therefore, that even in the heyday of Christian naturalistic art, there were some dangers in attempting to paint the nude that were not there in the same way in the Gothic or the iconographic styles.

Even if we accept that some of the nudes of this time can be considered reasonable representations (we will discuss how this might be possible in the context of Historical Man later), I would argue that we are much less likely to find artists capable of doing this today. When we draw and paint anything, the final painting is affected not only by what we see but also by similar imagery stored in the memory. This is what accounts for the unconscious development of individual style. Artists in the past were aware of this tendency and sought to control it. The baroque master Rubens, for example, stressed the importance of controlling the images in the memory of the artist by ensuring that the student train by drawing only the most beautiful and dignified sculptures of the human form. The modern person is bombarded by the imagery of film, television, and photography. So much of this is deliberately manipulated to conform to a negative ideal of overemphasized eroticism. In glossy magazines, for example, the figures are deliberately airbrushed so as to promote impurity. These disordered images stored in the memory of the artist will affect his final drawing, regardless of whether he is conscious of it. This influence is one that simply would not have been there four hundred years ago. Therefore, even given an identical training, the tendency of the artist to produce disordered imagery is greater today than it was in the past. I suggest therefore that we should err on the side of an even greater caution than was used in past times.

3. *The naked form is beautiful.* This is true, but it does not in itself justify the painting of it nude. This is the whole essence of the discussion relating to Original Man, Historical Man, and Eschatological Man given earlier. John Paul II argues that only "before the eyes of God"[18] should Historical Man, the form of man we are considering at this point, be seen without clothes. As mentioned, after consideration of Erik Peterson's article "The Theology of Dress," clothes do not hide the beauty of Historical Man, but rather enhance it so that it is closer to what it ought to be.

Conclusion

If the few articles I have read are anything to go by, the comments of John Paul II on nudity in art have been interpreted in some circles as a theology of Catholic permissiveness. Here was a groundbreaking theologian pointing to the need for nudity in art. One imagines cultured Catholics who did not want to be seen as puritanical by their liberal friends heaving a sigh of relief: now, when the subject came up at dinner parties, they could point gleefully to the words of this "right-on," pro-nude pope and hold their heads high.

While, as we have discussed, the pope was indeed very interested in artists portraying human sexuality visually in an ordered way, when one examines the sort of nudity he proposes, one sees that, rather than opening

18. Homily of His Holiness John Paul II, April 8, 1994, 6.

the door to a previously unseen permissiveness, he seems to be reinforcing a very traditional and conservative line (though certainly not puritanical).

Does this rule out the naked portrayal of Historical Man altogether? While all that I have described sets out the great difficulty of the task facing the artist, it seems to me that it does not rule out altogether the possibility that a skilled artist could paint Historical Man naked, provided he did so in a particular way. Historical Man is still essentially human and therefore if this can be revealed through a very careful and subtle abstraction that reveals the full humanity of the subject and his potential for glory then it will be legitimate, for this is man as God sees him. The artist must by means of idealization communicate this full truth to people who are themselves fallen and predisposed (to some degree) to look at the naked form with impure eyes. Strict adherence to natural appearances is out of the question, as the pope has said, but there must nevertheless be a high degree of naturalism in order for this to correspond to Historical Man. To give us a dignified portrayal of Historical Man, with just the right balance of naturalism and idealization that is not open to misinterpretation, therefore requires a highly skilled artist with a very clear idea of his purpose. We might argue that some of the great masters of the past were able to do this.

However, given all the pitfalls involved, I feel that it would be prudential for artists today to restrict the portrayal of the nude to those cases where it is necessary, such as Adam and Eve, and to do so in forms that are highly stylized, such as the iconographic or the Gothic. I would avoid the naturalistic forms that an academic training produces and I would remove the study of the nude from the training of artists in this form, so that they have training that is closer to that of the Spanish baroque masters.

15

Newman for a New Generation

Carol Zaleski

I'll never forget the day John Henry Newman's beatification was announced. My family and I were barreling along in a large van headed for Heathrow airport with Léonie Caldecott, an intrepid driver who was determined to get us to our plane despite major traffic jams. A text message appeared on her mobile phone, and from where I was sitting clutching my seat, I had a chance to read it aloud. It came from a priest of the Oratory: "Rome announces Newman's beatification." Spirits were high for the rest of the trip, and we did catch the plane.

Not all observers were ready to chime in with this festal mood. Coverage in the British press leading up to Newman's beatification looked very shabby compared to the outpouring of affection occasioned by Cardinal Newman's death on the eleventh of August, 1890. "A great man has passed away"; "a great link with the past has been broken," said the London *Times*. "Whether Rome canonizes him or not he will be canonized in the thoughts of pious people of many creeds in England." *The Evangelical Magazine* considered that "of the multitude of saints in the Roman calendar there are very few that can be considered better entitled to that designation than Cardinal Newman." His present and former coreligionists were eager to set aside differences and honor him for having been, at each stage of his journey from evangelical to Anglo-Catholic to Roman Catholic, a steady witness to the gospel as it was known to the apostles and the early church, to the development of doctrine by which the gospel has been safeguarded and unfolded over the centuries, to the harmony of the gospel with the voice of reason and conscience, and to the beauty of the gospel as source and guarantor of the greatest achievements of English literature and art.

A second *Times* obituary concluded by saying that "the Cardinal has long taken his position as a 'Father' of we know not what century in that constellation of acute and saintly minds that still illumines the dark interval between ancient and modern civilization." But I think we *do* know what century: ours. This, at least, is the conclusion I'm led to after three decades of friendship with the Caldecotts. Family visits to the series of Caldecott homes in Oxford have almost always included a Newman pilgrimage to Oriel, to Trinity, and out to Littlemore. It's possible that on one of these visits we established a new tradition: while paying our respects to the bust of Newman garlanded in foliage by the wall outside the Trinity College Garden Quad, our boys climbed into the flower bed and reached up to rub Newman's nose for good luck. A Japanese tour group that was passing by stopped to observe this act of homage. As we left, we saw a few of them approach the statue and try the experiment for themselves. Word of such things gets out. Newman's nose gets shinier every year.

Really, Newman does shine—there is a radiance of intellectual and spiritual beauty visible in the many portraits of him young and old, in George Richmond's 1840 chalk drawing of a handsome, soulful clergyman gazing out to the middle distance (minus the glasses without which he could not have seen anything at any distance), and also in the caricature by Sir Leslie Ward ("Spy") in an 1877 issue of *Vanity Fair* of an aged Newman crotchety but unbowed. The same intelligent beauty shines from his prose, in which he articulates and defends—not for specialists or professional theologians, but for ordinary Christians—the truths of faith and conscience that we attempt to live by but are hard-pressed to justify or explain: the existence of the triune God, the mystery of Christ's incarnation, passion, and resurrection, the indwelling of the Holy Spirit, the real presence of Christ in the Eucharist, the reality of sin, the essential connection between holiness and happiness, and the ground of our hope for the world to come. Newman defends these truths without resorting to the dry-as-dust rationalism of earlier ages. He knows that in the current climate of thought it may seem a tall order to believe the claims of Christianity; he recognizes that the standard rational arguments for faith, even when they are sound, often fail to reach the heart:

> The heart is commonly reached, not through the reason, but through the imagination, by means of direct impressions, by the testimony of facts and events, by history, by description. Persons influence us, voices melt us, looks subdue us, deeds inflame us. Many a man will live and die upon a dogma: no man will be a martyr for a conclusion.[1]

1. Newman, "The Tamworth Reading Room" (1841), Letter 6, "Secular Knowledge Not a Principle of Action." "The Tamworth Reading Room" refers to a series of letters

Above all, for Newman, the heart is reached by conscience, the internal arbiter, the aboriginal vicar of Christ—as we hear from Callista, the third-century convert and martyr heroine of Newman's 1855 novel of that name, when urged by her friends not to lay down her life for an unknown God:

"Well," she said, "I feel that God within my heart. I feel myself in His presence. He says to me, 'Do this: don't do that.' You may tell me that this dictate is a mere law of my nature, as is to joy or to grieve. I cannot understand this. No, it is the echo of a person speaking to me. Nothing shall persuade me that it does not ultimately proceed from a person external to me. It carries with it its proof of its divine origin. My nature feels towards it as towards a person. When I obey it, I feel a satisfaction; when I disobey, a soreness—just like that which I feel in pleasing or offending some revered friend. So you see, Polemo, I believe in what is more than a mere 'something.' . . . An echo implies a voice; a voice a speaker. That speaker I love and I fear."[2]

Many modern religious thinkers have sought to locate Christianity in the heart and in the moral sense; what is remarkable about Newman is that he does not, in so doing, abandon reason or "institutional" Christianity. He affirms the objectivity of revelation and the binding character of its authoritative expression without diminishing its mystery and its personal character—and he does all this in the most thrilling English prose. One can just imagine what it would have been like to hear him preach.

But Newman is easily misunderstood. He spent his whole adult life under a cloud of misunderstanding, from his Tractarian days (when he was suspected of popery), to his conversion (which looked like apostasy), to his dealings with Fr. Faber (which cast him as hyper-sensitive), to his trial for libel (when his archbishop hung him out to dry), to the heresy charge prompted by his 1859 article "On Consulting the Faithful in Matters of Doctrine." Not to mention the misunderstandings that dogged his efforts to found a Catholic university in Ireland, to make the *Rambler* an effective Catholic literary organ, and to provide a Catholic translation of the Bible. For decades he was regarded as a traitor by his Anglican supporters and only half-Catholic by his coreligionists. What turned the tide of public opinion, ironically, was one more colossal misunderstanding: Charles Kingsley's remark in *Macmillan's Magazine* in 1863 that "truth, for its own sake, had never been a virtue with the Roman clergy. Father Newman informs us that

---

Newman published in the *Times* under the name Catholicus.

2. Newman, *Callista*, 314.

it need not, and on the whole ought not to be"[3]—an assertion so outrageous that it providentially became the occasion for Newman to write the *Apologia pro vita sua*—passionate, indignant, delivered at breakneck speed, yet constituting a literary and spiritual classic that even George Eliot could not read without tears. That turned the tide; but not until Newman was created a cardinal at the end of his life were all the wrongs set right.

So if anyone deserves not to be misunderstood now it is Newman. Yet he is so complex, so subtle, so prolific (forty books, and over twenty thousand letters), so bold in his metaphors and tropes, and so downright funny at times, that he is easily misunderstood even by his admirers. Often it is a matter of not knowing exactly where to place the emphasis. Newman has justly been called the Father of the Second Vatican Council, but interpretations of the Council are varied and contested, and so, too, of Newman. For those who favor a liberal interpretation of Newman and of the Council, he is aligned with a movement to resist, as one distinguished Newman scholar puts it, "the tides of clericalism, over-centralisation, creeping infallibility, narrow unhistorical theology and exaggerated mariology" in favor of "freedom, the supremacy of conscience, the Church as a communion, the return to Scripture and the fathers, the rightful place of the laity, work for unity, and all the efforts to meet the needs of the age."[4]

The liberal perspective on Newman is for the most part just and generous in what it affirms but one-sided in what it denies. True, Newman resisted the Ultramontane version of papal infallibility, but he accepted the doctrine as it was defined at the First Vatican Council. True, Newman was put off by the Marian devotions he witnessed during his travels in Italy, but he was incessant in his praise of the Blessed Virgin, affirming that "nothing is too high for her to whom God owes His human life; no exuberance of grace, no excess of glory, but is becoming, but is to be expected there, where

3. Extract from a review of Froude's *History of England*, vols. 7 and 8, in *Macmillan's Magazine* for January 1864, signed "C. K."; quoted by Newman in Preface to *Apologia*, 4.

4. Nicholas Lash, quoting the great Newman scholar Father (Charles Jean) Stephen Dessain of the Birmingham Oratory. Lash comments, "But we are not there yet. There is poignancy in the thought that neither Christopher Butler nor Stephen Dessain seems to have noticed that tides never flow in the same direction for very long. The Curial resistance to renewal has not been broken and has been at the heart of the concerted attempt in recent years to argue that nothing of any great importance happened to the Catholic Church between 1962 and 1965. . . . At the heart of my hope that, with beatification swiftly followed by canonization, Newman may before too long be officially declared a doctor of the church, is the belief that such a declaration would be a powerful signal that the church has not abdicated its dedication to the movement of renewal and reform that the council so wholeheartedly initiated" ("Waiting for Dr. Newman," 14).

God has lodged Himself, whence God has issued."[5] True, Newman advocated a return to Scripture and the fathers, but not at the cost of rejecting as mere accretions significant medieval developments in Christian thought and worship. True, Newman advocated the rights of conscience. His letter to the duke of Norfolk has the famous toast "to the Pope, if you please,—still to Conscience first, and to the Pope afterwards."[6] But Newman never meant to interpret the rights of conscience in a libertarian sense. Conscience has rights because it has duties; it is a personal voice but not a subjective one, it elicits principally a fear and love of God, a desire to be holy, to surrender one's will and be of service. The freedom Newman prizes depends upon a wholehearted investment in the sacramental life, traditions, and authoritative teachings of the church; freedom is the dividend from that investment.

Pope Emeritus Benedict XVI has spoken of how, during his years as a seminarian, he first fell in love with Newman's writings on conscience. Having lived in the shadow of a totalitarian party—with leaders like Hermann Göring, who boasted, "I have no conscience. Adolf Hitler is my conscience"—Ratzinger craved the assurance that "the 'we' of the Church does not rest on a cancellation of conscience, but that, exactly the opposite, it can only develop *from* conscience."[7] As Ratzinger read more deeply in Newman's writings, he came to revere him as an ecclesial thinker for whom the church is the living body of Christ, a mystic for whom nothing is more real than the presence of God, and above all a witness to the truth of the gospel who speaks directly to modern doubts. Newman is aptly named in the title of the brief biography by Meriol Trevor and Léonie Caldecott: *John Henry Newman: Apostle to the Doubtful*.

The texts chosen for the Office of Readings for Newman's feast day (October 9, the day of his reception into the Catholic Church) are taken from the famous fifth chapter of the *Apologia* ("Position of my Mind since 1845"), in which he asserts that becoming Catholic "was like coming into port after a rough sea" and shows us exactly what that state of mind is like in which a doctrine of the faith becomes the object of joyful, instant, and unconditional assent—despite "difficulties":

> Many persons are very sensitive of the difficulties of Religion; I
> am as sensitive of them as any one; but I have never been able

5. Newman, *Discourses Addressed to Mixed Congregations*, Discourse 18, "On the Fitness of the Glories of Mary," 363.

6. Newman, *A Letter Addressed to the Duke of Norfolk on Occasion of Mr. Gladstone's Expostulation of 1874*, in *Certain Difficulties Felt by Anglicans in Catholic Teaching*, vol. 2, sec. 5, 261.

7. Ratzinger, "Newman Centenary Symposium."

to see a connexion between apprehending those difficulties, however keenly, and multiplying them to any extent, and on the other hand doubting the doctrines to which they are attached. Ten thousand difficulties do not make one doubt, as I understand the subject; difficulty and doubt are incommensurate. . . .

A man may be annoyed that he cannot work out a mathematical problem, of which the answer is or is not given to him, without doubting that it admits of an answer, or that a certain particular answer is the true one. Of all points of faith, the being of a God is, to my own apprehension, encompassed with most difficulty, and yet borne in upon our minds with most power.

Newman singles out Transubstantiation—rejected by Protestants as a medieval corruption and mercilessly parodied by David Hume—as the classic case of a difficult doctrine:

People say that the doctrine of Transubstantiation is difficult to believe; I did not believe the doctrine till I was a Catholic. I had no difficulty in believing it, as soon as I believed that the Catholic Roman Church was the oracle of God, and that she had declared this doctrine to be part of the original revelation. It is difficult, impossible, to imagine, I grant;—but how is it difficult to believe?

To be a Christian believer is to say *yes*, as Mary said at the Annunciation, not *maybe*, on the condition of adequate evidence. It is to repose in the secure possession of truth, to trust in the church as God's creation and instrument, and to meet death in this full conviction, as Gerontius does in Newman's *Dream*:

Firmly I believe and truly
    God is three, and God is One;
And I next acknowledge duly
    Manhood taken by the Son.
And I trust and hope most fully
    In that Manhood crucified;
And each thought and deed unruly
    Do to death, as He has died.
Simply to His grace and wholly
    Light and life and strength belong,
And I love, supremely, solely,
    Him the holy, Him the strong.
Sanctus fortis, Sanctus Deus,
    De profundis oro te,

Miserere, Judex meus,
    Parce mihi, Domine.
And I hold in veneration,
    For the love of Him alone,
Holy Church, as His creation,
    And her teachings, as His own.

Listen to all these adverbs: firmly, truly, fully, supremely, solely; they are not there merely for emphasis, but to make a point that Newman expounds systematically in *A Grammar of Assent*. There are no *degrees* of certitude, Newman tells us; religious certitude, when it is present, is absolute and unconditional. "I may love by halves," Newman tells us, "I may obey by halves; I cannot believe by halves: either I have faith, or I have it not."[8]

Newman certainly had an aptitude for believing. Ever since his first conversion at age fifteen, he had been convinced of the "luminous self-evidence" of his Creator. As his journey of faith unfolded, he went from strength to strength. To a modern sensibility, which regards faith as a venture and a hazard, this notion of firmly, truly, fully, supremely, and solely assenting to the teachings of the Catholic Church will seem a little strange. Yet Newman is indeed an apostle to the doubtful. He is full of sympathy for the honest doubter. He admits to hard facts and dilemmas that many believers would prefer to hush up; he admits to these facts and dilemmas in the very same breath with which he expresses his unreserved assent, in chapter 5 of the *Apologia*:

> Starting then with the being of a God, (which, as I have said, is as certain to me as the certainty of my own existence, though when I try to put the grounds of that certainty into logical shape I find a difficulty in doing so in mood and figure to my satisfaction,) I look out of myself into the world of men, and there I see a sight which fills me with unspeakable distress. The world seems simply to give the lie to that great truth, of which my whole being is so full; and the effect upon me is, in consequence, as a matter of necessity, as confusing as if it denied that I am in existence myself. If I looked into a mirror, and did not see my face, I should have the sort of feeling which actually comes upon me, when I look into this living busy world, and see no reflexion of its Creator. This is, to me, one of those great difficulties of this absolute primary truth, to which I referred just now. Were it not for this voice, speaking so clearly in my conscience and my

8. Newman, *Discourses Addressed to Mixed Congregations*, Discourse 11, "Faith and Doubt."

heart, I should be an atheist, or a pantheist, or a polytheist when I looked into the world.[9]

The world seems to give the lie to what he knows to be true; the truth would remain hidden from him had he not heard the voice speaking in his conscience; having heard the voice speaking in his conscience, he is able to hear the whole revealed message that God has entrusted to the church. His certitude is absolute, but it does not prevent him from understanding what it is like to be in doubt.

Newman's sympathy for skepticism has several sources. For one thing, he had a vivid imagination, which enabled him to enter into other people's mental landscapes. As a young boy he lived in his imagination, visualizing scenes from the family Bible and from stories of a more fantastic kind: "I used to wish the Arabian Tales were true; my imagination ran on unknown influences, on magical powers and talismans. I thought life might be a dream, or I an angel; my fellow angels, by a playful device, concealing themselves from me, and deceiving me with the semblance of a material world."[10] For another, he had a flair for analytical thinking, and had read widely in the English philosophical tradition, which grounded insight in sense experience and valued common sense and empirical reasoning over metaphysical abstractions. As a fourteen-year-old, he tells us,

> I read Paine's Tracts against the Old Testament, and found pleasure in thinking of the objections which were contained in them. Also, I read some of Hume's Essays; and perhaps that on Miracles. So at least I gave my father to understand; but perhaps it was a brag. Also, I recollect copying out some French verses, perhaps Voltaire's, against the immortality of the soul, and saying to myself something like "How dreadful, but how plausible!"[11]

And he knew skeptics—his brother Charles, William Froude—too intimately to write them off. Most importantly, his intellectual integrity made him unwilling to settle for inadequate defenses of the faith. To follow reason wherever it leads seemed to Newman a noble ideal, and he could readily understand how casting off the faith might feel like a liberation, as if a great weight were removed. To this feeling—an epidemic in our time, Newman observed to a friend, and a "wonderfully catching" one—religion needs to offer a "counter-fascination." From Saint Philip Neri, the joyful sixteenth-century

9. Newman, *Apologia*, ch. 5, "Position of my Mind since 1845," 216.

10. Newman, *Apologia*, ch. 1, "History of my Religious Opinions up to 1833," 23.

11. Newman, *Apologia*, ch. 1, "History of my Religious Opinions up to 1833," 25.

father of the Congregation of the Oratory, Newman learned that it was better to rely upon the attractive beauty of the Christian life than on hectoring
appeals to the unchurched.[12]

Newman's fullest treatment of how we come to believe and are justified in believing unconditionally is the book he called *An Essay in Aid of a
Grammar of Assent*. Unlike most of his other writings, this book was not
occasioned by a controversy but was a project dear to him, which he mulled
over through all the phases of his Anglican and Catholic career. It is "a subject which has teased me for these twenty or thirty years," he told a friend.
"I felt I had something to say upon it, yet, whenever I attempted, the sight
I saw vanished, plunged into a thicket, curled itself up like a hedgehog, or
changed colors like a chameleon."[13]

Grammar of Assent anticipates the great Victorian "Ethics of Belief"
debate—so named because of an essay titled "The Ethics of Belief" published in 1877 by Cambridge mathematician W. K. Clifford. Clifford had
renounced his Christian faith after reading Darwin, Huxley, and Hume.
He was an ardent rationalist whose maxim (Clifford's Law, it is sometimes
called) was that "it is wrong always, everywhere, and for anyone, to believe
anything upon insufficient evidence."[14] Against Clifford, the American philosopher William James wrote a famous essay titled "The Will to Believe" in
which he argued that religious faith was too vital to human well-being to be
held to Clifford's strict standard. We cannot have certainty, James said, but
we do have the right to believe for the sake of the moral and psychic benefits
it confers. James was a very attractive thinker who helped many people—
including the founders of Alcoholics Anonymous—overcome their intellectual obstacles and open themselves to the saving presence of a higher power
in their lives. But for James, as for Kierkegaard and many other modern
thinkers, faith had to make do without certainty: it was a wager, a leap in the
dark. While Clifford gave up faith for the sake of certainty, James gave up
certainty for the sake of faith: they embody the two types—the rationalist
and the humanist—most familiar to modern thought.

Newman has something radically different and far more subtle to offer.
He thought he could show that one can be rationally and morally certain of
a belief, without being able to prove it; that uneducated believers, though
they may not be able to make their reasons explicit, are not for all that simply resorting to blind faith; that at age fifteen he really did experience the

12. Newman, *Idea of a University*, Part 1, Discourse 9, 178–81.

13. Newman to Aubrey de Vere, August 1870, in Ward, *Life of John Henry, Cardinal
Newman*, 2:245.

14. Clifford, "Ethics of Belief," 346.

luminous self-evidence of God; that Gerontius is rational in saying, "Firmly I believe"; that belief may be strong and intact and rational even when there is a persistent and troubling sense of intellectual difficulty and—harder still—a spiritual temptation to doubt (Lord, I believe; help Thou my unbelief). Belief was no less strong, rational, and intact for Mother Teresa, and for her namesake, Saint Thérèse, however occulted during their long dark nights.

Accounting for the rational character of belief required, Newman realized, making fine distinctions between different kinds of reasoning. "Formal logical sequence is not in fact the method by which we are enabled to become certain of what is concrete,"[15] Newman says (and for Newman, religious belief has always to do with what is concrete—with experienced realities, seen and unseen, rather than general conceptions). A more informal kind of reasoning is involved: "It is the cumulation of probabilities, independent of each other, arising out of the nature and circumstances of the particular case which is under review; probabilities too fine to avail separately, too subtle and circuitous to be convertible into syllogisms, too numerous and various for such conversion, even were they convertible."[16]

The ability to see, as it were at a glance, the truth to which the converging probabilities are tending, Newman calls the "illative sense," from the past participle of the Latin verb *ferre* with the prefix *in*, suggesting that which is brought in (or brought *home*) to the mind. The illative sense, in a well-disposed mind, judges rightly; certitude is attained, even where the evidence is meager and the means of logical demonstration wanting.

"The best illustration of what I hold," Newman wrote in a letter, "is that of a *cable*, which is made up of a number of separate threads, each feeble, yet together as sufficient as an iron rod. An iron rod represents mathematical or strict demonstration; a cable represents moral demonstration, which is an assemblage of probabilities, separately insufficient for certainty, but, when put together, irrefragable. A man who said, 'I cannot trust a cable, I must have an iron bar,' would *in certain given* cases, be irrational and unreasonable:—so too is a man who says 'I must have a rigid demonstration, not moral demonstration, of religious truth.'"[17]

The technicalities of his argument, involving fine distinctions between apprehension and assent, between assent and inference, and between notional and real assent, are beyond the scope of this essay; but the gist of his

15. Newman, "Informal Inference," in *An Essay in Aid of a Grammar of Assent*, Part 2, ch. 8, sec. 2, 230.

16. Ibid.

17. Newman to Canon Walker, July 1864, in Ward, *Life of John Henry, Cardinal Newman*, 2:43.

approach is already present in the University Sermons Newman gave as an Anglican.

In Sermon 13, "Implicit and Explicit Reason," for Saint Peter's Day, 1840, Newman takes as his text 1 Peter 3:15: "Sanctify the Lord God in your hearts; and be ready always to give an answer to every man that asketh you a reason of the hope that is in you, with meekness and fear." Always be ready to give a reason for the hope that lies within: this has long been the motto for Christian apologetics; countless arguments for theistic belief from morality, from causality, from design, and from the statistically improbable "fine-tuning" of the physical constants have begun with an appeal to 1 Peter 3:15 as the mandate for Christians to supply evidence-based arguments for their faith. But Newman interjects into his account of reasons to believe a note of Christian personalism rarely found in rational apologetics.

"St. Peter's faith was one of his characteristic graces," Newman begins. "It was ardent, keen, watchful, and prompt. It dispensed with argument, calculation, deliberation, and delay, whenever it heard the voice of its Lord and Savior: and it heard that voice even when its accents were low, or when it was unaided by the testimony of the other senses."[18] Saint Peter, in other words, is the model of immediate assent, person to person, heart to heart: "If in any one Faith appears in contrast with what we commonly understand by Reason, and with Evidence, it so appears in the instance of Peter. When he reasoned, it was at times when Faith was lacking."[19] But Newman will not lead us into fideism:

> Faith and Reason, then, stand in strong contrast in the history of Peter: yet it is Peter, and he not the fisherman of Galilee, but the inspired Apostle, who in the text gives us a precept which implies, in order to its due fulfillment, a careful exercise of our Reason, an exercise both upon Faith, considered as an act or habit of mind, and upon the Object of it. We are not only to "sanctify the Lord God in our hearts," not only to prepare a shrine within us in which our Saviour Christ may dwell, and where we may worship Him; but we are so to understand what we do, so to master our thoughts and feelings, so to recognize what we believe, and how we believe, so to trace out our ideas and impressions, and to contemplate the issue of them, that we may be "ready always to give an answer to every man that asketh us an account of the hope that is in us." In these words,

18. Newman, Sermon 13, "Implicit and Explicit Reason," in *Fifteen Sermons*, 251.
19. Ibid., 252.

I conceive, we have a clear warrant, or rather an injunction, to
cast our religion into the form of Creed and Evidences.[20]

What looks like a contradiction is resolved by a *distinguo*:

> Here, then, are two processes, distinct from each other,—the
> original process of reasoning, and next, the process of investi-
> gating our reasonings. All men reason, for to reason is nothing
> more than to gain truth from former truth, without the inter-
> vention of sense; to which brutes are limited; but all men do not
> reflect upon their own reasonings, much less reflect truly and
> accurately, so as to do justice to their own meaning; but only
> in proportion to their abilities and attainments. In other words,
> all men have a reason, but not all men can give a reason. We
> may denote, then, these two exercises of mind as reasoning and
> arguing, or as conscious and unconscious reasoning, or as Im-
> plicit Reason and Explicit Reason. And to the latter belong the
> words, science, method, development, analysis, criticism, proof,
> system, principles, rules, laws, and others of a like nature. . . .
>
> Faith, then, though in all cases a reasonable process, is not
> necessarily founded on investigation, argument, or proof; these
> processes being but the explicit form which the reasoning takes
> in the case of particular minds.[21]

In short, Saint Peter knew our Lord intimately and bore witness unreservedly to his recognition of our Lord's true nature: "Thou art the Christ, the
Son of the Living God." But he did not make explicit all that this recognition
involved; that would be the work of centuries of doctrinal development.

If Sermon 13 is a condensed version of the argument in *Grammar of
Assent*, Sermon 15, Newman's final University Sermon, gives us *An Essay on
the Development of Doctrine* in a Gospel miniature. The text is from Luke
2:19—"But Mary kept all these things, and pondered them in her heart"—
and the starting point is similar to that of Sermon 13: "Little is told us in
Scripture concerning the Blessed Virgin, but there is one grace of which
the Evangelists make her the pattern, in a few simple sentences—of Faith."
The Blessed Virgin, like Saint Peter, is graced with an ardent, spontaneous
faith. No matter for deliberation could be stranger or more troubling than
the one the Angel gave her; no answer could be more blessed than Mary's
fiat. And yet, Newman tells us, "Mary's faith did not end in a mere acqui-
escence in Divine providences and revelations: as the text informs us, she

20. Ibid., 258–59, 262.
21. Ibid., 262.

'pondered' them."[22] Again, hearing her twelve-year-old son explain why he was in the temple discussing the things of God, "she kept all these sayings in her heart"; and by this deep pondering was prepared, when the wine ran out at Cana, to foresee Christ's first miracle: "Whatsoever He saith unto you, do it." Therefore the Blessed Virgin is the pattern of faithful reasoning to an even more marvelous degree of perfection than Saint Peter:

> She does not think it enough to accept, she dwells upon it; not enough to possess, she uses it; not enough to assent, she developes it; not enough to submit the Reason, she reasons upon it; not indeed reasoning first, and believing afterwards, with Zacharias, yet first believing without reasoning, next from love and reverence, reasoning after believing. And thus she symbolizes to us, not only the faith of the unlearned, but of the doctors of the Church also, who have to investigate, and weigh, and define, as well as to profess the Gospel; to draw the line between truth and heresy; to anticipate or remedy the various aberrations of wrong reason; to combat pride and recklessness with their own arms; and thus to triumph over the sophist and the innovator.[23]

Once Newman became a Catholic, he understood Mary's response more deeply; having uttered a *fiat* of his own, he could accept the 1854 definition of her Immaculate Conception; having accepted it with good will, he could discover its deep coherence with all the truths of the faith.

Newman is the apostle to the doubtful in that he offers a path to believing that is at once rational and personal, objective and affective. It does not base itself upon "evidences" such as those offered by the "physical theology" popular in Newman's day and under different guises in our own. Therefore it does not stand or fall with changing scientific perspectives on the physical world. "I believe in design because I believe in God," Newman wrote, "not in a God because I see design."[24] In an 1868 letter discussing Darwin's *Origin of the Species*, Newman is unflappable:

> I do not fear the theory. . . . It does not seem to me to follow that creation is denied because the Creator, millions of years ago, gave laws to matter. He first created matter and then he created laws for it—laws which should *construct* it into its present wonderful beauty, and accurate adjustment and harmony of parts

22. Newman, Sermon 15, "The Theory of Developments in Religious Doctrine," in *Fifteen Sermons*, 312.

23. Ibid., 313–14.

24. Newman to Brownlow, April 1870, in Ward, *Life of John Henry, Cardinal Newman*, 2:269.

gradually.... Mr Darwin's theory need not then to be atheistical, be it true or not; it may simply be suggesting a larger idea of Divine Prescience and Skill. . . . at first sight I do not [see] that "the *accidental* evolution of organic beings" is inconsistent with divine design—It is accidental to *us*, not to *God*.[25]

Newman predicted that there would be plenty of followers of Darwin prepared to conclude (as the American paleontologist George Gaylord Simpson once put it) that "man is the result of a purposeless and natural process that did not have him in mind."[26] But as Newman pointed out in *The Idea of a University*, scientists outrun their actual competence and discredit themselves by making such metaphysical claims; the doubts thus sown are not genuine, and need not alarm us:

He who believes Revelation with that absolute faith which is the prerogative of a Catholic, is not the nervous creature who startles at every sudden sound, and is fluttered by every strange or novel appearance which meets his eyes. He has no sort of apprehension, he laughs at the idea, that any thing can be discovered by any other scientific method, which can contradict any one of the dogmas of his religion. He knows full well there is no science whatever, but, in the course of its extension, runs the risk of infringing, without any meaning of offence on its own part, the path of other sciences: and he knows also that, if there be any one science which, from its sovereign and unassailable position can calmly bear such unintentional collisions on the part of the children of earth, it is Theology.[27]

The believer "is sure, and nothing shall make him doubt, that, if anything seems to be proved by astronomer, or geologist, or chronologist, or antiquarian, or ethnologist, in contradiction to the dogmas of faith, that point will eventually turn out, first, not to be proved, or, secondly, not contradictory, or thirdly, not contradictory to any thing really revealed, but to something which has been confused with revelation."[28] There is ample room in Newman's vision for the sciences to enjoy autonomy; and nothing but delight in the thought that where the sciences flourish, fresh and unsettling discoveries will continually be made, such that "the conclusions of today"

25. Newman to Canon Walker, May 1868, in Newman, *Letters and Diaries*, 24:77–78.

26. Simpson, *Meaning of Evolution*, 345.

27. Newman, *Idea of a University*, 8.

28. Ibid., 351.

are "nothing more than starting points of to-morrow"[29] and that a methodological doubt is the better part of wisdom. Ultimately knowledge is one,
and its end cannot be doubted: the divinizing vision of God, All in All.
What the *Times* expressed with such warmth and prescience in 1890 is
now clearer than ever: John Henry Newman, the apostle to the doubtful, is
a Father to our troubled century; God willing, it will not be long before we
can call him doctor to the universal church.

29. Newman, "God Is All in All," in *Meditations and Devotions*, 589.

16

The Prayer of Saint Francis
and the Grammar of Communion

Derek Cross

Lord, make me an instrument of thy peace.
Where there is hatred, let me sow love;
Where there is injury, pardon;
Where there is doubt, faith;
Where there is despair, hope;
Where there is darkness, light;
Where there is sadness, joy.

O divine Master, grant that I may not so much seek
To be consoled as to console,
To be understood as to understand,
To be loved as to love;
For it is in giving that we receive;
It is in pardoning that we are pardoned;
It is in dying to self that we are born to eternal life.

The well-known "Prayer of Saint Francis" is, even if a nineteenth-century construction rather than a Franciscan autograph, a guide to encountering Christ on several levels. It can well serve as material for *lectio divina*, by dint of simple repetition with accompanying attention. This prayer has three sections. As we move from one section to the next, the prayer signals the ongoing transformation of the self by the grammatical constructions it employs. The prayer begins with the objective pronoun "me," moves to the subjective pronoun "I," and finishes with the collective pronoun "we"—this time in the context of a gravely impersonal background: "it is." We can see that these three sections correspond to the classical threefold path of spiritual development: the purgative, the illuminative, and the unitive ways.

Saint Francis's prayer begins with a number of petitions for *me*, the first person expressed in the objective (or, if you like, the accusative) case. Self-objectification is not necessarily the best place to *be*, but it is a realistic place to *begin*. At first, we think we know ourselves, our wants and needs. We regard all this as personal, if fixed, in nature. We think of the self as an object, *me*; we suppose we have a picture of this *me* before our minds and can unerringly identify it. It is such an objective self we invoke when we say to someone, "I want you to understand *me*," that is, I want you to endorse the judgments I make about *myself* as an object. There may, however, be both more and less to ourselves than we think. But on this occasion the *me*-word occurs in a prayer, where the *me*-self from the very first acknowledges that it finds itself in a situation striated with enmity and opposition, where this *me*-self prays that it can help make a difference for the better. Listen. *Lord, make* **me** (Saint Francis would have us pray) *an instrument of thy peace. Where there is hatred, let* **me** *sow love; where there is injury, pardon; where there is doubt, faith; where there is despair, hope; where there is darkness, light; where there is sadness, joy.* In every instance, the pray-er discerns something negative and begs God to make his *me* an instrument to heal the wounds and illumine the darkness of his surroundings. In fact, it is a little difficult to make out from the words of the prayer whether the me-self recognizes much more than a vague distinction between its self-image and the situation it confronts. It is not really clear whether it regards the objects of its prayer as lying outside or included within. Is the hatred mine or the world's? What about the sadness? This vagueness is perhaps characteristic of the me-self, which presumes rather than clearly perceives the distinction between self and other. But when injury and pardon are in question, it would seem that the pray-er is speaking about injuries done to his *me*. How else could the *me* be an instrument of pardon? (We shall be very interested when the prayer must repeat the word *pardon* later, in another context.) But conceiving the *me* objectively also means conceiving its role objectively. The pray-er asks that God wield him as a separated instrument to mitigate certain ills. Our first impression is that we are dealing with three clearly delimited things: God, me, and evil. And yet the act of healing strangely involves bringing these closer together. The location of love, pardon, faith, despair, light, and joy is determined by identifying the present lack of those things. As God grasps the *me* instrumentally, these opposites are joined, and the negative becomes the soil for the growth of the positive. Let me *sow*, the pray-er asks. The obstacles and the sufferings of this world become the soil wherein virtuous acts flower.

Now let's move to the second part of the prayer. Here no longer are negative deficiencies the soil of positive acts, but a deepening presence of

Christ makes itself known in the soul's own activity. *O divine Master* (Saint Francis asks us to continue) *grant that **I** may not so much seek to be consoled as to console, to be understood as to understand, to be loved as to love.* Here we have moved from the *me* to the *I*, from the self as an object to the self as a subject. The object must be something conceived (even if as an instrument of goodness); it is all there (you think) in front of you. The subject, on the other hand, is one who *acts*. Far from being simply conceived and delimited (perhaps wrongly), the subject can even afford to be an actor somewhat heedless of itself. Now the self petitions not *for* the *me* but asks that the *I* may act—that *I* may *console*, that *I* may *understand*, that *I* may *love*. This *I*-self is fully given over to its acting, with no concern that anyone (even God) console, understand, or love the *me* as an object. The *I*-self seeks no gratification or approval for itself. Does the pure *I*-subject then act alone and bereft of God's help? By no means. The *I*-self no longer thinks of itself as an object external to God, but as a participation in the consoling, understanding, loving action of God bestowing itself in self-donating activity.

In the final section of the Prayer of Saint Francis, the expletive subject *it* and the existential verb *is* govern the corporate subject *we* (subject of a passive verb) by inclusion. This juxtaposition suggests both communion and ultimacy. Thus, the comprehensive receiver of the act, the *we*-community, is united with the act itself. We are no longer separate competitors—haves and have-nots. Whatever *we* give away redounds to us. We are forgiven by ourselves participating in the act of forgiveness. In the life of communion, action and passion are one. Death itself opens onto life. Christ is born in us, and we dare to utter the sacrificial paradoxes of his divine humanity: *For **it** is in giving that* we *receive;* **it is** *in pardoning that* we *are pardoned;* **it is** *in dying to self that* **we** *are born to eternal life.* This is the divine peace.

17

Stratford Caldecott

A Brief Biography

Philip Zaleski

Stratford Stanley Francis Caldecott was born at King's College Hospital in south London on November 26, 1953. His father was Oliver Caldecott (1925–1989), one of the leading publishers and editors in England, and his mother Moyra Caldecott, née Brown (1927–), a poet and novelist best known for her fantasy trilogy *Guardians of the Tall Stones*.

Stratford's parents came from South Africa, immigrating to England around 1950 partly on account of his father's anti-apartheid activities; at least one linguist, a Benedictine monk, claims to discern traces of the veldt in Stratford's soft, musical voice. Stratford was raised, with two siblings (Julian, b. 1956; Rachel, b. 1960), in a lively London household piled high with books and frequented by well-known writers, a number of them in the vanguard of New Age thought as Oliver Caldecott's publishing interests ran increasingly in that direction. As a young child, Stratford suffered from poor eyesight, eczema, and asthma—once a lung collapsed, requiring a stay in hospital—reasons enough for his favoring intellectual endeavors over sports. Nonetheless, upon entering Dulwich College on a state scholarship he learned to love cricket, and he also developed an interest in history and science, astronomy in particular (the seed of this fascination with the heavens may have been planted in early youth, when one night his parents woke him up and led him to a front room where a telescope had been set up to view the moon through an open window: a beautiful, haunting image).

Stratford was not baptized, as his father wished him to determine his own religious beliefs. Instead, he drew early spiritual nourishment from literature, including fantasy novels and American comic books, and from dreams of a most peculiar nature, "dreams that seemed to be more than dreams . . . bearing revelations that can never be expressed in words," as he later described them.[1] These influences awoke in him a firm if fledgling belief in God. At the age of fourteen, while questioning the claims of materialism during a family visit to South Africa, he had a realization that transformed his life that "the very awareness of the question" was itself nonmaterial. "It is hard to convey," he wrote, "the force with which this insight impacted upon my life, or the horizons it opened up for me." This profound, if adolescent and as yet untutored insight, combined with another into the unity of "matter, consciousness, and time," set him upon a metaphysical and religious path to which he has kept ever since. He studied arguments for the existence of God, devoured counter-cultural religious texts—many of them published by his father—and spent a year in America, working as a male au pair and exploring the country by bus and hitchhiking, before arriving in Oxford on a scholarship to study psychology and philosophy at Hertford College.

At the time, behavioral psychology and analytical philosophy dominated at the university. They proved thin gruel for a young man on the lookout for spiritual truth, and Stratford soon grew disillusioned with his studies. Instead, he pored over the writings of Sufis, in particular Jalaluddin Rumi and Ibn Arabi, along with the books of the modern Traditionalist school of René Guenon, Frithjof Schuon, and Ananda Coomaraswamy, and he encountered followers of the Russian esotericist G. I. Gurdjieff. He sensed in the Traditionalists and Gurdjieffians a spiritual elitism that troubled him, and yet he learned to his benefit, through these unconventional explorations, the dangers of religious syncretism on the one hand and of a religionless "spiritual search" on the other. While at Oxford, he also enjoyed a far more important encounter, "the event that would truly change my life": he met his future wife, Léonie Caldecott (née Richards), destined to be his partner in so many endeavors on behalf of the church. She came up to Oxford a year after him, entering Hertford to read philosophy and theology. Stratford was assigned as her mentor and the two fell in love, their romance surviving the occasion when the smitten man, demonstrating to his young angel his skills with a punt, plunged headfirst into the river, ruining his black suede jacket.

The couple married in 1977 at Oxford's Anglican church, Saint Mary Magdalen. After a brief stint as a sales assistant and clerk in a London bookstore, Stratford followed in his father's footsteps by beginning a career as a publisher and editor. He had developed a deep interest in the teachings of the nineteenth-century Persian religious leader Bahá'u'lláh and found his

---

1. Caldecott, "Gnosis and Grace," 169.

first job as an assistant editor for the small Bahá'í publishing firm of George Ronald in Kidlington. Upon losing his faith in Bahá'í, Stratford moved on to the London firm of Routledge & Kegan Paul, famed for its impressive philosophy and spirituality lists. Meanwhile, Léonie worked as a journalist, writing on the arts, nuclear issues, and ecofeminism.

As the next phase in what had become by now a mutual religious quest, Stratford and Léonie explored Buddhism under the Tibetan Rinpoche Namkhai Norbu, a practitioner in the rDzogs-chen lineage. They valued the meditational serenity imparted by this tradition but harbored serious reservations; Léonie was convinced that the sacramental element, such as one finds in Christianity, had to be at the core of any spiritual path. Stratford then began to read intensely in Saint Thomas Aquinas and his most prominent modern interpreters, Étienne Gilson and Jacques Maritain, and eventually came to realize that Christianity "is not to do with states of consciousness," that it "is about salvation . . . an ontological change, a change in the substance of reality itself, brought about by the sacrifice of the Son of God."[2] At around the same time, he experienced a powerful dream of the Holy Grail appearing in his parents' Dulwich home: "In the dream, or vision, I prostrated myself before it: the sense of a sacred presence was overwhelming." Thus spurred on by reason and imagination, philosophy and art, theology and vision, he received instruction from a local priest and, in November 1980, on his twenty-seventh birthday, was received into the Roman Catholic Church. "The Absolute had always loomed on my interior vision as the source and goal of my thinking," he wrote. "But it was only in the Church that this interior God approached me from outside and invited me to trust him as absolutely as a God ought to be trusted. In the teaching of the Church I recognized the God of my interior horizon . . . to reject the invitation of that God would have been to deny my true self." Léonie, after much prayer and discernment, entered the church three years later.

In 1984 the Caldecotts moved to Boston, where Stratford worked as philosophy and social sciences editor for the American branch of Routledge & Kegan Paul, while Léonie continued her journalism career. Here they encountered the Harvard Catholic scene, attended meetings of the newly founded branch of Communion and Liberation, and studied the works of John Henry Newman, Hans Urs von Balthasar, G. K. Chesterton, Romano Guardini, Henri de Lubac, Joseph Ratzinger, and other outstanding nineteenth- and twentieth-century intellectuals. Here, too, they discovered the international Catholic review, *Communio*, founded by Ratzinger, von

2. All the quotations in this paragraph come from Caldecott, "Gnosis and Grace," 175–77, 180.

Balthasar, Louis Bouyer, and others, and began their long, intensive, and fruitful relationship with the journal and the circle around it.

Pope John Paul II influenced them profoundly with his brilliant encyclicals and his emphasis upon cultural evangelization; on a brief trip back to Europe, they attended a private papal Mass and afterwards met the pope in his library. On the same journey, they encountered Carlo Cardinal Caffara, who told them that "the most important thing you can do for the church is to work in the area of faith and culture."[3] These words entered their hearts; they felt that they had been given their mission.

A year or so later, they returned to England, an infant daughter (Tessa) in tow. They lived first in Wimbledon and then in Oxford, and two more daughters (Sophie and Rosie) entered the family. At this time their work for the church began in earnest, exploring and elucidating the marriage of faith and culture. Stratford shouldered this task with the same astonishing energy and enthusiasm that permitted him, in his youth, to leap down stairs four or five steps at a time. He worked as an editor at HarperCollins, then for T. & T. Clark. He organized conferences, beginning with one in Zagreb on the economy. He and Léonie founded a Centre for Faith and Culture, initially located at Westminster College near Oxford, and convened a number of important gatherings: on Saint Philip Neri, on Chesterton, on Christopher Dawson and the Catholic vision of history (leading to the 1997 book *Eternity in Time*), and, most notably, on the liturgy, resulting in the Oxford Declaration on the Liturgy,[4] a document that wielded considerable influence upon Catholic thought in Britain and abroad. Stratford also put together a series of Hans Urs von Balthasar lectures at the Oxford Chaplaincy and worked on the organization and maintenance of the Chesterton Library (created by Aidan Mackey and now owned by the Chesterton Library Trust), the principal collection of that great and benevolent writer's books, manuscripts, and personal artifacts.

Meanwhile, the Caldecotts established a journal of faith and culture, the finest English-language Catholic effort of its kind, titled *Second Spring* after Newman's celebrated sermon. From 1992 to 1999 it appeared as an eight-page insert in *Catholic World Report*, but with the new millennium, it took on new life as a full-scale independent journal. The first issue appeared in 2001, designed, edited, and mailed from the Caldecott kitchen table. It continues to this day, a venerable, widely read journal, each issue offering some of the best Catholic writing in the English-speaking world. The *Second Spring* website (www.secondspring.co.uk) became and continues to be a

3. Interview with Léonie Caldecott.
4. See http://www.secondspring.co.uk/spirituality/declaration.htm.

nexus of Catholic intellectual life—and a place for Stratford to offer not only theological and social reflections, but also pastoral advice.

Perhaps here the author of this memoir may be permitted a brief personal aside: one of Stratford's most striking characteristics, which my wife and I have had the opportunity to observe on many occasions, is his generosity and gentleness in conversation with those seeking to understand (or undermine) the Christian faith. During one very long car ride across snowy Massachusetts, for example, we watched him, when challenged on abortion and birth control, provide on the spot a cogent, insightful explanation of orthodox teaching combined with a humble admission that he and the church need to do better in communicating the truth—the last not the sort of self-deprecating remark many would willingly advance.

While engaged in *Second Spring*, Stratford moved his center of operations for a time to Plater College, a Catholic educational institution for adults in Headington, Oxford. There he taught, directed the G. K. Chesterton Institute, and oversaw the G. K. Chesterton Library. He and Léonie initiated at Plater a series of summer schools, including a memorable one in 2001 on the Mission of the Baptised, with James Cardinal Stafford, then head of the Pontifical Institute for the Laity; Angelo Cardinal Scola also visited at Stratford's invitation, but before the two could develop a planned association between Plater and the Lateran University in Rome, Stratford's relationship with the college came to an end. Plater closed in 2005; since then, the Caldecotts have organized other summer schools under other auspices, including one on Shakespeare with Clare Asquith and Fr. Peter Milward, SJ, at Saint Benet's Hall (where Stratford is a G. K. Chesterton Fellow), and they have offered for many years a regular Oxford summer program in partnership with Thomas More College on such subjects as the cultural crisis of the Reformation and the nineteenth-century Catholic revival.

When Pope Benedict XVI paid his "Cor ad Cor Loquitur" visit to the United Kingdom, culminating in the beatification of John Henry Newman on the nineteenth of September, 2010, a special international English edition of *Magnificat* (a liturgical journal founded in France in 1992) was launched, containing the text of the liturgies and public prayers for that historic occasion. Since then the editing of the UK/Ireland *Magnificat* (based upon the existing U.S. edition) has been the shared responsibility of Stratford, Léonie, and Tessa, the latter serving as managing editor. *Magnificat* embodies the sensitivity to beauty in word and image and the conviction of Christ's presence at the heart of the church's liturgy, the same qualities that are the hallmark of *Second Spring*.

The labors described above have occupied much of Stratford's time, but for many, his greatest accomplishment is his writing. His books, essays, and reviews have made major and lasting contributions to the evangelization of culture across an unusual number of fields, ranging from social ethics, economic development, and education to literary criticism, biblical exegesis, and metaphysics. His books on education have helped contemporary parents and teachers rethink what it means to shape young minds, and his books on the Catholic mythopoeia of J. R. R. Tolkien have been an eye-opener for fans of *The Lord of the Rings*. In all his writings on theology, society, and culture, Stratford embodies an irenic *intellectus fidei* very welcome in these embattled times.

The following bibliography of Stratford's major writings is provided for students of his work:

- Stratford Caldecott and John Morrill, editors, *Eternity in Time: Christopher Dawson and the Catholic Idea of History* (London: T. &. T Clark, 1997).

- Stratford Caldecott, editor, *Beyond the Prosaic: Renewing the Liturgical Movement* (London: T. & T. Clark, 2000).

- Stratford Caldecott, *Catholic Social Teaching: A Way In* (London: Catholic Truth Society, 2001).

- Stratford Caldecott, *Secret Fire: The Spiritual Vision of J. R. R. Tolkien* (London: Darton, Longman & Todd, 2003), together with its American edition:

- Stratford Caldecott, *The Power of the Ring: The Spiritual Vision behind The Lord of the Rings* (New York: Crossroad, 2005). Second edition: Stratford Caldecott, *The Power of the Ring: The Spiritual Vision behind The Lord of the Rings and The Hobbit* (New York: Crossroad, 2012).

- Stratford Caldecott, *The Seven Sacraments: Entering the Mysteries of God* (New York: Crossroad, 2006).

- Stratford Caldecott and Thomas M. Honegger, editors, *Tolkien's The Lord of the Rings: Sources of Inspiration* (Zurich: Walking Tree, 2008).

- Stratford Caldecott, *Companion to the Book of Revelation* (London: Catholic Truth Society, 2008).

- Stratford Caldecott, *Beauty for Truth's Sake: On the Re-enchantment of Education* (Grand Rapids: Brazos, 2009).

- Stratford Caldecott, *Catholicism and Other Religions: Introducing Interfaith Dialogue* (London: Catholic Truth Society, 2009).

- Stratford Caldecott, *Fruits of the Spirit* (London: Catholic Truth Society, 2010).

- Stratford Caldecott, *All Things Made New: The Mysteries of the World in Christ* (San Rafael, CA: Angelico/Sophia Perennis, 2011).

- Stratford Caldecott, *Beauty in the World: Rethinking the Foundations of Education* (Tacoma, WA: Angelico, 2012).

- Stratford Caldecott, *The Radiance of Being: Dimensions of Cosmic Christianity* (Tacoma, WA: Angelico, 2013).

- Stratford Caldecott, *Not as the World Gives* (Kettering, OH: Angelico, 2014).

A partial list of the journals and magazines that have published Stratford's work includes *Communio, The Chesterton Review, The Tablet, The Catholic Herald, Parabola, Sacred Web, Catholic World Report, Inside the Vatican, Thirty Days, National Catholic Register, The Sower,* and *St. Anthony's Messenger.*

Links to Stratford's three blogs ("Beauty in Education," "All Things Made New," and "The Economy Project") can be found on the Second Spring website.

Afterword

Léonie Caldecott

Deus, qui nobis dilectum Filium tuum audire praecepisti, verbo tuo interius nos pascere digneris, ut, spiritali purificato intuitu, gloriae tuae laetemur aspectu.

I

How does it hold?
Armies have crossed it.
Dowries sacked,
Fragile wings flailing
And ploughed under.
Failing.

Oh you who have ears

A cell. Now three.
She spins in the darkness,
A whirling dervish of haecceity.

I see and it is good

Her feet are sure
(a sign of contradiction)
Lightly she dances across the bridge.

My eyes like the eyes of your handmaid

His hands are white upon the coverlet.
The keys fall silent.
The hours of the night absorb him.

For my eyes have seen

The barbarians gather.
Plundering cuckoos
Plucking at notions.

And the gates of hell shall not prevail

II

How can it hold?
A well-booted legion marches,
Their relentless stride effecting fractures.

See how the mighty are fallen

Who am I? Give it no mind.
This is the answer the lame
Must give to the blind.

O taste and see if any grief

We struggle to span
A raging torrent,
This hail-wracked spring.

He is not in the storm

I have set my face
Against the darkness,
My sandals on my feet.

Dust to dust

III

How shall I hold
The anamnesis of our days?
They fell like leaves, carpeting the ground.

I asked the watchman
Have you seen him?

In the land of milk and honey
The mother bee spells out
A semaphore of grace.

That we may rejoice to behold

In the darkness before the dawn
The disarmed face rests.
The byssus as yet unstirred.
My flame, a solitary vigil.

Rare-veined traveller
I take you as my witness.

Bibliography

Alexander, Christopher. *The Nature of Order: An Essay on the Art of Building and the Nature of the Universe.* 4 vols. Berkeley: Center for Environmental Structure, 2002.

Amar, Joseph P., translator. *A Metrical Homily on Holy Mar Ephrem, by Mar Jacob of Sarug.* Patrologia Orientalis 47, 1, no. 209. Turnhout: Brepols, 1995.

———, editor and translator. *The Syriac Vita Tradition of St. Ephrem the Syrian.* Corpus scriptorum Christianorum Orientalium 629, Scriptores Syri 242. Louvain: Peeters, 2011.

Anatella, Tony. *Le règne de Narcisse.* Paris: Gallimard, 2005.

Aquinas, Thomas. *De veritate.*

———. *Summa theologiae.*

———. *Summa Contra Gentiles.*

Aristotle. *De Anima.* Translated, with an introduction and notes by Mark Shiffman. Newburyport, MA: Focus, 2010.

———. *Metaphysics.*

———. *Physics.*

Artigas, M., T. F. Glick, and R. A. Martinez. *Negotiating Darwin: The Vatican Confronts Evolution, 1877–1902.* Baltimore: Johns Hopkins University Press, 2006.

Augustine. *De Trinitate.*

Balthasar, Hans Urs von. *Epilogue.* Translated by Edward T. Oakes. San Francisco: Ignatius, 1987.

———. *Glaubhaft ist nur Liebe.* Einsiedeln: Johannes, 1963. English translation: *Love Alone Is Credible.* Translated by D. C. Schindler. San Francisco: Ignatius, 2004.

———. *The Glory of the Lord: A Theological Aesthetics.* Vol 1, *Seeing the Form.* Translated by Erasmo Leiva-Merikakis. Edinburgh: T. & T. Clark, 1982.

———. *The Glory of the Lord: A Theological Aesthetics.* Vol. 4, *Theology: The Old Covenant.* Translated by Brian McNeil. San Francisco: Ignatius, 1991.

———. *The Grain of Wheat: Aphorisms.* Translated by Erasmo Leiva-Merikakis. San Francisco: Ignatius, 1995

———. *Homo Creatus Est.* Skizzen zur Theologie 5. Einsiedeln: Johannes, 1986.

———. *New Elucidations.* Translated by Mary Theresilde Skerry. San Francisco: Ignatius, 1986.

———. *Razing the Bastions: On the Church in This Age.* Translated by Brian McNeil. San Francisco: Ignatius, 1993.

———. "Spirit and Institution." In *Explorations in Theology,* 4:209–44. Translated by Edward T. Oakes. San Francisco: Ignatius, 1995.

———. *Theo-Drama: Theological Dramatic Theory.* Vol. 2, *The Dramatis Personae: Man in God.* Translated by Graham Harrison. San Francisco: Ignatius, 1990.

———. *Theo-Drama: Theological Dramatic Theory.* Vol. 4, *The Action.* Translated by Graham Harrison. San Francisco: Ignatius, 1994.

———. *Theo-Drama: Theological Dramatic Theory.* Vol. 5, *The Last Act.* Translated by Graham Harrison. San Francisco: Ignatius, 1998.

Barrow, J., and F. Tipler. *The Anthropic Cosmological Principle.* Oxford: Oxford University Press, 1986.

Basil, Saint. *On the Holy Spirit.* Translated by Stephen Hildebrand. Yonkers, NY: St. Vladimir's Seminary Press,

Beck, E. "Asketentum und Mönchtum bei Ephräm." In *Il Monachesimo Orientale,* 341–62. Orientalia Christiana analecta 153. Rome: Pont. Institutum Orientalium Studiorum, 1958.

———. "Das Bild vom Spiegel bei Ephräm." *Orientalia Christiana Periodica* 19 (1953) 1–24.

———. *Des heiligen Ephraem des Syrers Hymnen De Virginitate.* 2 vols. Corpus scriptorum Christianorum Orientalium 223–24, Scriptores Syri 94–95. Louvain: Peeters, 1962.

———. "Ein Beitrag zur Terminologie des ältesten syrischen Mönchtums." In *Antonius Magnus Eremita,* 254–67. Studia Anselmiana 38. Roma: 1956.

———. *Ephraems Reden über den Glauben, ihr theologischer Lehrgehalt und ihr geschichtlicher Rahmen.* Studia Anselmiana 33. Roma: Pontificium Institutum S. Anselmi, 1953.

———, translator. *Hymnen de fide.* 2 vols. Corpus scriptorum Christianorum Orientalium 154–55, Scriptores Syri 73–74. Louvain: L. Durbecq, 1955.

———. "Symbolum-Mysterium bei Aphraat und Ephräm." *Oriens Christianus* 42 (1958) 19–40.

———. "Zur Terminologie von Ephraems Bildterminologie." In *Typus, Symbol, Allegorie bei den östlichen Vätern und ihren Parallelen im Mittelalter,* edited by M. Schmidt, 239–77. Eichstätter Beiträge 4. Regensburg: Pustet, 1982.

Benedict XVI, Pope. *Caritas in Veritate.* June 29, 2009.

———. "Faith, Reason, and the University—Memories and Reflections." Lecture at Aula Magna of the University of Regensburg, September 12, 2006, http://www.vatican.va/holy_father/benedict_xvi/speeches/2006/september/documents/hf_ben-xvi_spe_20060912_university-regensburg_en.html.

———. Homily to the Consistory, March 25, 2006, http://www.vatican.va/holy_father/benedict_xvi/homilies/2006/documents/hf_ben-xvi_hom_20060325_anello-cardinalizio_en.html.

———. *Spe Salvi.* November 30, 2007.

———. *The Spirit of the Liturgy.* San Francisco: Ignatius, 2000.

———. *Truth and Tolerance.* San Francisco: Ignatius, 2004.

Blignières, L.-M de. "Un regard thomiste sur l'Evolution." *Sedes Sapientiae* 106 (2008) 57–77.

Bonaventure, Saint. *Breviloquium.* Translated by Dominic V. Monti. Works of St. Bonaventure 9. St. Bonaventure, NY: Franciscan Institute, 2005.

Bou Mansour, T. "Aspects de la liberté humaine chez saint Ephrem le Syrien." *Ephemerides Theologicae Lovaniensia* 60 (1984) 252–82.

———. "La défense éphremienne de la liberté contre les doctrines marcionite, bardésanite et manichéenne." *Orientalia Christiana Periodica* 50 (1984) 331–46.

———. "La Liberte chez S. Ephrem le Syrien." *Parole de l'Orient* 11 (1983) 89–156.

———. *La pensée symbolique de Saint Éphrem le Syrien.* Bibliothèque de l'Université Saint Esprit 16. Kaslik: Université Saint-Exprit, 1988.

Brock, Sebastian P. *The Luminous Eye: The Spiritual World Vision of St. Ephrem.* Cistercian Studies 124. Kalamazoo, MI: Cistercian, 1990.

————. "The Mysteries Hidden in the Side of Christ." *Sobornost* 7 (1978) 464–72.

————, editor and translator. "Ephrem's Letter to Publius." *Le Muséon* (1976) 261–305.

Brock, Sebastian P., and George A. Kiraz, translators. *Ephrem the Syrian: Select Poems.* Eastern Christian Texts 2. Provo: Brigham Young University Press, 2006.

Bruns, P. "Arius hellenizans?—Ephraem der Syrer und die neoarianischen Kontroversen seiner Zeit." *Zeitschrift für Kirchengeschichte* 101 (1990/91) 21–57.

Bulgakov, Sergei. *The Bride of the Lamb.* Translated by Boris Jakim. Grand Rapids: Eerdmans, 2002.

Cabasilas, Nicholas. *Sermo in Nativitatem Deiparae, Sermo in Annunciationem Deiparae,* and *Sermo in Assumptionem Deiparae.* In *Homélies mariales byzantines: textes grecs,* edited by Martin Jugie. Patrologia Orientalis 19. Paris: Firmin-Didot, 1922.

Caldecott, Stratford. *All Things Made New: The Mysteries of the World in Christ.* San Rafael, CA: Angelico/Sophia Perennis, 2011.

————. "At Home in the Cosmos: The Franciscan Redemption of Ecology." Greyfriars Lecture, Taylor Institution, Oxford, May 24, 2010.

————. "At Home in the Cosmos: The Revealing of the Sons of God." *Nova et Vetera,* English edition, 10 (2012) 105–20.

————. "Beauty for Truth's Sake and the Children of Wisdom." Lecture given at the University of Notre Dame, November 2, 2010, http://www.secondspring.co.uk/books/Caldecott%20talk%20at%20ND.pdf.

————. *Beauty for Truth's Sake: On the Re-enchantment of Education.* Grand Rapids: Brazos, 2009.

————. *Beauty in the World: Rethinking the Foundations of Education.* Tacoma, WA: Angelico, 2012.

————. "Beyond Left and Right: A Politics of Life." *Communio* 22 (1995) 381–88.

————, editor. *Beyond the Prosaic: Renewing the Liturgical Movement.* Edinburgh: T. & T. Clark, 2000.

————. "*Caritas in veritate* and 'Integral Human Development.'" *Communio* 36 (2009) 182–85.

————. *Catholic Social Teaching: A Way In.* London: Catholic Truth Society, 2001.

————. *Catholicism and Other Religions: Introducing Interfaith Dialogue.* London: Catholic Truth Society, 2009.

————. "Christian Ecology." *Catholic World Report,* August-September 1996, http://www.ewtn.com/library/ISSUES/CHRISECO.TXT.

————. *Companion to the Book of Revelation.* London: Catholic Truth Society, 2008.

————. "Cosmology, Eschatology, Ecology." *Communio* 15 (1988) 305–18.

————. "Creation and the University: Educating for a Human Ecology." Earth Day Lecture, University of St. Thomas, Houston, Texas, April 15, 2010.

————. "Creation as a Call to Holiness." *Communio* 30 (2003) 161–67.

————. "A Deeper Ecology." http://theeconomyproject.blogspot.com/2012/10/a-deeper-ecology.html.

————. "A Distributist Manifesto?" http://theeconomyproject.blogspot.com/2009/07/controversies-5-third-way.html.

————. "The Family at the Heart of a Culture of Life." *Communio* 23 (1996) 89–100.

————. *Fruits of the Spirit.* London: Catholic Truth Society, 2010.

————. "Gnosis and Grace." In *The Path to Rome: Modern Journeys to the Catholic Church,* edited by Dwight Longenecker, 169–80. Leominster, UK: Gracewing, 1999.

———. "The Lord and Lady of the Rings: The Hidden Presence of Tolkien's Catholicism in *The Lord of the Rings*." *Touchstone* 15 (2002) 51–57. http://touchstonemag.com/archives/article.php?id=15-01-051-f.

———. "Lost in the Forest? Some Books on Ecology." *Priests and People* 9 (1995). Reprinted in *Second Spring*, 2002. http://www.secondspring.co.uk/articles/scaldecott8.htm.

———. "Love in Truth." Given as a talk for the permanent diaconate in the archdiocese of Southwark, UK, May 1, 2010. http://www.secondspring.co.uk/economy/Love%20in%20Truth%202.pdf.

———. "The Marian Dimension of Existence." In *Being Holy in the World: Theology and Culture in the Thought of David L. Schindler*, edited by Nicholas J. Healy and D. C. Schindler, 281–94. Grand Rapids: Eerdmans, 2011.

———. "New Sins: Technology and the Frontiers of Catholic Social Teaching." *Communio* 28 (2001) 488–504.

———. *The Radiance of Being: Dimensions of Cosmic Christianity*. Tacoma, WA: Angelico, 2013.

———. "The Science of the Real: The Christian Cosmology of Hans Urs von Balthasar." Revised version of *Communio* 25 (1998) 462–79. http://www.secondspring.co.uk/articles/scaldecott11.htm.

———. *Secret Fire: The Spiritual Vision of J. R. R. Tolkien*. London: Darton, Longman & Todd, 2003; American edition: *The Power of the Ring: The Spiritual Vision Behind The Lord of the Rings*. New York: Crossroad, 2005. Second edition: *The Power of the Ring: The Spiritual Vision Behind* The Lord of the Rings *and* The Hobbit. New York: Crossroad, 2012.

———. "Session V. Response from Mr. Stratford Caldecott." Colloquium, The Ethics of Climate Change. Blackfriars Hall, Oxford, November, 17 2007.

———. *The Seven Sacraments: Entering the Mysteries of God*. New York: Crossroad, 2006.

———. "Theological Dimensions of Human Liberation." *Communio* 22 (1995) 225–41.

———. "A Theology of Gift." http://www.secondspring.co.uk/uploads/articles_15_592693109.pdf.

———. "Theories of Evolution." http://www.secondspring.co.uk/articles/Evolution.pdf.

———. "Trinity and Society: The Search for a 'New Way.'" *Second Spring*. http://www.secondspring.co.uk/articles/scaldecott25.htm. Originally published in *The Chesterton Review* 19 (1993) 463–89.

———. "To the Editor: On the Distribution of Property." *Communio* 17 (1990) 628–30.

Caldecott, Stratford, and Léonie Caldecott. "Theosis: The Final Mystery of the Rosary." http://www.christendom-awake.org/pages/faithcul/theosis.html.

Caldecott, Stratford, and Thomas Honegger, editors. *Tolkien's* The Lord of the Rings: *Sources of Inspiration*. Zurich: Walking Tree, 2008.

Cáoimh, P. Ó. "Roman Catholicism and the World of Science." *Downside Review* 128 (2010) 129–49.

Chandebois, R. *Pour en finir avec le darwinisme. Une nouvelle logique du vivant*. Montpellier: Harmattan, 1993.

Chesterton, G. K. *Heretics*. In vol. 1 of *The Collected Works of G. K. Chesterton*. San Francisco: Ignatius, 1986.

———. *Orthodoxy*. London: Bodley Head, 1906.

———. *The Outline of Sanity*. Norfolk, VA: IHS, 2001.

Clarke, Lindsay. "Afterword: Wolfram's Parzival: A Myth for Our Time." In *Parzifal and the Stone from Heaven: A Grail Romance Retold for Our Time*, 207–29. London: HarperCollins, 2001.

Claudel, Paul. *I Believe in God: A Meditation on the Apostles' Creed*. Edited by Agnes du Sarment. Translated by Helen Weaver. New York: Holt, Rinehart & Winston, 1963.

———. *Lord, Teach Us to Pray*. Translated by Ruth Bethell. London: Dennis Dobson, 1947.

———. "Religion and the Artist: Introduction to a Poem on Dante." *Communio: International Catholic Review* 22 (1995) 357–67.

Clément, Olivier. *The Roots of Christian Mysticism: Text and Commentary*. New York: New City, 1996.

Clifford, William Kingdon. "The Ethics of Belief." In *Lectures and Essays*, 339–63. London: Macmillan, 1886.

Coles, Romand. "Ecotones and Environmental Ethics: Adorno and Lopez." *In the Nature of Things: Language, Politics, and the Environment*, edited by Jane Bennet and William Chaloupka, 226–49. Minneapolis: University of Minneapolis Press, 1993.

Congregation for the Doctrine of the Faith (CDF). *Instruction on Christian Freedom and Liberation*. March 22, 1986.

Corbon, Jean. *The Wellspring of Worship*. Translated by Matthew J. O'Connell. New York: Paulist, 1988.

Cramer, W. *Die Engelvorstellung bei Ephräm dem Syrer*. Orientalia Christiana Analecta 173. Rome: Pontificio Instituto Orientale, 1965.

Crean, T. *A Catholic Replies to Professor Dawkins*. Oxford: Family Publications, 2007.

Darwin, C. *On the Origin of Species*. 6th ed. London: John Murray, 1872.

Dávila, Nicolás Gómez. *Notas*. Bogotá: Villegas, 2003.

Dawkins, Richard. *The God Delusion*. London: Houghton, Mifflin, 2006.

Dawson, Christopher. *Judgment of the Nations*. New York: Sheed & Ward, 1942.

Day, Dorothy. *On Pilgrimage*. Ressourcement. Grand Rapids: Eerdmans, 1999.

D'Costa, Gavin. "The Impossibility of a Pluralist View of Religions." *Religious Studies* 32 (1996) 223–32.

Dennett, D. C. *Breaking the Spell: Religion as a Natural Phenomenon*. New York: Viking, 2006.

———. *Darwin's Dangerous Idea: Evolution and the Meaning of Life*. New York: Simon & Schuster, 1995.

Dover, G. *Dear Mr. Darwin: Letters on the Evolution of Life and Human Nature*. Berkeley: University of California Press, 2000.

Eliade, Mircea. *The Sacred and the Profane: The Nature of Religion*. Translated by Willard R. Trask. New York: Harcourt, Brace, 1959.

Ephrem. *Sermo IV in Hebdomadam Sanctam*. Corpus scriptorum Christianorum Orientalium 413. Leuven: Peeters, 1979.

Evagrius, Ponticus. *The Praktikos; Chapters on Prayer*. Translated by John Eudes Bamberger. Kalamazoo, MI: Cistercian, 1981.

Faucon de Boylesve, Pierre. *Aspects néoplatoniciens de la doctrine de saint Thomas d'Aquin*. Paris: Librairie Honoré Champion, 1975.

Flannery, M. A., editor. *Alfred Russel Wallace's Theory of Intelligent Evolution: How Wallace's World of Life Challenged Darwinism*. Riesel, TX: Erasmus, 2008.

Florensky, Pavel. "Iconostasis." http://www.vehi.net/florensky/ikonost.html.

———. *The Pillar and Ground of the Truth: An Essay in Orthodox Theodicy in Twelve Letters.* Translated by Boris Jakim. Princeton: Princeton University Press, 1997.

Gadamer, Hans-Georg. *The Relevance of the Beautiful and Other Essays.* Translated by Nicholas Walker. Edited by Robert Bernasconi. Cambridge: Cambridge University Press, 1986.

Gandillac, Maurice de. *Philosophie de Nicolas de cues.* Paris: Aubier, 1942.

Gill, Eric. *A Holy Tradition of Working.* Ipswich, Suffolk, UK: Golgonooza, 1983.

Goodenough, Ursula, and Terrence E. Deacon. "The Sacred Emergence of Nature." In *The Oxford Handbook of Religion and Science,* edited by Philip Clayton and Zachary Simpson, 854–71. Oxford: Oxford University Press, 2006.

Goethe, Johann Wolfgang von. "Studie nach Spinoza." In *Werke* 13. Munich: C. H. Beck, 1981.

Granados, José. "Taste and See: The Body and the Experience of God." *Communio* 37 (2010) 292–308.

Griffith, Sidney H. "Asceticism in the Church of Syria: The Hermeneutics of Early Syrian Monasticism." In *Asceticism,* edited by V. L. Wimbush and R. Valantasis, 220–45. Oxford: New York, 1995.

———. *Faith Adoring the Mystery: Reading the Bible with St. Ephraem the Syrian.* The Père Marquette Lecture in Theology, 1997. Milwaukee: Marquette University Press, 1997.

Guardini, Romano. *Letters from Lake Como: Explorations in Technology and the Human Race.* Translated by Geoffrey W. Bromiley. Grand Rapids: Eerdmans, 1994.

Harris, Sam. *The End of Faith: Religion, Terror, and the Future of Reason.* New York: Norton, 2004.

Harrison, Peter. "Introduction." In *The Cambridge Companion to Science and Religion,* edited by Peter Harrison, 1–17. Cambridge: Cambridge University Press, 2010.

Hart, David Bentley. *The Beauty of the Infinite.* Grand Rapids: Eerdmans, 2003.

Hawking, Stephen, and Leonard Mlodinow. *The Grand Design.* London: Bantam, 2010.

Heidegger, Martin. "On the Origin of the Work of Art." In *Philosophies of Art and Beauty: Selected Readings in Aesthetics from Plato to Heidegger,* edited by Albert Hofstadter and Richard Kuhns, 650–700. Chicago: University of Chicago Press, 1976.

Hitchens, Christopher. *God Is Not Great: The Case against Religion.* London: Twelve, 2007.

Hick, John. *God and the Universe of Faiths.* 2nd rev. ed. London: Oneworld, 1993.

Hodgson, Peter. *Christianity and Science.* Oxford: Oxford University Press, 1990.

Hopkins, Gerard Manley. *The Poems of Gerard Manley Hopkins.* Edited by W. H. Gardner and N. H. MacKenzie. 4th ed., revised and enlarged. Oxford: Oxford University Press, 1967.

International Theological Commission. "Communion and Stewardship: Human Persons Created in the Image of God." Vatican City· Libreria Editrice Vaticana, 2002.

Jaki, S. *The Origin of Science and the Science of Its Origin.* Edinburgh: Scottish Academic Press, 1978.

John Paul II, Pope. *Dominum et Vivificantem.* Letter on the Holy Spirit in the Life of the Church and the World. May 18, 1986.

———. *Ecclesia de Eucharistia.* London: Catholic Truth Society, 2003.

———. Homily of His Holiness John Paul II, April 8, 1994. http://www.vatican.va/ holy_father/john_paul_ii/homilies/1994/documents/hf_jp-ii_hom_19940408_restauri-sistina_en.html.

———. *Letter to Families.* http://www.vatican.va/holy_father/john_paul_ii/letters/ 1994/documents/hf_jp-ii_let_02021994_families_en.html.

———. *Man and Woman He Created Them: A Theology of the Body.* Translated by Michael Waldstein. Boston: Pauline, 2006.

———. *Reconciliation and Penance.* Apostolic Exhortation. December 2, 1984.

Keller, E. F. *Making Sense of Life.* Cambridge: Harvard University Press, 2002.

Khan, Muhammad Muhsin, translator. *Sahīh al-Bukhārī: Arabic-English.* Vol. 1. Chicago: Kazi, 1976.

Kronholm, T. *Motifs from Genesis 1–11 in the Genuine Hymns of Ephrem the Syrian with Particular Reference to the Influence of Jewish Exegetical Tradition.* Coniectanea Biblica. OT 11. Lund: Gleerup, 1978.

Lamy, Thomas Joseph. *Sancti Ephraem Syri Hymny et Sermones.* 4 vols. Malines: 1882–1902.

Lash, Nicholas. "Waiting for Dr. Newman." *America* 202.3 (2010) 12–14.

Latouche, Serge. *L'Invention de l'économie.* Paris: Albin Michel, 2005.

Latour, Bruno. *We Have Never Been Modern.* Translated by Catherine Porter. Cambridge: Harvard University Press, 1993.

Le Fanu, James. *Why Us? How Science Rediscovered the Mystery of Ourselves.* New York: Vintage, 2009.

Leopold, Aldo. "The Land Ethic." In *A Sand County Almanac.* New York: Oxford University Press, 1949.

Lewis, C.S. *The Lion, the Witch, and the Wardrobe.* New York: HarperCollins, 1994.

Lings, Martin. *A Sufi Saint of the Twentieth Century: Shaikh Ahmad al-'Alawī: His Spiritual Heritage and Legacy.* 2nd ed. London: George Allen & Unwin, 1971.

Lossky, Vladimir. "Panagia." Translated by E. Every. In *The Mother of God: A Symposium,* edited by E. L. Mascall, 24–36. Westminster: Dacre, 1959.

Latour, Bruno. *We Have Never Been Modern.* Translated by Catherine Porter. Cambridge: Harvard University Press, 1993.

Losurdo, Domenico. *Liberalism: A Counter-History.* Translated by Gregory Elliott. London: Verso, 2011.

Lubac, Henri de. *Corpus Mysticum: The Eucharist and the Church in the Middle Ages.* Translated by Gemma Simmonds with Richard Price and Christopher Stephens. Edited by Laurence Paul Hemming and Susan Frank Parsons. Notre Dame: University of Notre Dame Press, 2007.

Lynch, William. *Christ and Apollo: The Dimensions of the Literary Imagination.* New York: Sheed and Ward, 1960.

MacAuliffe, Jane D. "Exegetical Identification of the Sābi'ūn." *The Muslim World* 72 (1982) 95–106.

MacDonald, George. *Epea aptera = Unspoken Sermons: Series I, II, and III in One Volume.* Whitehorn, CA: Johannesen, 1999.

Maddox, J. "The Unexpected Science to Come." *Scientific American,* December 1999. http://www.scientificamerican.com/article/the-unexpected-science-to/.

Marcel, Gabriel. "The Mystery of the Family." In *Homo Viator: Introduction to a Metaphysic of Hope,* translated by Emma Craufurd, 68–97. New York: Harper, 1962.

Martin, John Rupert. *Baroque*. New York: Harper & Row, 1977.

Mathews, Edward G., Jr. "General Introduction." In *St. Ephrem the Syrian: Selected Prose Works*, edited by E. G. Mathews, Jr., and J. P. Amar, 3–56. Washington, DC: Catholic University of America Press, 1994.

McGrath, Alister. *Dawkins' God: Genes, Memes, and the Meaning of Life*. Oxford: Blackwell, 2007.

McMullin, E., editor. *The Church and Galileo*. Notre Dame: University of Notre Dame Press, 2005.

McVey, Kathleen E. "Ephrem the Syrian." In *The Early Christian World*, edited by Philip F. Esler, 2:1228–50. London: Routledge, 2000.

———. *Ephrem the Syrian: Hymns*. Classics of Western Spirituality. Mahwah, NJ: Paulist, 1989

———. "Were the Earliest *madrāšē* Songs or Recitations?" In *After Bardaisan: Studies in Syriac Christianity in Honour of Professor Han J. W. Drijvers*, edited by G. J. Reinink and A. C. Klugkist, 185–99. Orientalia Lovaniensia Analecta 89. Leuven: Peeters, 1999.

Michéa, Jean-Claude. *The Realm of Lesser Evil*. Translated by David Fernbach. Cambridge: Polity, 2009.

Milbank, John. "The Politics of the Soul." Paper originally delivered to the Temenos Academy, London, November 2012.

Mongrain, K. "The Eyes of Reason: Intelligent Design Apologetics as the New *Preambula Fidei*?" *Heythrop Journal* 52 (2011) 191–210.

Moore, James R. *The Post-Darwinian Controversies: A Study of the Protestant Struggle to Come to Terms with Darwin in Great Britain and America, 1870–1900*. Cambridge: Cambridge University Press, 1979.

Mounier, E. *A Personalist Manifesto*. Translated by the Monks of Saint John's Abbey. London: Longmans, Green, 1938.

Murray, John Courtney. "This Matter of Religious Freedom." *America*, January 9, 1965, 40–43.

Murray, R. *Symbols of Church and Kingdom: A Study in Early Syriac Tradition*. Cambridge: Cambridge University Press, 1975; 2nd ed. with corrections, Piscataway, NJ: Gorgias, 2004.

Nasr, Seyyed Hossein. *Science and Civilization in Islam*. 2nd ed. Cambridge: Islamic Texts Society, 1987.

Newman, John Henry. *Apologia Pro Vita Sua*. Edited by Ian Ker. London: Penguin, 1994.

———. *Callista*. New ed., with an introduction by Alan G. Hill. Notre Dame: Notre Dame University Press, 2000.

———. *Certain Difficulties Felt by Anglicans in Catholic Teaching*. London: Longmans, Green, 1900.

———. *Discourses Addressed to Mixed Congregations*. Edited by James Tolhurst. Birmingham Millenium Oratory Edition. Leominster: Gracewing, 2002.

———. *The Dream of Gerontius*. 1st ed. London: Burns, Lambert, and Oates, 1866.

———. *An Essay in Aid of a Grammar of Assent*. Edited with introduction and notes by I. T. Ker. 1870. Reprint, Oxford: Clarendon, 1998.

———. *An Essay on the Development of Christian Doctrine*. Introduction by Ian Ker. Notre Dame: University of Notre Dame Press, 1989.

―――. *Fifteen Sermons Preached before the University of Oxford between A.D. 1826 and 1843.* Reprint of 3rd ed. of 1872. Notre Dame Series in the Great Books. Notre Dame: University of Notre Dame Press, 1997.

―――. "God Is All in All." In *Meditations and Devotions of the Late Cardinal Newman.* London: Longmans, Green, 1907.

―――. *The Idea of a University.* Introduction and notes by Martin J. Svaglic. Notre Dame Series in the Great Books. Notre Dame: University of Notre Dame Press, 1997.

―――. *The Letters and Diaries of John Henry Newman.* Vol. 24. Edited by Charles Stephen Dessain and Thomas Gornall. New York: Oxford University Press, 2009.

―――. *Prayers, Verses, and Devotions: The Devotions of Bishop Andrewes, Meditations and Devotions, Verses on Various Occasions.* San Francisco: Ignatius, 1989.

―――. "The Tamworth Reading Room." In *Discussions and Arguments on Various Subjects,* 298–305. London: Longmans, Green, 1907. ("The Tamworth Reading Room" refers to a series of letters addressed to the Editor of the *Times* and published under the name Catholicus. Letters. *The Times.* 5 February 1841: 5; 9 February 1841: 6; 10 February 1841: 5; 12 February 1841: 5; 20 February 1841: 5; 22 February 1841: 5; 27 February 1841: 5.)

Numbers, Ronald L., editor. *Galileo Goes to Jail—and Other Myths about Science and Religion.* Cambridge: Harvard University Press, 2009.

O'Meara, Dominic. *Platonopolis: Platonic Political Philosophy in Late Antiquity.* Oxford: Oxford University Press, 2003.

Ostheimer, Anthony L. *The Family: A Thomistic Study in Social Philosophy.* Washington, DC: Catholic University of America Press, 1939.

Ouellet, Marc. *Divine Likeness: Toward a Trinitarian Anthropology of the Family.* Translated by Philip Milliga and Linda M. Cicone. Grand Rapids: Eerdmans, 2006.

―――. "Trinity and Eucharist: A Covenantal Mystery." *Communio: International Catholic Review* 27 (2000) 262–83.

Paul VI, Pope. *Letter Enciclica Mysterium Fidei.* Rome: Editrice Studium, 1966.

Péguy, Charles. *Basic Verities: Prose and Poetry.* Translated by Anne Green and Julian Green. New York: Pantheon, 1943.

―――. *Porche du mystère de la deuxième vertu.* Paris: Gallimard, 1986.

Perl, Eric. "The Presence of the Paradigm: Immanence and Transcendence in Plato's Theory of Forms." *Review of Metaphysics* 53:2 (1999) 339–62.

Peterson, Erik. "A Theology of Dress." Reproduced in *Communio* 20 (1993) 558–68.

Pickstock, Catherine. *After Writing: On the Liturgical Consummation of Philosophy.* Oxford: Blackwell, 1998.

Pieper, Josef. *Living the Truth.* San Francisco: Ignatius, 1989.

Pius XII, Pope. "Christmas Message of 1942." *Catholic Mind* 41.961 (1943) 49–50.

―――. *Mediator Dei.* Encyclical Letter on the Sacred Liturgy. November 20, 1947.

Plotinus. *Ennead.* Translated by A. H. Armstrong. Cambridge: Harvard University Press, 1994.

Polanyi, Karl. *The Great Transformation: The Political and Economic Origins of Our Time.* 1944. Reprint, Boston: Beacon, 2001.

―――. *The Tacit Dimension.* 1966. Reprint, Gloucester, MA: Peter Smith, 1983.

Prufer, Thomas. "Creation, Solitude, and Publicity." In *Recapitulations: Essays in Philosophy,* Washington, DC: Catholic University of America Press, 1993.

Raine, Kathleen, and George Mills Harper, editors. *Thomas Taylor the Platonist: Selected Writings*. Princeton: Princeton University Press, 1969.

Ratzinger, Joseph. "The Feeling of Things, the Contemplation of Beauty." Message to the Communion and Liberation Meeting at Rimini, August 24–30, 2002. http://www.vatican.va/roman_curia/congregations/cfaith/documents/rc_con_cfaith_doc_20020824_ratzinger-cl-rimini_en.html.

———. *Introduction to Christianity*. San Francisco: Ignatius, 1990.

———. *A New Song to the Lord*. New York: Crossroad, 1996.

———. "Presentation by Joseph Cardinal Ratzinger on the Occasion of the First Centenary of the Death of John Henry Cardinal Newman." In *Shadows and Images: The Papers of the Newman Centenary Symposium, Sydney, 1979*, edited by B. J. Lawrence Cross. Melbourne: Polding, 1981.

———. *The Spirit of the Liturgy*. San Francisco: Ignatius, 2000.

Reese, Thomas. "The Hidden Exodus: Catholics Becoming Protestants." *National Catholic Reporter*, April 18, 2011. http://ncronline.org/news/faith-parish/hidden-exodus-catholics-becoming-protestants.

Romeyer, Blaise. "Philos, chrétienne III." *Archives de philosophie chrétienne* (1928) 144–62.

Rousselot, Pierre. *The Eyes of Faith: With Rousselot's Answer to Two Attacks*. Translated by Joseph Donceel and Avery Dulles. New York: Fordham University Press, 1990.

Sahlins, Marshall. *The Western Illusion of Human Nature*. Chicago: Prickly Paradigm, 2008.

Schindler, D. C. *The Catholicity of Reason*. Grand Rapids: Eerdmans, 2013.

———. "Truth and the Christian Imagination: The Reformation of Causality and the Iconoclasm of the Spirit." *Communio* 33.4 (2006) 521–39.

Schindler, David L. "The Anthropological Vision of *Caritas in veritate* in Light of Economic and Cultural Life in the United States." *Communio* 37 (2010) 430–49.

———. "Freedom, Truth, and Human Dignity: What Did *Dignitatis Humanae* Affirm Regarding the Right to Religious Liberty?" *Communio* 40 (2013) 208–316.

———. *Heart of the World, Center of the Church*: Communio *Ecclesiology, Liberalism and Liberation*. Grand Rapids: Eerdmans, 1996.

———. *Ordering Love: Liberal Societies and the Memory of God*. Grand Rapids: Eerdmans, 2011.

———. "The Repressive Logic of Liberal Rights." *Communio* 38 (2011) 523–47.

Schmitz, Kenneth. *The Gift: Creation*. Milwaukee: Marquette University Press, 1982.

———. *The Recovery of Wonder*. Montreal: McGill-Queen's University Press, 2005.

Schuon, Frithjof. "The Contradiction of Relativism." In *Logic and Transcendence*, edited by James S. Cutsinger, 6–15. Bloomington: World Wisdom, 2009.

———. *The Transcendent Unity of Religions*. Translated by Peter Townsend. London: Quest, 1953.

Sertillanges, Antonin Gilbert. *Saint Thomas d'Aquin*. 2 vols. Paris: Alcan, 1912.

Shah-Kazemi, Reza. *Common Ground between Islam and Buddhism*. Louisville: Fons Vitae, 2010.

———. *The Other in the Light of the One: The Universality of the Qur'an and Interfaith Dialogue*. Cambridge: Islamic Texts Society, 2006.

———. *The Spirit of Tolerance in Islam*. London: I. B. Tauris, 2012.

Shaw, Gregory. *Theurgy and the Soul: The Neoplatonism of Iamblichus*. University Park: Pennsylvania State University Press, 1995.

Simpson, George Gaylord. *The Meaning of Evolution*. New Haven: Yale University Press, 1967.

Smith, C. H., editor. *Alfred Russel Wallace: An Anthology of His Shorter Writings*. Oxford: Oxford University Press, 1991.

Solovyov, Vladimir. *Lectures on Godmanhood*. London: Dennis Dobson, 1948.

————. "Theosis: The Final Mystery of the Rosary." Online: http://www.christendomawake.org/pages/faithcul/theosis.html.

Spaemann, Robert. "Die Unvollendbarkeit der Entfinalisierung." In *Schritte über uns hinaus. Gesammelte Reden und Aufsätze II*, 102–25. Stuttgart: Klett-Cotta, 2011.

————. "Natur." In *Philosophische Essays*, 19–40. Stuttgart: Reclam, 1994.

————. "Naturteleologie und Handlung." In *Philosophische Essays*, 41–59. Stuttgart: Reclam, 1994.

————. *A Robert Spaemann Reader: Philosophical Essays on Nature, God, and the Human Person*, edited by D. C. Schindler and Jeanne Schindler. Oxford: Oxford University Press, forthcoming.

Speltz, George H. *The Importance of Rural Life according to the Philosophy of St. Thomas Aquinas: A Study in Economic Philosophy*. Lexington: St. Pius X Press.

Speyr, Adrienne von. *Magd des Herrn*. Einsiedeln: Johannes, 1948.

————. *Maria in der Erlösung*. Einsiedeln: Johannes, 1984.

Steele, D. R. "Is God Coming or Going?" *Philosophy Now* 78 (2010) 9–12.

Tabari, Tafsir al. *Jāmi 'al-bayān*. Vol. 1. Beirut: Dar al-Firk, 2001.

Tarot, Camille. "Rèperes pour une histoire de la naissance de la grace." *La revue de Mauss semestrielle* 1 (1992–93) 91–116.

Tawney, R. H. *The Acquisitive Society*. New York: Harcourt, Brace, 1920.

————. *Religion and the Rise of Capitalism*. New Brunswick, NJ: Transaction, 1998.

Taylor, Charles. *A Secular Age*. Harvard: Harvard University Press, 2007.

Taylor, M. "A Deeper Ecology: A Catholic Vision of the Person in Nature." *Communio* 38.4 (2011) 583–620.

Theodoret, Bishop of Cyrrhus. *Correspondance*. Vol. 3. Translated by Yvan Azéma. Sources chrétiennes 111. Paris: Cerf, 1965.

Theokritoff, E. "Embodied Word and New Creation: Some Modern Orthodox Insights Concerning the Material World." In *Abba: The Tradition of Orthodoxy in the West: Festschrift for Bishop Kallistos (Ware) of Diokleia*, 221–38. Crestwood, NY: Saint Vladimir's Seminary Press, 2003.

Tolkien, J. R. R. *The Letters of J. R. R. Tolkien*. Selected and edited by Humphrey Carpenter, with the assistance of Christopher Tolkien. Boston: Houghton Mifflin, 1981.

————. *The Lord of the Rings*. 3rd ed. London: Unwin Hyman, 1989.

Tolkien, C. R., and J. R. R Tolkien. "Athrabeth Finrod ah Andreth." In *The History of Middle-Earth*, part 3. London: HarperCollins, 2002.

Trevor, Meriol, and Léonie Caldecott. *John Henry Newman: Apostle to the Doubtful*. CTS Biographies. London: Catholic Truth Society, 2001.

Ward, Wilfrid. *The Life of John Henry, Cardinal Newman Based on His Private Journals and Correspondence*. Vol. 2. New York: Longmans, Green, 1912.

Weigel, George. "*Caritas in Veritate* in Gold and Red." *National Review Online*, July 7, 2009. http://www.nationalreview.com/articles/227839/i-caritas-veritate-i-gold-and-red/george-weigel.

Weikart, R. *From Darwin to Hitler: Evolutionary Ethics, Eugenics and Racism in Germany.* New York: Palgrave Macmillan, 2004.

———. "A Recently Discovered Darwin Letter on Social Darwinism." *Isis* 86 (1996) 609–11.

White, Lynn. "The Historical Roots of Our Ecological Crisis." *Science*, March 10, 1967, 1203–7.

Zwick, Mark, and Louise Zwick. *The Catholic Worker Movement: Intellectual and Spiritual Origins.* Mahwah, NJ: Paulist, 2005.

———. *Mercy Without Borders.* Mahwah, NJ: Paulist, 2010.

www.ingramcontent.com/pod-product-compliance
Lightning Source LLC
Chambersburg PA
CBHW030946150426
42814CB00031B/395/J